Alan Lennox-Boyd

For Joan and Leo Murphy

ALAN LENNOX-BOYD

A Biography

Philip Murphy

I.B.TAURIS *Publishers*
LONDON•NEW YORK

Published in 1999 by I.B.Tauris & Co Ltd
Victoria House, Bloomsbury Square, London, WC1B 4DZ
175 Fifth Avenue, New York, NY 10010
Website: http://www.ibtauris.com

In the United States and Canada distributed by St Martin's Press
175 Fifth Avenue, New York NY 10010

ISBN 1 86064 406 6

A full CIP record for this book is available from the British Library
A full CIP record for this book is available from the Library of Congress

Library of Congress catalog card: available

Typeset in Bookman by The Midlands Book Typesetting Company, Lougborough
Printed and bound in Great Britain by WBC Ltd, Bridgend

Contents

List of Illustrations

1. Alan Lennox-Boyd, his mother, Florence, and his elder brother, George.

2. At the Oxford Union, 1926.

3. Three quarters of the 'Lennox-Boyd Mutual Admiration Society': Francis, Alan and Donald Lennox-Boyd at Henlow Grange in the 1930s.

4. Alan Lennox-Boyd with his mother at Sway in the 1930s.

5. Vicky's attack on Franco's British apologists, *Daily Herald*, 1938.

6. Alan Lennox-Boyd introducing his fiancée, Lady Patricia Guinness, to constituents in Mid-Bedfordshire in 1938.

7. Alan Lennox-Boyd with the crew of Motor Launch 113.

8. Churchill, with Alan and Patsy Lennox-Boyd, addressing an election rally in Biggleswade Market Square, 1955.

9. Alan Lennox-Boyd bidding farewell to Kwame Nkrumah and his Cabinet at the end of his visit to the Gold Coast, 1957.

10. The Secretary of State downs a quart tankard of *tuak* in Sarawak, 1955.

11. A weekend at Chequers during the March 1957 Constitutional Conference on Singapore.

12. At the East African Governors' Conference at Chequers, January 1959.

13. Alan Lennox-Boyd sailing with his sons, 1959.

14. Alan and Patsy Lennox-Boyd with Nnamdi Azikiwe and his wife, Nigeria, 1963.

Acknowledgements: 1, 4, 7, 11, 12 & 14 courtesy of Viscount Boyd of Merton; 2 courtesy of the Oxford Union Society; 3 courtesy of the *Luton News*; 5 courtesy of Solo Syndication; 6 & 8 courtesy of the *Bedfordshire Times & Citizen*; 9 Crown copyright, courtesy of the Controller of Her Majesty's Stationary Office; 10 courtesy of Sir John Johnston; 13 courtesy of *The Herald*, copyright Scottish Media Newspapers Ltd.

Preface and Acknowledgements

Ask friends or colleagues of Alan Lennox-Boyd what he was like, and the first thing they are likely to tell you is that 'he was very tall'. Sometimes, you will be told this as though it were a special confidence. You might think it a rather elementary point; but perhaps information of a different order is also being conveyed. Lennox-Boyd's exuberance and generosity of spirit, his astonishing drive and energy, his grandiose imperial dreams, his ability to absorb large quantities of alcohol with no visible effect, even his rounded, oversized handwriting, all suggested a determination to operate on a rather larger scale than the rest of humanity.

An elegant man who took great pains about his appearance, Lennox-Boyd could never quite compensate sartorially for the slightly comical impression created by his great height. The sight of the Colonial Secretary towering over colonial dignitaries and guards of honour always tended to puncture the solemnity of great occasions. The journalist Charles Foley recalled the impression he made during a press conference in Nicosia:

> The Minister was accompanied by the Governor, a man of more moderate height, whose head was level with the visitor's collar, and Larry Durrell, who came in a little lower again. The sight of the Secretary of State stooping to talk to the Director of Information was reminiscent of a Beerbohm cartoon, 'Watts-Dunton reprimanding Swinburne for drinking absinthe'.[1]

So let us get this out of the way at the very beginning: Alan Lennox-Boyd was *very tall*. Six feet five inches to be precise.

Friends and colleagues will list other endearing characteristics of the man. His willingness to entertain people of all races at his London residence impressed many contemporaries. His skills as a parliamentary performer won praise from both sides of the House of Commons. His collection of walking sticks, gathered from around the world, provided an accessible point of interest for those to whom politics did not appeal. He also collected proverbs from across the British Empire, examples of which appear in this book as chapter headings. Above all, his admirers will recall his extraordinary charm, kindness and generosity.

Ask some of Lennox-Boyd's adversaries their impressions of him and you will probably be told that he was complacent, unreflective and *very right wing*, someone for whom, in Barbara Castle's words, 'the British ruling class, both at home and overseas, could do no wrong'.[2] In a profile of him written in May 1952, Michael Foot provides a characteristically elegant summary of some of the main charges:

In short he is a real Tory without prefix, suffix, qualification or miti-
gation. His Tory instincts work in response to any proposition,
however strange or unaccustomed, as if operated by an electrical ap-
pliance. There is nothing complicated in his nature. He is simplicity
itself. Indeed, he would be the despair of the most amateur psycholo-
gist. Nothing bizarre or appalling happened to him in his infancy apart
from membership of the Junior Imperial League. The real question is
whether he has ever escaped the atmosphere of those childish capers.
He is a Junior Imp who never grew up, a Primrose League Peter Pan...[3]

These sentiments were not entirely confined to Lennox-Boyd's political
opponents. In a rare (although by no means unique) moment of irritation with him, Harold Macmillan complained in his diary that
Lennox-Boyd was 'a great overgrown boy without judgement or pro-
fundity'.[4]

Yet if their dominant impressions of him vary, admirers and de-
tractors tend to agree on one thing: that during his time as Colonial Secretary from 1954 to 1959, Lennox-Boyd consciously sought
to impede progress towards self-government in Britain's colonial
territories. In the words of Nigel Fisher, by 'a combination of
personal charm and considerable wealth, Lennox-Boyd had sat on
the safety valve of African nationalism for five years'.[5] Lennox-Boyd
was quite happy to portray himself as a 'brake' on the process of
decolonization in subsequent accounts of his political career.[6]
Under the circumstances, it is understandable that so many historians should have taken Lennox-Boyd at his word and portrayed
his departure from the Colonial Office in October 1959 as a necessary precondition for the acceleration of the transfer of power
particularly in Africa.

As this book seeks to demonstrate, however, Lennox-Boyd's
record as Colonial Secretary deserves to be viewed in a less negative light. In practice, he proved remarkably pragmatic in his
approach to political advance. Indeed, power was so widely distributed within the British system of colonial rule that Lennox-Boyd's
longevity as Secretary of State is in itself indicative of a talent for
conciliation and a willingness to compromise. He was consistently
in advance of his Cabinet colleagues in recognizing the strength of
colonial nationalism and need for Britain to grant political concessions. Yet it is both anachronistic and unhelpful to judge his
performance on the basis of the number of colonies that achieved
their independence during his time in office. Many of the territories for which he was responsible – including Cyprus, Malta,
Uganda, Somaliland and the Southern Arabian Protectorates –
raised far more complex problems than whether simply to devolve
power to a dominant nationalist movement. While he was certainly
keen to maintain a leading role for European politicians in the

affairs of East and Central Africa, it was not until the very end of the 1950s that even those on the liberal wing of the Conservative party began to contemplate the possibility of African majority rule in these areas.

Events in Britain's remaining colonies in the years 1954–59 could form the basis of an infinite number of far more specialized studies. A book of this kind cannot hope to do justice to more than a fraction of the Colonial Secretary's responsibilities. In deciding which areas to examine, it seemed to me that the most pressing task for his biographer was to address Lennox-Boyd's reputation as a 'brake' on constitutional change. I therefore decided – rightly or wrongly – to concentrate largely upon political developments. In the process, other significant aspects of Lennox-Boyd's Ministerial duties have had to be excluded from the study. One important omission, for example, is his role in debates over the Government's policy on immigration. As with a number of other aspects of his work, however, this subject is more than adequately considered elsewhere.[7]

The section of this book dealing with Lennox-Boyd's time at the Colonial Office seeks to explore both the political evolution of specific territories and how, in a broader sense, British policy evolved over the course of these five years. It consists of an introductory chapter, followed by four chapters arranged in broadly chronological order, but each containing a number of separate case studies. The latter are, in effect, 'snap-shots' of some of the issues that concerned Lennox-Boyd most during the years in question. In some cases – like Cyprus or Kenya – it will be necessary to return to a territory more than once. In most instances, however, a colony will be examined in detail only once. I have therefore sought to provide some basic background detail and to suggest how Lennox-Boyd's involvement with the territory in question might have influenced later political developments there.

During the course of writing this book I have incurred many debts of gratitude. The project began for me when I was hired by the Bodleian Library in Oxford to catalogue Alan Lennox-Boyd's papers. Helen Langley and Stephen Tomlinson patiently oversaw my efforts. Judith Priestman, Martin Kauffmann and Allison Pennell did their best to keep me sane. I then enjoyed the luxury of two years as a Senior Associate Member of St. Antony's College, Oxford, during which time the bulk of the research for this book was completed. Thanks to Terence Ranger and Anne Grocock for helping to arrange this. Thanks in particular to Tony and Helen Kirk-Greene for welcoming me back into the fold and for innumerable other acts of kindness. Sir Edgar Williams and Professor Kenneth Kirkwood provided invaluable help and encouragement.

The following people kindly shared with me their recollections of Lennox-Boyd: Mark Amory, Humphry Berkeley, Lord Boyd-Carpenter, Piers Brendon, Ian Buist, Baroness Castle, Lord Clark of Kempston, Lord Elton of Headington, Terence Gavaghan, Herbert Ferdinando, Lord Fraser of Kilmorack, Sir Stephen Hastings, Sir Edward Heath, Oliver Holt, Lord Kelvedon, Keith Kyle, Lord Longford, Bryan Magee, Sir John Moreton, Lord and Lady Perth, John Profumo, David Sandys-Renton, Lord Sherfield, Lady Thatcher. Thanks to them all. Sir John Moreton allowed me to see a transcript of his diary of a tour of East Africa with Lennox-Boyd. Ian Buist kindly read through an early draft of this study and made valuable comments. I am grateful to Sir John Johnston for permission to quote from his privately published memoir and to Nigel Salmon for permission to quote from his unpublished account of Lennox-Boyd's time at Guinness. Sir Peter Smithers answered a series of queries and provided me with a set of notes on Lennox-Boyd. Professor David Dilks provided advice and encouragement during the early stages of my research. His series of lectures on Lennox-Boyd at Rhodes House, Oxford, in Hilary term 1993 played a significant part in shaping my own impressions of the man. I suspect that had he produced a full-length biography, his approach to Lennox-Boyd's political career would have been quite different from my own. I nevertheless hope he sees some value in the current study.

Grateful thanks to the staff of the Bodleian Library, Oxford, particularly to Martin Maw, the former archivist of the Conservative Party's papers, and to Colin Harris and his colleagues in the Modern Manuscripts reading room. John Pinfold and his predecessor as librarian at Rhodes House, Alan Bell, were both enormously helpful and encouraging. Thanks also to the reading room staff of Rhodes House, and those at the Public Record Office, the House of Lords Record Office, and the Modern Records Centre of Churchill College, Cambridge. I am grateful to Peter Lapping for allowing me to consult the archives of Sherborne School, and to George Tatham for his generous assistance during my visit to Sherborne.

I am grateful to Lady Avon for permission to quote from two of Anthony Eden's letters, to Michael Bloch for permission to reproduce part of a letter from James Lees-Milne, to Viscount Chandos for permission to quote from a letter from Oliver Lyttelton, to the Clerk of the Records at the House of Lords Record Office on behalf of the Beaverbrook Foundation Trust for permission to quote from Lord Beaverbrook's correspondence, to the Macmillan Trustees for permission to quote unpublished extracts from the diaries of Harold Macmillan, and to Mrs Pamela Powell for permission to reproduce a letter from Enoch Powell. Crown copywright material in the Public Record Office is reproduced by kind permission of the Controller of Her Majesty's Stationary Office.

My principal debt of gratitude is to the Lennox-Boyd family who commissioned this book and provided generous support and hospitality during its production. Patricia, Viscountess Boyd, Lord and Lady Boyd, Sir Mark Lennox-Boyd and Charles and Charlotte Mitchell all gave me extensive interviews, read drafts of the work and provided valuable comments. At the same time they made no attempt to alter my judgements and they bear no responsibility for the views expressed in subsequent pages.

Many thanks to Lester Crook of I. B. Taurus for the faith he has displayed in this book and his help in the final stages of its production. Thanks also to Stephen Howe who kindly agreed to read the final manuscript. Friends and colleagues at the Universities of Keele and Reading have given generous help and encouragement. My wife, Christina Britzolakis, has helped in every possible way. As always, my parents have provided invaluable support, and I gratefully dedicate this book to them.

Notes

1   Charles Foley, *Legacy of Strife: Cyprus from Rebellion to Civil War* (Harmondsworth, Penguin, 1964), p. 31.
2   Barbara Castle, *Fighting all the Way* (London, Macmillan, 1993), p. 262.
3   Lord Boyd's scrapbooks, Ince Castle, Cornwall, Jan-June 1952, p. 31.
4   The Macmillan Diaries, Bodleian Library, Oxford, 3 April 1955 (I am grateful to Peter Catterall for bringing this passage to my attention).
5   Nigel Fisher, *Iain Macleod* (London, André Deutsch, 1973), p. 142.
6   Lennox-Boyd suggested this to a seminar in Oxford on 15 March 1978. See A.H.M. Kirk-Greene (ed.), *Africa in the Colonial Period, III – The Transfer of Power: The Colonial Administrator in the Age of Decolonization* (Oxford, University of Oxford, 1979), p. 5.
7   Among the most recent is Ian R. G. Spencer, *British Immigration Policy since 1939: The Making of Multi-Racial Britain* (London, Routledge, 1997).

1

The Boyds of Merton Hall

The man who goes ahead stumbles that the man who follows may have his wits about him.[1]

In 1928, Alan Lennox-Boyd made his first visit to the United States. He toured the country, taking part in a series of debating competitions as part of a team from Oxford University. At each campus town on his itinerary he provided the local press with a colourful, not to say imaginative account of his Scottish ancestry. His arrival in Cornell was announced by the headline 'A. T. Lennox-Boyd — Descended from Ancient House'. The article below made much of his 'brilliant historical background' managing to include the names of Wallace, the Bruce and the Young Pretender.[2] The truth is slightly more mundane; but there can be no doubting the pride and interest Lennox-Boyd took in his Scottish heritage. And this Scottish heritage was also an imperial one.

Lennox-Boyd's earliest identifiable ancestor on his father's side was the Rev. William Boyd, Minister of the parish of Dalry in Kirkcudbridgeshire who died in 1741 at the age of 83.[3] William was educated at the University of Glasgow and spent some time in Holland where, according to family legend, he formed a friendship with William of Orange. His grandson, also called William Boyd, acquired lands in Wigtownshire including the estate of Merton Hall which he purchased from Charles Gordon in 1772.

In 1798, William's second son, Edward – Alan Lennox-Boyd's great-grandfather – was bequeathed the bulk of the family

1

property following a dispute between his father and elder brother.[4] Edward, like his father before him, incurred large debts on his estates. In an attempt to restore the fortunes of his family, he invested in maritime insurance and trade with the West Indies.[5] He became part of a network of lowland Scots merchants, including William Jardine and James Matheson, whose interests reached out into the British Empire and other parts of the extra-European world. According to his son, Mark, Edward was frequently consulted by Pitt the Younger on matters relating to America and the West Indian trade.[6] Among other things, Edward used his connections with government to lobby on behalf of the West Indian plantation owners against the abolition of slavery. His business activities prospered and his family lived in some comfort, dividing their time between Merton Hall and their London home in Waterloo Place.[7]

Edward's children continued the family's involvement in the British Empire. His eldest son, William Sprott Boyd, left England in 1819 to take up a post in the East India Company. He rose to reach the position of Political Commissioner in Gujarat and Resident at Baroda and even seems to have been considered as a possible candidate for the Presidency of Bombay. Edward's second son, Benjamin, earned fame and indeed notoriety as founder of the Royal Bank of Australia. A London stockbroker, Benjamin brought together a group of investors to found the bank in February 1840, and the next year set sail for Sydney on board the *Wanderer*. Once in Australia, Benjamin purchased large tracts of land on behalf of the company and became, for his time, the largest 'squatter' in the Australian colonies.

In 1843, Benjamin founded Boyd Town in New South Wales as a base for his fleet of whaling ships. He built his settlement with characteristic ambition and showmanship. With its Elizabethan-style hotel, and imposing Gothic church, Boyd Town appeared to testify to the great prosperity of its founder.[8] In reality, Benjamin's position was far more precarious. His attempts to import cheap labour from the Pacific Islands proved neither very popular with the Australians nor sufficiently lucrative to solve his mounting financial problems. In 1849, his shareholders in London finally lost patience with him. He was removed from the board of the Banking Company of Australia, and the venture was subsequently wound up, leaving debts of £80,000. Undeterred, Benjamin sailed for California to seek his fortune in the gold rush. He had no more success there. His thoughts returned to the Pacific Islands, and to another grandiose scheme – of establishing a South Sea Republic. The indigenous inhabitants of Boyd's intended republic, however, proved uncooperative.

In 1851 Benjamin was killed shortly after having set foot on the Isle of San Cristoval, now Guadalcanal, in the Solomon islands. It was rumoured that he had been eaten by cannibals. Only his belt was ever found.[9]

Benjamin's unhappy career seems not to have detracted unduly from the prosperity or respectability of his brothers. Mark established himself as a tireless lobbyist on behalf of the colonists of Australia and New Zealand. According to his own account, he was told by the Colonial Secretary, Lord Derby, 'to call upon him at all times', and made the fullest use of this invitation to promote his chosen causes.[10] Benjamin's brother, Edward, lived the life of a successful businessman. He inherited Merton Hall and also maintained a London house in Cleveland Square.

Edward's only son, Alan Walter Lennox Boyd — Alan Lennox-Boyd's father — was sent to Rugby public school, and from there went up to St. John's College, Oxford, in 1874. Like his son, he read history at university and then studied for a career in the law. In 1881, he was called to the bar. He settled in Bournemouth and practised as a barrister on the Southern Circuit. By the time he married Alan Lennox-Boyd's mother in 1901, he was already 46 and a widower. Alan Walter had married his first wife, Clementina Louisa Whittingham, in 1886. She died 10 years later, leaving him with a daughter, Phyllis, who was 11 when her father married for a second time. Despite sharing some of her step-brother's political interests — she was a life-long Conservative activist in Bournemouth — Phyllis was never especially close to Alan and his brothers.

When Alan Walter married for a second time, he chose as his bride Florence Annie Begbie, a cousin of his first wife. Fifteen years his junior, Florence had been born in 1870 into a family of eminent Scottish physicians. Her father, Dr James Warburton Begbie, rose to be President of the Royal College of Physicians of Edinburgh, while her grandfather served as Physician-in-Ordinary to the Queen. James Warburton Begbie died when Florence was still a child, apparently worn out by his work. The family's medical tradition was continued by Florence's brother, Francis, who served as an officer in the Royal Army Medical Corps in both the Boer War and in Mesopotamia during the First World War. Florence's other brother, George, was also serving as an officer in South Africa at the time of her wedding. Through her mother's side of the family, Florence could claim descent from the Napier family. Her grandmother was the Hon. Caroline Napier, daughter of Francis, the 8th Baron Napier. Francis was among the British troops who surrendered to General Gates at Saratoga in October 1777. Among Francis's half-cousins were the brothers Sir Charles Napier, who conquered Sind for the British in 1844, Sir George Napier, who as Governor of the Cape of Good Hope from 1837 to 1843 enforced the abolition of slavery there, and Sir William Napier, the historian of the Peninsular war.

Alan Lennox-Boyd's family saga was, then, a miniature history of the British Empire itself, encompassing heroism, chicanery, conquest, revolt, slavery, abolition, high principle and low profiteering. His mother, to whom he was devoted, maintained a particular interest in her Napier ancestors and it was probably through her that Alan first began to acquire his passionate identification with Britain's imperial past.

Alan Walter and Florence were married at St. Clement's Church, Bournemouth, on 31 October 1901. A little under 10 months later, Florence gave birth to her first son, George. Alan Tindal Lennox Boyd, their second child, was born on 18 November 1904. Two more sons were to follow: Donald in 1906 and Francis in 1909. Up until about the time he graduated from Oxford in 1927, Alan's family lived in Roysdean in Bournemouth. They — or at least his mother and brothers — then moved to Broadley House in Sway, Hampshire. By that time, Alan Walter and Florence were estranged. Alan Walter spent long periods away from the family, apparently with a mistress in Germany; and when Florence moved to Sway, he retained a house in Bournemouth. In 1925, Alan Walter adopted the surname Lennox-Boyd by deed poll. Quite why, at the advanced age of 70, he should suddenly have felt the need for a state-sanctioned hyphen is unclear.

The little evidence which survives about him suggests that Alan Walter was a distant figure who quickly lost interest in his young family. His principal contribution to his sons' welfare seems to have been to provide them with fairly generous financial allowances. It is far easier to describe Alan's relations with his mother. James Lees-Milne, who first got to know the Lennox-Boyd brothers soon after the family had left Bournemouth, recalls that they 'worshipped their old mother at Sway where I imagined her to be enshrined like a deity. They consulted her over everything they did or contemplated doing — or so I imagined'.[11]

From the diaries he kept intermittently between 1928 and 1934, Alan Lennox-Boyd emerges as enormously possessive of his mother, resenting any other claims on her affection — even those made by his brothers.[12] The overriding emotion he conveys is his desire to be with her. A typical entry reads: 'FALB [Florence] in London so a happy day'. [13] In her letters to Alan, Florence sometimes almost seemed to assume the conspiratorial voice of a secret lover. As he was returning from a trip to Africa in the autumn of 1934 she wrote to tell him that on his return, his brothers would be meeting their father, who by then was within a couple of months of death. This would mean, she added, that 'U and I will be alone. O Len — it is too wonderful. Oh good angels keep you safe till I have you in my arms and ever after too!'[14] Donald's relationship with his mother was equally intense. Departing on one of his overseas trips, he told her, 'I can see the towns of England slipping away and can't conceive of what a fool I've been, utterly mad to go voluntarily away from you — my utter own.'[15] The possessive instinct operated in both directions. Alan records in his diary having monitored a telephone conversation between Donald and a female friend, on 'maternal instructions'.

Of her four sons, it was probably Francis, the youngest, whose feelings for Florence were most passionate. On 3 May 1944, as he was preparing to leave with his parachute regiment to spearhead the invasion of Europe, he and his mother had one final meeting. After she had left, he wrote to her,

> My Darling, you were so sweet and kind today as always. You have never failed me once in any way at all and I shall love you for ever in this world and the next.[16]

Francis disappeared on the day of the invasion and it was not until some months later that it was known he had been killed. Before her son's death was confirmed, Florence talked about him to Hugh Molson, a family friend. She told him that Francis had claimed he would not want to go on living if she died. Molson, quite understandably, was troubled by this. Yet he comforted Florence with the thought that if Francis had indeed been killed, he would have been spared this bereavement which he most dreaded.[17]

In encouraging the development of such an intense relationship with her sons, Florence seems to have been seeking to satisfy a need for affection which was not being met by her husband. It is difficult to imagine that this combination of an absentee father and an overbearing mother did not have an impact on the emotional development of the Lennox-Boyd brothers. Despite the fact that Donald was 32 when he died, Francis 35 and George 41, none of them married. They certainly had girlfriends and George acquired a reputation as a womanizer. Yet rumours of homosexuality almost inevitably attached themselves to the brothers. The mysterious circumstances of Donald's death in Germany in 1939 added to these rumours. Although Alan married in 1938, a number of friends and acquaintances believed that he too was homosexual. This is vehemently denied by others who knew him well. The truth of such allegations is impossible to establish with any degree of accuracy, and the term 'homosexual' is probably unhelpful given the prevalence of homoeroticism in the public schools and Oxbridge colleges of Lennox-Boyd's time. Nevertheless, it is clear that the extraordinary hold Florence exerted over her sons overshadowed their relations with women of their own age. One would-be girlfriend of Francis complained bitterly of the malign influence of the 'Witch of Sway'. At least in part because of this, the strongest emotional ties established by the Lennox-Boyd brothers outside the immediate family unit tended to be with other men.

The brothers' later careers took very different directions. Alan went into politics. George and Donald became professional soldiers. Francis took a job in the city, while nurturing the ambition to be an artist. Their public personas were in some respects quite distinct: George, the tough if eccentric man of action; Francis the aesthete, remembered by James Lees-Milne as 'tall, languid, a bit of a dandy'.[18] All the brothers shared a taste for danger, although in the cases of George and Donald this seems to have been particularly pronounced, bordering on the reckless. James Lees-Milne remembered George as 'almost lunatic, though very amusing and eccentric'. In the obituary he produced for *The Times,* Lees-Milne described George as 'a vividly wayward, romantic perhaps almost picaresque figure, naturally akin to a more incautious, yet far more genuinely constituted century than our own.'[19] It was a description that could apply equally well to Alan. Above all, the brothers remained fiercely loyal to each other. Friends knew that, however close they might get, they would never wholly penetrate what one described as the 'mutual admiration society' of the Lennox-Boyd brothers.[20]

Alan Lennox-Boyd began his education at a prep-school in Bournemouth. When he arrived at Sherborne School in the autumn of 1918, a few weeks before his 14th birthday, it was the first time he had been sent away from home for any length of time. He seems to have found the separation from his mother particularly difficult to bear. In a letter which seems to date from this period, she urged him, 'try to settle little Dearest, it will all pass quicker if you do and you have no real worries Pet so you will try best to take each day as it comes'.[21] Florence herself made quite an impression at the school. She earned a glowing reference as 'the sweetest of mothers' in the memoirs of Alan's housemaster.[22] Clearly, she remained fairly close at hand.

The power structure of Sherborne, like most other public schools, had a devolved character, resembling that of the colonial empire over which Lennox-Boyd was later to preside. Throughout Lennox-Boyd's time at Sherborne, the post of headmaster was occupied by C. Nowell

Smith. By all accounts a gentle, scholarly and enlightened figure, albeit one given to occasional displays of fury, Nowell Smith managed,
in the words of one of Lennox-Boyd's contemporaries, to guide the
school 'from barbarism into civilized ways'.[23] Yet like a reforming
Colonial Secretary, Nowell Smith's capacity to shape events in his
dominions was severely restricted by the authority exerted by his
subordinates. The adult of whose guiding influence Sherborne school-
boys were most immediately and constantly aware was their
housemaster. He was generally able to operate with only occasional
interference from his superior; but Lennox-Boyd's housemaster, Alick
Trelawny-Ross, the head of Lyon House, seems to have demanded
an extreme form of autonomy. Some people, with only slight exag-
geration, took to referring to 'Sherborne School and Ross's House'.[24]

Trelawny-Ross was educated at Sherborne and after an undis-
tinguished three years at Oxford, returned as a teacher in 1911 and
remained there for the rest of his working life. He never married.
Instead, his boys, with whom he kept in regular touch after they
left the school, became a surrogate extended family. At the outbreak
of the First World War he had attempted to enlist but was rejected
on medical grounds. As he explained in his memoirs,

> ...it seemed to me that, *as I could not kill Germans, I must try to build
> up Englishmen.* That became my purpose in life, and the House was
> the instrument which I could best use both for that objective and to
> help the School.[25]

Lennox-Boyd arrived at Lyon House just as the First World War was
nearing its end. The Armistice was a cause of general rejoicing
throughout the school. The poet Louis MacNeice, who spent a brief
spell as a pupil at Sherborne, recalled the carnival spirit, with 'little
boys whooping and junketing' and effigies of the Kaiser being con-
signed to the flames.[26] Yet Trelawny-Ross saw no reason to relax
his efforts to 'build up Englishmen'. He complained in his memoirs
that the end of the First World War witnessed a 'lowering of standards', a phenomenon he regarded as common to all wars and which
he blamed, in part, on the long separation of boys from their fa-
thers.[27] Both in the way he ran his house and in his broader political outlook, he clearly placed great emphasis on the maintenance
of authority and discipline. He saw challenges to this principle not
only in the specific circumstances of the war but also in the spread
of democratic values in society as a whole. 'As democracy advances,'
he once suggested, 'morals and manners recede.'[28] Trelawny-Ross
liked to believe that he had played a part in shaping the political
outlook of the young Lennox-Boyd, and the distinctly authoritarian
slant of the latter's subsequent views tends to bear this out.[29]

So far as one can judge, Lennox-Boyd's career at Sherborne
was untroubled, even exemplary. This was despite the fact that
Sherborne valued sporting achievement above all else and
Lennox-Boyd was, by his own admission, 'no sort of athlete'.[30] In
the sixth-form, while studying for a history scholarship at Oxford,
Lennox-Boyd managed to pick up the school's Bowen Prize for
History, its Longmuir Prize for English and its Parson's Prize for
Divinity.[31] He became a school prefect and in 1923 was made
head of Lyon House. He proved both capable and at ease in his
new role. Trelawny-Ross described him as an 'excellent Head [of
House] and, without loosing any of his power, the best tempered
fellow one could meet'.

The subtle deployment of authority was one skill he developed
during his time at Sherborne. Another was a facility for constructing an argument. When he left the school in 1923, Trelawny-Ross
commented that he would miss Lennox-Boyd's 'dinner-dialectics'.[32]
What else he took away with him when he left for Oxford in 1923
is difficult to say. Imperial mythology would have permeated every
aspect of life at Sherborne, as it did at the other major public
schools. The project of 'building up Englishmen' was justified at
Sherborne, as elsewhere, by the need to create an imperial ruling
class. The cult of the sporting hero, so pronounced at Sherborne,
was itself intimately connected with the growth of imperial ideology at Britain's public schools.[33]

Among Lennox-Boyd's friends at Sherborne was the future poet
laureate, Cecil Day Lewis. They can be seen sitting next to one
another in the 1923 school photograph, grinning at the camera with
the confident expressions of two clever young men contemplating
future triumphs. Their subsequent careers were to take radically
different courses. Yet their shared experiences at public school seem
to have left certain common traits. Writing of his father, Sean Day
Lewis suggests that the influence of Sherborne could be detected
in Cecil's,

> developed sense of responsibility; his worship of heroes, especially
> games-playing heroes; his willingness to live or work with others in a
> position of leader or follower; his wish to belong as an insider and the
> concomitant tendency towards conformity.[34]

Although a keen admirer of male physical beauty, Lennox-Boyd's
own particular form of hero worship tended not to focus particularly upon sportsmen. Otherwise he displayed all these attributes
to a high degree. Unlike many of his more intelligent contemporaries, however, the imperial mythology which underpinned
Sherborne's obsession with sporting prowess remained central to

his political outlook. His experiences as an undergraduate at Oxford would, if anything, magnify its importance.

Notes

1 Bondei proverb from Kenya, collected by Lord Boyd, Papers of the first Viscount Boyd of Merton, Bodleian Library, Oxford (hereafter indicated by the abbreviation PBM), Ms. Eng. c. 3796, f. 264.
2 Lord Boyd's scrapbooks, Ince Castle, Cornwall (hereafter indicated by the abbreviation SB), *America 1928*, p. 32.
3 Preliminary Report on the Family of Boyd of Merton Hall, PBM, Mss. Eng. c. 3778, ff. 55 – 63.
4 Marion Diamond, *The Sea Horse and the Wanderer: Ben Boyd in Australia* (Carlton, Melbourne University Press, 1988), p. 6.
5 Diamond, p. 6.
6 Mark Boyd, *Reminiscences of Fifty Years* (London, Longmans, Green and Co., 1871), cited in Diamond, p. 9.
7 Diamond, p. 5.
8 J.H. Watson, 'Benjamin Boyd, Merchant', *Journal and Proceedings of the Australian Historical Society*, vol. 2, part 6, 1907, p. 133.
9 Hence the joke that there is a tribe of South Sea islanders who are Scottish by absorption.
10 Boyd, p. 73.
11 James Lees Milne to the author, 28 May 1996.
12 Diary of Alan Lennox-Boyd (hereafter referred to simply as Diary), 18 Feb. 1928, PBM, Ms. Eng. c. 3338, f. 34.
13 Diary, 22 Feb. 1933.
14 Florence Lennox-Boyd to Alan Lennox-Boyd, undated (autumn 1934), PBM, Ms. Eng. c. 3758.
15 Donald Lennox-Boyd to Florence Lennox-Boyd, undated, PBM, Ms. Eng. c. 3759.
16 Francis Lennox-Boyd to Florence Lennox-Boyd, 3 June 1944, PBM, Ms. Eng. c. 3762.
17 Molson to Florence Lennox-Boyd, 19 Aug. 1944, PBM, Ms. Eng. c. 3762.
18 James Lees-Milne to the author, 28 May 1996.
19 *The Times*, 17 Nov. 1943. George's waywardness was not to everyone's taste. In 1934, Lord Baden-Powell intervened in an attempt to break off the engagement between his daughter, Heather, and George after hearing rumours of George's womanizing and that he had undergone a character change after falling on his head. George and Heather were eventually 'disengaged' (Tim Jeel, *Baden-Powell* (London, Hutchins, 1989), pp. 536—38).
20 Molson to Lennox-Boyd, 27 Feb. 1938, PBM, Ms. Eng. c. 3387, f. 25.
21 Florence Lennox-Boyd to Alan Lennox-Boyd, undated, PBM, Ms. Eng. c. 3758.
22 A.H. Trelawny-Ross, *Their Prime of Life: A Public School Study* (Winchester, Warren & Son, 1956), p. 66.
23 C. Day Lewis, *The Buried Day* (London, Chatto & Windus, 1960), p. 106. For other accounts of Nowell Smith see Alec Waugh, *The Early Years of Alec Waugh* (London, Cassell, 1962); Oliver Holt, *Nowell Smith and his Sherborne: A Memoir* (private publication, 1955).
24 Interview with Oliver Holt, 25 June 1996.
25 Trelawny-Ross, p. 17.
26 Louis MacNeice, *The Strings are False: An Unfinished Autobiography* (London, Faber and Faber, 1965), p. 71.
27 Trelawny-Ross, p. 60.

28 Trelawny-Ross, p. 22.
29 Brown to Lennox-Boyd, 27 Feb. 1938, PBM, Ms. Eng. c. 3386, f. 245
30 Trelawny-Ross, p. 66.
31 *The Sherborne Register* (6th Edn., 1982), p. 39.
32 Trelawny-Ross, p. 68.
33 For a discussion of this connection, see J.A. Mangan, '"The grit of our forefathers": invented traditions, propaganda and imperialism', in John M. Mackenzie (ed.), *Imperialism and Popular Culture* (Manchester, Manchester University Press, 1986), pp. 113–139.
34 Sean Day Lewis, *C. Day Lewis: An English Literary Life* (London, Weidenfeld & Nicolson, 1980), p. 19.

2

The House

A coconut shell full of water is a sea to an ant.[1]

In February 1923, shortly after learning that he had won an honorary scholarship in Modern History to Christ Church, Lennox-Boyd received a letter of welcome to 'the House' from J. C. Masterman, the Senior Censor. Masterman, a quintessential establishment 'insider', left him in no doubt of the pride he should feel in his award, telling him that there was, a 'kingly' character about Christ Church which no other college possessed.[2] While other Oxford colleges might have disputed this claim, 'the House' certainly included, during Lennox-Boyd's time there, a rich cross-section of the British establishment-in-waiting. There was Alec Douglas-Home, who would be Secretary of State for Commonwealth Relations during Lennox-Boyd's time as Colonial Secretary and later Prime Minister; Roger Makins, who would become British Ambassador in Washington and Joint Permanent Secretary of the Treasury; and Dick White, who served as Director-General of MI5, and then as head of SIS (Secret Intelligence Service) at the time of the Suez Crisis. There were also some of the country's more exotic sons: the prince of the aesthetes, Harold Acton, the poet, W. H. Auden, the historian, A. L. Rowse, and the journalist, politician and homosexual rake, Tom Driberg.

Lennox-Boyd made a quiet start to his Oxford career. During his first year he appears to have taken no part in politics and it was only at the beginning of his second that he was coaxed out of obscurity by James Scrimgeour-Wedderburn. Wedderburn invited him to attend a meeting of the Canning Club, a society which still exists as a forum for discussion among students and academics of High Tory leanings. At the end of October 1924, he was

11

elected a member of the Canning. He also made his first speech at the Oxford Union Society, again apparently at the instigation of Wedderburn. He was an instant success, 'fluent and confident' according to the University magazine, *Isis*.[3] Having thus dipped his toe in the murky waters of Oxford politics, Lennox-Boyd now plunged in with a vengeance. Within the course of the next six terms he was to attain the Presidency of the Union via the posts of Junior Treasurer and Junior Librarian, whilst in the meantime becoming Secretary of the Canning Club, and President of both the Oxford Carlton Club and the University Conservative Association. This record of success was attributed by Frank Pakenham, in a profile in the *Oxford City Chronicle*, to a variety of Lennox-Boyd's talents. Within the Union it was due to 'his commanding presence, his fine delivery and his manifest sincerity', in the Canning to his 'reputation for tact and broad-mindedness', and in the Conservative Association to his 'indefatigable industry' and his 'ability to strike a happy mean between impudence and obsequiousness in his dealings with great visitors'.[4]

Coverage of his performance in Union debates repeatedly stressed the natural charm and sincerity that Lennox-Boyd brought to his speeches. So far as technique was concerned, he seems to have taken full advantage of the opportunity which the Union provided to practise and refine his oratory. While an early *Isis* commentary complained that he should learn to arrange his speech more carefully (and realize that Archbishops and drunkenness were not inherently funny), a report dating from the time when he was running for President describes Lennox-Boyd as 'incisive and impressive'.[5] Another of Lennox-Boyd's talents which emerged at the Union was 'his unusual power of absorbing and understanding detail'.[6] It was a capacity which aroused expectations of a brilliant career in the law; but it was in the political sphere that this was to manifest itself in later life.

The 'Isis Idol' profile of Lennox-Boyd, also apparently by Pakenham, suggests that his private life at Oxford outside the political sphere was equally colourful and energetic:

> Whether he is engaged in some lightening motor dash to Corsica and back, in some impersonation of a foreign grandee (an incident from whose unpleasant consequences he is still trying to escape), in the locking up in the Balliol telephone box of one of that college's most respected members, in the quelling by the most brutal physical force of a recently departed...humorist in the Union 'Silence' Room – whether engaged in any of these things, he always shows the same unflagging energy and most noticeably the will that wins.[7]

This lifestyle was made possible by an allowance from Lennox-Boyd's father of £500 a year, a considerable sum at that

time. Yet if Alan Walter Lennox-Boyd provided his son with financial support, he seems to have given him little else. Nor did
he show much willingness to recognize and applaud his son's
considerable achievements at Oxford. On learning of his election
as president of the Union, Lennox-Boyd's father apparently
remarked that in his day no gentleman would have been a member of the Society.

Lennox-Boyd's flamboyant existence certainly kept him in the
public eye; but it also encouraged suspicions that his success in
the field of Oxford politics represented a victory of style over sub-
stance. 'If I had not listened so carefully' claimed an *Isis* correspondent after witnessing one of his performances at the Union
'I should have thought it a better speech'.[8] Nor is it ever recorded
that his arguments were strikingly original. One account referred
to 'a certain simplicity of thought that enables him to dispense
with the ordinary frills and furbelows of Union oratory'.[9] He
also lacked the desire – so pronounced among many of his
contemporaries – to be either shocking or subversive. 'There is no
nonsense about Mr Lennox-Boyd,' complained another *Isis* scribe,
'he is essentially sane.'[10]

The High Tory Imperialist views Lennox-Boyd expressed in
Union debates and Canning meetings were certainly neither especially original nor sophisticated. In tone and content they seemed
to owe less to the writings of Burke and Disraeli than to those of
his friend and mentor, John Buchan. Buchan's home, Elsfield
Manor, four miles outside Oxford, provided Lennox-Boyd and a
number of his contemporaries with an important window on the
wider political world. Lennox-Boyd joined a stream of visitors including fellow undergraduates like Frank Pakenham, Roger Makins
and James Scrimgeour-Wedderburn, treading what Pakenham
described as 'the pilgrim way' across the fields to Elsfield.[11] For
Buchan's young son, William, the sight of these exceptionally tall
young men converging on the house was proof that the outside
world was peopled largely by giants.[12] For the students themselves,
Elsfield was a place were they might encounter L. S. Amery or T.
E. Lawrence and converse with them on equal terms.

Buchan, both in his free-lance capacity as a popular novelist,
and in his official role as a government propagandist, was among
the most influential exponents of what one might call the Empire
of the imagination.[13] This rose and declined roughly in parallel to
the 'real' Empire, but it remained, in a sense, quite distinct from
it. The Empire that presented itself to British policy makers was a
vast patchwork of territories, some acquired almost by default, some
by distinctly shady means, and each presenting complex, often

intractable problems of negotiation and administration. The Empire of imagination, by contrast, was a great patriotic myth, essentially for domestic consumption, which drew upon a quasi-religious vocabulary of chivalry and self-sacrifice. Buchan's writings breathed new life into this mythology. The men who served in Britain's navy were, for example, in Buchan's terms, 'modern crusaders, the true defenders of the faith, doing battle not only for home and race and fatherland, but for the citadel and sanctities of Christendom'.[14] Pitted against them were the deadly foes of Bolshevism, Prussianism and Anarchism.

The political assumptions that shaped Buchan's novels were broadly shared by many of Lennox-Boyd's contemporaries, and not just those on the 'radical right'. Lennox-Boyd, however, expressed them with a romantic zeal and theatricality that were very much his own; so much so, in fact, that one might suspect that his principal aim was to amuse his listeners. Perhaps it was. Yet it would be unwise to dismiss his views as mere undergraduate posturing. Many of the values he championed at this time were to guide him throughout the rest of his political career.

A common theme of these pronouncements was that Britain was threatened by sinister and anarchic revolutionary movements. Reporting to the Canning Club in October 1925 on the events of the vacation, he pointed to 'proof of the international movement for revolution' and argued that the Government should adopt a stronger policy of hostility to Britain's national enemies 'from bolsheviks to profiteers'. At the centre of this web of subversion he saw Communist Russia. In June 1926, he spoke forcefully against a motion in the Union which urged the recognition of Russia. He denounced the Russians as 'barbaric' and looked forward to a Czarist restoration.[15] To his colleagues in the Canning 'he unmasked the vague assumptions of Bolshevik morality and proved that in Russia, family life had been completely abandoned'.[16]

At the heart of his political outlook was a conception of patriotism rooted in established institutions. He devoted one of his papers to the Canning to a self-consciously eccentric defence of the divine right of kingship.[17] He urged members of the Canning to cultivate the 'splendid spirit of the Cavaliers – the ancestors of the Conservative party' and argued that 'the adoption of a theory of divine right would give the Conservative party a continuity and an historical development that would greatly strengthen it'. This reactionary romanticism drew him at least temporarily towards the wilder fringes of British politics. His first paper to the Canning Club, delivered in February 1925, was a defence of

'Fascismo'.[18] This he defined as 'in its essence...a manifestation of the true spirit of patriotism and the regulation of all class war'. It was based on the assumption that democracy could go too far and that above any allegiance to party or faction should be loyalty to the state. The same month, he wrote to the British Fascists, suggesting that there was a chance of doing something for fascism in Oxford. This elicited a warm letter of thanks from Brigadier General R. G. D. Blakeney, president of the organization.[19] The British Fascists had been founded in 1923 by Rotha Lintorn-Orman, who quickly surrendered the leadership of the movement to Blakeney, a former manager of the Egyptian State Railways.[20] The movement's avowed enemies were the agents of Socialism, Anarchism and Bolshevism. It was not as overtly anti-semitic as some of the other proto-fascist organizations in Britain, although its spokesmen increasingly identified these enemies with 'alien internationalists'.[21]

There is no evidence to suggest that, following his exchange of letters with Blakeney, Lennox-Boyd took an active role in the British Fascists. It is certainly true, however, that the outlook of the kind of 'fascist' organization which Blakeney was attempting to construct had many points in common with Lennox-Boyd's own political views. It is also true that he continued to regard fascism as being on the side of order and patriotism in their constant struggle against the dark forces of Anarchism and Bolshevism. In June 1926, a month after the General Strike, he prepared a speech for the Union debate which immediately preceded his election as president, in which he argued that although 'extreme' trades unionists denounced fascism, 'I am sure that fascism at the height of its power is not so great a menace to the security of any country as is the dominance of the Trades Union Congress in political affairs'.[22] Ten years later, as a young MP, he told an audience in Chester-le-Street that if it ever came to a crisis between Bolshevism and Fascism 'one would inevitably be on the side of the Fascists, for the Fascists would be a little bit better than the other side'.[23] Of course, when this great confrontation did occur Lennox-Boyd found himself fighting as part of an avowedly anti-fascist alliance which included the Soviet Union.

In his speeches to the Union and papers to the Canning, Lennox-Boyd was able to play with political ideas without ever having to worry about putting them into practice. At midnight on 3 May 1926, however, there began a brief but decisive industrial conflict which was to draw him and many of his contemporaries from the safe confines of Oxford and challenge them to express their views through action. This was the General Strike. It was an event which divided Oxford, not so much, according to A. J. P. Taylor, between those who backed the strikers and those who supported the Government, but between those who acted and those who did not.[24]

Lennox-Boyd himself needed little encouragement to act. He left Oxford for London to work as a guard for the Great Western Railway at Paddington Station. A rumour which found its way into the student press suggested that he had reported for duty in a top hat, tail coat and white trousers and carrying a tennis racket. He also enrolled with the Metropolitan Special Constabulary at St. George's Club in London on 11 May, the day before the strike ended. One contemporary recalled that 'nothing more impressive could be imagined than his continual appearances in his huge car striving unwearyingly to find some work to do'.[25] His brother, Francis, also took part in the confrontation, acting as a conductor for the Bournemouth Corporation Tramways.

Back in Oxford, Imperial affairs had already emerged as Lennox-Boyd's principal passion and area of expertise, and in this field Lennox-Boyd's undergraduate pronouncements appear relatively level-headed. In 1926, he won the Beit prize for Imperial history with an essay which took as its subject *The Development of the Idea of Trusteeship in the Government of Backward Peoples*. The piece was heavily influenced by the ideals and preoccupations of the Round Table movement. In Lennox-Boyd's day, the Oxford branch of the Round Table included among its members Reginald Coupland, Lionel Curtis's successor as Beit Professor, and Keith Feiling, Lennox-Boyd's tutor.[26] Their work combined the idealism of the Empire of imagination with a more practical concern for specific problems of colonial administration. Central to it was the notion of Britain's historic mission to nurture liberty among colonial peoples on the basis of a flexible and benevolent system of law.

In the course of his essay, Lennox-Boyd dutifully echoed the Round Table doctrine that the ultimate aim of British trusteeship was to advance colonial peoples to a stage when they would be capable of governing themselves. This was, he claimed, 'an ideal, adherence to which alone can justify the maintenance of the British power in India'. He expressed approval for the 1919 Government of India Act, which implemented the recommendations of the Montagu-Chelmsford Report, as being wholly consistent with this principle. The Act increased the unofficial element within the provincial legislative councils which were to operate alongside the Governor and his Executive Council under a system of diarchy, and provided for a bi-cameral legislature at the level of central government. Lennox-Boyd recognized that the Act could only be a temporary measure and that the power of the elected element within the system would necessarily increase with a corresponding reduction in the control which the Imperial government would be able to exercise. Yet he clearly believed, along with the authors of the Montagu-Chelmsford Report, that when further extensions in the power of those representative institutions occurred they would be, in the first instance, at the level of the provincial governments. As such, this position was not necessarily incompatible with his subsequent opposition to the 1935 Government of India legislation.

What mattered above all was the pace of political development. In the course of his essay, Lennox-Boyd offered a formula which could easily have been lifted from one of his speeches on Africa during the 1950s:

> The greatest test of the genuine trustee is a resolute determination to make, as far as possible, the evolution of democratic institutions synchronize with the growth in the political capacity of those who will be responsible for their efficient working.[27]

A strand of Round Table thought which Lennox-Boyd embraced with rather greater enthusiasm was the notion of the Englishman's innate capacity for colonial administration. He quoted with approval Lord Cromer on 'the singular political adaptability of the Englishman' and Lord Milner on 'the practical instinct which enables men of British birth...to fit into the most incongruous situations, and to make the best of limited opportunities without troubling their heads about theoretical interpretations of system'.[28] He maintained that the Empire was a profoundly benevolent entity and that it obtained its moral force, not so much through the effectiveness of its institutions but through the personal integrity of its officials. 'The history of the development of trusteeship,' he concluded 'is largely the history of individual efforts.'[29] In his discussion of Burke's speech at the impeachment of Warren Hastings, Lennox-Boyd reiterated, in even stronger terms his belief in the importance of individuals:

> The greatest test of any government in its dealings with backward races is to be found in the character of the men whom it appoints to positions of authority and trust.[30]

Lennox-Boyd may have accepted, with a certain degree of reluctance, that in practical terms democracy was the only possible form of government for modern Britain, however fragile it might appear. Yet both in his Beit essay and elsewhere he conveys a sense that

his ideal form of government consisted of the *best* people being
given the maximum scope for the exercise of benevolent authority. One of the reasons why Imperial politics so appealed to him
was that it was here, rather than in the domestic sphere, that this
ideal could, and he believed did, exist.

The fact that the Empire rallied behind Britain during the Great
War was, for Lennox-Boyd conclusive proof 'that in their government of backward nations the British people had been progress-
ing upon just and statesmanlike lines'.[31] It was a theme to which
Lennox-Boyd was repeatedly to return later in his career, particularly during the debates over the India Bill in the 1930s. Indeed,
this seems to have been the aspect of his research for the Beit essay
which had the most significant impact on his political development.
He later explained how impressed he had been in the course of his
reading by the benevolence of the rule of the Indian princes and
the great contribution which they had made to the Imperial war
effort. He had also noticed and admired the work of Moslem leaders such as Jinnah and the chief minister of Hyderabad. On the
other hand, his research on the period of the War left him with a
suspicion of the Hindus of the Congress Party which was never
entirely dispelled:

> I felt strongly for the martial tribes and admired the fighting men of
> the Punjab more than the clerks of Bengal. I was told that in the year
> of the Simon Commission the Punjab sent 86,000 men to serve in the
> army while Bengal sent none.[32]

These early impressions were clearly a factor behind Lennox-Boyd's
defence of the position of the princes during the debates over the
1935 Government of India Bill. Even as Colonial Secretary in the
1950s, there was a strong sense in which he retained a natural
sympathy for 'martial races' and traditional rulers of the colonies
whose position was sometimes threatened by the 'clerks' of the new
nationalist movements. In particular, he believed that Britain owed
a debt of loyalty towards the peoples of Northern Nigeria and the
Northern territories of the Gold Coast who had played a disproportionate role in their countries' armed forces during the Second
World War.

During the course of 1926, as well as winning the Beit prize,
Lennox-Boyd also achieved his ambition of becoming President of
the Union. During his term as President he arranged one great
occasion 'so that' in the words of one contemporary 'he should have
had the opportunity of rising to it'.[33] The event in question was
the unveiling in the Union chamber on 26 October 1926 of a bust

of Lord Curzon, the former Viceroy of India and Foreign Secretary. The inspiration seems to have come from Lord Birkenhead, then Secretary of State for India, an outstanding product of the Union's school of oratory who kept a close and somewhat obsessive eye on Oxford student politics.[34] Lennox-Boyd persuaded the former Prime Minister, Herbert Asquith (by then Earl of Oxford and Asquith), to unveil the bust. The ceremony itself was attended by Curzon's widow and by his daughter Cynthia, accompanied by her husband Sir Oswald Mosley. Lennox-Boyd opened the proceedings with a short speech which despite being merely the prelude to contributions by some of the Union's most distinguished sons, earned enthusiastic praise for its eloquence, style and dignity. As *Isis* said of him, recalling the occasion:

> Where all...were well dressed, he was the best dressed. Where all were dignified, he was most dignified. Where all played their parts well, he played his magnificently.[35]

In retrospect there was to be a certain cruel irony attached to Lennox-Boyd's participation in this event. For Curzon, although he was later to return to Oxford in triumph, had left it at the end of his undergraduate career tainted, as he saw it, with an indelible mark of mediocrity – a second-class honours degree. This was to be the fate of Lennox-Boyd also, and he felt it no less.

Signs that his immersion in Oxford politics might prejudice his academic performance appeared relatively early. By Christmas 1925, concerns were already being expressed that Lennox-Boyd was taking on too many extra-curricular activities. Hugh Molson told him that his tutor, Keith Feiling, was uneasy about the prospect of him assuming the Presidency of the Union at too late a stage in his Oxford career, fearing that his work might suffer.[36] Molson agreed that nothing should be allowed to get in the way of him achieving his First. He believed that Lennox-Boyd could combine distinction in Schools with the Union presidency but warned that involvement in too many small clubs could thwart these twin ambitions. In the event, Lennox-Boyd assumed the presidency of the Union only in the first term of his final year at Oxford, raising further concerns about his likelihood of achieving a First.[37]

The release of the Modern History class lists in August 1927 proved that the concerns of Feiling and Molson had been well placed. Lennox-Boyd was devastated to discover that he had only got a Second. His friends attempted to draw what comfort they could from the result. Hilda Grenfell told him she was pleased about his Second and argued that the recipients of first-class degrees were

liable to drift into sloppy academic or bohemian ways.[38] The Dean
of Christ Church offered rather more headmasterly sympathy, suggesting that all life was an examination and that in the end he was
sure that Lennox-Boyd would be marked Alpha Plus.[39] Masterman
wrote of his own bitter disappointment at the result, but claimed,
not entirely convincingly, that it did not necessarily damage
Lennox-Boyd's chances of obtaining a fellowship at All Souls.[40]

Lennox-Boyd sat the examination for All Souls in the autumn
of 1927, but was unsuccessful. Meanwhile, he had embarked upon
a career in the law having entered the Middle Temple on the nomi-
nation of Colonel Sparkes, whom he had first encountered during
the General Strike.[41] Initially, he intended to pursue this for three
years and then make another attempt at the All Souls examination. In the event, however, he appears to have accepted Molson's
advice that this would be a mistake, and to have made no further
efforts to return to academic life in Oxford.[42] Within three years
he would, in any case, be a seasoned political campaigner with a
highly promising constituency. The fact remained, however, that the
failure to gain entry to All Souls was another severe blow to his
confidence. At the end of 1927, Masterman was prompted to tell
him that he must cultivate greater confidence in himself.[43] He had
a considerable record of success behind him and yet, Masterman
feared, failure was uppermost in his mind. It was a sad end to a
glittering Oxford career.

Notes

1   Swahili proverb from Zanzibar collected by Lennox-Boyd, PBM, Mss. Eng. c.
    3796, f. 276.
2   Masterman to Lennox-Boyd, 12 Feb. 1923, PBM, Mss. Eng. c. 3456. This was
    not, incidentally, the view of the King himself, who selected Magdalen for his
    son, the Prince of Wales, after having been advised by Lord Derby that Christ
    Church was becoming a den of *nouveaux riches* (Frances Donaldson, *Edward
    VIII* (London, Futura, 1976), p. 39).
3   *Isis*, no. 663, 29 Oct. 1924, p. 8.
4   *Oxford City Chronicle*, 18 June 1926.
5   *Isis*, no. 671, 4 Feb. 1925, p. 7; Ibid., no. 708, 16 June 1926, p. 10.
6   *Oxford City Chronicle*, 18 June 1926.
7   *Isis*, no. 711, 3 Nov. 1926, p. 7.
8   *Isis*, no. 667, 26 Nov. 1924, p. 10.
9   *Isis*, no. 694, 27 Jan. 1926, p. 17
10 *Isis*, no. 694, 27 Jan. 1926, p. 17.
11 Lord Pakenham, *Born to Believe* (London, Jonathan Cape, 1953), p. 36.
12 William Buchan, *John Buchan: A Memoir* (London, Harrap, 1982), p. 160.
13 Buchan served in the final months of the First World War as Director of Intel-
    ligence at the Ministry of Information – essentially as press liaison officer for
    MI5 (Anthony Masters, *The Man Who Was M* (London, Grafton, 1986), p. 30).
14 Juanita Kruse, *John Buchan and the Idea of Empire: Popular Literature and
    Political Ideology* (Lampeter, The Edwin Mellon Press, 1989), p. 99.

15 *Isis*, no. 682, 3 June 1925, p. 2.
16 Canning Club Minutes, Bodleian Library, Oxford, vol. 14, 1129th meeting, 3 June 1925, Dep. d. 782, f. 148.
17 Oxford Canning Club Minutes, vol. 14, 1137th meeting, 27 Jan. 1926, ff. 176–7.
18 Canning, vol. 14, 1123rd meeting, 18 Feb. 1925, ff. 131–3.
19 Blakeney to Lennox-Boyd, 17 Feb. 1925, PBM, Mss. Eng. c. 3456.
20 Colin Cross, *The Fascists in Britain* (London, Barrie and Rockliff, 1961), pp. 58–9.
21 Cross, p. 60.
22 Undated speech in Lennox-Boyd's hand, PBM, Mss. Eng. c. 3794.
23 *Newcastle Journal*, 20 Oct. 1936.
24 A.J.P. Taylor, *My Personal History* (London, Coronet Edn., 1984), p. 104.
25 *Oxford City Chronicle*, 18 June 1926.
26 Paul B. Rich, *Race and Empire in British Politics* (Cambridge, Cambridge University Press, Second Edition, 1990), p. 61.
27 Alan Lennox-Boyd, *The Development of the Idea of Trusteeship in the Government of Backward Peoples* (Beit Prize essay, 1926), pp. 96–7.
28 *The Development of the Idea of Trusteeship*, p. 120.
29 *The Development of the Idea of Trusteeship* p. 156.
30 *The Development of the Idea of Trusteeship*, p. 45.
31 *The Development of the Idea of Trusteeship*, p. 3.
32 Notes by Lord Boyd for Oxford Colonial Records Project Interview on his early career, PBM, Mss. Eng. c. 3429, f. 7.
33 *Isis*, no. 711, 3 Nov. 1926, p. 7.
34 John Parker, 'Oxford Politics in the Late Twenties', *Political Quarterly* (vol. 54, no. 2, April – June 1974), pp. 220–1.
35 *Isis*, no. 711, 3 Nov. 1926, p. 7.
36 Molson to Lennox-Boyd, 25 Dec. 1925, PBM, Mss. Eng. c. 3456.
37 Molson to Lennox-Boyd, 14 Aug. 1926, PBM, Mss. Eng. c. 3456.
38 Grenfell to Lennox-Boyd, 16 Aug. 1927, PBM, Mss. Eng. c. 3456.
39 White to Lennox-Boyd, 13 Aug. 1927, PBM, Mss. Eng. c. 3456.
40 Masterman to Lennox-Boyd, 15 Aug. 1927, PBM, Mss. Eng. c. 3456.
41 Grenfell to Lennox-Boyd, 24 Nov. 1927, PBM, Mss. Eng. c. 3456.
42 Molson to Lennox-Boyd, 1 Dec. 1927, PBM, Mss. Eng. c. 3456.
43 Masterman to Lennox-Boyd, 14 Dec. 1927, PBM, Mss. Eng. c. 3456.

3

The Wrecker of Mid-Beds

He who does not lie never grows up.[1]

In what may have been an attempt to ward off depression after his failure to achieve a First or win election to All Souls, Lennox-Boyd threw himself into a variety of activities after coming down from Oxford. His immediate objective was to qualify for the Bar. Although his legal studies occupied by no means all of his time, they were sufficient to earn him a first-class result in Roman Law in November 1929. He dabbled in the law during the early 1930s. In January 1932, for example, during the Parliamentary recess, he acted as judge's marshal on a tour of the Northern Circuit. Yet he was not called to the bar until November 1941 and does not appear to have practised thereafter.

His overriding ambition remained that of entering mainstream politics. In this, he continued to receive the support and encouragement of his mentor John Buchan. He also entered the orbit of a far more significant figure in British politics: Winston S. Churchill. They were brought together by the Christ Church don, Frederick Lindemann, who recommended Lennox-Boyd to Churchill when the latter was looking for a research assistant.[2] Plans that Lennox-Boyd should begin work for Churchill in October 1927 eventually came to nothing; but the two men struck up a warm if turbulent friendship, unquestionably the most important of Lennox-Boyd's political career. He made frequent visits to Chartwell as the guest not only of Winston but of other members of the

22

Churchill family. Winston's daughter, Diana, seems to have been particularly fond of him. His wife, Clementine, also fell for Lennox-Boyd's charms. In August 1929, she told her husband that the family had had 'that nice, tall young man, Alan Lennox-Boyd' to stay with them.[3]

In May 1928, less than a year after coming down from Oxford, Lennox-Boyd sought to be adopted as Conservative candidate for Southampton. He was already on sufficiently good terms with Churchill to persuade him to write a letter of recommendation to Lord Apsley, a local grandee. Apsley replied that although he had the greatest admiration for Lennox-Boyd, he thought that the executive committee of the Southampton Conservative Association would think him too young.[4] This assessment proved disappointingly accurate.

Lennox-Boyd's quest for a Parliamentary seat was interrupted in the autumn of 1928 by his first visit to the United States. He was part of a team from the Oxford Union which had been invited to take part in a series of debating competitions on American university campuses. His colleagues were two other former Presidents of the Union: Malcolm Brereton and Dingle Foot. Churchill briefed Lennox-Boyd on the virtues of the American political system. He explained that American Presidential elections were fought on a 'nobler' basis than British Parliamentary contests, the latter relying too much on demagogic 'catchwords'.[5] He also provided Lennox-Boyd with various introductions including one to his old friend Bernard Baruch, the financier and advisor to successive US Presidents. As is apparent from the notes which Lennox-Boyd made during the trip he was duly impressed; although more by the sheer scale and energy of America's city-scapes than by her form of government.

The tour involved an exhaustingly heavy schedule of speaking engagements covering over 20 universities across the United States. The motions for debate were generally chosen from a list of four. Two of these were non-specific showcase questions: 'that this house believes in duties rather than rights' and 'that this house believes that the best life is a public life'. The other two dealt with the League of Nations. Significantly, Lennox-Boyd along with both his colleagues always spoke in favour of the proposition 'that America should join the League of Nations'; but the motion 'that governments should adopt a system of compulsory arbitration in the settlement of international disputes' was opposed by Lennox-Boyd and Brereton and supported by Foot.

Lennox-Boyd and his colleagues managed to draw large and attentive audiences. A press report of their debate at Cornell University claimed that the 'Memorial Hall was wedged tight with those curious to see an Oxford man in the flesh'. All of this must have been particularly gratifying for a young man still struggling to make himself known at home and used to the more critical attentions of Conservative constituency associations.

In the course of the tour, the Oxford debating team visited the Ford motor works in Detroit. Lennox-Boyd was amazed at how clean and modern the shop floor appeared, 'more like an exhibition building' than a factory.[6] Detroit itself seemed a hive of energy where 'little men hurry hither and thither to serve it and to reap rich rewards'. What impressed Lennox-Boyd above all, however, was the idea that all of this had been set in motion by the creative genius of a single individual:

> Never was such power acquired by any man to mould according to his wishes the lives of thousands as Henry Ford has today. Everything is Ford or Fordian; his is the greatest industry; his was the incentive for the creation of a new city; his is the land that stretches for miles on either side of the neighbourhood...[7]

His impressions of Detroit find their strongest echo in the account he wrote of his first visit to Rome in 1933. What excited him most about both cities was that they bore the imprint of a 'Great Man', Ford and Mussolini respectively. In seeking to gauge the influence which this visit to the United States had upon Lennox-Boyd we are faced, as so often during his career, with a series of paradoxes. As Churchill had hoped, he did indeed learn a great deal, not only about the political system but also about how the democratic spirit in America permeated the most elementary forms of social interaction. Yet Detroit, like Rome, appeared to embody a very different lesson – that of the redemptive potential of one man's untrammelled authority.

Perhaps the most startling discovery of his tour for Lennox-Boyd was the extent to which racial segregation and racial hatred were everyday facts of life in the United States. On 27 November, Lennox-Boyd, Foot and Brereton took part in what was billed as an 'Inter-Racial – International' debate at the Bethel African Methodist Episcopal Church in Baltimore against a team from Lincoln, the segregated university in Pennsylvania. The team and almost the entire audience were Afro-American. This was the only debate of the tour which was not conducted on the basis of one of the four motions mentioned above. Instead, the question for discussion was 'Resolved: That prohibition is the most effective means of controlling the liquor traffic'. The Oxford team spoke against the motion, the Lincoln team for. Among Lincoln's representatives was the young Thurgood Marshall, who was to become the first black justice in the US Supreme Court, nominated by Lyndon Johnson at the height of the civil rights protests of the 1960s.[8] At the 1960 Lancaster House Conference on Kenya, shortly after Lennox-Boyd's retirement from the Colonial Office, Marshall served as a special adviser to the African nationalist delegation.

On the night of the debate, Lennox-Boyd and his colleagues were booked into a 'whites-only' hotel. When a senior member of the Lincoln faculty called for them he was rudely turned away by the hotel porter and called a 'nigger'.[9] While at Oxford, Lennox-Boyd had made flippant remarks about the need for 'racial purity' and the desirability of sending all the American negroes to Liberia.[10] Yet he was not prepared for the ugly reality of racial segregation and he found it extremely disturbing. This was the most important formative influence of his time in the United States. It left him more sensitive to the whole issue of race relations. It was also an experience he was to remember when as Colonial Secretary in the 1950s he had to field American criticism of British colonial rule in Africa.

Lennox-Boyd's tour of America was a great success and it was swiftly followed by another: his adoption in January 1929 as prospective Conservative Parliamentary candidate for the Gower Division of Glamorgan. He was one of four or five young men who had been asked to fight solidly Labour seats in the area. Their election expenses were to be met by Lord Kyslant, the chairman of the Wales and Monmouthshire Unionist Council. This appeared to absolve Lennox-Boyd from any financial worries. Unfortunately, shortly after the election Kyslant went bankrupt and was sent to jail, leaving Lennox-Boyd concerned that he might have to meet the costs of the election himself.[11]

Lennox-Boyd's friendship with Churchill helped to sway the Gower selection committee as did his confident performance. According to a local press report:

> The new candidate, a tall slight young man, gave the meeting a most able and comprehensive address, which delivered in his clear voice with a faint sibilant lisp, aroused an enthusiastic response. He is a brilliant orator.[12]

Gower was a predominantly industrial area of South Wales with a large mining community, hardly promising territory for the Conservatives at the best of times; and by 1929, Conservative fortunes were flagging. It was represented by a former miner, Dai Grenfell, an extremely popular Labour member. Nevertheless, Lennox-Boyd threw himself into the campaign with characteristic enthusiasm.

He arranged with the President of the Gower Conservative Association to take up residence with his mother at Parc-le-Breos in
Glamorgan. In the pages of the local press, he even confessed to a
hitherto unrevealed interest in the Welsh language. He harnessed
the energies of his brothers behind a literally exhausting round of
canvassing and public meetings. Not for the first time, and certainly
not the last, he overestimated his own physical fitness and pushed
himself to the point of collapse. He had to cancel at least one speaking engagement on at the advice of his doctor.[13]

Quite how seriously he took the campaign is apparent from the
election address that he drafted. This was no doomed but heroic
defence of his own decidedly right-wing brand of Conservatism but
a programme carefully designed to appeal to an industrial
working-class audience. The first item on the agenda was 'PEACE
IN THE WORLD'. Lennox-Boyd boldly stated 'I am an ardent supporter of the LEAGUE OF NATIONS, of the WORLD COURT OF
ARBITRATION TREATIES and will support all schemes of systematic world DISARMAMENT'.[14] As with his new-found interest in
the Welsh language, this would have come as a surprise to anyone who had followed his career up to that point. The rest of the
address was devoted to proving the commitment of the Conservative Government and their candidate in Gower to improving
housing, health care, pensions and education, and reducing unemployment. While it promised that Lennox-Boyd would work 'for
the Development of our Empire and the multiplication of our colonial markets', no mention was made of the possibility of using
tariff barriers to advance these objectives. When he was questioned about his attitude towards tariff reform at his selection
meeting, Lennox-Boyd hedged expertly. He suggested that, if an
industry appeared to be subject to unfair foreign competition
based on subsidies or sweated labour, then an investigation
should be made 'by an impartial tribunal to see whether in the
interests of the country it should not be protected'. One can hardly
criticize Lennox-Boyd for shaping his platform to appeal to the
views of his electorate. All the same, the Gower campaign suggests that Lennox-Boyd's views might have been modified or at
least muted if, like Harold Macmillan, he had been faced with the
problem of defending a seat outside the relatively prosperous
South of England.

Lennox-Boyd's sterling efforts were not particularly well rewarded at the polls. He came third in the contest with 6,554 votes
to Grenfell's 20,664 – more than the Conservative and Liberal to-
tals combined. The Vice-Chairman of the Gower Conservative Association, in congratulating Lennox-Boyd on his excellent campaign,

took some comfort from the fact that the anti-Socialist vote had increased. He had, however, to admit that from a purely Conservative standpoint the result was disappointing. Yet by a strange turn of events the Gower defeat was to lead to Lennox-Boyd's adoption to a far more promising seat.

Shortly after the 1929 General Election, Lennox-Boyd spent a weekend with the Churchills at Chartwell. While he was there, he received the news that his former agent in Gower had forgotten to submit the election returns and that these had to be in by the following Monday. There followed a hair-raising car journey to London, with Randolph Churchill behind the wheel, apparently driving in the capital for the first time. They arrived at Conservative Central Office and Lennox-Boyd completed the necessary forms, only to find that these also required the signature of a magistrate. On a Saturday afternoon in Central London, magistrates suddenly seemed thin on the ground. Lennox-Boyd's suspicion that one might be found lurking in the Junior Carlton Club proved correct. 'I asked the porter there whether there was a magistrate in the house,' he later recalled. 'He said "Mr Wingfield, a big landowner in Bedfordshire is here – I am sure he would sign anything you like".'[15]

A.H. Wingfield was not only a landowner and magistrate but also chairman of the Mid-Bedfordshire Conservative Association. He took an instant liking to the young but already battle-hardened campaigner and not only signed the forms but invited him to spend a weekend at his home. On Lennox-Boyd's first visit to Ampthill House, Wingfield showed him something of the Mid-Beds constituency. Brigadier General W.W. Warner, who had held the seat for the Conservatives in the previous Parliament had been ousted by the Liberals and had announced that he would not be standing for re-election. Mid-Beds was a classic marginal seat which had not been held by the same party in two consecutive general elections since its formation in 1918. Yet it at least offered an enterprising candidate a reasonable chance of success. The second time Lennox-Boyd visited Ampthill, he and Wingfield dined with Brendan Bracken, the Conservative MP for North Paddington and a close associate of Churchill. According to Lennox-Boyd, Bracken, who lived just outside the constituency, said to Wingfield, 'Why don't you ask Alan to fight this seat?' 'Well, I'm summoning up the courage to ask him this afternoon,' Wingfield replied.[16]

The Duke of Bedford, the Conservatives' principal benefactor in the constituency, approved of Wingfield's choice. Thereafter, the official selection procedure represented something of a formality. Conservative Central Office was consulted only as an afterthought. Lennox-Boyd was unanimously adopted as prospective Conservative

candidate for Mid-Beds on Saturday 30 November 1929. His acceptance speech could not have been further removed from his speeches
in Gower earlier in the year. He claimed that the Conservative party
was without a policy and that if they were 'content to play the game
of politics as at present, they would remain in the wilderness'.[17] The
policy of 'Safeguarding' (the protection of domestic production by
tariff barriers) had, he argued, proved its worth under the previous
administration, but the Government had been afraid to take it to its
natural conclusion. Now it should be the basis of a concerted drive
to develop the economic potential of the   Empire.

This policy, which was to become the central plank of
Lennox-Boyd's campaign, was well suited to the needs of the constituency. The area around Biggleswade and Sandy was an important centre for market gardening, and voters there had reason to
resent competition from overseas farmers. Unlike the industrial
workers of Gower, they could expect to be net beneficiaries from a
system which raised food prices by imposing tariffs on foreign
imports. The policy also served to distinguish Lennox-Boyd from
his main opponent, the sitting Liberal MP, Milner Gray, a convinced
free trader. Yet the course which Lennox-Boyd adopted also reflected
wider conflicts within the Conservative Party itself.

The 1929 General Election had resulted in a minority Labour
Government with 287 seats against the Conservatives' 261 and the
Liberals' 59. There was widespread dissatisfaction within the Conservative party at Baldwin's leadership and this expressed itself in
two direct challenges to Baldwin's leadership. The first was the
campaign for tariff reform. This was spearheaded by the Empire
Economic Union, whose founders included the former Conservative Ministers Lords Brentford and Birkenhead, and by the Empire
Free Trade campaign of the press barons Lords Rothermere and
Beaverbrook. The latter organization declared itself ready to field
candidates in by-elections against Conservatives who opposed its
cause.[18] The second challenge was over India. It reflected a genuine fear within the party that Baldwin was conducting a policy of
surrender to nationalist agitation on the sub-continent. Yet for some
of its leaders, particularly Churchill, it was essentially a pretext to
attack Baldwin.[19]

At a meeting in Stotfold at the beginning of May 1930,
Lennox-Boyd implicitly endorsed Beaverbrook's stand.[20] The speech
was noticed by Beaverbrook himself, who wrote to Lennox-Boyd to
say how pleased he was with it, and to express the hope that he
would continue to make propaganda for the cause. Lennox-Boyd
replied that he would do what he could to help.[21] Nevertheless, he
recognized the need to tread carefully on this issue. In July 1929,

Conservative Central Office had withdrawn official support from Sir John Ferguson, the Conservative candidate at the Twickenham by-election who had become too closely associated with the cause of Empire Free Trade.[22] As Lennox-Boyd later recalled, he himself was 'a little bit hard to get in signing on the dotted line with Beaverbrook or Rothermere'.[23] At least until the establishment of the National Government in August 1931, he attempted to balance his support for tariff reform with a display of loyalty to the party leadership. As Baldwin re-established his authority within the party, Lennox-Boyd had to step back from complete identification with the Beaverbrook campaign. This was despite the fact that his local Conservative Association made clear its own firm support for protectionism.[24]

On the issue of India, Lennox-Boyd proved more willing to defy the party leadership. In December 1929, the Viceroy, Lord Irwin, declared that the ultimate objective of British policy in India was Dominion status. The Congress party responded by raising the stakes. They demanded full independence. A new campaign of civil disobedience was launched and Gandhi and many of his supporters were jailed. In June 1930, the Simon Commission recommended the introduction of responsible government for the Indian provinces and new negotiations to determine the shape of the central administration. These began in November with the first Round Table conference in London. Although Congress boycotted the conference, Irwin persuaded other Indian representatives, including the princes, to attend. The decision of the conference to agree in principle to a federal constitution put pressure on Congress and the British to resume negotiations. Irwin released Gandhi and talks began. From the time of Irwin's declaration of December 1929, Baldwin had supported the Viceroy, in the face of mounting criticism from within the Conservative party, and from Churchill in particular. Gandhi's release was the final straw for Churchill who resigned from the Shadow Cabinet in protest on 27 January 1931.

In his Beit essay, Lennox-Boyd had displayed a relatively tolerant attitude towards Congress and an acceptance that Britain's role was to guide India towards an ever greater degree of self-government. Churchill's attitude was, to say the least, far less nuanced. Indeed, as Baldwin once suggested, his views often seemed a reversion to the mess-room prejudices of his days as a young subaltern in the Bombay of the 1890s. Following a visit to Chartwell in June 1931 Lennox-Boyd recorded an extraordinary diatribe by Churchill:

Of their religion: The time to cure it was after the mutiny. We won't
touch your religion!! Pah! We should have said we will cleanse your
dirty religion. What w[oul]d you think if Westminster, St. Paul's and
York had brothels attached, for the delectation of worshippers... Oh,
but it's Eastern, mysterious, sublime! But I call it damned dirty. And
Irwin – all this stuff had sent him fuzzy. He's done for and will not be
heard of again... Irwin? Lord worming and squirming is a better
name.[25]

Despite being regarded with extreme suspicion by the Conservative leadership, Churchill's views struck a chord with ordinary
party activists, not least those of Lennox-Boyd's constituency.
On 25 February 1931 the Conservative Party's Central Council
passed a resolution which called on the party to make a strong
stand for law and order in India. The annual meeting of the
Mid-Beds Conservative Association debated a motion which
endorsed this decision and expressed approval for Churchill 'in
his endeavour to marshal British opinion on the subject of   India
by formally dissociating himself from any complicity in the weak,
wrong-headed administration of India by any party, or by the
Socialist Government and the Viceroy acting under its orders'.[26]
The motion was passed by an overwhelming majority with only
three votes against. Lennox-Boyd's reaction to the motion was
that Churchill had performed 'an immense public service' by his
stance on India.

Lennox-Boyd's own position undoubtedly hardened during this
period. In place of the inevitability of constitutional development,
his speeches increasingly stressed the importance of the static
elements of the political settlement – the Indian Civil Service and
the personal rule of the princes. He also raised the position of the
'untouchables', for whom, he implied, the continuation of British
rule was the only guarantee of impartial government. The fact that
his principal opponent in Mid-Beds, the sitting MP Milner Gray,
supported Government policy, was a further incentive to question
the wisdom of reform. Over the next few months, Lennox-Boyd's
political centre of gravity was to swing ever more firmly away from
Conservative Central Office towards a dependence upon the support of his constituency party and of anti-Baldwinites like Churchill
and Beaverbrook. This almost certainly contributed to his subsequent adoption of a resolutely 'die-hard' position on India.

Lennox-Boyd's decisive break from the bonds of party discipline
was brought about by the circumstances of the 1931 General Election. Although the offer of a winnable Parliamentary seat had come
to him quite fortuitously, he grasped it with all the force that youth-
ful ambition and energy could confer. Twelve months after his
adoption as prospective candidate, Lennox-Boyd was able to claim

that he had addressed nearly 60 meetings and would soon have visited every village in the constituency. When in October 1931 he was officially adopted to fight the forthcoming election, he could boast of having made 12–13,000 personal visits across Mid-Beds.

Yet after two years of intense effort, there arose the possibility of the candidature being snatched away from him as suddenly as it had been offered. In August 1931, the Labour Prime Minister, Ramsay MacDonald, faced with a revolt within his Cabinet over spending cuts, was persuaded to lead a rump of his colleagues into a 'National' coalition government with the Liberals and Conservatives. Among the Liberals who entered government with the formation of this administration was the member for Mid-Beds, Milner Gray. At the beginning of October, a general election was called with the purpose of enabling the National Government to obtain 'a doctor's mandate' for measures to restore the economy. Not surprisingly, Gray felt that the Conservative candidate should make way for him as the official National Government representative. Equally unsurprising was Lennox-Boyd's determination not to allow two years of political campaigning to go to waste. As he later recalled, his attitude to Gray was dismissive:

> He was Parliamentary Secretary to the Minister of Labour and of course that was an important ministerial appointment, but I was very young and very rude and I said the fact that he was a bottle washer in the Government was no reason why he should be treated with great respect.[27]

During the ensuing campaign, Lennox-Boyd claimed that Conservative Central Office had not requested him to step down as a candidate. Whether or not any formal request was made, Central Office certainly made it clear to him that, given Gray's membership of the National Government, they could not support Lennox-Boyd. He came under pressure to retire from the contest from a number of quarters. The Lord Lieutenant of Bedfordshire, Howard Whitbread, sought to persuade Lennox-Boyd that it would be improper for him to challenge the National candidate. Lennox-Boyd replied that it was improper for the Lord Lieutenant to intervene in Parliamentary politics whereupon Whitbread issued a public statement deploring his candidature. The Duke of Bedford sent an emissary to Baldwin who was staying with Lord Derby at Knowsley, begging him to send Lennox-Boyd a message of support. Baldwin replied that he could not.

Despite all of this, however, the dispute as to whether Lennox-Boyd should stand does not appear to have extended in any major sense to the Mid-Beds Conservative Association, which on 9 October adopted him as their candidate. The mood of this meeting was enthusiastic and Lennox-Boyd was given a warm reception.[28] The patronage of the Duke of Bedford acted as a counterbalance to those voices urging Lennox-Boyd to stand down. Bedford's family, the Russells, had feuded with the Whitbreads ever since another electoral dispute a century and a half before. The intervention of the Lord Lieutenant served, therefore, only to endear Lennox-Boyd further to the Duke. It was, however, contemporary political arguments which had the greater bearing upon the mood of the constituency party activists. Apart from their natural desire to field a candidate, they were aware that the alternative was to support a politician whose views diverged widely from their own on the key issues of India and Imperial preference.[29]

Even before the campaign was announced, Lennox-Boyd had already sought the assistance of Beaverbrook. Early in September he asked him to come and address a meeting in his constituency. Beaverbrook was happy to do so but was clearly concerned that his intervention might damage Lennox-Boyd's standing with his party.[30] Lennox-Boyd assured him:

> No embarrassment in any way would be caused to me by your powerful advocacy of a policy which I have tried myself to preach down here.[31]

When the General Election was called at the beginning of October and pressure was placed on him to step down, he again consulted Beaverbrook. As he reminded Lennox-Boyd some years later, Beaverbrook advised him 'to tell the Tory machine to go to the furthermost part of hell'.[32] The Beaverbrook press threw its support behind Lennox-Boyd and tariff reform became the central element of his campaign. Beaverbrook provided practical help in the form of the loan of a car and a van. He also made a personal appearance in Mid-Beds on 15 October, when he addressed a mass meeting in Leighton Buzzard. Lennox-Boyd later recalled travelling up to the constituency with his patron. 'Tell me what Mid-Bedfordshire produces,' demanded Beaverbrook. 'Brussel sprouts,' Lennox-Boyd replied. Beaverbrook turned to his secretary. 'Find me something in the Bible about brussel sprouts,' he snapped.[33]

The day before the General Election, at Lennox-Boyd's request, the *Daily Express* carried a message of support for him from Beaverbrook, praising his efforts to 'protect British market gardeners against crushing importation of foreign produce'.[34] Although they were to remain friends, Beaverbrook and Lennox-Boyd were never again as close as they were during this election. When it was over Beaverbrook telegraphed 'I am as happy as if you were my own son.'[35] It was a phrase which Lennox-Boyd recalled many years later. As someone with a tendency to worship strong men and seek out father figures, it must have struck a particularly deep chord.

Milner Gray was not without his own high-ranking supporters. Shortly before the election, he published letters of endorsement from the Prime Minister, Ramsay MacDonald, and the Chancellor of the Exchequer, Philip Snowden. MacDonald claimed to be 'amazed' that as a former Minister in the National Government, Gray was being challenged by someone who purported to support that administration.[36] Snowden denounced the challenge as 'deplorable'. The press took up this theme, accusing Lennox-Boyd of damaging the prospects of a National Government victory by splitting the anti-Socialist vote in his constituency. They provided him with the label which he was to wear defiantly for many years to come – 'The Wrecker of Mid-Beds'.

The interest which this bitter contest had aroused was reflected in an unusually high turn out in Mid-Beds, about 79%. The Court House at Amphill where the count was taking place was surrounded by supporters of Gray and Lennox-Boyd, both camps confident of victory; but when, at about 2.20 in the morning of the 28th, the candidates emerged from the building, it was Lennox-Boyd whose broad smile betrayed the result. The returning officer announced Lennox-Boyd's poll – 15,213 – and barely had time to pronounce the first two digits of Milner Gray's result – 13 – when a roar went up from Conservative supporters which was to drown out any further results.

Lennox-Boyd made a triumphal progress through the surrounding towns and villages with his mother and three brothers. Even Baldwin responded to his victory with a telegram of congratulation.[37] The mood of celebration among Conservatives was not shared by some of the local newspapers. *The Bedfordshire Times and Independent* bemoaned the fact that their new MP had been elected on the basis of protection rather than support for the National Government adding, with a certain pomposity,

> The Duke's protégé has stood avowedly for nothing more than 'tariffs and the quota system': his constituents have no right to expect the wider or more 'national' or statesmanlike outlook from Mr Lennox-Boyd.[38]

How far Lennox-Boyd's subsequent record as a young MP could be judged to be 'statesmanlike' is really a matter of individual taste. The people of Mid-Beds had, however, elected someone who by his own admission was 'very young and very rude'. He was not about to turn overnight into a compliant piece of National Government lobby fodder.

Notes

1   Ganda proverb from Uganda collected by Lennox-Boyd, PBM, Mss. Eng. c. 3796, f. 274.
2   Lindemann to Lennox-Boyd, 15 July 1927, PBM, Mss. Eng. c. 3456.
3   Clementine Churchill to Winston S. Churchill, 31 Aug. 1929, reproduced in Martin Gilbert, *Winston S. Churchill*, vol. 5, Companion, Part 2 (London, Heinemann, 1981), p. 65.
4   Eddie Marsh to Lennox-Boyd, 5 May 1928, PBM, Mss. Eng. c. 3457.
5   Diary, undated Sept. 1928, PBM, Mss. Eng. c. 3338, f. 62.
6   Diary, 13 Oct. 1928, PBM, Mss. Eng. c. 3338, f. 92.
7   Diary, 13 Oct. 1928, PBM, Mss. Eng. c. 3338, ff. 92–3.
8   SB, *America 1928*, p. 47.
9   Conversation with Patricia, Viscountess Boyd, 6 Sept. 1994.
10 Minutes of the Chatham Club, vol. 9, 912th meeting, 18 Nov. 1925, Mss. Top. Oxon. d. 727, f. 113; Diary, 1 March 1933, PBM, Mss. Eng. c. 3338, f. 226.
11 Interview on Lord Boyd's early career conducted by Gillian Peele, 20 Feb. 1975, PBM, Mss Eng. c. 3432, f. 1.
12 SB, *Gower and Mid-Beds 1929–1930*, p. 3.
13 *South Wales Daily Post*, 25 March 1929.
14 Undated draft in Lennox-Boyd's hand of Gower Election Address, PBM, Mss. Eng. c. 3794.
15 Interview on Lord Boyd's early career, PBM, Mss. Eng. c. 3432, f. 2.
16 Interview with Lord Boyd on his early career, PBM, Mss. Eng. c. 3432, f. 19.
17 *Bedfordshire Standard*, 6 Dec. 1929.
18 Carl Bridge, *Holding India to the Empire: The British Conservative Party and the 1935 Constitution* (New York, Envoy Press, 1986), p. 33.
19 Bridge, p. 34.
20 *Bedfordshire Standard*, 9 May 1930.
21 Beaverbrook Papers, House of Lords Record Office, BBK C/55, Beaverbrook to Lennox-Boyd, 17 May 1930; Lennox-Boyd to Beaverbrook, undated.
22 Anne Chisholm and Michael Davie, *Beaverbrook: A Life* (Hutchinson, London, 1992), p. 281.
23 Interview with Lord Boyd on his early career, PBM, Mss Eng. c. 3432, f. 3.
24 *Bedfordshire Standard*, 21 Nov. 1930.
25 Diary, 7–8 June 1931, PBM, Mss. Eng. c. 3338, ff. 149–50.
26 *Luton News*, 5 March 1931.
27 Interview on Lord Boyd's early career, PBM, Mss. Eng. c. 3432, f. 11.
28 *The Leighton Buzzard Observer*, 13 Oct. 1931.
29 *The Leighton Buzzard Observer*, 13 Oct. 1931.
30 Beaverbrook to Lennox-Boyd, 14 Sept. 1931, BBK C/55.
31 Lennox-Boyd to Beaverbrook, 15 Sept. 1931, BBK C/55.
32 Beaverbrook to Lennox-Boyd, 8 May 1944, BBK C/55.
33 I am grateful to Piers Brendon for this story.
34 *Daily Express*, 26 Oct. 1931.
35 Interview on Lord Boyd's early career, Mss. Eng. c. 3432, p. 3.
36 SB, *Mid-Beds 1930–1*, p. 50.
37 SB *1930–31*, p. 60.
38 *The Bedfordshire Times and Independent*, 30 Oct. 1931.

4

Bad Company

It is no good asking the spirits to help you run if you do not mean to sprint.[1]

Lennox-Boyd was sworn in as a new MP on 5 November 1931. There is a story, perhaps apocryphal, that Donald Lennox-Boyd smuggled himself into the Chamber and sat waving at his brother from the benches opposite. Whether or not this is true, it would have been quite easy for an interloper to go unnoticed on the Government benches in the immediate aftermath of the October Election. National Government supporters had gained 554 out of the 615 seats. Conservative MPs alone totalled 473. The Labour opposition, by contrast, numbered only 52.

As one of a large crop of new Government backbenchers, Lennox-Boyd's prospects of making a mark and gaining promotion appeared frustratingly remote. At the end of his first parliamentary session, he recorded in his diary, 'How I long for a hard job and stern sentries to watch my performance at it'.[2] When Parliament resumed he noted:

> I have made a series of resolutions actively to engage in Parliamentary life this year – it is the easiest place in the world in which to slack off and become an onlooker.[3]

Yet the Government's impregnable majority, combined with the circumstances of his election, also left Lennox-Boyd feeling free to follow his own conscience.[4] If he required some further encouragement to take advantage of his freedom it was close at hand in the form of his old friend, Winston Churchill.

The first test of Lennox-Boyd's allegiance came only two weeks after the General Election. 1931 saw the enactment of the Statute

35

of Westminster which formally ended the sovereignty of the British Parliament over the Dominions except where the latter specifically asked for restrictions on their powers. It also gave Dominions' parliaments the right to pass legislation with extra-territorial effect. Churchill and his allies feared that this would allow the Irish Free State to repudiate the Government of Ireland Act of 1920 and the Articles of Agreement of 1922. They were particularly concerned that Britain might lose her rights of access to Irish ports in time of war. They therefore tabled an amendment to the Statute of Westminster which provided that nothing in the Act should be deemed to authorize the Irish Free State to repeal, amend or alter the 1920 or 1922 legislation.

Lennox-Boyd was highly tempted to vote with Churchill but was unready to defy the Government whips so early in his career. The Government opposed the amendment and it was defeated by a large majority.[5] Rather than voting against the Government, Lennox-Boyd abstained. As he later recalled,

> I met Winston in the lobby immediately afterwards. He said something to the effect that I had been screwing up my courage but hadn't screwed it up enough, and I remember feeling rather mortified.[6]

Churchill was soon to provide Lennox-Boyd with an opportunity to redeem himself. On 1 December, at the close of the second Round Table Conference, the Government published a White Paper setting out its revised constitutional proposals on India. These were considered by Conservative die-hards to be a retreat in the face of pressure from Indian nationalists. The following day, Churchill tabled a hostile amendment. This time Lennox-Boyd's courage did not fail him. He was one of 43 MPs who supported the amendment.

When Parliament reassembled in February 1932, Lennox-Boyd found himself already marked out as a rebel without having even spoken in the Chamber. He actually waited until 10 May to deliver his maiden speech. This came in the course of the debate on Neville Chamberlain's April 1932 budget. Not only did he disregard the convention that maiden speeches should be uncontroversial but he took the opportunity to criticize the performance of his own front bench. Lennox-Boyd voiced the concerns of many in the Conservative party that the Government had not taken full advantage of the mandate it received in the October General Election to make further drastic cuts in public expenditure. He argued that the current level of spending was beyond the country's means and that high taxation was crippling British industry. Indeed, he questioned whether 'the enormous expenditure we are incurring on social services is necessarily synonymous with social progress':

> Why spend £100,000,000 a year on education? Why imagine that if
> we continue to spend £100,000,000 a year on education and keep the
> parents out of work that the children in the future will be more grateful
> to us or the country better off than if we spend a little less and give
> their fathers employment.[7]

In a telling intervention in March 1933 during a Commons debate
on the subject of rural industries, Lennox-Boyd made it clear that
his objections to Government spending on education were not solely
based on economic arguments. He also believed that popular education served to undermine traditional social relations:

> ...our charcoal burners are living in huts which are almost exact rep-
> licas of the hut-circle habitations of our primitive ancestors. But a
> Government inspector comes round and finds that, though these men
> have worked for generations in those huts and have taken no harm
> from the woods, the huts do not conform to some regulation of the
> Ministry of Health, or that a small boy in the hut is ignorant of some
> algebraic problem, and the whole force of Parliament is brought to bear,
> an Act is prepared, the Government Whips are brought on, a new red
> villa is built in the woods, an asphalt path is laid from the villa to the
> school, and there the child learns of the day when William the Con-
> queror came to the Throne, but he will be taught to despise a trade
> which was old at the time of the Conquest.[8]

He condemned what he regarded as the educational bias against
rural employment and the assumption 'that the only man whose
education had justified itself is the person who can wear a black coat
– and then finds when he looks for work that there is none at hand'.

Lennox-Boyd was by no means unique in his nostalgia for an
imagined golden age when authority within English society grew
naturally from traditional bonds of duty and deference. Yet by
the 1930s, most Conservatives recognized that they could not
hope to fight a rear-guard action against the encroachment of
modern, state-sponsored individualism. In looking further afield
to the pre-industrial societies of the British Empire, Lennox-Boyd
found a more fruitful outlet for his romantic ultra-conservatism.
The rhetoric which he had applied to the charcoal burners trans-
lated remarkably easily to the colonial sphere where it would
command wide-spread acceptance within the Conservative Party
for many years to come. The party's 1949 statement on colonial
affairs, *Imperial Policy*, which Lennox-Boyd helped to draft,
noted:

> The Conservative Party considers that in the past there has been too much
> rigidity and lack of imagination in Colonial education policy, and that while
> the aim is to combat the illiteracy, the introduction of a purely European
> type of education has encouraged the growth of a class of black-coated
> workers who grow up to despise those who work with their hands.[9]

It was an irony which was probably lost on the drafting committee that this 'European' education had been regarded by one of its members as almost equally unsuitable and subversive when applied to British rural communities.

In a similar way, the concerns Lennox-Boyd was later to express about the wisdom of establishing democratic forms of government in the colonies contained echoes of his earlier fears about the advent of full democracy in Britain. It was only in 1929 that the British themselves first went to the polls on the basis of universal adult suffrage, a development which clearly afforded the young Conservative candidate for Gower some unease. He began the draft of his address for the 1929 General Election with the following statement:

> For the first time we are a complete democracy of men and women, and political leaders are already endeavouring to outdo one another in the offering of BRIBES. Yet as I am venturing to offer myself as the Conservative and Unionist Candidate for the Gower Division, I shall not take part in a game of this kind.[10]

The Labour Party's subsequent victory did nothing to dispel Lennox-Boyd's doubts regarding the collective wisdom of the newly enlarged electorate. The Labour Government's collapse in August 1931 and the formation of an emergency administration suggested to him that the whole system was extremely fragile. Shortly after entering Parliament he recorded his belief that, should the new government not succeed, there would be 'a wave of popular disillusionment which may cripple parliamentary institutions and lead to startling changes in our forms of government'.[11]

His profound suspicion of democratic innovations found an outlet in his continuing opposition to the Government's policy towards India. The Government's White Paper on India of March 1933 had resulted in the establishment a Parliamentary Joint Select Committee to investigate constitutional reform. This reported in the autumn of 1934, and the Government introduced a bill based on its recommendations. It provided for the granting of elected self-government in the provinces, and for the creation of a federal system of government for India as a whole, with the Viceroy retaining control over a number of key areas including defence and foreign affairs. Churchill and his allies coordinated their opposition to these proposals through the extra-Parliamentary India Defence League and its Parliamentary counterpart, the India Defence Committee of which Lennox-Boyd became joint secretary. On 4 December 1934, they put their case before the Party's Central Council in the form of an amendment, tabled by Lord Salisbury, to the leadership's motion accepting the principles of the Select Committee's report. The amendment directed its criticism at the proposal for a central representative government in India.[12] Disappointingly for the rebels, it was decisively rejected by 1,102 votes to 390.

Defeat in the Commons was more of a formality. Lennox-Boyd was among 37 MPs who, the same month, put their signatures to an amendment to the White Paper. It was, perhaps, a mark of the diehards' frustration that this adopted an even more extreme position than the one tabled before the Central Council. Unlike Salisbury's amendment, it did not even accept the provisions for provincial autonomy which many of them, including Lennox-Boyd, had previously been prepared to tolerate. Indeed, it did not even command the support of all the India Defence League members in the Commons, five of whom voted against it.[13] The amendment was lost by 410 votes to 127.

Despite this defeat, Churchill and his supporters continued to harry the Government during the second reading and report stage of the Bill from February to May 1935. Few engaged more actively in the struggle than Lennox-Boyd. In his arguments against the assumptions behind the Bill one can identify three principles which were to continue to guide his approach to colonial affairs. The first of these was that the 'Westminster model' of government was not necessarily appropriate for extra-European cultures. During the debate on the second reading of the bill, Lennox-Boyd told the House that although he and his allies accepted that democracy was the most suitable form of government for Britain,

> ...we are neither democrats nor Parliamentarians when we approach the problem of India until the Indian people, by a sense of responsibility, have proved to us that Western institutions of this kind are suitable to the genius of the East.[14]

The second principle was that 'traditional' systems of government should be protected from the modernizing ambitions of nationalist politicians. In the case of the India Bill, the diehards' attentions focused upon the rulers of the princely states, at least half of whom had to give their assent in order for the federation proposed by the legislation to be put into effect. Churchill and his allies saw their opportunity to wreck the Bill and made every effort to persuade the rulers to reject the constitution. Nevertheless, as he recorded in his journal in January 1933, Lennox-Boyd sincerely believed that contact with more democratic systems would be destabilizing for the princely states.[15]

The third prong of Lennox-Boyd's attack on the principles behind the Bill was the argument that the British Government was

paying too much attention to a vocal minority of Westernised nationalist politicians. The mass of the population were, by contrast,
interested not in politics but in their immediate material wellbeing
which could be best safeguarded by the preservation of colonial rule.
During the February 1935 India debate, Lennox-Boyd joked that
Indian peasants were saying, 'If Mr Gandhi is a saint let him raise
the price of our corn.' The problem with this argument, as the British discovered elsewhere in the world, was that their continued presence in and orderly retreat from the colonies required them to make
deals with local politicians, not with stoical peasants. Furthermore,
Gandhi and his successors proved remarkably successful in persuading their peoples that they could not live by bread alone.

Like Churchill, Lennox-Boyd viewed the problems of India from
a distance. He did not visit India until after his retirement from
active politics. His enthusiasm for the Empire in general and traditional rulers in particular was, however, boosted by a visit he
made to Uganda and Tanganyika in August 1934 as a member of
a delegation from the Empire Parliamentary Association. The
group's first port of call was Buganda, the most powerful of
Uganda's kingdoms. Although the 1900 Agreement with the British had resulted in a significant revision of the system of
government there, it still appeared to outsiders to be the epitome
of a 'traditional African kingdom'. The MPs met its ruler, the
Kabaka, Daudi Chwa. They were introduced to one of the widows
of Daudi Chwa's grandfather, the Kabaka Mutesa, at whose court
Stanley had arrived in 1875. The delegation also visited the other
Ugandan kingdoms of Bunyoro, Toro and Ankole. In a further
incident, calculated to excite Lennox-Boyd's romantic imagination,
the MPs witnessed the District Commissioner returning to the
Mukama of Bunyoro the standards which Captain Thruston had
captured when seeking to 'pacify' the kingdom in the 1890s.

Although the chiefs outside Buganda notionally derived their authority from their traditional status they became, under the colonial system, little more than government appointees. To a delighted
Lennox-Boyd, however, they seemed to inhabit a world in which the
'divine right of kings' was still a governing principle of society. As
he recalled much later in his life:

> I didn't find the existence of the four princely states, Buganda,
> Bunyoro, Toro and Ankole an anachronism in any way. I liked the little
> gilded courts and I didn't find the people there any less happy than
> in the directly administered areas.[16]

Yet he did more than merely project onto Uganda romantic notions
of Britain's ancient traditions. The presence of these kingdoms

within the Empire became, for Lennox-Boyd, an argument for Britain to preserve and enhance the mystique of her own monarchy.
During his visit to Bunyoro he witnessed the Mukama's reaction
on being presented with a signed photograph of the 'King Emperor'.
He recalled shortly afterwards:

> Every inch of the photograph was scanned greedily. It was a Royal
> photograph, the King blazing with Orders. 'This is a King indeed.' I
> felt greatly relieved that the bowler-hat conception of Monarchy has
> not yet penetrated to Great Britain with her world-wide Empire.[17]

The report that the MPs drafted after their return to England supported Lennox-Boyd's view that the peoples of Uganda were
perfectly contented with the 'traditional' structures of indirect rule.
The chiefs understood 'the workings of the native mind' better
than any European and little benefit would accrue from the
importation of Western practices. In particular, the MPs asserted
that 'the native prefers speedy justice, be it rough and ready,
rather than all the refinements so near to the heart of the legal
fraternity'.[18] The report's comments on education in Uganda were
fully consistent with Lennox-Boyd's general hostility towards the
imposition of formal schooling on traditional communities both
at home and abroad:

> The delegation are particularly pleased to notice that the Government
> are making a strenuous effort to prevent the formation of a 'failed B.A.'
> class of native and have realized the value of vocational training.

Lennox-Boyd's overriding belief in the need to consolidate the British Empire exercised a strong influence on his attitude to domestic
economic questions. He continued to champion the cause of tariff
reform. A speech to the Commons on the subject in May 1934,
prepared with Beaverbrook's assistance, drew enthusiastic praise
from the great Imperial statesman, L. S. Amery. Beaverbrook himself told Lennox-Boyd that his had been the most valuable
contribution during the whole debate adding, 'The leadership of the
Empire movement in the House is vacant. It is a place you can
make your own if you choose to do so.'[19] He underlined his genuine regard for Lennox-Boyd by agreeing to speak on his behalf
during the 1935 General Election campaign, a service he
apparently performed for no other Conservative candidate.[20]

Lennox-Boyd's loyalty to the cause of Empire Free Trade did not
earn him universal approbation within his constituency. During the
debate of May 1934, he referred to 'unscrupulous people in rural
districts' who were using the controversy over imports of dairy
produce from New Zealand to argue that the prosperity of British

farmers was incompatible with Imperial agricultural development.[21] It was at about this time that Lennox-Boyd hit upon a novel device to demonstrate that the problems faced by British farmers were due to factors other than Dominion imports. In the summer of 1936, this scheme became a reality with the opening of 'Bedfordshire Producers', a greengrocers' shop in Somers Town, London. The shop was a joint venture between Lennox-Boyd and William Rapley, an agricultural correspondent from the *News Chronicle*. Its purpose was to show that the market gardeners of Mid-Beds were not receiving fair prices from London merchants and that their food could be made available to consumers more cheaply while at the same time bringing them higher returns.[22] The scheme proved so successful that he was able to open a second shop in the West End in November.

Lennox-Boyd's high-profile brand of politics and his unquestionable devotion to his constituency paid off in electoral terms. Given his reputation as a rebel, he was afraid that Conservative Central Office might attempt to sabotage his re-election. In July 1934, he recorded:

> Bad news at the C[entral] O[ffice]. They want to take my agent and promote him to London and so I fear imperil my organization in Mid-Beds perhaps damaging it fatally for the next election.[23]

Yet when the General Election did come in November 1935, Lennox-Boyd was able to put up an impressive fight. He managed to persuade both Beaverbrook and Churchill to speak on his behalf. In the event, he actually managed to increase his majority. He was told by a friend that when his result was announced in the Carlton Club, a great whoop of joy rang out and even one of the Party whips sang his praises.[24] In June 1936 he felt sufficiently secure to lease a house in the constituency – Henlow Grange – and settle his mother there. His increased majority also consolidated his position in the Commons and he took full advantage of the licence that it afforded him.

He was at his most outspoken in matters of foreign policy. His apparent sympathy for the fascist dictatorships was never forgotten or forgiven by his opponents. He distinguished clearly, however, between Mussolini and Franco whom he admired, and Hitler towards whom he was always suspicious. In April 1933, Lennox-Boyd had joined a delegation of British MPs to the International Parliamentary Commercial Conference in Rome. It was his first visit to the Italian capital and he was deeply impressed by what he saw there. He recorded that the city 'far outdoes all my expectations'.[25] As well as being treated to a stream of anecdotes by senior fascists about Mussolini's brilliant achievements, Lennox-Boyd also had the opportunity to dine with the Duce and came away dazzled by 'his amazing eyes'. An entry in his diary demonstrates how enthusiastically he had absorbed the propaganda surrounding the Italian leader:

> A master man – Pontine Marshes, recreation of old Rome, youth enlivened...and industrial peace. Press restriction is not a heavy price to pay.[26]

Also in Rome at the same time were Oswald and Cynthia Mosley with a small group from the British Union of Fascists (BUF). Lennox-Boyd found himself at one with the Mosleys in finding many lessons for Britain in the Italian experiment. He recorded in his diary:

> Cynthia Mosley bitter on Parliament – spoke of Pontine drainings and released capital and the leadership so lacking in our pedestrian policies. Heartily agreed with nine-tenths of what she said.[14]

Lennox-Boyd's visit to Rome clearly reinforced his admiration for the Italian fascist movement. It was a sentiment shared by a large section of the British political élite, including Churchill; and Oswald Mosley was keen to exploit this in order to attract prominent supporters to the BUF. One of the organizations through which the BUF attempted to foster contacts with potential sympathizers outside their movement was the January Club. This was established in 1934 with the intention of providing 'a platform for leaders of Fascist and Corporate State thought'.[28] When Lennox-Boyd's membership of the Club was revealed in the press, he and a fellow Conservative MP, Michael Beaumont, were labelled 'Genteel Fascists'.[29] Beaumont, while denying that he was a fascist, was an avowed 'anti-democrat' who defended the BUF in Parliament after its violent rally at Olympia in June 1934. Yet many of its members were, like its first chairman, Sir John Squire, admirers of Mussolini who were at the same time uncomfortable with the poorly disguised extremism of the BUF. The Club was particularly keen to distance itself from Hitler's brand of fascism. Indeed, it drew to its meetings not only Zionists but also stalwart supporters of Churchill like Brendan Bracken and Duncan Sandys.

Lennox-Boyd's own feelings towards Nazi Germany were decidedly mixed. He made a number of visits there before the war and included occasional references in his speeches to the lessons which could be learned from this and other 'continental dictatorships'. Predictably, he saw Germany as a bulwark against the spread of Bolshevism from the East. At the same time, he was repelled by the brutality of the Nazis. In the summer of 1934, at the height of

the BUF's drive for respectability, two events occurred which alien-
ated many of those in Britain who had initially inclined towards
sympathy for the Nazis: the Night of the Long Knives in Germany
and the murder of Chancellor Dollfuss of Austria. In July,
Lennox-Boyd met the wife of Sir Charles Petrie, Foreign Editor of
the high Tory *English Review*. He noted that she and her husband,
although 'initially favourable' to the Nazis, had been 'repelled
by the Hitler massacre', particularly 'the linking of so many
incongruous victims'.[30] Later that month Lennox-Boyd recorded his
own 'great distress' at hearing of the death of Dollfuss.[31] Two days
later he noted that Hitler was 'doing everything to suggest innocence of the Dollfuss murder' but concluded that 'his campaign
inspired it all'.[32]

In contrast to his cautious view of Hitler, Lennox-Boyd's attitude towards General Franco was and remained one of virtually
uncritical admiration. From the time of the attempted coup by
a group of Spanish Generals in July 1936, he was a leading supporter of the Nationalist cause on the Conservative benches.
Lennox-Boyd made no apologies for his support for Franco either at the time or subsequently. He maintained that the alternative to Franco was a Communist government threatening
Gibraltar. He did not advocate direct British military involvement
on the side of Franco but he repeatedly urged the Government
to provide indirect support for the Nationalists. As early as 11
November 1936, he was urging the Foreign Secretary, Anthony
Eden, to recognize Franco's government.[33] In July 1937,
Lennox-Boyd argued that Franco's forces should be granted bel-
ligerency rights by the British Government.[34] Besides arguing
Franco's case in the Commons, he also became actively involved
in the pressure group, The Friends of National Spain, along with
other 'diehard' Tory MPs like Sir Henry Page Croft, Patrick
Donner and Victor Cazalet.

As a young MP, Lennox-Boyd's attitude towards his left-wing opponents was hardly emollient and his stance on Spain gave them
particular reason to hate him. He was described in *Tribune* as
'Franco's Little Friend'[35] and in the *Daily Worker* as 'Franco's
Deputy'.[36] His old Liberal opponent Milner Gray got in on the act,
calling Lennox-Boyd a 'playboy dictator'.[37] The *Daily Herald* printed
a cartoon by Vicky showing Lennox-Boyd and Page Croft
goose-stepping behind a pantomime horse which bore the head of
Franco and the jack-boots of Italy and Germany.[38] The cartoon was
reproduced by Lennox-Boyd's Labour opponent in the 1945 General Election as part of a leaflet reminding voters of his record of
support for the Nationalists.

It was not only on the left that the issue of Spain provoked strong reactions. In May 1941, Lennox-Boyd dined with his brother in law, Henry 'Chips' Channon, and the American Ambassador, John Winant. Channon recorded his surprise that Winant,

> did not seem as pleased to see Alan as I had supposed he would: during dinner it came out that they had differed over Franco. Nothing so divides people, not even Munich. Never have passions run so high on an issue.[39]

Indeed, it even divided Lennox-Boyd's family. George, his brother, visited Spain in 1938 and was shocked to find evidence of atrocities committed by both the Nationalist and Republican sides. On his return to Spain at the beginning of the following year, his sympathy for the Republicans increased as he witnessed the fall of Barcelona and the many refugees attempting to reach safety in France. He assisted in the evacuation of at least two Spanish citizens with the cooperation of the Republican government. Lennox-Boyd's relations with George although close, tended to be rather less so than with his other brothers and the emotive accounts of the situation in Spain which George published in the press can have done nothing to add to the warmth between them.

In 1934, Lennox-Boyd joined a group of Conservative MPs, calling themselves the Imperial Policy Group, to launch what they described as 'A New Patriotic Policy'. One of their key objectives was 'to free Great Britain from all unnecessary commitments in Europe: the British Empire to be the sole reason for entering or not entering any new alliance'.[40] Central to their approach was the belief that Britain should concentrate on the defence and development of her Empire and on strengthening her navy. At the same time, Britain should not allow the League of Nations to circumscribe her freedom of action. In February 1937, Lennox-Boyd went as far as to question publicly whether British interests might not be best served 'by washing our hands of world-wide universal obligations and confining ourselves at first, anyhow, to combining the British people into a real imperial League of Nations'.[41]

This attitude to the League was also in evidence following Mussolini's invasion of Abyssinia in October 1935. There was widespread agreement on the Government benches that the cooperation of Mussolini was essential if German ambitions were to be held in check and the stability of Europe maintained. Opinions differed, however, as to how far this strategy should be subordinated to the need to respond firmly to Mussolini's flagrant violation of international law. Senior back benchers like Austen Chamberlain and Winston Churchill believed that it was vital that the Government express support for collective action by the League. Lennox-Boyd, by contrast, was one of a group of MPs who met at the Constitutional Club on 11 October and urged the Government to reject 'any sanctions in any way likely to lead to war'.[42]

Lennox-Boyd and his colleagues differed from the Government not so much in their underlying analysis of the situation as in their lack of interest in any superficial compliance with the protocols of the League. Throughout Eden's period as Foreign Secretary, Lennox-Boyd maintained a consistent position of opposing sanctions against Italy and urging the Government to make concessions to Mussolini over Abyssinia. Although this seemed somewhat at odds with the Government's stated policy, it did not differ markedly from the private views of Chamberlain. In February 1938, Chamberlain's determination to reopen talks with Mussolini caused a final breach with Eden who resigned. During the Parliamentary debate on the issue on 21 February, only days before his appointment to the Government, Lennox-Boyd took the opportunity to argue that it was time for Britain to recognize the King of Italy as Emperor of Abyssinia.[43]

In one respect, however, Lennox-Boyd disagreed profoundly with the policy of 'appeasement'. After sending troops into the Rhineland on 7 March 1936, Hitler issued a series of proposals for the possible re-entry of Germany into the League of Nations. These included discussion of 'the question of colonial equality of rights'.[44] To Lennox-Boyd and those on the Conservative benches who shared his belief in the primacy of the British Empire, the idea of surrendering colonies to Germany was unthinkable. In April, he joined two arch anti-appeasers, Churchill and Sandys, in seeking from the Government an assurance 'that no application by Germany for the return of Tanganyika will be considered, at least during the lifetime of the present Government'.[45] The Government was seriously embarrassed by representations of this kind since an official committee under Lord Plymouth was currently considering the feasibility of any such return. The Plymouth Committee eventually concluded that the problems involved in any transfer of colonies would be formidable, and in July, the Government announced that it had not been able to resolve the 'moral, political and legal' difficulties posed by any such policy.[46] Yet it remained on the political agenda until the outbreak of war.

The Imperial Policy Group, whose views on foreign policy Lennox-Boyd largely endorsed, also had a domestic social agenda. This emerged in part from the emphasis placed by the Group on the need for Britain to rearm. In October 1936, Lennox-Boyd and four other members of the Group – Victor Raikes, A. R. Wise and

John and Kenneth de Courcey – visited Merthyr Tydfil at the invitation of W. Bertram Harris, a local landowner. They heard representations from the mayor and from other local dignitaries urging
the Government to do more to reduce the high level of unemployment in the region. At the Conservative Party Conference in the
same month, Lennox-Boyd and Wise supported an amendment to
the main resolution on the economy which called for 'renewed
vigour' in Government action to ease the problems of economically
deprived 'Special Areas' like Merthyr.

Returning for the new session of Parliament, Lennox-Boyd certainly appeared chastened by his visits to South Wales and
Durham. He told the Commons that he had 'seen sights which have
shaken me out of any complacency into which I might have been
inclined to drift because of my own more happy personal and
political surroundings'. He was, he claimed, determined to do what
he could to alleviate these conditions.[47]   L.M. Hawkins of the
Bedfordshire Times gleefully congratulated him on his speech and
suggested that he might yet end up as leader of the Liberal Party.[48]
Closer inspection would, however, have revealed that Lennox-Boyd's
social conscience was informed by a distinctively right-wing popu-
lism. In his first remarks on the issue in the Commons, he carefully distanced himself from the left's efforts to exploit the issue of
unemployment. He defended Baldwin's refusal to receive the Jarrow
marchers on the grounds that it was the job of MPs to raise this
question. Yet he also rejected the notion that an ordinary trade
revival without Government intervention could make a significant
impact on levels of unemployment like those in South Wales. He
demanded greater state intervention although, unlike the
Government's left-wing critics, he wished to see much of this new
investment coming in the form of arms production.

Lennox-Boyd was keen not appear to be taking his cue in all of
this from the policies of Hitler and Mussolini. He told an audience in
Seaham that 'he viewed with horror the establishing in England of
any system remotely resembling the dictatorships of the continent'.[49]
Yet in his stress on rearmament, Government investment and peace
in industry he clearly had something of Mussolini's 'corporate state'
in mind. He argued in his Seaham speech that 'there was much we
could with advantage learn from the Fascists overseas such as discipline and arbitration instead of bitter disputes'. He also, inevitably,
associated job creation with the economic development of the Empire
as a whole through a system of Imperial preference.

The Government responded to this kind of agitation with vague
promises of reform. They ensured, however, that Parliament did not
have the chance to make far-reaching amendments to the Special

Areas Act by refusing to allow it to be debated separately from the Expiring Laws Continuance Bill. A group of Conservative MPs responded by establishing a Depressed Areas Committee. Lennox-Boyd was a member along with Harold Macmillan and Bob Boothby from the left of the Conservative Party. When the Expiring Laws Continuance Bill was debated on 17 November, Macmillan voted against the Government. Lennox-Boyd spoke, urging the Government to take some of the measures outlined above, but did not cast a vote. The day after this debate, the King, Edward VIII, visited Merthyr and made his famous remark that 'something must be done' to find work for the men of South Wales. The timing of this apparently innocuous remark made it highly embarrassing for the Government.

An interesting feature of Edward VIII's abdication only three weeks later was that the Imperial Policy Group was apparently prepared to take up arms against the Government on his behalf. On 7 December the leaders of the Group called an emergency meeting of MPs. They gathered together many of Churchill's allies over India and rearmament, including Lennox-Boyd. It was suggested in the press that they were taking their lead from Churchill who acted as an adviser to Edward during the crisis.[50] Some members of the Group probably saw the occasion as another opportunity to embarrass the Government. For the ultra-monarchist Lennox-Boyd, however, this was too important a matter to be used as a political pawn. He publicly dissociated himself from the views of the Group and made clear his support for Baldwin. Like the Prime Minister, he was utterly opposed to Parliament passing legislation to allow Edward to make a morganatic marriage. Clearly upset by the whole affair, he let it be known that he was 'considering his future relationship' with the Group.[51]

The term 'right-winger' is a notoriously slippery one in British politics. In the absence of a more precise set of criteria, it is tempting merely to assert that 'I know one when I see one'; and never more so than in the case of Alan Lennox-Boyd. At the centre of his political universe was the concept of authority. He believed that the soundest basis for authority was tradition rather than democratic legitimation. He was also deeply attracted by the charismatic aspects of leadership, whether embodied by the British King Emperor, the Kabaka of Buganda, or, in a more provisional sense, by Mussolini and Franco. He had little time for modern concepts of international conciliation, believing that Britain's best chance of security lay with the development of her navy and her Empire.

During his time on the backbenches he had certainly succeeded in making an impact on the House of Commons. He had yet to prove, however, that he was much more than a flamboyant and amiable self-publicist. Over the seven years from the spring of 1938, he was to have ample opportunity to do so. In the process, the private and public life he had hitherto known collapsed around him and a new one began to take its place.

Notes

1   Ganda proverb from Uganda collected by Lennox-Boyd, PBM, Mss. Eng. c. 3796, f. 275.
2   Diary, 4 July 1932, PBM, Mss. Eng. c. 3338, f. 187.
3   Diary, 18 Oct. 1932, PBM, Mss. Eng. c. 3338, f. 189.
4   Interview by Gillian Peele on Lord Boyd's Early Career, 20 Feb. 1975, PBM, Mss. Eng. c. 3432, f. 5.
5   Philip Williamson, *National Crisis and National Government: British Politics, the Economy and Empire, 1926–1932* (Cambridge, Cambridge University Press, 1992), p. 493.
6   Interview on Lord Boyd's early career, PBM, Mss. Eng. c. 3432, p. 6.
7   *HC Deb*, 265, col. 1801, 10 May 1932.
8   *HC Deb*, 275, cols. 2063–4, 15 March 1933.
9   *Imperial Policy: A Statement of Conservative Policy for the British Empire and Commonwealth* (June 1949), p. 47.
10 Draft Election Address, Gower, May 1929, PBM, Mss. Eng. c. 3794.
11 'How Parliament Impresses the New MP', PBM, Mss. Eng. c. 3794.
12 R.T. McKenzie, *British Political Parties* (London, Mercury Books, 1964), p. 204.
13 John Charmley, *Lord Lloyd and the Decline of the British Empire* (London, Weidenfeld and Nicolson, 1987), p. 192.
14 *HC Deb*, 297, col. 1493, 8 Feb. 1935.
15 Diary 16 Jan. 1933, PBM, Mss. Eng. c. 3338, f. 204.
16 Interview with Lord Boyd on East Africa conducted by Alison Smith, 13 Dec. 1974, PBM, Mss. Eng. c. 3433, f. 273.
17 SB, *Africa 1934 (I)*, p. 28.
18 Proofs of the Report of the Empire Parliamentary Association Delegation to the Association's Executive Committee, 14 Feb. 1935, CO 822/60/4, f. 61.
19 Beaverbrook to Lennox-Boyd, 8 May 1934, BBK C/55.
20 A.J.P. Taylor, *Beaverbrook* (London, Hamish Hamilton, 1972), p. 357.
21 *HC Deb*, 289, cols. 861–2, 7 May 1934.
22 *Daily Sketch*, 4 July 1936.
23 Diary, 18 July 1934, PBM, Mss. Eng. c. 3338, f. 268.
24 Taylor to Lennox-Boyd, 18 Nov. 1935, PBM, Mss. Eng. c. 3385, f. 142.
25 Diary, 19 April 1933, PBM, Mss. Eng. c. 3338, f. 251.
26 Diary, 24 April 1933, PBM, Mss. Eng. c. 3338, f. 253.
27 Diary, 18 April 1933, PBM, Mss. Eng. c. 3338, f. 250.
28 Richard Griffiths, *Fellow Travellers of the Right: British Enthusiasts for Nazi Germany, 1933–39* (Oxford, Oxford University Press, 1983), p. 51.
29 SB, *1934-5*, p. 2.
30 Diary, 17 July 1934, PBM, Mss. Eng. c. 3338, f. 266.
31 Diary, 25 July 1934, PBM, Mss. Eng. c. 3338, f. 273.
32 Diary, 27 July 1934, PBM, Mss. Eng. c. 3338, f. 274.
33 *HC Deb*, 317, cols. 845–6, 11 Nov. 1936.
34 *HC Deb*, 326, col. 1619, 15 July 1937.
35 *Tribune*, 27 May 1938.
36 *Daily Worker*, 26 March 1938.
37 SB, *1937*, p. 10.
38 *Daily Herald*, 29 March 1938.

39 Robert Rhodes James (ed.), *Chips: The Diaries of Sir Henry Channon* (Harmondsworth, Penguin Books, 1970), p. 371, 7 May 1941.
40 SB, *1934–5*, p. 2, newspaper cutting, 30 June 1934.
41 *Lymington Times*, 13 Feb. 1937.
42 L.S. Amery to Baldwin, 11 Oct. 1935, PREM 1/177B, ff. 17–19.
43 *HC Deb*, 332, col. 92, 21 Feb. 1938.
44 R.A.C. Parker, *Chamberlain and Appeasement: British Policy and the Coming of the Second World War* (London, Macmillan, 1993), p. 69.
45 *HC Deb*, 310, col. 2751, 8 April 1936.
46 Parker, *Chamberlain and Appeasement*, pp. 71–2.
47 *HC Deb*, 317, cols. 969–70, 11 Nov. 1936.
48 Hawkins to Lennox-Boyd, 13 Nov. 1936, PBM, Mss. Eng. c. 3459, f. 122.
49 *Sunderland Echo*, 23 Oct. 1936.
50 *News Chronicle*, 8 Dec. 1936.
51 SB, *1936*, p. 45.

5

Into the Blue

Fire does not produce fire; it produces ashes.[1]

In February 1938, Lennox-Boyd entered the Government as a junior Minister. Having secured such a respectable outlet for his considerable energies he might have been expected to fade somewhat into the Conservative establishment. Yet neither the circumstances of his appointment nor their immediate aftermath did much to compromise his public image as a right-wing maverick.

Lennox-Boyd's entry into Government was occasioned by the resignation of the Foreign Secretary, Anthony Eden. This was the culmination of growing disagreements with Chamberlain over the handling of Britain's relations with Italy. The immediate cause of Eden's departure was Chamberlain's determination to open negotiations with the Italians which would include consideration of Mussolini's demand for *de jure* recognition of Italian sovereignty over Abyssinia. On 21 February, during the Commons debate on Eden's resignation, Lennox-Boyd argued that it was 'the height of folly to continue to dwell in an unreal world and to deny that the king of Italy is now Emperor of Abyssinia'.[2] Three days later, Chamberlain brought Lennox-Boyd into the Government.

Eden was replaced as Foreign Secretary by Lord Halifax, the uncle of Lady Patricia Guinness, Lennox-Boyd's future wife. In appointing a member of the House of Lords to this position, Chamberlain ensured that he himself would be the Government's main spokesman on foreign affairs in the Commons and thus strengthened his own control over foreign policy.[3] Along with Eden, Lord Cranborne (later Lord Salisbury), the Parliamentary Under-Secretary for Foreign Affairs, also resigned. He was replaced by R.A. Butler who was moved from the Ministry of Labour where

he had served as Parliamentary Secretary. Butler chose as his
Parliamentary Private Secretary, Henry 'Chips' Channon,
Lennox-Boyd's close friend and future brother-in-law.

Like Lennox-Boyd, Chips was firmly on the right of the Conservative party and made no secret of his admiration for Mussolini.
Lennox-Boyd was staying with Channon in his house at 5 Belgrave
Square when the new appointments were announced. Channon's
comment on hearing of Eden's departure from government was that
'the doctrinaire "Leftist" policy of the Foreign Office has received a
check'.[4] Lennox-Boyd was brought into Government to take over
Butler's job as Parliamentary Secretary to the Ministry of Labour.
Despite having described this position as that of a Government
'bottle-washer' when it was occupied by his Liberal rival in
Mid-Beds, Milner Gray, Lennox-Boyd was apparently pleased with
the appointment. It made him among the first of his Parliamentary intake to achieve office. He told Chamberlain, 'I most deeply
value your confidence in me and I shall do all I can to justify it.'[5]

Although it was a cause of celebration for his many friends in
the Commons, Lennox-Boyd's entry into government was not universally applauded. It provoked a number of letters of protest from
those on the left who regarded him as a fascist sympathizer. It also
attracted criticism from the former Prime Minister, Stanley Baldwin.
Baldwin felt that in the circumstances of Eden's resignation, the
Government should have been particularly sensitive in its choice
of candidates for promotion. It was important, he maintained, that
Eden's departure should not be seen as indicative of a general swing
to the right. To Baldwin, the junior posts for Lennox-Boyd and
Channon and the Cabinet position for Lord Winterton seemed 'as
bad a set of appointments as you could conceive'.[6]

In the long term, Lennox-Boyd's friends were to find plenty of
justification for the confidence they had placed in him. In the short
term, however, it was the fears of those who believed that his
right-wing agenda might embarrass the Government which were
more fully vindicated. One of Lennox-Boyd's main roles in his new
job was to be the human face of the Ministry of Labour, opening
labour exchanges and visiting training schemes for the young and
unemployed. He fulfilled these duties with a characteristic flair for
public relations. Yet it was his past record and continued pronouncements in the field of foreign policy that received the most
publicity. On 7 March, in what was a clear reference to
Lennox-Boyd, the Labour MP, George Strauss, asked Chamberlain
to give an assurance that he would not again appoint anyone to
his Government who had been closely associated with General
Franco. Chamberlain's claim that this description did not apply to

any Minister gave the press an opportunity to publish a recent circular letter from 'The Friends of National Spain' bearing Lennox-Boyd's signature.[7] Lennox-Boyd had, of course, resigned from this organization on his appointment to the Ministry of Labour. His resignation came too late, however, to prevent it issuing another circular naming him among its speakers for a meeting on 23 March.[8]

At about the same time as The Friends of National Spain letter appeared in the press, the *Daily Worker* published a story alleging that Lennox-Boyd had provided assistance to Prince Mario Colonna, a frequent visitor to London, whom the paper described as an 'Italian agent'.[9] Whatever the truth of this report, Lennox-Boyd had, like many other Conservative backbenchers, undoubtedly maintained friendly contacts with the Italian Ambassador in London, Count Dino Grandi, and these contacts continued after he joined the Government.[10] Reports of this kind could, of course, easily be dismissed as left-wing mischief-making. The greatest blow to Lennox-Boyd's standing in the Commons during his first weeks in office was an event very much of his own making and one which suggested that promotion had rather gone to his head.

On Friday 18 March, less than a month after his appointment to the Government and five days after the announcement of Germany's *Anschluss* with Austria, Lennox-Boyd made a monumentally indiscreet speech in his constituency. This was reported fully in *The Times* the following day. He opened his address by commenting that now he was a Minister he had to be more careful about what he said than had hitherto been necessary.[11] Quite what he would have included in his subsequent comments had he been *less* careful is difficult to imagine. He rejected as impractical the suggestion that Britain should guarantee the borders of Czechoslovakia against German aggression, adding that 'from what he knew of Mr Chamberlain he did not think he would make a move to give a guarantee of that kind'. He pointed to the ethnic divisions within Czechoslovakia, suggesting that if the country were threatened by a German invasion, only a minority of its citizens would be ready to resist Hitler's troops. Germany could, he suggested, absorb Czechoslovakia without posing a threat to Britain or France.

His remarks cannot have endeared him to his former mentor, Winston Churchill. Churchill was sent a newspaper cutting about the speech by the MP Robert Boothby, who described it as 'an incitement to Germany to get on with the job.'[12] Indeed, the sentiments expressed by Lennox-Boyd were all the more damaging for being a lamentably accurate reflection of Cabinet opinion. On the same day as his speech, the Foreign Policy Committee of the Cabinet considered the possibility of undertaking, conditionally, to go to the aid of France were she to be attacked by Germany in the process of assisting Czechoslovakia to resist a German invasion. Chamberlain and his new Foreign Secretary both spoke forcefully against the proposals citing objections similar to those elaborated by Lennox-Boyd.[13] Only two members of the Committee saw any virtue in giving such an undertaking to France. Sir Alexander Cadogan, Permanent Under-Secretary at the Foreign Office, recorded in his diary that the Committee was 'unanimous that Czechoslovakia is not worth the bones of a single British Grenadier. And they're quite right too'.[14]

Not surprisingly, the Labour Opposition seized on Lennox-Boyd's speech. When, on the following Monday, he got up to answer questions on labour policy, the House was considerably less interested than it might otherwise have been in what he had to say about employment permits in the rubber footwear industry. He and the Prime Minister were challenged by a number of Opposition members including the leader of the Labour party, Clement Attlee, to comment on the Biggleswade speech. Chamberlain initially suggested that Lennox-Boyd's speech had not been accurately reported. A Liberal member asked the Speaker whether it would be in order for Lennox-Boyd to make a personal statement on the matter ('Not that anybody takes any notice of what he says, really!' interjected the Labour MP, Ellen Wilkinson). The Speaker agreed that this would be permissible. Later in the day, Arthur Henderson raised the matter again in an adjournment motion. He noted that sections of the speech had been broadcast over the German radio system and that the report had been compiled in such a way as to suggest that Lennox-Boyd's remarks represented Government policy.

Not for the last time in his political career, Lennox-Boyd extricated himself from a tight corner by a mixture of charm and contrition. He told the House:

> ...I have been so recently translated to an important position that I have not perhaps begun properly as yet to realize the importance which may be attached to chance words of mine. When the Hon. member for Jarrow [Ellen Wilkinson] said this afternoon that nobody took any notice of what I said, I suppose she was giving expression to a thought in my own mind, and that I have not been able to rid my mind of since my Right Hon. friend did me the honour to ask me to join his Administration.

Chamberlain claimed to be satisfied with his admission of 'frank and full regret' and professed himself 'sure that he will be extremely careful not to repeat his indiscretion'.

In the light of Lennox-Boyd's views on Czechoslovakia, it was only to be expected that he should have been an enthusiastic supporter of the Munich agreement reached at the end of September. On 5 October, the day upon which German troops crossed the Czech border to occupy the Sudetenland, he told readers of a local paper in his constituency that Britain's duty now was 'to make friends with Germany and understand their point of view'.[15] Not surprisingly, Churchill treated Lennox-Boyd as a 'renegade' over the issue of appeasement, and their relationship rapidly deteriorated.

If Lennox-Boyd's entry into the Government in 1938 raised a few eyebrows, so did the other major event in his life that year: his decision to marry. His bride to be was Lady Patricia Guinness. Born in 1918, Patsy, as she was known to friends and family, was the second daughter of the Earl and Countess of Iveagh. Her father, Rupert Guinness, the second Earl of Iveagh, was chairman of Arthur Guinness, Son and Co. and head of the wealthy and influential Guinness family. From 1912 to 1927 when he succeeded to the earldom, Iveagh had served as MP for Southend-on-Sea. The seat became something of a family heirloom. When Rupert was elevated to the Lords, his wife was elected in his place. On her retirement, Southend passed to their son-in-law, Henry 'Chips' Channon; and when Channon died in 1958, his son, Paul, stepped in to continue the family tradition. He remained the Member for Southend until the 1997 General Election.

Lady Gwendolen, Patsy's mother, came from a family with a long political pedigree. The eldest daughter of the fourth Earl of Onslow, she could claim to be the 22nd member of her family to sit in the House of Commons. Her sister was the wife of Lord Halifax, the Foreign Secretary. Following her election for Southend in 1927 she began to play a leading role within the Conservative Party organization, becoming first Vice-Chairman, and then, in 1930, Chairman of the National Union of Conservative and Unionist Associations. Her rise to prominence within the party reflected the recognition by senior Conservatives of the importance of capturing the women's vote following the 1918 and 1928 reform acts. For Patsy, it meant a close acquaintance with the world of high politics combined with a relatively distant one with her mother.

At the time of her marriage to Alan in December 1938, Patsy was 20, 14 years younger than her husband. They had met over a year before at a party but had only got to know one another well after Alan's appointment to the Ministry of Labour. Patsy's early life had been a fairly nomadic one. Parliamentary sessions, the London 'Season' and the shooting season divided the year into a series of migrations. The family moved between their home in St. James's Square and a number of other houses: Farmleigh in Dublin, Pyrford near Woking, Elveden near Thetford, Bosham where they sailed, and a villa in Asolo in Northern Italy. Patsy's education seems to have been provided largely by governesses. At 16 she was sent to Munich to improve her German. She also spent time in Rome and Paris in lodgings strictly vetted by her mother. Her upbringing thus gave her a command of European languages (one not shared by her husband), but probably did insufficient to engage her very considerable intelligence or allow her to assert her independence. In retrospect, she particularly regretted that she had received no encouragement from her parents to go to university.

There was a considerable age gap between the Iveagh's two older children – Honor and Arthur – and Patsy and her sister Brigid. Honor, nine years Patsy's senior, had married Lennox-Boyd's close friend 'Chips' Channon in 1933. Channon, described by Tom Driberg as 'one of the better known homosexuals in London', was an amusing companion and a devoted father, but hardly the ideal husband, and the marriage was eventually to end in divorce.[16] In her teens, however, Honor and Chips must have appeared to Patsy to occupy a charmed position in the glamorous world of adulthood. She, by contrast, continued to be treated by her family as a child. At one of the first parties she attended with Lennox-Boyd, her uncle, Lord Halifax, approached her and asked, 'Patsy, what are you doing here?' Her parents were rather suspicious of Lennox-Boyd's quixotic and unmistakably ambitious style of politics. Gwendolen told her daughter, 'I married a tortoise, but you're marrying an electric eel.' Yet her relationship with Lennox-Boyd, an exciting figure and a close friend of Chips, must have seemed to Patsy a means of propelling herself into the adult world of her sister.

Patsy was warned by friends that she would be mad to marry into the Lennox-Boyd family. Certainly the 'mutual admiration society' of the Lennox-Boyd brothers supervized by their strong-willed and fiercely protective mother was a daunting prospect for any outsider. Yet, understandably, Florence Lennox-Boyd was not inclined to prevent her deeply ambitious son from marrying into one of the wealthiest and most influential families in Britain.

Alan and Patsy were married on Thursday 29 December in Elveden in Suffolk, the home of Lord and Lady Iveagh. A magnificent house set in a 23,000 acre shooting estate, Elveden Hall had been bought by Edward Guinness, the first Lord Iveagh, in 1894 at the suggestion of his friend the Prince of Wales.[17] Before the First

World War, Elveden had been the scene of some magnificent social gatherings. By the 1930s, however, the house was already
enjoying a 'twilight existence'.[18] Rupert Guinness regarded Elveden
as a 'mausoleum' and was relieved when, a year after his daughter's
marriage, he was able to abandon it for good. Gwendolen used it
occasionally to entertain political friends, and Honor held all-night
parties there before her marriage to Chips. The house was specially
opened for Patricia and Alan's wedding, and something of its former
glory was recaptured for the occasion. One guest, the Iveaghs' old
friend, Freya Stark, recorded the scene, the night before the ceremony:

> The dining room very gorgeous with gold griffins and pale green or-
> chids all down the table and Patsy with her new diamonds round her
> neck. Lovely tiaras and sapphires and emeralds among the gifts. Ev-
> eryone a little hectic except Lady Iveagh who keeps her perfect and
> beautiful calm.[19]

There must have been quite a few of those present who viewed
the marriage with a certain amount of scepticism. Stark's account
reflects a distinct sense of concern for Patsy. She commented to
her mother on 'Patsy looking so serious under her huge veil. Such
a small boat, a girl's heart at 20, to sail out to sea'.[20] Perhaps she
and many others would have been surprised to learn that the
marriage would last until Alan's death over 44 years later.

The wedding brought together some old political adversaries.
Lord Halifax, who as Viceroy of India had attracted fierce criticism
from Lennox-Boyd and fellow 'die-hards', presented the couple with
a tea set and table. The members of the India Defence League contributed a silver tray inscribed 'In recognition of a gallant endeavour'. Alan and Patsy took great pleasure in placing the tea set on
the silver tray and arranging both on Halifax's table. In a more
esoteric gesture, another of Alan's allies from the battles over India, Lord Lloyd, presented him with an umbrella – apparently a
'traditional' wedding gift to a homosexual.

Even Lennox-Boyd's honeymoon had an element of political controversy attached to it. Having stopped at Paris and Rome en route,
he and Patsy travelled to Bengasi, and from there to Cairo. They
were met in Egypt by Francis Lennox-Boyd. The presence on a
honeymoon of the groom's brother is hardly conventional, but it
was wholly characteristic of the Lennox-Boyd clan. Illness had
prevented Francis from attending the wedding, so he was invited
to join in the honeymoon by way of compensation. The party visited Luxor and Aswan before travelling down the Nile into the
Sudan. While in Khartoum, Alan had the idea of taking a flight to

Addis-Ababa in Italian controlled Abyssinia. He telegraphed the
British Consul there telling him that he, Patsy and Francis wished
to arrive there on Thursday and asking him to make the necessary
arrangements.[21] The authorities in the Sudan disapproved of a
Minister visiting a regime which was not recognized by the British
Government. This did not discourage the Lennox-Boyds. The next
flight back to Khartoum did not leave for another couple of days,
so if the Italians decided to deport them this would fit perfectly into
their travel arrangements.[22]

In the event they were given an extremely warm reception. So
infrequent were foreign visitors to Abyssinia that the British Consul and the Italian Viceroy were both keen to have the honour of
entertaining them. The Viceroy was the Duke of Aosta, a cousin of
King Victor Emmanuel. Aosta had succeeded the notorious Marshal Graziani in November 1937 and was to remain in the post until
May 1941 when he surrendered to British forces and was sent into
extremely comfortable exile in Kenya. On his return to England,
Lennox-Boyd sought to portray this little adventure as a serious
'fact-finding' mission. He told the *Daily Telegraph* that as a member of the British Government he had been given every facility 'for
inspecting the work being done by the Italian Ministry of Labour'.
He added that he had found 'competent officials who had reduced
their problems, in Addis Ababa at least, to smooth working order'.
In a speech to his constituents he argued that his recent experiences had demonstrated the Italians' desire to 'bury the hatchet'
and hoped that Britain would take the opportunity to establish
friendly relations with the Government of Abyssinia.

Patsy had little time to adjust to married life before she and Alan
were confronted with a terrible and sinister tragedy. In April 1939,
Donald Lennox-Boyd died during a visit to Nazi Germany. The circumstances of his death remain obscure as does the purpose of
his visit although he appears to have been involved in some form
of espionage. As a Lieutenant in the Scots Guards, Donald seems
to have been singled out for intelligence work fairly early in his
military career. He was posted to Palestine in October 1933 as
aide-de-camp to the British High Commissioner. In April 1935, he
was sent to Tallinn in Estonia where he remained for nine months
learning Russian. The Baltic states enjoyed a brief spell of independence in the years between the Wars and became a favoured
training ground for members of the Western intelligence community. During his stay there, Donald paid a number of brief visits
to Leningrad.[23] On his return to England in January 1936, his
interest in Eastern Europe led to his appointment as liaison officer
to the Polish delegation at the funeral of George V. The following

year, he was granted leave to spend two months in Poland.

In 1937, he resigned his commission and began work as an Air Raid Precautions officer in Wiltshire. In February 1939, he was interviewed for the job of Civilian Assistant Camouflage Officer by the War Office. The selection procedure required him to be politically vetted.[24] According to the War Office, Donald was not chosen for the post. Nevertheless, in March he resigned from his job in Wiltshire and later that month travelled to Stuttgart with his brother George. One can only conclude that the War Office had offered him some alternative task.

A report in the *New York Times* suggested that Donald's visit to Germany was part of a reciprocal arrangement between the British and German Governments under which they agreed to allow each others' officers to inspect their air raid shelters.[25] It coincided, however, with a new low-point in Anglo–German relations. In the middle of March, German troops had occupied what remained of Czechoslovakia and at the end of that month Chamberlain announced that Britain would defend Poland from attack. The German officers selected to inspect British shelters had cancelled their visit in the light of the worsening international conditions. Donald, however, went ahead with his plans. As he left for Germany, he reportedly told one friend, 'I am going into the blue.' It was against this background that Donald's family heard the news that he had died suddenly in Stuttgart on 6 April.

Having lived something of a charmed life, this was Alan's first real taste of personal tragedy. For Patsy, the episode provided a harsh introduction to married life. She accompanied her husband to Germany in order both to provide emotional support and to act as a translator. On their arrival in Stuttgart, Alan broke down completely and the British Consul had to arrange for him to be taken home. Patsy remained in the city until the Germans were ready to surrender Donald's ashes. The family told the British press that no attempt had been made by the German authorities to prevent them from seeing the body. In fact, it appears to have been cremated long before Alan and Patsy arrived in Germany.

Patsy learned that George and Donald had both been arrested and accused of spying. George was subsequently released and was told that his brother would follow.[26] Donald, however, died in custody. The timing and nature of Donald's visit and the subsequent behaviour of the authorities gave rise to widespread rumours that Donald had been murdered by the Nazis in the course of an intelligence mission. These were strenuously denied by Donald's family and by British officials. They maintained in public that Donald had died of a heart attack after suffering from a bout of influenza.

Donald's occupation was also kept secret. On his death certificate, witnessed by the British Consul General in Frankfurt, he was described as a 'merchant'. Nevertheless, alternative accounts of Donald's death abounded. Shortly after his return from Germany, Alan was contacted by Michael Wardell, of the *Evening Standard*. According to Wardell, his newspaper had what appeared to be definitive proof of Donald's murder by the Nazis. The source and nature of this evidence is unclear, although it seems highly likely that it reached Wardell via the *Standard*'s proprietor, Lord Beaverbrook, in which case it may well have come from Lennox-Boyd himself. The two men met to discuss the question of publication, after which Alan wrote to Wardell to tell him that 'the official version does still stand'.[27] The 'official version' was largely accepted by the rest of the British press, although the *New York Times* revealed the existence of rumours that Donald had 'died from injuries received in a fight with Nazi guards'.

The efforts by Donald's family and the British authorities to conceal the incident can be explained in a number of ways. First, there was still something of a reflex reaction on the part of those in Government to try to suppress material which might inflame public opinion against Germany. Nevertheless, after the outbreak of the war, no attempt seems to have been made to publicize the incident. The murder of a British officer had obvious propaganda value, irrespective of the truth of the story. The fact that no further revelations were made points to a further reason for secrecy: that Donald had been engaged in some form of intelligence operation.[28] It is, of course, possible that Donald had been on a private mission which was not expressly authorized. A third reason why the family might have been keen to avoid publicity concerns another piece of information which Patsy received from the German authorities. They claimed that Donald had been arrested in a bar popular with homosexuals and had committed suicide in custody out of a sense of honour. That Donald might have been discovered in such a bar was not, as the family would have known, entirely out of the question.

Among Alan Lennox-Boyd's friends and relatives it was accepted that Donald had died at the hands of the Nazis in the course of some covert operation.[29] This belief was shared by the Iveaghs' old friend, Freya Stark, herself no stranger to the world of espionage. She and Donald had met at Alan's wedding and had developed a close friendship based on a shared sense of adventure. In her book of memoirs, *Dust in the Lion's Paw*, she described how, while travelling through Syria in April 1939, she had received two letters: the first from an unnamed man, asking her to marry him; and the second, two days later, containing the 'obscure news' of his death. Her only reference to the circumstances of his death was that 'his service was ... beyond the law'.[30] The unnamed man was Donald. His letter supposedly proposing marriage does not survive, and Alan seems to have regarded it as a mere figment of Stark's imagination.[31] Nevertheless, she was clearly devastated by the news of Donald's death. She told a friend, 'I don't think in this whole world there was a truer, more chivalrous, more absolutely true and gallant soul'. When she wrote this account of him on 19 April, she was in no doubt that he had died at the hands of the Germans. 'Among my friends,' she claimed 'he is the first victim of this war.'[32] Her editor, Sir Sydney Cockerell shared this belief. Beside a reference to Donald in Stark's correspondence, he scribbled tersely, 'shot as a spy'.[33]

Alan himself confided in a number of people that Donald had died at the hands of the Germans. When, in 1950, Christ Church was in the process of erecting a monument to old members who had died in the course of the War, he was asked by Sir Roy Harrod whether he thought Donald's name should appear on the list of the fallen. Harrod asked him two further questions: whether, to the best of his knowledge, Donald was in Germany on duty; and whether he was killed by the Nazis as a consequence of this. Alan's answer to all three questions was 'yes'. He added, however, that his old friend from Christ Church, Roger Makins, whom he had consulted at the Foreign Office, held a different view.[34] In September 1954, he gave a fuller account of the incident to A.H. Trelawny-Ross, his old House Master at Sherborne. Lennox-Boyd mentioned that the family had been asked to treat the matter with the greatest secrecy at the time. He believed that Donald had probably been strangled in gaol.[35]

Hitler's flagrant violation of the Munich agreement in March 1939 when German troops occupied Prague, came as a shock to many supporters of Appeasement. Lennox-Boyd later recalled that when Hitler repudiated his undertakings, 'I changed completely along with a lot of my fellow countrymen, and by the time of the dreadful days before the declaration of war, I was a passionate intervener'.[36] Donald's death, coming so soon after the annexation of Czechoslovakia, must have added a strong personal element to his newly found support for a policy of resisting Hitler.

When war finally came in September, Lennox-Boyd felt it was his duty to volunteer for military service. Chamberlain, however, refused to accept his resignation, believing that it would undermine the Government's policy of keeping certain people in 'reserved occupations' in civilian life. Lennox-Boyd alluded to this in a speech in his constituency the following March. He told his audience, 'While some of us hanker after more romantic occupations the best thing is to do what we are told – in my case by my leader...' Instead of being allowed to enter the services he was transferred, four days after the war broke out, to the Ministry of Home Security. On hearing of his departure from the Ministry of Labour, some of Lennox-Boyd's opponents claimed that he had been debarred as a fascist. As he later recalled, 'John Anderson [the Home Secretary] suggested I should be photographed at my desk in the Home Office – "not locked up but in the department that does the locking up".'[37]

Perhaps, however, Lennox-Boyd's appointment to this sensitive Ministry was not universally welcomed, as he remained there for only six weeks before being transferred, in November 1939, to the Ministry of Food. Despite his undoubted talent for public relations, as a tall, wealthy and manifestly well-nourished junior Minister, he was not ideally suited to the task of justifying austerity measures. In March 1940, he publicly hinted that the Government might no longer be prepared to keep the price of butter artificially low, since it was a luxury product for which margarine was a perfectly adequate substitute. He was challenged in the Commons by the Labour MP, Edith Summerskill, who said she did not believe he had ever tasted margarine: 'I know he could never have been brought up on margarine otherwise he could never have attained the height of 6 ft. 4 in.'[38]

Nineteen thirty-nine, a year of personal tragedy and disappointed hopes, closed for Lennox-Boyd on a positive note with the birth of his first son. He used this as the occasion for an act of piety towards his beleaguered chief, Neville Chamberlain. Chamberlain was invited to be a godfather and the boy was baptized Simon Donald Rupert Neville. The Prime Minister accepted, but did not actually attend the christening service which took place at Pryford Church near Woking the following February. Luckily, there were three other godfathers, all close friends of Alan: Anthony Wingfield, Patrick Buchan-Hepburn and Chips Channon. Freya Stark acted as one of the godmothers. As well as that of the Premier, Alan and Patsy's son received the names of his maternal grandfather and his dead uncle. The decision to add 'Neville' to the list appears to have been an afterthought. It did not appear on Simon's birth certificate, something which was to cause a certain amount of confusion later in his life.

In May 1940, discontent on the Conservative back benches at his conduct of the war forced Chamberlain from Downing Street, and Churchill assumed the premiership. Lennox-Boyd chose this moment to leave the Government. Some time before, Lennox-Boyd had raised his desire to join the armed forces with Churchill, then First Lord of the Admiralty. Churchill, like Chamberlain, had urged him to remain in the Government, but promised to find him a commission in the RNVR should he decide to resign. Lennox-Boyd was now anxious that this promise should be honoured, but did not wish to appear to be demanding special favours from the new premier.

Lord Woolton, his former chief at the Ministry of Food, wrote directly to Churchill, telling him of Lennox-Boyd's determination to enlist and reminding the Prime Minister of his undertaking.[39] He was full of praise for Lennox-Boyd's performance as his parliamentary secretary. Woolton appears to have been concerned that in his eagerness to don a uniform, Lennox-Boyd would simply join the militia and be assigned a post unworthy of his abilities. At the foot of Woolton's letter, Churchill directed that the matter be referred to the Admiralty, adding, 'I suggest Commander rank.' When Lennox-Boyd rejoined the Government three and a half years later, Churchill showed him the subsequent correspondence with the Admiralty. Scribbled on a memorandum explaining the Prime Minister's wishes, in the spidery handwriting of an Admiralty clerk, it was recorded, 'he was today made temporary probationary sub-lieutenant RNVR'. 'And one day,' Churchill lamented, 'history will call me a dictator.'[40]

Lennox-Boyd began his naval career by spending three months at the King Alfred training centre in Hove. He then served aboard HMS Derbyshire for a couple of months followed by a brief spell of Motor Torpedo Boat (MTB) training with HMS Hornet. He continued his service with Hornet from December 1940 to June 1941 on board MTB 102. It was a dangerous and demanding life as Chips Channon found when, in April 1941, he visited him at his headquarters - the Lord Warden Hotel in Dover. The previous night, Lennox-Boyd had sailed to the French coast and shelled Boulogne. Dover itself was subject to heavy and frequent bombing. None of this was to Channon's taste: 'I cannot imagine a more horrible existence; and he [Lennox-Boyd] does not look well or enjoy it.'[41] Towards the end of his visit, Channon came uncomfortably close to enemy fire as he accompanied Lennox-Boyd through Dover:

> About 11 o'clock we walked down to the jetty where his torpedo boat is moored, and at that moment planes appeared, guns roared, everyone ducked, a balloon came down, and in the midst of the excitement – my baptême du feu – I saw 13 parachutes descend; they were mine-laying ones. Alan jumped aboard and called out 'good-bye'.

Channon retreated back to London, reflecting that active service was not for him.

Channon's judgement that Lennox-Boyd was reacting badly to
life in the navy may have been heavily coloured by his own lack of
enthusiasm for what he had seen. While there were certainly periods of great stress and hardship during his naval career, Lennox-
Boyd looked back on this period of his life with a great deal of
satisfaction and affection. Service on the torpedo boats, however
demanding, was in a sense the fulfilment of a childhood ambition.
Lennox-Boyd had hoped to enter the Royal Naval College at
Dartmouth at the age of 13 but had been turned down because of
poor eyesight. His talent for leadership, and his ability to inspire
confidence and loyalty in subordinates made him, in some respects,
a model officer. Yet he was not a very accomplished mariner, and
in particular never really got the hang of navigation. The resumé
of his service career which Churchill obtained at the time of
Lennox-Boyd's return to Government in November 1943, makes
clear his strengths and weaknesses:

> The officer's record shows that he had very little sea experience be-
> fore joining the RNVR but that he quickly developed a very good man-
> ner in dealing with men. He did not seem, at the same time, to make
> the progress that might have been expected in seamanlike matters.
> This comparative slowness in developing sea sense has continued
> throughout his reports and he is still reported on as being 'out of his
> depth' in these matters. His strong personality and general high stan-
> dard of intelligence have, however, never been questioned.[42]

A temporary break from the rigours of the Channel came i
n June 1941 when Lennox-Boyd was sent to the United States.
His task over the next few months was to arrange, via the British
Purchasing Commission, for the acquisition of 12 patrol torpedo
boats. It was intended that he would then serve with one of these
in the Mediterranean.[43]

In 1938, the Admiralty had sought to ensure that it could obtain torpedo boats from America in time of war. As a result, the
Power Boat Company of Great Britain had made arrangements for
the Electric Boat Company of Bayonne, New Jersey, to manufac-
ture one of its designs under licence in America. When, however,
the Power Boat Company approached the Admiralty in February
1940 offering to supply boats from the Bayonne factory they were
told, with staggeringly complacency, that the Royal Navy was fully
able to supply all its needs from its own building establishments.[44]
Three months later, with German troops pushing inexorably towards the French coast, the Admiralty changed its mind and decided to buy as many torpedo boats as it possibly could from
America.[45] Efforts to obtain these boats foundered, however, following opposition from the Senate Naval Affairs Committee. Members

of the Committee objected to the apparent breach of American neutrality and claimed that the boats were needed for the US Navy. On 24 June Roosevelt, who was facing Presidential elections later in the year, intervened to stop the sales.

Ironically, Lennox-Boyd publicly opposed one of the Government's efforts to overcome American resistance to the sale of military hardware to Britain. In the middle of August, Churchill negotiated an agreement whereby the United States would provide Britain with 50 destroyers in return for the use of bases in the Caribbean and Newfoundland on 99 year leases. This surrender of British territory proved unacceptable to some Conservative backbenchers and Lennox-Boyd's old friend Somerset de Chair tabled a motion aimed at shortening the leases.[46] Lennox-Boyd was one of a number of Chamberlainite Imperialists who signed the motion. The fact that as a serving member of the Royal Navy he should have publicly engaged in this sort of criticism of the Prime Minister says much both about the kind of resistance Churchill still faced from the Chamberlainite right of the Conservative party and about Lennox-Boyd's own peculiar status as both an MP and a serviceman.

Following Roosevelt's re-election in November, a far more positive attitude was adopted by the American Government towards sales of arms to Britain, and plans were initiated for new purchasing arrangements which were to culminate in the 'Lend-Lease' agreement. It was against this more optimistic background that in June 1941 Lennox-Boyd set out for Canada and from there to the United States. Patsy was in the final stages of pregnancy and shortly after his arrival in Canada, Lennox-Boyd heard news of the birth of his second son, Christopher. 'CHRISTOPHER COLOSSAL AND MAGNIFICENT', telegrammed Chips Channon. Later on in the summer, Lennox-Boyd visited Chips's son Paul who was staying at East Hampton, Long Island along with some of the Roosevelt children. Paul had been evacuated to America the year before to his father's very great distress.

Lennox-Boyd's mission was not a success. As negotiations dragged on, tension between the United States and the Axis powers escalated. Well before the Japanese attacked Pearl Harbour on 7 December, the United States Government had become extremely wary about providing Britain with boats likely to be required by its own forces. When Lennox-Boyd arrived back in Britain on 15 November 1941, he did so empty handed. Plans that he should serve in the Mediterranean had to be revised and instead he was assigned to a motor launch protecting convoys in the Channel. Before taking up his new command he was able to take some unpaid leave to look after constituency business and spend some time with his young family.

At the beginning of February 1942, Lennox-Boyd went to Gosport to take over Motor Launch 113 as a Temporary Lieutenant. His flotilla was responsible for escorting the Channel convoys which operated between Southend and Falmouth. The passage through the Straits of Dover was particularly dangerous and could take place only at night.[47] One of the tasks of Lennox-Boyd's flotilla was to escort ships joining at Newhaven or Shoreham and link them on to the back of the convoys, a particularly hazardous job without the use of navigation lights. In the summer of 1942, his flotilla was moved from Portsmouth to Newhaven and in August it took part in the ill-fated raid on the French port of Dieppe.

At the beginning of 1943, Lennox-Boyd was appointed commanding officer of MTB 650, a D Class vessel then under construction at Falmouth. On its completion, Lennox-Boyd took it to Brixham for gunnery trials and to Weymouth for working up exercises before beginning normal duties from Great Yarmouth. In May, Patsy gave birth to Mark, their youngest son. This was a brief moment of joy in a difficult and dangerous year. Lennox-Boyd's final command provided him with some close encounters with death. In August, his boat along with three others took part in a raid on a German convoy off Scheveningen, just north of The Hague. Attacking under the cover of mist, they came under heavy fire from the German boats escorting the convoy. In the course of the engagement one of the British vessels was blown up and sunk. MTB 650 was less seriously damaged but was left with a gaping hole in the side of Lennox-Boyd's cabin.

Three months later, Lennox-Boyd's naval career came to an abrupt end after his motor torpedo boat was damaged by a large shell while on operations off the Dutch coast. His was one of a number of boats which attacked a German convoy off the Hook of Holland. They penetrated the outer-escort and managed to destroy a couple of enemy trawlers. As they tried to get away, however, they again encountered the outer-escort and came under fire from some heavily armed minesweepers. MTB 650 was badly damaged and Lennox-Boyd and his crew returned to Great Yarmouth and were sent on leave pending the repair of their boat. When he arrived there, he found a telegram from his mother to say that George, his eldest brother, was critically ill in a military hospital in Scotland. George had contracted pneumonia while on service in the Middle East and had been brought home for treatment. Lennox-Boyd immediately travelled North to be at his brother's bedside. George died two days later. He was delirious for the final 24 hours of his life, talking continually and begging Alan and their mother to take him home. The building in which he was being treated was a mental hospital requisitioned by the army, and George was convinced that he had been incarcerated in a lunatic asylum.

The experience of watching his brother die in such extreme distress was a draining and traumatic one for Alan. A few days later, James Lees-Milne found him looking 'grey and very tired'.[48] By that stage, his life had taken yet another twist. In October, Duff Cooper, the Chancellor of the Duchy of Lancaster, was offered the post of British Representative to the French Committee of National Liberation in Algiers. Churchill took the opportunity of a minor reshuffle to bring Lennox-Boyd back into Government. His decision to do so may have been influenced by a spot of lobbying from one of Lennox-Boyd's old political allies, Henry Page Croft, by then Lord Croft. Writing to Churchill shortly after Cooper had accepted his new post, Croft argued that insufficient young men were being allowed to gain administrative experience in preparation for a role in post-war Government. He singled out Lennox-Boyd as someone who had in the past displayed both courage and talent, and recommended that he be offered a Ministerial post.[49] Churchill discussed the matter with the Chief Whip and the wheels were set in motion. By 5 November, Chips Channon knew that Lennox-Boyd was in line for a job.[50] He was considered for Under-Secretaryships at the Ministry of Supply, the Home Office and the Ministry of Food before the decision was finally made to send him to the Ministry of Aircraft Production.[51]

On 10 November, Lennox-Boyd received a telephone call from Churchill.[52] The Prime Minister had heard of George's death, and he asked Lennox-Boyd what his youngest brother was doing. Francis was commanding a parachute regiment. Churchill must have realized that Francis's chances of surviving the impending offensive against the French mainland were not good. He told Lennox-Boyd, 'You go and wake your mother up and tell her that you are joining the Government tomorrow. It would be good to have someone who had heard shots fired in anger in this Government.'[53] On the same day, Churchill wrote to Sir Stafford Cripps, the Minister of Aircraft Production. He told Cripps that he was sending Ben Smith, his department's current Parliamentary Under Secretary, to Washington and was replacing him with Lennox-Boyd.[54] Perhaps anticipating trouble, he stressed Lennox-Boyd's 'very active service' at sea and described him as 'a most capable man'. By an administrative oversight, the Admiralty was not informed of this decision and for some hours Lennox-Boyd was technically a deserter.

Lennox-Boyd returned from Edinburgh to Bedfordshire with his mother. There he found a message from Churchill telling him to go straight to London. He was summoned to the underground cellar of the Admiralty where Churchill was in bed. The Prime Minister was due to leave the following day on his way to Teheran for his meeting with Stalin and Roosevelt. Churchill informed Lennox-Boyd that he was to go to the Ministry of Aircraft Production where he would serve under Cripps. Cripps had been a leading figure on the Labour left during the 1930s. In 1939 he was expelled from the Labour Party because of his advocacy of a 'Popular Front' of anti-Chamberlainite forces to overthrow the policy of appeasement. The presence at the Ministry of Aircraft Production of such an ardent socialist caused some disquiet among Conservative politicians and industrialists. In February 1943, five Tory MPs forwarded to Churchill an unsigned memorandum which complained that Cripps was using his position as Minister to put into effect 'policies which he has not been able to get accepted from the platform'.[55] Although Churchill backed Cripps on this occasion, he clearly shared some of these doubts and was keen that the new Parliamentary Secretary should help curb some of his radical tendencies. 'Keep an eye on him', he instructed Lennox-Boyd, 'he will try to use the war to nationalize all sorts of things.'

It would be difficult to imagine two men less likely to establish an immediate rapport, and indeed, the early indications were that Lennox-Boyd's relations with Cripps would not be easy. Only a few hours after telling Lennox-Boyd of his new appointment, Churchill showed him a letter he had received from Cripps. Cripps was not happy about losing Ben Smith. As for Lennox-Boyd, he remarked,

> ...I imagine that you have satisfied yourself that he no longer holds the pro-Nazi and pro-Fascist views which led to so much comment as a result of a speech he made just before the war. I am afraid that this will handicap him seriously with the workers in the aircraft industry, as it is of course widely known and was much discussed in working class circles when it was made. I could not work in comfort with such a person unless I was assured that he no longer holds such views.[56]

'He doesn't seem to like you very much,' muttered Churchill, clearly amused by Lennox-Boyd's predicament.[57] He then summoned one of his secretaries and instructed Lennox-Boyd to dictate a reply.

In his response, Lennox-Boyd claimed never to have 'held Nazi or Fascist views' and always to have 'regarded them with abhorrence'. He added that he had fought two general elections calling for rearmament to guard against German aggression.[58] Only on the basis of a very sympathetic reading of some of Lennox-Boyd's very early political pronouncements could the first part of this statement be said to be strictly true. The second part, though, was certainly fair comment. Lennox-Boyd went on to claim that during his time at the Ministry of Labour, his relations with the Trades Union Movement and with the rank and file of the Parliamentary Labour Party had been extremely good. Churchill forwarded the letter to Cripps with the comment 'This seems alright [sic]'. Early the following morning, according to Lennox-Boyd, he received a handwritten message from Cripps. It said simply 'Dear Lennox-Boyd, welcome to the Department'.

Cripps does not appear to have borne any grudges and almost immediately he was commending Lennox-Boyd to others who harboured similar suspicions about his political record. A week after his appointment, Lennox-Boyd spoke to Bill Stevenson, the Secretary of the Boilermakers' Union. Stevenson told him that he had just been to see Cripps as part of a delegation from the London Works Council protesting against Lennox-Boyd's appointment. An approach of this kind was hardly surprising given the amount of hostile comment which had appeared in the left-wing press. Both *Tribune* and the *New Statesman* made a great deal of Lennox-Boyd's far-right credentials with the latter going as far as to link his appointment with Mosley's recent release from internment in order to suggest that Britain's leaders did not regard fascism as the true enemy. Cripps's response to the union delegation, according to Lennox-Boyd, was to tell them, 'While you were chalking up "Open a Second Front Now" on the walls in London, the new Parliamentary Secretary was commanding a torpedo boat in the Channel, and I always think he has done more to bring this dreadful war to an end than any of you.'[59]

In June 1944, there came yet another crushing personal blow. Lennox-Boyd knew that when the 'second front' was launched, his brother Francis was likely to be among the first troops dropped over France. Francis, a Major in the Royal Scots Greys, had been posted to Palestine at the beginning of the war. He helped to establish the Palestine Corps with which he served in the Sudan and the Western desert campaign. He then worked for a while as a military liaison officer with the Scottish public schools before volunteering to help form a paratroop company. On 5 June, realizing that the invasion was at hand, Alan Lennox-Boyd drove at great speed from an aircraft factory he had been visiting to Brize Norton where his brother was stationed. He was able, briefly, to see his brother for what was to be the last time. Shortly after midnight, Francis left England in command of the 22nd Independent Parachute Company of the 6th Airborne Division.

As so often in war, fate intervened to render meaningless the months of intensive training. As the plane in which his company were travelling reached their target, the trap door through which they were to jump failed to open.[60] The plane circled, but before it was again over the target area the trap door opened prematurely and Francis was pushed out by the force of people behind him. Although his parachute seems to have opened, he fell some distance away from the rest of the company in an area which had not yet been cleared of German troops. He was probably shot as he reached the ground.[61]

The anguish of Alan Lennox-Boyd and his mother was exacerbated by the fact that confirmation of Francis's death did not reach them for many months. One member of Francis's company, who also disappeared during the mission, turned up in a German prisoner of war camp. Inevitably, this raised hopes that Francis might also have been captured, and Alan tried to obtain further information about his brother through the Red Cross. It was not until February 1945 that Francis's death was officially confirmed.[62] His body had been discovered and buried by a family in the village of Ranville near Caen. In the space of only six years, Lennox-Boyd gained a wife and three sons and lost his three beloved brothers.

Notes

1   Swahili proverb from Zanzibar collected by Lennox-Boyd, PBM, Mss. Eng. c. 3796, f. 278.
2   *HC Deb*, 332, col. 92, 21 Feb. 1938.
3   R.A.C. Parker, *Chamberlain and Appeasement: British Policy and the Coming of the Second World War* (London, Macmillan, 1993), p. 122.
4   Robert Rhodes James, (ed.) *Chips: The Diaries of Sir Henry Channon* (Harmondsworth, Penguin, 1970), p. 182.
5   Lennox-Boyd to Chamberlain, 24 Feb. 1938, PREM 5/206.
6   Keith Middlemas and John Barnes, *Baldwin: A Biography* (London, Weidenfeld and Nicolson, 1969), p. 1043.
7   SB, *1938 (I)*, p. 7, unidentified press clipping, 8 March 1938.
8   Lord Phillimore to Lennox-Boyd, 4 March 1938, PBM, Mss. Eng. c. 3387, f. 65.
9   *Daily Worker*, 9 March 1938.
10 Grandi to Lennox-Boyd, 6 May 1938, PBM, Mss. Eng. c. 3459, f. 161.
11 *Biggleswade Chronicle*, 28 March 1938.
12 William Manchester, *The Caged Lion: Winston Spencer Churchill, 1932-1940* (London, Michael Joseph, 1988), p. 295.
13 R.A.C. Parker, pp. 135-6.
14 Robert Shepherd, *A Class Divided: Appeasement and the Road to Munich, 1938* (London, Macmillan, 1988), p. 147.
15 SB, *1938 (I)*, p. 49.
16 Tom Driberg, *Ruling Passions* (London, Jonathan Cape, 1977), p. 186.
17 Piers Brendon, *Head of Guinness: The Life and Times of Rupert Guinness, 2nd Earl of Iveagh* (privately published, 1979), p. 28.
18 Brendon, p. 159.
19 Freya Stark, *Letters, Vol. 3, The Growth of Danger 1935-1939* (Tisbury, Compton Russell, 1976), p. 238.
20 Stark, *Letters, vol. 3*, p. 238.
21 SB, *Wedding and Honeymoon 1939*, p. 57.

22 Interview with Patricia, Lady Boyd, 10 July 1995.
23 *Daily Express*, 13 April 1939.
24 Donald Lennox-Boyd to Alan Lennox-Boyd, 20 Jan. 1939, PBM, Mss. Eng. c. 3759.
25 *New York Times*, 13 April 1939.
26 A.H. Trelawny-Ross, p. 238.
27 Wardell to Lennox-Boyd, 14 April 1939; Wardell to Lennox-Boyd, 18 April 1939; Lennox-Boyd to Wardell, 19 April 1939, PBM, Mss. Eng. c. 3760.
28 MI6 denies holding any information on the incident in its archives. Indeed, apart from a newspaper clipping in a Foreign Office file, it has proved impossible to unearth any documentary material relating to Donald's death among the papers of any Government department. No doubt, however, such material does exist under lock and key. Irrespective of whether Donald was working as an agent, it seems impossible to believe that the British Government would not have taken at least a passing interest in the death of the brother of a Minister in such very highly suspicious circumstances.
29 See for example Iveagh to Lennox-Boyd (undated), PBM, Mss. Eng. c. 3760.
30 Freya Stark, *Dust in the Lion's Paw* (London, John Murray, 1961), p. 7.
31 Molly Izzard, *Freya Stark: A Biography* (London, Hodder and Stoughton, 1993), p. 129.
32 Stark, *Letters, Vol. 3*, p. 249.
33 Izzard, p. 128.
34 Harrod to Lennox-Boyd, 14 March 1950; Lennox-Boyd to Harrod, 19 March 1950, PBM, Mss. Eng. c. 3760.
35 Trelawny-Ross, p. 238. In June 1996 when I visited Sherborne I noticed that although it appeared on the Lyon House war memorial, Donald's name was not included on the school's main war memorial.
36 Lord Boyd interviewed about his early career by Gillian Peele, 20 Feb. 1975, PBM, Mss. Eng. c. 3432, f. 31.
37 SB, *1939-40*, p. 21.
38 *Daily Mail*, 13 April 1940.
39 Woolton to Churchill, 14 May 1940, Churchill Papers, Churchill College, Cambridge, CHAR 20/4A, f. 86.
40 Lord Boyd interviewed about British Prime Ministers by Gillian Peele, 21 Feb. 1975, PBM, Mss. Eng. c. 3432, f. 43.
41 Robert Rhodes James, *Chips: The Diaries of Sir Henry Channon* (Harmondsworth, Penguin, 1970), p. 366.
42 Resumé of Alan Lennox-Boyd's service record, obtained by Downing Street from the Admiralty on 11 Nov. 1943, PREM 5/212.
43 SB, *America 1941*, vol. 1, p. 1.
44 Minute by Deputy Controller, 9 Feb. 1940, ADM 1/11134.
45 Jarrett to Seal, 26 May 1940, ADM 1/11134.
46 Andrew Roberts, *Eminent Churchillians* (London, Weidenfeld and Nicolson, 1994), p. 177.
47 Harold Watkinson, *Turning Points: A Record of Our Times* (Salisbury, Michael Russell, 1986), p. 9.
48 James Lees-Milne, *Diaries 1942-1945: Ancestral Voices and Prophesying Peace* (London, John Murray, 1995), pp. 242-3.
49 Croft to Churchill, 21 Oct. 1943, CHAR 20/103, f. 7.
50 Rhodes James, *Chips*, p. 463.
51 Lists of proposed Ministerial appointments, undated but probably drafted from 3-10 November 1943, PREM 5/212.
52 Rhodes James, *Chips*, p. 463.
53 Lord Boyd interviewed about British Prime Ministers by Gillian Peele, 21 Feb. 1975, PBM, Mss. Eng. c. 3432, p. 4.
54 Churchill to Cripps, 10 Nov. 1943, PREM 5/212.
55 'Probable Fall in Aircraft Production', undated memorandum, PREM 4/34/5.

56 Cripps to Churchill, 11 Nov. 1943, PREM 5/212.
57 Lord Boyd interviewed about British Prime Ministers by Gillian Peele, PBM, Mss. Eng. c. 3432, f. 44.
58 Lennox-Boyd to Churchill, 11 Nov. 1943, PREM 5/212.
59 Lord Boyd interviewed about Prime Ministers, Mss. Eng. c. 3432, p. 6.
60 James Lees-Milne, *Diaries 1942-45*, p. 355.
61 Lennox-Boyd to Dowager Lady Amphill, 25 Oct. 1944, Lycett to Lennox-Boyd, 17 May 1957, PBM, Mss. Eng. c. 3762.
62 *The Times*, 26 Feb. 1945.

6

An Active
Backbencher

Fight a cat with the weapons you would use in fighting a lion.[1]

In May 1945, Britain celebrated the end of the War in Europe and prepared for its first general election in 10 years. Labour withdrew from the coalition Government, and Churchill established a caretaker administration. Lennox-Boyd, who remained for the time being at the Ministry of Aircraft Production, geared himself up for the fight ahead.

In Mid-Bedfordshire, Lennox-Boyd's Labour opponents at last had the chance to arraign him for his pre-War political sympathies. The tone of the campaign was set by a Labour party leaflet which quoted excerpts from Lennox-Boyd's speeches to accomplish the not especially difficult task of proving that he was 'a Supporter of Franco'. Overleaf was a reproduction of a Vicky cartoon from the *Daily Herald* of March 1938 depicting Lennox-Boyd and Henry Page Croft goose-stepping behind a pantomime horse effigy of the Spanish leader. E.K. Martell, Lennox-Boyd's Liberal challenger, took up this theme. In a clear attempt to prevent Lennox-Boyd benefiting from Churchill's popularity, Martell reminded voters of that the two men had taken opposite sides on the issue of appeasement. Lennox-Boyd countered this charge by pointing out that he had voted against the Government over 80 times between the wars, often following Churchill's lead at a time when it was unpopular do so.

On the weekend before the General Election results were announced, Lennox-Boyd indulged in an unfortunate piece of sooth-saying. He published an article in the *Sunday Despatch* entitled 'Why Churchill Has Won'.[2] 'A Gamble that Failed!' was the terse comment he scribbled on the copy which he pasted into his scrapbook. Indeed it did. Labour gained an overwhelming majority (albeit on the basis of only 46.8% of votes cast) winning 393 seats against the Conservatives' 213. Lennox-Boyd's own share of the vote fell slightly, but even in this most unpromising election he still managed to hold Mid-Beds.

Meanwhile, the war with Japan continued. Its conclusion in the middle of August was marked, for Lennox-Boyd, by one particularly poignant scene. Churchill had arranged a dinner at Claridges for former Tory Ministers. There were not many of them and Lennox-Boyd was the most junior. Suddenly, the Prime Minister's Private Secretary, John Colville, arrived with a note from Attlee to say that Japan had surrendered. Churchill read this out and commented that it was a pity they did not have a radio to hear the Prime Minister's announcement. Lennox-Boyd and Ralph Assheton managed to find one in the hotel. So it was, as Lennox-Boyd was later to recall, that:

> on a borrowed wireless set in a hired room in Claridges, Winston heard of the end of the war, and I think there wasn't a single of his former colleagues who wasn't near to tears at the irony of the situation. Then he went out into the rain and there were three old ladies under an umbrella who had heard he was there and gave him a cheer. Well, that was the end of war cooperation.[3]

The appearance of the Commons Chamber when the House reassembled on 20 August 1945 was in marked contrast to the scene which had confronted Lennox-Boyd after his election to Parliament in 1931. The Conservative Opposition certainly had an impressive front bench team including Churchill, Eden, Oliver Stanley, Oliver Lyttelton and Rab Butler; but this was, as John Boyd-Carpenter observed, an army of generals without troops. Of those Conservative candidates who were returned to Parliament in 1945 many were older members with safe seats. These were not the sorts of people most likely to take to the barricades. Churchill's eccentric and unpredictable leadership did not help matters. Lennox-Boyd was among the younger and more dynamic Conservative members who attempted to demonstrate that their party was still a political force to be reckoned with. He became the *de facto* leader of a group of MPs, organized by Sir Herbert Williams, who called themselves the Active Back Benchers.

Lennox-Boyd and his colleagues waged a form of guerrilla warfare against the Labour Government. During the war, the Government had arrogated to itself the power to legislate through statutory instruments. Most of these would automatically come into operation without being debated in Parliament unless a motion to annul them – a 'Prayer' – was tabled within 40 days of their being laid before the House. Prayers were usually taken at around 10 pm, after the main business of the House had been completed, and there was, in those years, no limit on the time during which they could be debated. To terminate such a debate the Government had to obtain a motion for closure which required 100 votes in favour. Hence, a handful of Tory MPs bombarding the Government with prayers could keep Government managers and a 100 Labour members hanging around the House until the early hours of the morning.[4]

However juvenile these adventures might appear to outsiders, they certainly helped to restore the morale of Conservative members and provided a further source of irritation to a Government beset by plenty of extra-Parliamentary problems. They did, however, take their toll on Lennox-Boyd himself. James Lees-Milne who dined at the Lennox-Boyds' one evening in July 1947 found that his host was so exhausted after a Commons sitting which had lasted until 7 am that he fell asleep after the meal.[5]

If their experiences during the Second World War had persuaded some Conservatives of the need for a new approach to domestic policy, Lennox-Boyd's views show few signs of having altered. He was utterly opposed to the Attlee Government's policy of nationalization and had little inherent sympathy for its domestic social programme. He opposed Government expenditure on education and welfare, as he had done in the 1930s, on the basis that Britain needed to channel her resources towards achieving economic recovery. In March 1947, he complained that proposals to raise the school leaving age would take out of industry 300,000 young people whose efforts might make the difference between the country surviving or perishing.

In economic affairs, much of his attention was concentrated in the field of civil aviation. Here his opposition to the Government was fuelled in part by a very personal sense of grievance. As Parliamentary Secretary at the Ministry of Aircraft Production he had been responsible for introducing the Civil Aviation White Paper of March 1945, the so-called 'Swinton Plan'. During the inter-war period, privately owned British companies had faced the greatest difficulty operating international air routes on a profitable basis and had become dependent upon state subsidies. Hence, despite the Conservatives' aversion to nationalization, the Chamberlain Government's decision to take Imperial Airways and British Airways under public ownership and merge them to create the British

Overseas Airways Corporation (BOAC), had proved largely uncontroversial. The wartime coalition had recognized that BOAC in its existing form would be inadequate to deal with the rapid expansion of demand for air passenger transport which was bound to follow the conclusion of the war. The Swinton plan therefore proposed some diversification: BOAC would remain responsible for Commonwealth services. Other overseas routes would be operated by BOAC in partnership with the shipping companies, while domestic and continental services would be operated by a single corporation consisting of BOAC, the travel agencies, railway and shipping companies and the pre-war private air companies. The Government would exercise overall control of the establishment of new companies and general matters of policy but would not involve itself in day-to-day management decisions.

To Lennox-Boyd's dismay, following the General Election of July 1945, the Labour Government, rather than implementing the Swinton plan, introduced their own legislation. This was not presented to Parliament until May 1946, and it represented a significant change from the proposals of the previous year. It adhered to the Swinton plan in seeking the creation of three new companies with distinct geographical spheres of operation: a revised BOAC covering Commonwealth, North Atlantic and Far Eastern routes; the British European Airways Corporation; and the British South American Airways Corporation.[6] Unlike the March 1945 White Paper, however, it vested ownership of all three companies in the state and excluded private capital from any involvement. The three public companies were to have exclusive rights to operate scheduled air services. The remaining private firms were relegated to operating rescue and training flights and certain narrowly defined charter services. In justifying this new arrangement, the Government argued that the development of civil aviation should not be constrained by the financial interests of private railway and shipping companies.[7] Logic of this kind did not impress Lennox-Boyd, who led for the Opposition when the proposals were put before Parliament on 6 May. He naturally deplored the exclusion of private capital and expertise. In particular, however, he complained that the Swinton plan 'was agreed on 14 precious months ago, months during which foreign friendly but active competitors have been conquering air routes all over the world'.[8]

Lennox-Boyd continued to take a close interest in civil aviation policy throughout his period on the Opposition benches, making use of the contacts in the industry which he had established while at the Ministry of Aircraft Production. When Swinton resigned as chairman of the Conservative back bench Civil Aviation

Committee in November 1946, Lennox-Boyd was elected in his place and he played a key role in the often highly contentious business of devising party policy on the issue.

An indication of Lennox-Boyd's success in harrying the Attlee administration was the amount of personal abuse he attracted from the Government benches. This had one overriding theme: his supposed fascist sympathies. Memories of the 1930s were still fresh, and Lennox-Boyd himself tended to provoke criticism by the sheer recklessness of his personal attacks on Labour Ministers. During a debate in July 1946, he launched into an impromptu diatribe against John Strachey, the Minister of Food, suggesting that Strachey's failure to provide the House with details about Food supplies might owe something to the fact that he had 'at one time a close association, as his first lieutenant, with Sir Oswald Mosley in his early Fascist days'.[9] This was, of course, quite unfair; Strachey's association with Mosley dated from the time of the New Party and was abruptly terminated by him when Mosley began to transform the party into a quasi-fascist organization. It also displayed remarkable cheek given Lennox-Boyd's own activities in the 1930s. Labour members were inevitably quick to remind the House that Lennox-Boyd had been 'closely associated with Franco and Fascist Spain' and a furious row ensued.

Lennox-Boyd got himself into a similar scrape only two weeks later in another attempt to goad the Government benches. Following an answer by the Chancellor of the Exchequer, Hugh Dalton, to a Labour question suggesting the establishment of a May Day holiday as a tribute to the efforts of the workers during the war, Lennox-Boyd asked whether this would be an appropriate occasion for speeches by 'conscientious objectors of the last war, now serving in His Majesty's Government'. This was a clear reference to the Lord President of the Council and Leader of the House, Herbert Morrison. Dalton responded that the question was 'malicious as well as irrelevant' and came from 'a friend of an enemy of this country'.[10] Quintin Hogg attempted to whip up some indignation at this, but after a sharp exchange of views the Speaker stepped in to defuse the row.

Lennox-Boyd never missed an opportunity to attack the 'drab and standardized' atmosphere of Attlee's Britain. His own private circumstances, however, were far from austere. When in February 1947, Lady Gammans dined with the Lennox-Boyds in their new London home in Chapel Street, she was amazed, not only by the size of the house, but by the fact, so she claimed, that the family retained no less than five butlers.[11] Yet Chapel Street was far more than a symbol of personal wealth; it became for Lennox-Boyd an important political resource. He kept open house for visitors from around the Empire and Commonwealth, in the process constructing an impressive network of personal contacts. Members of delegations to London, often quite junior and unknown outside their own territories and sometimes markedly unsympathetic to British colonial rule, would be surprised to find themselves invited to dine or even to stay at Chapel Street.

For some of Lennox-Boyd's colleagues, the sight of coloured people being treated with such warmth and respect, came as even more of a surprise in the London of the 1940s than the grandeur of Chapel Street itself. This generated an enormous fund of goodwill among colonial politicians upon which Lennox-Boyd was able to draw for many years to come. In January 1956, during the final round of negotiations for Malaya's independence, the Malayan politician Toh Eng Hoe wrote to him, recalling the time five years before when as part of a delegation to London he had been entertained at Chapel Street and introduced to senior figures in the Conservative party including Churchill. 'It was,' he added, 'a most memorable occasion which all of us will long remember.'[12] In September 1955, in the middle of some tense negotiations over his country's constitutional future, the premier of the Gold Coast, Kwame Nkrumah, found time to recall the 'very happy occasion' four years before when Lennox-Boyd had thrown a party for him in Chapel Street.[13]

Lennox-Boyd also cultivated links with overseas political leaders through a series of informal overseas visits. One of the most important friendships which he nurtured during this period was with the Regent of Iraq, Crown Prince Abd al-Ilah, who had been restored to power by the British following the revolution of 1941. In February 1946, Lennox-Boyd flew to Iraq on a private visit as the Regent's guest. As well as sight seeing, he was also taken on shooting expeditions by the Regent himself. Lennox-Boyd's visit to Iraq coincided with growing tension in the Middle East which focused upon Soviet intentions in the area. On 1 March, the Soviet Union announced that it would not withdraw its troops from northern Iran, raising understandable fears in Washington and London that Stalin had designs on the region's oil wells. Britain depended on imported oil and the Anglo-Iranian oil company provided the British exchequer with an important source of revenue. In the course of his travels, Lennox-Boyd crossed into Iran and pointedly made a visit to the Anglo-Iranian company's refinery at Abadan.

Business and pleasure took Lennox-Boyd to a variety of locations within the British Empire and Commonwealth during the years of Opposition. These visits reflected Lennox-Boyd's continuing interest

in Commonwealth and colonial affairs. During the period of Opposition, he occupied the important position of chairman of the Parliamentary Committee of the Empire Industries Association. The
Association had been established in 1923 by Leo Amery, Neville
Chamberlain and Lord Lloyd to campaign for protectionist policies.
Although notionally 'non-partisan', the Parliamentary committee was,
during its heyday in the 1940s and early 1950s, a virtual extension
of the Conservative parliamentary party.[14] It represented an important constituent part of the network through which Conservative MPs
could discuss Imperial policy. In November 1946 the Conservative
back bench Imperial (later Commonwealth) Affairs Committee established a special sub-committee to consider economic matters and in
particular 'Imperial Preference'. Since one of the duties of the
sub-committee was to liaise with the Parliamentary Committee of the
Empire Industries Association, Lennox-Boyd was the natural choice
to be its first chairman, and he duly added this to his list of responsibilities.

He reaffirmed his faith in protectionism in an article entitled,
'Broad Imperial Thinking', published in April 1948. The piece combined a characteristically romanticized defence of the Empire with
a pointed attack on the United States over her determination to
break down tariff barriers:

> We should say also to the USA, 'You have the trade all over your vast
> territory. We do not question your rights. Yours is a great Empire
> united by land. Ours is linked together by sea. You have also prefer
> ential arrangements with Cuba and Hawaii. You even have them with
> your independent Philippine Islands, with whom you have signed a 20
> year preference agreement. You cannot ask us to abandon what you
> have no intention of abandoning yourself.'[15]

This was the so-called 'salt-water heresy' about which Conservatives activists and Colonial Office mandarins complained well into
the 1950s: that irredentist tendencies across land-masses such as
those of America and the Soviet Union were regarded as legitimate,
while those across the scattered territories which constituted the
British Empire were not. It was a sentiment strongly echoed by an
early draft of *Imperial Policy*, the Conservative party's 1949 pamphlet on colonial affairs, of which Lennox-Boyd was one of the
authors. The draft asserted that the British Empire had as much
right to make its own economic arrangements as did the 'landlocked
empires' of the United States and the USSR.[16]

As one of his party's most active spokesmen on Imperial affairs,
Lennox-Boyd's inclination, in common with that of some of his
senior colleagues, was to fight a rear-guard action against the
Labour Government's more far-reaching constitutional reforms. In

practice, however, he was restrained by a number of factors. First, the Conservatives largely accepted the doctrine that colonial affairs should, so far as possible, be kept outside the arena of party political disputes. This was based upon the assumption that the moral authority of Britain's representatives in the colonies could be undermined if the policies they were charged with implementing were subject to concerted criticism within the Imperial parliament. Another factor tending to limit Conservative attacks on the Government's colonial policies was the influence of Oliver Stanley. Having been Colonial Secretary from 1942–45, he naturally became the principal Opposition spokesman on colonial affairs, as well as leading for the Conservatives on financial matters. A pragmatic figure on the left of the party, Stanley was fully aware of the growing strength of colonial nationalism and was disinclined to attack the Government for its efforts to reach an accommodation with it. Despite their differences on other issues, Stanley and Lennox-Boyd formed a close friendship based on their shared sense of the overriding importance of Imperial policy.

Stanley held the influential post of chairman of the Imperial Affairs Committee. His capacity to take an active role in shaping party policy was, however, increasingly undermined by ill-health. According to the characteristically uncharitable judgement of another imperial enthusiast, Lady Gammans, Stanley still hoped to return to the Colonial Office and was therefore keen that a mediocre figure who would not overshadow him should chair the Imperial Affairs Committee in his absence. He had therefore selected Lord Tweedsmuir as his understudy.[17] Whether or not this was true, it was certainly Tweedsmuir rather than Lennox-Boyd who was given principal responsibility for drafting the Conservatives' most important statement on colonial affairs in Opposition, the 1949 document, *Imperial Policy.* It was only in the final months of Stanley's life that he appears to have chosen Lennox-Boyd as his anointed successor and preferred candidate for the job of Colonial Secretary. Shortly before Stanley's death in December 1950, Lennox-Boyd took over as temporary Chairman of the Imperial Affairs Committee. He continued to chair the Committee until the 1951 General Election.

That Stanley did not bring Lennox-Boyd forward earlier probably owed more to policy differences between the two rather than to any desire on Stanley's part to retain the limelight. Stanley's ability to appreciate both sides of an argument left him prone to what R. A. Butler caricatured as 'an almost physical incapacity for making up his mind'.[18] Lennox-Boyd, by contrast, brought to Imperial affairs a quasi-religious fervour which still produced flashes of die-hard rhetoric. His views on the granting of independence to

a Congress-governed India rivalled those of Churchill in their ve-
hemence and were aired in public with far more abandon. The
Attlee Government's announcement in February 1947 that British
rule in India would end by June of the following year brought an
angry reaction from the member for Mid-Beds. In March, he told
Conservative party workers that,

> To give to a Constituent Assembly in India full self-Government and
> the right to leave the British Empire, and then to 'pack up' and leave
> without first ensuring that all the great Indian races were represented
> on that Assembly was to give India over to carnage and pillage and to
> wipe out in a few months of criminal weakness and cowardice the
> achievements of the last 150 years.[19]

Subsequent events did nothing to reconcile him to the
Government's policy. The following year at a meeting in his constituency he bemoaned the fact that every month 'enough people
to equal the population of Biggleswade were being slaughtered in
India', while the British Government had surrendered their responsibilities to 'that old fraud', Gandhi.

His growing interest in the affairs of the Middle East and distinct lack of sympathy for the Zionist cause made Lennox-Boyd no
less critical of the Labour Government over its policy towards Palestine. During his trip to Iraq in 1946 he had told a news conference that all parties in Britain realized that Palestine could not
absorb European Jewish immigration and were determined to ensure that the Arabs would not receive a raw deal.[20] On another
occasion, he criticized Labour for their 'reckless election promises
to give the Jews a country which for 1,000 years had been inhab-
ited by Arabs'. Following the Government's decision in September
1947 to withdraw from the Palestine mandate, he complained that
'we were leaving our friends the Arabs to a blood bath'.[21]

From a personal perspective, the period in Opposition was a particularly difficult and troubling one for Lennox-Boyd. In the autumn
of 1949, he had once again to endure the pain of bereavement. On
11 November, his mother died of heart failure. The loss of three of
her sons had taken its toll on her health. Particularly difficult was
the period between the disappearance of Francis, her favourite son,
in June 1944 and the official confirmation of his death almost a
year later. Alan Lennox-Boyd had spoken of this at the inquest into
his mother's death. 'Physically there was no reason why she should
live,' he told the coroner, 'it was only her spirit that kept her alive.'[22]
A frequent visitor to Henlow Grange in the final years of Florence's
life was her son's new friend and companion, Major Alexander
Beattie, a former officer in the Coldstream Guards and bodyguard
to Winston Churchill. Beattie accompanied Alan on a tour of Iraq

in 1948. Two years later, they went on holiday to Malta together, and in 1951 Beattie travelled with him on a tour of the West Indies. Beattie's presence on these trips was public knowledge. It was mentioned in press reports, and the two men received joint invitations to social events, for example to a reception at the US embassy in Baghdad in April 1948.

This was not the first time Lennox-Boyd had formed a very close and very public friendship with another man. From the 1930s onwards he remained in almost daily contact with his brother-in-law, Henry 'Chips' Channon. When Channon died in 1958, Lennox-Boyd wrote candidly to his friend, Lord Hailes,

> I know you understand how I feel about Chips. I miss him more every day. I suppose it is a great pity to get too tied up with anyone, but life would be very gloomy if we planned it in that sort of way.[23]

Beattie, however, seems to have been less discreet about his sexuality than Channon, as James Lees-Milne discovered when he dined with Beattie and Lennox-Boyd in January 1949:

> Beattie is a good-looking amiable ass. He asked me if I had ever been in love, and when I said, 'Yes, of course', seemed surprised. He vouchsafed that he liked sleeping in one bed with people he was fond of, but did not care much for sex. It left him cold. Is, I suspect, a Narcissus. 'As for women,' he said, 'they are so damned soft. Their bodies have no firmness. This is what I dislike.'[24]

Beattie's presence inevitably placed a strain on Lennox-Boyd's marriage. Staying with him in Dublin shortly after his visit to Iraq in 1948, Lees-Milne noted, 'Late at night Alan said what a tiresome necessity of life dissimulation was. He kept saying, "Isn't Patsy a wonderful wife?"'[25] Many of Lennox-Boyd's friends agreed, and at least one warned him that he was in danger of losing her if the relationship with Beattie continued. He was also placing his whole political career in danger. At around the time he rejoined the Government in the autumn of 1951, he appears to have decided to exercise rather more discretion in his private life, and the holidays with Beattie came to an end. Yet the two continued to see one another, and they maintained a regular if sometimes strained correspondence throughout the rest of Lennox-Boyd's life.

The quickening tempo of British politics which accompanied the death throes of the Labour Government may have provided Lennox-Boyd with a welcome relief from his personal problems. Only two months after Florence's death, Attlee called a general election for 23 February 1950. It seemed likely to be a difficult one for Lennox-Boyd. His majority had been reduced to less than 2,000 in 1945, and, as always, he faced the problem of how to canvas an electorate spread among a large number of small towns and villages. One of his solutions was to tour Mid-Beds with a caravan equipped with a loudspeaker, large quantities of Conservative literature and a bed on which he could catch a few moments sleep between engagements. In the middle of the campaign disaster struck when he suffered a severe attack of laryngitis and was advised by his doctor to refrain from making speeches for a week. With typical showmanship he turned this handicap into an extremely successful publicity stunt, enlisting the help of Patsy in a bizarre vaudeville act. He produced a speech for his wife to read on his behalf at election meetings which began:

> I have only lost my voice for five days. The Socialists have lost their heads for five years. I will get my voice back; they won't get their heads back.[26]

When questions were asked at the end of the meetings, Lennox-Boyd adopted two means by which to transmit his replies. The first was to whisper his them to his wife who would then 'interpret' them for the audience. The second, slightly more technologically advanced method was through a modified microphone which would amplify his whispers in a sinister baritone. The tactic generated a gratifyingly large number of silly newspaper headlines including 'A wife does all the talking', 'Speechless candidates' and 'Tories answer the whispers'.

Lennox-Boyd's whispering campaign proved successful. He comfortably held off his Labour rival, William Howell, and emerged with a slightly increased majority. Nationally, Labour remained in Government but with its huge majority of 1945 reduced to only five seats. It seemed highly likely that the new Government would not serve a full term in office. In contrast to the dismal picture which confronted them after the 1945 General Election, the Conservatives could take comfort in the belief that events were moving in their direction.

In September 1950, Lennox-Boyd visited Singapore and Malaya with five other members of a delegation of MPs from the Commonwealth Parliamentary Association (CPA) led by the Labour peer Lord Listowel. They were particularly concerned to study the state of military operations against the Communist guerrillas in Malaya. At one point during their three week tour, the party came rather too close for comfort to their intended object of study. Three minutes after Lennox-Boyd and his colleagues had passed the 39th milestone on the Jahore road, the spot was the target of a Communist ambush which killed a special constable. In another well-publicized incident, the MPs flew with the Royal Air Force on airdrops of supplies to the security forces in the jungle. Like the CPA delegation to Kenya in 1954, the visit was a great public relations success for the British counter-insurgency campaign. At the conclusion of their visit, the MPs gave a press conference at which they expressed their full support for the way in which the campaign was being conducted and denied that there was any friction between the population of Malaya and the British.

By the summer of 1951, it was clear that another election was imminent. On 24 June, Attlee had told the King that he would ask for a dissolution of Parliament in the autumn. The prospect of another election campaign may not have been far from Lennox-Boyd's mind when he entered hospital in July for a haemorrhoid operation. Nevertheless, having recovered from this, he went ahead with another foreign visit. On 30 August 1951, he sailed from Southampton for New York on the Queen Mary. From New York he flew to Jamaica. This, his first visit to the West Indies, was advertised as a fact finding mission in his capacity as Chairman of the Conservative Imperial Affairs Committee. Lennox-Boyd knew that a General Election might be declared in Great Britain at any time, but did not expect one until November. In the event, on 19 September a General Election was called for 25 October. Having managed to visit Barbados, Antigua and St. Kitts, Lennox-Boyd was forced to abandon his tour and return to England.

Back home, he was thrust into another exhausting round of electioneering. The BBC selected Mid-Beds for detailed coverage as a typical marginal constituency in which the result was impossible to predict. Once again, the campaign caravan was trailed around the Bedfordshire countryside. Lennox-Boyd claimed to have attended over 100 meetings in the course of the campaign. Again, he had problems with his voice but this did not pose as big an obstacle as it had the previous year. On the eve of poll the Conservatives arranged eight meetings in the constituency, five of which Lennox-Boyd attended himself. Once again his efforts were rewarded. He gained 19,681 votes to his Labour opponent's 17,818. His majority was slightly down on 1950 but he was able to claim that he had polled more votes than any other Conservative candidate in the history of the seat. Overall, the Conservatives obtained a majority of 17. After a break of six years, Lennox-Boyd could look forward to the prospect of returning to Government.

Notes
1 Swahili proverb from Zanzibar collected by Lennox-Boyd, PBM, Mss. Eng. c. 3796, f. 276.
2 *Sunday Despatch*, 22 July 1945, SB, *1945 General Election*, p. 37.
3 Lord Boyd interviewed about Prime Ministers, Mss. Eng. c. 3432, f. 46.
4 John Boyd-Carpenter, *Way of Life* (London, Sidgwick and Jackson, 1980), pp. 76–7.
5 James Lees-Milne, *Caves of Ice* (London, Faber and Faber, 1983), p. 186.
6 Kenneth O. Morgan, *Labour in Power 1945–1951* (Oxford, Oxford University Press, 1985), p. 102.
7 W.H.P. Canner, *The Air Transport Industry* (London, Brown, Son, Ferguson Ltd., 1986), p. 17.
8 *HC Deb*, 422, col. 621, 6 May 1946.
9 *HC Deb*, 425, col. 614, 11 July 1946.
10 *HC Deb*, 425, col. 1873, 23 July 1946.
11 The Diary of Lady Gammans, 14 Feb. 1947, Gammans Papers, Rhodes House, Oxford, Mss. Brit. Emp. s. 506, 8/2, f. 120.
12 Toh Eng Hoe to Lennox-Boyd, 24 Jan. 1956, PBM, Mss. Eng. c. 3463, f. 12.
13 Nkrumah to Lennox-Boyd, 30 Sept. 1955, CO 544/806, no. 112, in Richard Rathbone (ed.), *British Documents on the End of Empire, Series B, vol. 1, Ghana Part II, 1952–1957* (London, HMSO, 1992), p. 179.
14 Philip Murphy, *Party Politics and Decolonization: The Conservative Party and British Colonial Policy in Tropical Africa, 1951–1964* (Oxford, Oxford University Press, 1995), pp. 101–2.
15 *Life Line*, April 1948, p. 36.
16 Murphy, p. 34.
17 Gammans Diary, 30 March 1949, Mss. Brit. Emp. s. 506, 10/4, f. 13. Her views on this matter deserve to be treated with some caution partly because Stanley seems to have coveted the Treasury rather than the Colonial Office and partly because of her overriding conviction that her husband, David Gammans, rather than Tweedsmuir, should really have been in charge of policy making.
18 R.A. Butler, *The Art of the Possible* (London, Hamish Hamilton, 1971) p. 144.
19 SB, *1947*, p. 18.
20 *Iraqi Times*, 23 Feb. 1946; *Al Zaman*, 3 March 1946.
21 SB, *1948, 9, & 50 & Malaya and Singapore*, p. 4.
22 *Biggleswade Chronicle and Bedfordshire Gazette*, 18 Nov. 1949.
23 Lennox-Boyd to Hailes, 21 Nov. 1958, PBM, Mss. Eng. c. 3465, f. 270.
24 James Lees-Milne, *Midway on the Waves* (London, Faber & Faber, 1985), pp. 149–50.
25 Lees-Milne, *Midway on the Waves*, p. 45.
26 SB, *Election 1950*, p. 15.

7

Exile

A good thing sells itself; a bad thing wants advertising.[1]

As Chairman of the back bench Imperial Affairs Committee, Lennox-Boyd had some reason to hope that he might be offered the Colonial Office after the Conservative victory in the 1951 General Election. In the event, he was considerably lower down in the pecking order when Ministerial positions were allotted at the end of October. Once Oliver Lyttelton had accepted the post of Secretary of State for the Colonies, Lennox-Boyd let it be known that he would be prepared to serve at the Colonial Office as Minister of State. Had he not done so, the post itself, which had only existed since 1948, might very well have disappeared. Shortly before the 1951 General Election, Sir Thomas Lloyd, the Permanent Under-Secretary at the Colonial Office, recommended that it be abolished. He had been surprised when the job of Minister of State was retained after the 1950 election, believing it to have been created merely 'to provide a billet' for Lord Listowel, Britain's last Secretary of State for India.[2] Lloyd felt that there were too many Ministers and that, as a consequence, the Parliamentary Under-Secretary at the Colonial Office had 'nothing at all' to do.

The Cabinet Secretary, Norman Brook, took up this point as Churchill turned his mind to the more junior Ministerial appointments. He told the Prime Minister that there was no need for a Minister of State for the Colonies and that, indeed, it might be inconvenient to appoint one. The number of members of the Commons who could hold the title of 'Minister of State' was limited by statute to three. Churchill had already appointed two – for Foreign and Economic Affairs – and seemed likely to want to appoint a third to Defence.[3] Churchill, however, ignored these objections. When,

at the beginning of November Lennox-Boyd was summoned to
Downing Street, Churchill told him, 'I hear you want to be Minister of State in the Colonial Office; I didn't know there was such a
post.' Lennox-Boyd assured him that indeed there was. He was
offered the job and gladly accepted it.

The most pressing problem for the Colonial Office was the emergency in Malaya. In October 1951, shortly before the British
General Election, Sir Henry Gurney, the British High Commissioner
in Malaya, had been killed in a guerrilla ambush. Lennox-Boyd, who
was canvassing in Mid-Bedfordshire at the time, was horrified by
the news. Gurney's murder seemed to pose a direct threat to
Britain's ability to maintain control of the situation. Lyttelton was
equally concerned, and took the earliest opportunity to visit Malaya. In his absence, Lennox-Boyd was left in charge of the Colonial
Office for much of December.

On Lyttelton's return, Lennox-Boyd embarked on a tour of East
Africa. He left London on 3 January and arrived in Nairobi the
following day. From there, with only a break for lunch, he flew to
Tanganyika in a Government plane specially provided for his tour
of the territory. He spent 12 days in Tanganyika following a crowded
schedule which took him 2,000 miles. High on Lennox-Boyd's
agenda was the question of constitutional development. A recent
constitutional commission had recommended the introduction of
racial 'parity' among the unofficial members of the Legislative Council, with the European, African and Asian communities each having
seven seats. This stopped far short of representing accurately the
numerical strengths of the different racial groups, and in particular the overwhelming preponderance of the Africans. Yet in giving
non-Europeans a combined majority among the unofficials it went
too far for many settlers in the territory.

Lennox-Boyd's visit did much to pacify the settlers who were
impressed by his very public and emphatic message to African leaders that they could not expect their political representation to reflect
their numerical superiority.[4] It also set the pattern for the tours
he was to undertake as Colonial Secretary. He made a point of lis-
tening to the views of relatively junior colonial officials. This allowed
him to canvas alternative opinions, and it gave tremendous encouragement to the officers themselves. Lennox-Boyd was equally
attentive to the non-officials he met. He always carried with him a
pad on which he would write down any requests and grievances
that were put to him, promising that these would be considered
on his return to England.

Lennox-Boyd's general impression of Tanganyika was extremely
favourable. Towards the end of his tour, he told members of the

Tanganyikan Government how impressed he had been both by the respect with which officials in the territory were regarded and by the lack of inter-racial animosity.[5] He was surprised, however, by the extent to which political interest was focused almost exclusively upon the recommendations of the Constitutional Committee for parity in the legislature. In Opposition, the Conservatives had hoped that a large proportion of the political energies both in East and West Africa could be deflected towards local government activity, thus decreasing somewhat the pace of constitutional advance at a territorial level. Lennox-Boyd was left in no doubt that this was not going to be feasible in Tanganyika and that, as a consequence, 'parity' of representation in the legislature would almost certainly have to be granted.

From Tanganyika, Lennox-Boyd travelled to Kenya. Here the Tanganyikan constitutional proposals had already caused alarm among European politicians, afraid that a similar policy might be applied to their own territory. In contrast to the warmth with which he had been received by the Governor of Tanganyika, Sir Edward Twining, Lennox-Boyd found the Kenyan Governor, Sir Philip Mitchell, 'a rather aloof and Olympian figure'. Mitchell was deeply sensitive about what he regarded as Colonial Office interference in his colony, and was less than welcoming towards the Minister of State. When Lennox-Boyd arrived in Kenya, he was surprised to find that the Governor had made no provision for him to give a single speech. He did, however, make an impromptu speech to a large gathering of Europeans, having decided that it would be embarrassing if he did not say a few words. Afterwards, Mitchell told him, rather patronizingly, that had he known the Minister would handle the situation so well he would have arranged for him to make one or two speeches.[6]

At the time of Lennox-Boyd's visit, unrest within the Kikuyu reserves had risen to such a level that European settlers were beginning to press for firm action from the Kenya Government. Junior administrative officers were also warning of discontent within their districts. During his talks with Mitchell, Lennox-Boyd asked him about the rumours of instability. Mitchell replied that he was slightly concerned about the towns but that the countryside was peaceful. Lennox-Boyd later claimed that no mention was made of illegal 'Mau Mau' assemblies among the Kikuyu. His comments to reporters on his departure from Nairobi reflected some of Mitchell's complacency. He told them,

> If there are people who feel that race relations in Kenya are bad, the best thing such people can do is to come and see for themselves.[7]

These were words which Lennox-Boyd was soon to regret. On 20 October 1952 a state of emergency was declared in Kenya and the Government embarked upon a major counter-insurgency operation.

Back in London, one of the main areas which commanded Lennox-Boyd's attention was Central Africa. The settlers of Northern and Southern Rhodesia had for many years been pressing for the amalgamation of the two territories. Given Northern Rhodesia's rich mineral deposits and the high degree of political autonomy which the settlers of Southern Rhodesia had already achieved, this would have opened the way for the creation of an extremely wealthy, European-dominated state in Central Africa. The idea had not been welcomed by the Colonial Office which feared not only for the interests of the region's Africans but for Britain's own capacity to maintain control over a united Rhodesia. The leader of the Northern Rhodesian Europeans, Roy Welensky, had little success in his efforts to sell the idea of amalgamation to the Attlee administration. Oliver Stanley, for the Conservatives, proved no more encouraging. Instead, Welensky was persuaded to press for a revised scheme for a federation in Central Africa. This commanded the support of influential officials within the Colonial and Commonwealth Relations Office, leading industrialists, and some of the Conservative party's colonial specialists, among them Alan Lennox-Boyd.

For the British Government, the scheme appeared to offer a way to wean the settlers of Southern Rhodesia away from closer contacts with South Africa in the wake of the National Party victory of 1948. It also provided them with a solution to the problem of what to do with the small but densely populated colony of Nyasaland which was in urgent need of substantial investment. Very much against the wishes of the European settlers of Rhodesia, Nyasaland was to be included in the new federation. To Conservatives like Lennox-Boyd, the federal proposals seemed an attractive alternative to the course which already seemed virtually inevitable in West Africa: that of gradually liquidating British imperial power and of transferring control to African nationalist Governments. In the longer term it was hoped that the East African territories of Kenya, Uganda and Tanganyika might also adopt a policy of federation.

Until October 1951, the principal obstacle to the rapid implementation of Federation was the widespread concern within the British Labour party at the prospect of giving the European settlers greater control over the fate of the region's Africans. While still in Opposition, Lennox-Boyd had proved happy to help pro-federal European settlers argue their case in London. In July

1951 for example, he sought to arrange a meeting between Roy
Welensky and Anthony Eden.[8] In the months preceding the 1951
General Election, he gave Welensky and his allies enthusiastic
support and advice on Parliamentary tactics. Following the election, the Conservatives pressed ahead with the federal proposals
and Lennox-Boyd took the closest interest in negotiations
between the British Government and settler politicians. In April
1952, a conference opened in London to draw up specific proposals for a federal constitution. Welensky's hopes that
Lennox-Boyd would be able to exert a positive influence over
these talks were, however, to be dashed. To his and
Lennox-Boyd's own great disappointment, Churchill chose this
moment to move the Minister of State.

Lennox-Boyd's sudden translation from the Colonial Office after just a few months was caused by the illness of John Maclay,
the Minister for both Transport and Civil Aviation. Maclay had
suffered a breakdown, partly as a result of Churchill's bullying
interventions.[9] Two factors made it imperative that Maclay should
be replaced as soon as possible. First, the Minister of Transport
was invested by statute with certain quasi-judicial powers that only
he could perform. There was a backlog of cases requiring the
Minister's decision. The Government was advised that, although in
normal circumstances a responsible official could exercise these
powers on the Minister's behalf, decisions taken while the Minister was known to be seriously incapacitated might be challenged
successfully in the courts.[10] Secondly, the Ministry of Transport was
under great pressure from the Cabinet in general and Churchill in
particular to bring forward legislation for the denationalization of
road haulage. Norman Brook, the Cabinet Secretary, encouraged
the Prime Minister's impatience, telling him that it was vital to the
Government's standing that a bill be ready for introduction into the
House of Commons in the first half of June.[11] The drafting of legislation would, he suggested, be delayed unless officials received
clear and prompt instructions from their Minister.

Maclay submitted his resignation on 3 May, and the news spread
rapidly around Whitehall that Churchill wanted Lennox-Boyd to
replace him. This caused consternation in the Colonial Office.
Lyttelton rang Lennox-Boyd and advised him to get out of town as
quickly as possible. He said that Churchill had told him, 'I can't
have my two tallest ministers, 12 foot nine inches of you, being
wasted in the same department.' Lennox-Boyd fled to his flat in
Brighton but Churchill tracked him down and told him to come to
lunch at Downing Street the next day. It was then Churchill revealed what was in store for him. Lennox-Boyd was adamant that

he did not wish to go to the Ministry of Transport and suggested some other names.[12]Lyttelton added his own protest. He told Churchill,

> I think that my man is ideally suited to the job and with the Central African Federation and other pots on the boil this would be a very unhappy moment for a change. You know his general abilities and I need not dilate upon them. All his interests have for the past seven years been concentrated upon colonial affairs and he knows all the personalities both at home and overseas. He is also able to entertain extensively and has done so with admirable results ever since we took office.[13]

Other voices, however, prevailed. A few days after his interview with Churchill, Lennox-Boyd was summoned back to Downing Street and told that his fate was sealed; the Party whips had insisted that he should replace Maclay. By way of compensation, Lennox-Boyd managed to extract a promise from Churchill that when Oliver Lyttelton left the Colonial Office, he would return there as Secretary of State. Lennox-Boyd later recalled that at the end of this unhappy interview he stepped outside with Churchill. The Prime Minister gestured towards a group of flag sellers standing in the rain. 'Poor people,' he mused. 'No umbrellas,' and then, with a wicked smile, 'and no transport.'[14]

Lennox-Boyd found it difficult to turn his back on colonial affairs. His Private Secretary at the Ministry of Transport told the Colonial Office: 'Lennox-Boyd's body might be with us, but his heart is with you'.[15] Indeed, only three days after taking up his new job, he was writing to Lyttelton encouraging him to arrange a Ministerial visit to Malaya.[16] The following month he wrote again, asking forgiveness for 'intruding on my old love', but suggesting that arrangements should be made for the Conservative Research Department's colonial affairs expert, Gerald Sayers, to visit Nyasaland.[17] Shortly after moving to the Ministry of Transport, he gave public notice of his disenchantment at having been moved from the Colonial Office. He told young Conservatives at an Empire Day meeting in Hampstead, 'My main interest is in the Colonies. I hope my separation from the Colonial Office is only temporary.'[18] If his real love remained the colonies, there was, however, plenty to keep him occupied in the Ministry of Transport.

Lennox-Boyd was plunged straight into one of the Government's most difficult problems. The Conservatives had gone into the 1951 General Election committed to major reforms of the transport system put in place by the Labour Government. The 1947 Transport Bill had been among Labour's most important measures to extend public ownership. It had created the British Transport Commission which was to be responsible for the railways, the docks, the inland waterways, the London transport system and long distance road haulage. One of the aims of this Bill had been to provide for a fully integrated transport system. Yet in the first years of its operation, the Commission was unable to establish effective control over the 'Executives' which actually managed the various nationalized transport services. The Conservative Party's election manifesto of September 1951 had contained a commitment to reorganize nationalized rail and road transport into regions and to give private road hauliers the chance to return to business.

As the Conservatives discovered, however, when they were returned to power in October, there were serious obstacles in the way of such a policy. First, since the time of the 1941 Railway Control Agreement, financial control over the railways had been centralized. Any attempt to create area authorities on the lines of the pre-nationalization railway boards would therefore be highly complicated. Secondly, British Road Services, which constituted the road haulage side of the Commission's operations, was beginning to show a surplus. The Commission was obliged to pay substantial amounts in fixed interest charges on British Transport Stock as compensation to the former owners of the assets it had acquired through compulsory purchase. In the event of the return of British Road Services to private hands, the Commission would lose an important source of revenue, and a greater financial burden would fall upon the railways. The ability of the railways to bear this was itself likely to suffer as a private road haulage company, unencumbered by restrictions on its pricing policy, drew freight away from the railways and onto the roads.[19]

Despite the formidable problems in the way of change, Churchill was adamant that proposals for new legislation should be put in place without delay. On 8 May, the day on which the Prime Minister submitted Lennox-Boyd's name to the Queen, a White Paper on transport policy was placed before Parliament. Churchill explained to Lennox-Boyd what he regarded as his Government's principal aims in this field:

> First, not to strangle the expansion of road transport in the interests of making nationalized railways pay.

> Secondly, to preserve the railways in the most efficient form possible for the indispensable though diminishing duties they discharge.[20]

The White Paper's analysis of the existing arrangements was that the structure of the Road Haulage Executive was an impediment to the expansion of road transport. Its assets should therefore be returned to private ownership. The method it proposed for reconciling this course of action with the preservation of railway services was a levy on goods vehicles. The levy had two parts. The first part was designed to compensate the British Transport Commission for the immediate losses it would sustain in the sale of the Road Haulage Executive's assets. The second part was intended to compensate the Commission for losses which would be entailed by future transfers of traffic from rail to road. The Government's intention was that the levy would yield £4 million per annum. The White Paper also proposed that the railways should be given greater regional autonomy, although it did not set out detailed proposals for decentralization.

On 21 May, only a fortnight after arriving at the Ministry of Transport, Lennox-Boyd had to defend the White Paper in the House of Commons. A motion approving the White Paper was carried by 305 votes to 283. Outside Parliament, however, the proposals were greeted with almost universal hostility. The second part of the levy provoked fierce opposition, much of it from those interests which supported the principle of road haulage denationalization. Such was the force of criticism that on 10 July the Government announced that it was postponing further consideration of the Bill until the autumn.[21] Churchill was particularly concerned by the press reactions. On 11 July he told Lennox-Boyd that he hoped he was studying the press comments 'to see whether we can learn anything from their gruntings'.[22]

Lennox-Boyd took rather more extensive soundings and at the end of July told the Cabinet committee on Transport Policy, 'I am afraid it is true to say that outside of the Government and the Party, the Transport Bill has hardly a friend.'[23] He promised to spend most of the Parliamentary recess holding consultations about the Bill. While assuring the committee that he would not promise any modifications without referring his proposals to them, he asked for 'a considerable measure of freedom to consider any proposals put forward by those people who want our policy to succeed'.

This was a significant request. In attempting to salvage the Government's transport policy, he was to face resistance not only from the committee but from Lord Leathers, the Secretary of State for Transport and Aviation, and Fuel and Power, and Lennox-Boyd's immediate superior in the so-called 'Overlord' system. Overlord was a personal creation of Churchill, who wished to recapture something of the spirit of the wartime Cabinet. It entailed reducing the size of the Cabinet by appointing coordinating Ministers, responsible for a number of departments.[24] Yet the system proved satisfactory neither to Lennox-Boyd nor to his counterpart, Geoffrey Lloyd, the Minister of Fuel and Power. In contemplating Maclay's

replacement, Norman Brook had foreseen that Leathers might prove
an obstacle to the swift production of a new Transport Bill and had
recommended that, in effect, the 'Overlord' system should be
short-circuited.[25] As the Bill ran into problems and new proposals
were advanced, however, Lennox-Boyd began to encounter opposition both from Leathers and other members of the Transport
Committee.

When Lennox-Boyd returned to the Committee in September
it was with a strengthened belief that the Bill was badly flawed
and would be difficult to introduce in its existing form.[26] All the
evidence pointed to the unpopularity of the second part of the
levy. Since, however, the levy formed the corner-stone of their
bill, the Government could not abandon it, Lennox-Boyd argued,
without having some other 'positive and radical instrument' to
put in its place. In particular, conditions would have to be created in which the railways could operate competitively. This, in
Lennox-Boyd's view, would require three fundamental changes.
First, the railways should be given a very substantial measure
of freedom in fixing their rates and charges. On this point
Lennox-Boyd recommended a radical overhaul. He suggested
that, instead of asking which of the controls and restrictions
should be lifted, the Government should begin with the question of why the railways should not have complete freedom and
then demand that each restriction justify itself in the light of
current requirements. The Government should at least consider
whether the railways should be completely free in the setting of
rates for freight traffic. Secondly, and less controversially,
Lennox-Boyd stressed the importance of bringing about as soon
as possible, a 'drastic decentralization' of the railways. Thirdly,
he suggested that the railways' liability to pay guaranteed interest on British Transport Stock should be divorced from their
commercial and rate-fixing policy. He asked whether they could
not be relieved of a substantial part of their liability to meet fixed
interest charges.

Lennox-Boyd's invitation to the Government to consider such
far-reaching revisions to the Bill was not well received by some
of his Cabinet colleagues. The Chancellor of the Exchequer, R.
A. Butler, and David Maxwell-Fyfe, the Home Secretary, were
both hostile to the idea of dropping the levy.[27] Most importantly
of all, Leathers himself was not convinced that the alternatives
which Lennox-Boyd had advanced would prove adequate.
Lennox-Boyd did, however, win the support of Lord Swinton, the
Chancellor of the Duchy of Lancaster, who did not believe that
the Transport Bill in its present form would survive its passage

through Parliament.[28] Crucially, he also had the backing of the
Prime Minister. Churchill's principal concern was to get his
Government out of a potentially sticky situation rather than to
promote market-led reforms.

The Conservatives went into their Annual Conference in
Scarborough on 9 October with the transport issue still not resolved. It was one thing for Lennox-Boyd to have to defend an
unpopular policy, quite another to have to face the Conference with
no policy at all. Indeed, he and some of his colleagues had by this
stage begun to question the whole notion of denationalizing the
Road Haulage Executive. That he survived his appearance in
Scarborough unscathed says much about his own powers as a
speaker, and even more about the rather docile temperament of
Annual Conferences. The Conference motion, while blaming the
country's transport problems on nationalization, made no specific
reference to denationalization but merely affirmed its support for
the putative bill.[29]

On 16 October Churchill was stung into action, characteristically enough, by a newspaper cartoon. He asked Leathers whether
he had seen 'the silly cartoon' by David Low in that day's *Daily
Herald* . This depicted Churchill and Lennox-Boyd in the driving
seat of a lorry stuck on a level crossing and about to be wrecked
by an on-coming train. The Prime Minister told Leathers that he
was increasingly inclined to drop part two of the levy.[30] Leathers
replied that the Cabinet Transport Committee had already reached
the conclusion that it was necessary to rethink legislation from first
principles.[31] Indeed, Leathers was now prepared to consider leaving the Road Haulage Executive's undertaking with the Commission and dropping both parts of the levy.[32] Lennox-Boyd supported
this approach. Their ministerial colleagues, however, feared that the
abandonment of plans to denationalize road haulage would be too
drastic a reversal of policy and might shake public confidence in
the Government.[33] On 29 October, the Cabinet at last reached a
decision: the Government would proceed along the lines originally
envisaged but part two of the levy would be dropped entirely, the
existing 25 mile limit on the operations of private lorries would be
lifted, and the railways would be given greater freedom to fix
charges.[34]

The bill in its revised form received its Second Reading in Parliament on 19 November. It provided for the creation of a Road
Haulage Disposals Board, which would be responsible for dividing
the assets of the Road Haulage Executive into saleable units, generally not consisting of more than 50 vehicles.[35] The levy, to be
imposed on commercial freight vehicles, would now compensate the

Commission only for 'road haulage capital loss', and was intended
to raise a considerably smaller amount then had been proposed in
the White Paper. The bill also required the Commission to submit,
within 12 months, a scheme under which it would absorb the
Railway Executive and provide for the establishment of decentral-
ized 'area authorities'. More specific clauses were included in the
bill giving the railways freedom over the imposition of charges.

Although the bill's amendments served to consolidate support
on the Government benches, it did not enjoy an easy passage
through Parliament. Following its completion of the Report stage
on 28 April 1953, the Government forced a guillotine motion on the
Lords' amendments. This provoked the Labour Party into tabling
a motion of censure which was debated on 5 May; so the guillotine device did not save any time.[36] The bill finally received Royal
Assent on 6 May. The completion of the bill's passage was a personal triumph for Lennox-Boyd, although subsequent events tended
to vindicate his concern about the viability of attempting to liquidate the assets of the Road Haulage Executive. At the beginning
of July 1954, he reported to the Cabinet that the disposal of the
Transport Commission's road haulage assets had not proceeded as
quickly as had been hoped.[37] The Government's aim of encouraging small operators to move into the industry had proved difficult
to achieve. What demand there was for the Commission's assets
tended to come from existing operators who wished to add to their
fleets of vehicles. Hence there was no general demand for units with
premises. The Road Haulage Disposals Board reported a lack of
interested capital and it seemed likely that of roughly 32,000 vehicles for sale about 15,000 would remain unsold.

Although Lennox-Boyd's handling of the transport bill won him
praise, not all members of his party were satisfied that he had done
enough to promote Conservative principles. Brendan Bracken, one
of his early patrons, told Lord Beaverbrook that although
Lennox-Boyd had displayed considerable skill in the House, he had
not proved to be a particularly successful departmental minister.
He suggested that Lennox-Boyd spent too much of his time defending what Bracken regarded as the British Transport Commission's
disgracefully expensive monopoly bus and coach services.[38] In
Bracken's view, the Commission lacked the combined managerial
talent necessary to run a local bus service from Leatherhead to
Epsom.

As Minister responsible for civil aviation, Lennox-Boyd devoted
a considerable amount of time to the question of a new airport for
London. In July 1952, he explained to the Cabinet that aircraft
movements around London had increased by some 50% over the

previous four years and were expected to double again by 1960.[39] The airfield at Northolt was currently used to deal with some of this civil aviation traffic, but this was due to be returned to the Royal Air Force by 1955–56. The case for a new London airport was, therefore, pressing and Gatwick had been identified as a suitable site. The Government established a public enquiry into the proposed Gatwick site under the chairmanship of Sir Colin Campbell. Campbell's report, issued in July 1954, shortly before Lennox-Boyd left Civil Aviation, concluded that Gatwick was a suitable site providing the Government was satisfied on a number of points including the effect of noise on the surrounding area, planning procedures and the views of the airlines. On 17 July, Lennox-Boyd told the Cabinet that so far as those issues which came under his own Ministerial responsibility were concerned, he saw no objections, and he recommended that the Gatwick scheme should go ahead.[40]

Having criticized Labour's 1946 Aviation Bill for giving insufficient scope for private enterprise, especially in the field of scheduled flights, Lennox-Boyd was now in a position to redress the balance somewhat in favour of the private operator. He liberalized the regime, allowing private companies to apply for certain scheduled services on equal terms with the two state corporations, BOAC and BEA. He also introduced measures to provide limited financial relief for independent operators. Calls from the private sector for the full denationalization of the civil aviation industry were, however, resisted, and Lennox-Boyd was keen to stress that concessions towards independent operators would not adversely affect the position of BOAC and BEA.[41]

If Lennox-Boyd's successful piloting of the Transport Bill through Parliament was a great triumph, his final months at the Ministry were to be overshadowed by tragedy. He had already had to deal with a major disaster on the railways. In October 1952, a London commuter train which was about to leave Harrow and Wealstone station was struck from behind by an express train travelling at nearly 60 miles per hour. In the resulting crash, 112 people were killed and about 200 injured. A subsequent inquiry blamed the dead train driver for the incident, and its political and practical consequences were limited. By contrast, the air disasters of 1954 had serious repercussions for the British aviation industry and were the cause of a great deal of distress and remorse to Lennox-Boyd.

On 10 January 1954, a BOAC Comet jet airliner flying from Singapore to London crashed into the Mediterranean near the island of Elba about 20 minutes after leaving Rome on the final leg of its journey. Its 29 passengers and six crew were all killed. BOAC had been using Comets since May 1952. Built by the British firm

De Havillands, the Comet was a pioneering example of jet propelled passenger aircraft and an important symbol of national recovery and technical expertise. Yet it had already proved accident-prone. In the first incident, on 26 October 1952, a Comet had crashed without loss of life while taking off from Ciampino airport in Rome. This was attributed at the time to pilot error. In March 1953, a Canadian Pacific Airlines Comet crashed while taking off from Karachi airport killing all 11 on board.[42] Two months later, all 43 occupants of a Comet were killed when their aircraft crashed, a few minutes after leaving Calcutta. A court of enquiry found that this crash was due to structural failure in the air. It recommended that the wreckage be transferred to London for detailed examination and that modifications be considered to the Comet's flying control system. At the time of the BOAC Comet crash off Elba, an official from De Havilland's admitted to journalists that detailed examination of the wreckage of the Calcutta flight had still not been completed.

The day after the Elba disaster, BOAC announced the temporary suspension of their Comet passenger services pending an examination of the rest of their fleet. Lennox-Boyd assured the Cabinet that, had the company failed to do this, he would have felt obliged to order it himself.[43] He was keen that the inquiry into the crash should be conducted under British auspices despite the fact that the plane appeared to have gone down just within Italian territorial waters making it technically the responsibility of the Italian Government.[44] Some pressure was applied by the British Embassy in Rome. On 20 January, Lennox-Boyd was able to announce that the Italian preliminary inquiry had found that the crash occurred outside Italian waters. The British Government would assume responsibility for further investigations.

The following month, perhaps sensing that his Minister of Transport was becoming discouraged, Churchill dangled in front of his eyes the prospect of the Colonial Office. He told him that Lyttelton was going to resign as Colonial Secretary at the end of the Parliamentary session and that he intended to appoint Lennox-Boyd in his place. Lennox-Boyd was clearly overjoyed. He told Churchill, 'It is the one task in the world which I wish to undertake.'[45] In the difficult months that followed, however, Churchill's promise must actually have added to Lennox-Boyd's worries.

On 8 March, Lennox-Boyd told the Commons that, after extensive examination of their fleet and the incorporation of numerous modifications, BOAC had decided to resume Comet passenger services. He added that this decision had been made with his full concurrence. Such was the national prestige invested in the airliner that Lennox-Boyd was clearly under pressure to allow the

Comet to return to service without unnecessary delays. Privately, however, he harboured doubts about the aircraft's safety. His worst fears were soon to be realized. On 9 April, he rang Downing Street at half-past two in the morning and reported that another Comet, on its way from Rome to Cairo, had gone missing.[46] Later that morning, he told the Commons that although no wreckage had so far been found, oil had been sighted south-west of Naples. BOAC had again grounded its Comets. He expressly reminded the House that their decision to resume services the previous month had been taken with his full approval.

As Lennox-Boyd's statement to Parliament indicated, he felt a deep sense of responsibility for the disasters. As was to be the case over the Hola Camp affair five years later, he believed that the honourable course was to resign. In both cases he was discouraged from doing so by the Prime Minister of the day. Lennox-Boyd remembered two meetings with Churchill following the final Comet crash. On the first occasion he told the Prime Minister that he had foreseen the likelihood of another disaster. 'How very clever of you,' Churchill responded. Lennox-Boyd insisted that his failure to ground the Comets after the first crash had caused further loss of life and felt that he should resign. He must have known that in doing so he would not only be bringing an end – temporarily or otherwise – to his Ministerial career, but losing the chance to inherit the post of Colonial Secretary. Churchill, however, dismissed his offer to resign.[47]

Lennox-Boyd then had the grim task of representing the British Government at the memorial service for those who had been killed in Elba. He returned to London and saw Churchill again. The Prime Minister kept him at Downing Street for three hours, prompting press speculation that Lennox-Boyd was being carpeted. In fact, according to Lennox-Boyd's recollections, a more typically Churchillian scene took place. Mention of the visit to Elba ignited Churchill's historical imagination and for the next three hours he regaled his Minister of Transport with an account of Napoleon's flight to St. Fréjus, of Ney and of Louis XVIII. It was a reminder of days long gone, when as a young aspiring politician Lennox-Boyd would be entertained by Churchill with an account of the battle of Gettysburg mapped out with pepper pots on the dining table at Chartwell.

The Comet crashes were a sad end to Lennox-Boyd's time at Transport and Civil Aviation. As well as being terrible tragedies in their own right they were also a great blow to British engineering. The subsequent investigation revealed that they had probably been caused by metal fatigue. This was not the end of the Comet project:

Comet IV was brought into operation by 1958. Yet in the intervening four years, Britain had lost her technical lead to the Americans. The Boeing 707 and the Douglas DC8 had a larger seating capacity and lower operating costs than the Comet and soon achieved a dominant position in the world market.[48]

Yet Churchill was right to insist that Lennox-Boyd should not resign. He was too accomplished a politician for the Government to be without; and Churchill was shortly to reward him with the post which was to utilize his abilities to the full – and in the process satisfy a lifetime's ambition.

Notes
1   Swahili proverb from Zanzibar collected by Lennox-Boyd, PBM, Mss. Eng. c. 3796, f. 279.
2   Bridges to Pitblado, 11 Oct. 1951, PREM 5/223. Listowel became Secretary of State for India in April 1947. India's achievement of independence four months later did not quite render Listowel's job redundant, since he remained responsible for the fate of Burma. He held the rather incongruous title of Secretary of State for Burma from August 1947 to January 1948 when Burma became a republic. During his two years as Minister of State for the Colonies from 1948–50, he witnessed no similar contraction of his territorial responsibilities.
3   Brook to Churchill, 1 Nov. 1951, PREM 5/223.
4   *The Tanganyika Standard*, 17 Jan. 1952.
5   Record of a meeting held at Government House on Saturday 12 Jan. 1952, CO 822/712, f. 14.
6   Lord Boyd interviewed about East Africa by Alison Smith, 13 Dec. 1974, PBM, Mss. Eng. c. 3433, f. 208.
7   *The Times*, 22 Jan. 1952.
8   Lennox-Boyd to Welensky, 11 July 1951, The Papers of Sir Roy Welensky (hereafter indicated by 'WP'), Rhodes House, Oxford, 79/3, f. 9.
9   Anthony Seldon, *Churchill's Indian Summer* (London, Hodder and Stoughton, 1981), p. 227.
10 Note by the Treasury Solicitor (undated), PREM 11/175, ff. 25–7.
11 Brook to Churchill, 30 April 1952, PREM 11/287, f. 345.
12 Lord Boyd interviewed about British Prime Ministers, PBM, Mss. Eng. c. 3432, f. 48.
13 Lyttelton to Churchill, 5 May 1952, PREM 5/224.
14 Text of a speech in Edmonton, Alberta, to the Winston Churchill Society, 14 May 1973, PBM, Mss. Eng. c. 3719, p. 18.
15 Anthony Seldon, *Churchill's Indian Summer: the Conservative Government, 1951–55* (London, Hodder and Stoughton, 1981), pp. 227–8.
16 Lennox-Boyd to Lyttelton, 14 May 1952, CO 967/250.
17 Lennox-Boyd to Lyttelton, 17 June 1952, CO 967/250.
18 SB, *Jan.–June 1959*, p. 30.
19 Michael R. Bonavia, *The Nationalisation of British Transport: The Early History of the British Transport Commission, 1948–53* (London, Macmillan, 1987), pp. 152–3.
20 Churchill to Lennox-Boyd, 11 May 1952, PREM 11/175, f. 7.
21 Bonavia, p. 157.
22 Churchill to Lennox-Boyd and Leathers, 11 July 1952, PREM 11/287, f. 14.
23 'The Transport Bill', TP (52) 12, 30 July 1952, PREM 11/287, ff. 7–10.
24 Anthony Seldon, *Churchill's Indian Summer* (London, Hodder and Stoughton, 1981), p. 102.

25 Brook to Churchill, 30 April 1952, PREM 11/287, f. 345.
26 'Transport Bill: Note by the Minister of Transport and Civil Aviation', TP (52) 14, 18 Sept. 1952, PREM 11/559, ff. 217–224.
27 Minutes of the Cabinet Committee on Transport Policy, TP (52) 10, 19 Sept. 1952, PREM 11/559, f. 213–4; Minutes of the Cabinet Committee on Transport Policy, TP (52) 11, 22 Sept. 1952, PREM 11/559, f. 202.
28 Minutes of the Cabinet Committee on Transport Policy, TP (52) 11, 22 Sept. 1952, PREM 11/559.
29 *Report of the Proceedings of the Seventy Second Annual Conference of the National Union of Conservative and Unionist Associations* (1952), pp. 69–73.
30 Churchill to Leathers, 16 Oct. 1952, PREM 11/559, f. 169.
31 Leathers to Churchill, 17 Oct. 1952, PREM 11/559, f. 163.
32 'Transport Bill: Memorandum by the Secretary of State for Co-ordination of Transport, Fuel and Power', 20 Oct. 1952, CAB 129/55, C (52) 346.
33 Cabinet Conclusions, 22 Oct. 1952, CAB 128/25, CC (52) 88, min. 3.
34 Cabinet Conclusions, 29 Oct. 1952, CAB 128/25, CC (52) 91, min. 2.
35 Bonavia, p. 158.
36 Bonavia, pp. 157–8.
37 'Road Haulage Disposals: Memorandum by the Minister of Transport and Civil Aviation', 2 July 1954, CAB 129/69, C (54) 215.
38 Brendan Bracken to Beaverbrook, 7 Jan. 1953, BBK C/57.
39 'Gatwick Airport: Memorandum by the Minister of Civil Aviation', 22 July 1952, CAB 129/53, C (52) 220.
40 'Gatwick Airport: Memorandum by the Minister of Transport and Civil Aviation', 17 July 1954, CAB 129/69, C (54) 236.
41 Anthony Seldon, *Churchill's Indian Summer: The Conservative Government, 1951–55* (London, Hodder and Stoughton, 1981), p. 230.
42 *The Times*, 11 Jan. 1954.
43 Cabinet Conclusions, CC (54) 2, 12 Jan. 1954.
44 Foreign Office telegram to Rome, 11 Jan. 1954, PREM 11/802, f. 9.
45 Lennox-Boyd to Churchill, 14 Feb. 1954, Churchill Papers, CHUR 2/192.
46 DBP to Churchill, 9 April 1954, PREM 11/802.
47 Lord Boyd interviewed about British Prime Ministers, PBM, Mss. Eng. c. 3432, f. 49.
48 W.H.P. Canner, *The Air Transport Industry* (Glasgow, Brown, Son, Ferguson Ltd., 1986), p. 20.

8

Paradise Regained: Lennox-Boyd at the Colonial Office

He who has not carried your burden knows not what it weighs.[1]

Part I: Lennox-Boyd's approach to colonial policy

At the end of July 1954, Alan Lennox-Boyd became Colonial Secretary. The essential principles that guided his approach to colonial affairs had altered little since the 1930s. He continued to believe that the maintenance of British rule was in the best interests of her colonial subjects, and that the 'silent majority' of these people gave little thought to the goal of independence. He fully endorsed the prevailing wisdom that progress towards self-Government should ideally be delayed until social and economic development had prepared the ground for the establishment of stable democracies. If the maintenance of British control over peoples not yet ready to govern themselves occasionally necessitated use of force, this did not in itself disturb him. The methods of law-enforcement employed in the colonies sometimes appeared unacceptably harsh to the British public; but they were, he maintained, generally in accordance with the standards and expectations of the colonial peoples themselves. Looking back from the vantage point of the 1970s on the ruthless campaign against Mau Mau and the revelation of the massacre at the Hola detention camp, he claimed that although the Government's methods were attacked at home, he could remember seeing no letters of condemnation from Africans.[2]

In the light of these views, Lennox-Boyd's replacement as Colonial Secretary by Iain Macleod in October 1959 might of itself appear to offer an explanation for the rapid acceleration of decolonization in Africa after that date.[3] Macleod, after all, was fundamentally more sympathetic than Lennox-Boyd towards the desire of nationalist leaders to achieve full independence for their countries. Like his friend, Enoch Powell, he was reluctant to accept that Britain could enforce her rule in the colonies by means that would be unacceptable at home. Also like Powell, he came to regard the colonies as a potential source of political embarrassment to the Conservative Party and an impediment to modernizing its image.[4] In substituting Macleod for Lennox-Boyd, it might seem reasonable to suppose that premier Harold Macmillan was giving the Colonial Office notice to 'get a move on' in Africa.[5] Historians have gone in search of evidence to indicate the precise moment when the decision was made to 'abdicate' there.[6]

This interpretation of British decolonization contains important elements of truth. Indeed, Lennox-Boyd and Macleod both, in their different ways, subscribed to this version of history and were keen to cast themselves in the respective roles of constitutional 'brake' and accelerator.[7] Yet any account of this process which focuses exclusively on the political preferences of policy-makers in London is bound to prove unsatisfactory. The decisive factor shaping British policy during this period was the nature of the system of colonial Government itself rather than the character of the Secretary of State. This system relied upon often extremely finely balanced arrangements of consent and collaboration. The most sensitive and important set of relationships within the colonial system was between the territorial Governments and local political representatives – self appointed or otherwise – who seemed capable of delivering the cooperation of their people.

In the course of the 1950s, as the rise of colonial nationalism disrupted the existing mechanisms of consent and collaboration, British governors in Africa became increasingly keen to coopt nationalist movements into the colonial state. Given the slender resources at their command, this generally appeared the most reliable way of preserving peace and order. The price nationalist movements demanded for their cooperation was an ever greater share in legislative and executive power for their elected representatives. The

senior British representative on the ground – generally the governor – was in a strong position to justify these sorts of concessions
to Whitehall. His ultimate threat – that if his recommendations were
not accepted he could not guarantee the maintenance of law and
order in his territory – was an extremely powerful one which no
Colonial Secretary could ignore.

Lennox-Boyd claimed that he had 'an instinctive prejudice' in
favour of the governors' recommendations.[8] Indeed, it is difficult
to think of a single case when, at his own instigation, he overruled
the request of one of his governors for permission to introduce
constitutional advance. In some cases – particularly Cyprus and
Singapore – pressure from other Cabinet colleagues forced
Lennox-Boyd to disregard a governor's advice on the pace of constitutional change. An important question-mark must also remain
over whether he would have vetoed Richard Turnbull's request for
a major package of reforms in Tanganyika had he continued as
Colonial Secretary after October 1959. Otherwise, the principal
characteristic of Lennox-Boyd's five years as Colonial Secretary was
a willingness to defer to the 'man on the spot'.

This is not to say that the governor would always prevail. It did
mean, however, that, irrespective of his own political preferences,
the bulk of Lennox-Boyd's time was spent seeking to reconcile the
often conflicting demands of his governors with those of other,
sometimes more powerful, departments of state. Since British rule
in most of her colonies depended on a delicate and constantly shift-
ing bargaining process, there was little point indulging in long-term
planning. When drafting policy statements, the principal concern
of the Colonial Office was not so much 'what should be the future
of colony A?' but 'what is it currently expedient for our attitude
towards the future of colony A to be?' The essential question was
whether Britain's chances of avoiding trouble in the short-term
would be increased or diminished by the Government adopting a
particular attitude towards a territory's future status.

As has already been noted, comparison is often made with
Macleod to suggest that Lennox-Boyd's approach to colonial policy
was at best overly cautious and at worst complacent. Yet perhaps
the most striking feature of Lennox-Boyd's five years as Colonial
Secretary was that this quintessential Imperial diehard spent much
of his time attempting to persuade his Cabinet colleagues of the
need to surrender powers to colonial nationalist leaders. This was
not, however, the consequence of a sudden conversion to the cause
of national liberation. Rather, Lennox-Boyd recognized that this
bargaining process was essential if Britain was to retain the initiative and avoid a potentially damaging confrontation with the

forces of nationalism. For all his lofty rhetoric about Britain's Imperial mission, the extreme fragility of the colonial system by the 1950s meant that Lennox-Boyd's efforts were largely devoted simply to ensuring that Britain remained in day-to-day control over her colonial territories.

The notion that by securing the cooperation of colonial leaders 'power' could be exchanged for 'control' was at the heart not only of Lennox-Boyd's approach to constitutional reform but also that of his successor, Iain Macleod. To use the analogy of Sir Leslie Monson, who served as Assistant Under-Secretary of State under both men, the staff at the Colonial Office were like a man riding a bike: 'they had to keep up the impetus to stay in control of the machine'.[9] Concessions from the British Government usually secured no more than a temporary accommodation with the forces of nationalism. It was only a matter of time before nationalist leaders returned with more extensive demands. So more power was surrendered in the name of maintaining control. Of course, the logical outcome of this power for control exchange is that eventually all formal power will be relinquished in order, supposedly, to enable the colonial government to remain in control of the situation. This may sound like a ridiculous assertion, yet even when powers amounting to virtual self-government were granted to radical nationalist parties, this was often justified along these lines.

British Somaliland provides an interesting example of how this process worked in practice. The Somalis were as badly affected as any African peoples by the arbitrary territorial boundaries imposed by European colonization. By the mid-1950s, the area around the Horn of Africa occupied by the Somali peoples was divided between British Somaliland, French Somaliland, the Italian Trusteeship of Somalia, the Ethiopian Haud and Reserved Areas, and the Northern Province of Kenya. In 1946, the British had explored the possibility of creating a Greater Somalia, incorporating all the Somali territories. Although they rejected the idea at the time, the rise of pan-Somali nationalism during the 1950s forced the issue back onto the agenda. Tensions with Ethiopia and the impending withdrawal by the Italians from their trusteeship of Somalia by 1960 at the latest, led to demands within the British Protectorate for independence and union with Italian Somalia. Lennox-Boyd was initially reluctant to give any encouragement to the idea, at least in part because of the prospect of the Somalis of Northern Kenya also demanding incorporation into an independent Somali state. By any objective set of criteria, the Somalis were less 'ready' for independence than their Kenyan, Ugandan or Tanzanian neighbours for whom a rapid transfer of power was not on offer.

The Chiefs of Staff stressed the strategic importance of British Somaliland, while the Foreign Office was extremely concerned about the likely reaction of Ethiopia to the prospect of a Greater Somalia.

Yet the growth of unrest in the Protectorate convinced Lennox-Boyd of the need for a new initiative. In October 1958, he told some of his senior colleagues that as a result of talks with the Governor of Somaliland he was convinced that constitutional development in British Somaliland would have to be at a faster rate than he had hitherto regarded as desirable. The Governor wished to announce that there would, by the end of 1960, be an unofficial majority in the territory's legislature and that Somali ministers would be included on the Executive Council. Recognizing the strength of feeling in favour of union with Somalia, the Governor felt that he could not duck the issue in his statement. He therefore proposed to say that if, when the constitutional changes came into force, the Somali dominated legislative council of the Protectorate wished to open negotiations with the government of Somalia on union, the British would not stand in the way of these talks and would accept their outcome.

Lennox-Boyd's gloss on these proposals was a prime example of the way in which throughout the 1950s and early 1960s, British policy makers defended transfers of power in terms of the maintenance of control and influence. He told Cabinet colleagues,

> I fully realise that to adopt a policy of this kind would be to cast our bread upon the waters, but it is almost certain that, if we do not adopt this kind of policy, our position in the Protectorate will become increasingly difficult to hold and that in the end we shall have to go and the union will take place in circumstances which will make it very probable, if not certain, that the new Somali nation will be anti-British.[10]

Objections from the governors of neighbouring colonies who, understandably, feared that these developments would encourage nationalist and separatist movements in their own territories resulted in a slight watering-down of the statement. Yet they did not persuade Lennox-Boyd to alter the general direction of British policy, despite the fact that rapid constitutional change in Somaliland was bound to make it more difficult to justify more gradual political advance elsewhere in East Africa. British Somaliland achieved its independence on 26 June 1960. Five days later, it united with Italian Somalia to form the Somali Republic.

Viewed in this light, the policy adopted by Macleod after October 1959 differed little in its basic rationale from that of his predecessor. The essential aim was to allow Britain to retain control over her colonies until the moment all formal authority had been relinquished, and to exert influence over them thereafter. Yet Macleod was dealing with a very different set of conditions. The option of merely supporting the 'man on the spot' was not open to him. In Kenya and in Nyasaland, the system had recently delivered embarrassing blows both to the Conservative Government in London and to British prestige in Africa. A change of governor in Kenya and the continued presence of a discredited one in Nyasaland both encouraged and enabled Macleod to take the initiative himself and reach a new accommodation with local nationalist leaders. As we shall see below, changing political alignments within the East African territories during Lennox-Boyd's final months as Colonial Secretary meant that, at least in Kenya and Tanganyika, nothing short of the promise of African self-government was likely to secure the cooperation of those leaders. Indeed, it seems quite possible that had he remained in his post after October 1959, Lennox-Boyd himself, albeit more reluctantly, would have pursued a policy in East Africa similar to that adopted by Macleod. That he would have been prepared to champion constitutional reform in Central Africa as forcefully as did his successor is far less likely. Yet had Lennox-Boyd still been Colonial Secretary in the early months of 1960, it is difficult to see how he could have done other than release Hastings Banda and involve him in fresh negotiations on the future of Nyasaland. Like Makarios in Cyprus, Banda was the only person capable of delivering the cooperation of his people. The only other option was to continue to hold Nyasaland down by force, which in the wake of the Devlin report was no longer politically feasible. Banda's cooption could only have been achieved on the basis of the promise of African self-government. This, however, would have delivered a potentially fatal blow to the white-dominated Central African Federation.

If the logistics of colonial rule tended to force Britain to devolve powers to local politicians, then the countervailing argument – that she had a duty to remain in place in order to 'develop' her colonies economically and socially – became ever more difficult to sustain as the 1950s progressed. The years immediately following the Second World War had seen a massive increase in the attention given to economic planning. Economists, agronomists and 'experts' of every kind flooded into Britain's overseas dependencies in what became known as the 'second colonial occupation'. The structure of the Colonial Office itself reflected this change. Whereas in 1939, its involvement in the economic development was so slight that it could be handled by one section of a department, by the end of 1951 there were six departments concentrating exclusively on this work.

In practice, however, the investment needed to give economic development a priority over political advance was simply not made available. When the 1945 Colonial Development and Welfare Bill was put
in place, it was assumed that colonial governments would fund development spending from a combination of their own surpluses, loans,
and CDW grants in roughly equal proportion.[11] Initially, the situation
seemed extremely encouraging. Many colonies emerged from the Second World War with healthy surpluses and reduced levels of foreign
debt. A dramatic increase in commodity prices between 1946 and 1951
boosted their levels of export earnings. Yet their ability to draw on
these earnings to promote development was severely limited. They
faced strict restrictions on the import of capital and consumer goods,
particularly from the dollar area. This acted both as an impediment
and a disincentive to increases in output, and led to the accumula-
tion of large surpluses in the form of colonial sterling balances in
London. These had reached £1,454 million by 1956, and were mostly
held in the form of British Government securities. As a recent study
has noted, 'some of the poorest and least-developed countries were
effectively lending to one of the richest and most developed'.[12]
    The amounts flowing in the opposite direction, in the form of
grants and loans, appear distinctly unimpressive when compared to
the size of these sterling balances. The 1945 Act allocated £120
million for development over 10 years, a sum which was raised to
£140 million in 1950. In 1954, with the date for the renewal of the
act fast approaching, Lennox-Boyd made an impassioned bid for an
increase in development spending, arguing that a failure to provide
this 'could do much harm in the colonies themselves and to the
Imperial connections'.[13] He sought £150 million to extend the act to
1960. £115 million of this was to be new money to which would be
added £35 million in unspent grants. Coinciding as it did with a brief
period of optimism about the British economy, Lennox-Boyd's bid
proved successful in increasing the overall allocation. Nevertheless,
the Treasury was only prepared to provide £80 million of new resources. For the limited sums available in CDW grants to have any
significant impact they needed to be supplemented by money from
other sources, and this proved extremely difficult to obtain.[14] Hence,
the British Government's failure to secure adequate investment for
the socio–economic development of her colonies meant that this
process was bound to be overtaken by the pace of political advance.

Part II: Style and reputation

There can be few Colonial Secretaries who were held in higher regard by British officials within the department and across the

Empire than Alan Lennox-Boyd. His comprehensive knowledge of the department's business earned him immense respect. One of his senior officials echoed the views of many within the department when he recalled that Lennox-Boyd knew more about colonial affairs than any of them.[15] They, and the members of the colonial service overseas, appreciated that Lennox-Boyd regarded the post of Colonial Secretary not as a stepping stone to promotion but as his ultimate political ambition. Lennox-Boyd, for his part, genuinely admired and respected the colonial service, unlike many in Whitehall who regarded it as a distinctly second-rate body. In 1956, when the post of Permanent Under-Secretary at the Colonial Office fell vacant, Lennox-Boyd displayed his confidence in the colonial service by insisting that the job should go to one of its members, rather than to a prominent Treasury official nominated by the Cabinet Secretary.[16]

Lennox-Boyd imposed a punishing schedule upon himself. On his departure from the office in the evening, he would regularly take with him four red boxes packed with files. He would rise at five in the morning and sort through his official business until about eight, usually phoning his private secretary at home to arrange additional engagements.[17] After arriving at the Colonial Office (then based in Church House), his programme left virtually no time for paperwork. He preferred to be briefed by the official dealing most closely with the issue in hand, regardless of their seniority. It was clearly good for departmental morale that relatively junior officials were made to feel that their views counted. It also avoided 'bottle necking' at times when a number of problems surfaced in different parts of the world.[18] Issues were generally resolved without those involved having to set out their views in formal memoranda. This owed a great deal to the sense of confidence that Lennox-Boyd engendered in his subordinates. As his Permanent Under-Secretary, Sir John Macpherson, recalled:

> ...you didn't need to [produce policy documents]. You could ring him or walk in and show him the file, and say this and this. All right, and he'd back you up. There was never any question of needing it on paper.[19]

John Profumo, who served as Parliamentary Secretary at the Colonial Office under Lennox-Boyd recalls that his boss treated his civil servants as personal friends, inviting them to dinner or to the theatre. Jack Johnston, his Principal Private Secretary, answered the telephone late one evening and was greeted by the familiar voice of his boss, just back from Downing Street: 'Jack, Winston's given me a bottle of brandy – come round at once.' Indeed, Johnston virtually became a temporary member of the Lennox-Boyd family. On one occasion, Lennox-Boyd asked him to take his wife and children skiing. He had intended to go himself, but at the last moment found that the problems of Cyprus required his continued presence in London.[20] Johnston no doubt performed admirably in the role of surrogate father. Yet for Lennox-Boyd's sons, a civil servant, however genial, was a poor substitute. They were understandably resentful of the all-consuming demands that Parliament and the Colonial Office made on his time. Johnston remembers them waving their father goodbye as he was departing for Mid-Bedfordshire at the start of the 1955 General Election campaign, shouting, 'Goodbye Daddy – we hope you lose.'

The easy charm and quite incredible memory that made Lennox-Boyd such an effective Minister and constituency MP, also endeared him to the British personnel he met during his tours of the colonies. In October 1954, during a visit to Kenya, Lennox-Boyd inspected a camp for Mau Mau detainees in the company of its medical officer, W. L. Barton. Having spent just two hours together, Barton and Lennox-Boyd did not meet again until 14 years later when they were both present at a reception in London. Lennox-Boyd noticed Barton across the room and went up to him. 'We have met before, haven't we?' he exclaimed; 'Which colony?' 'Kenya,' Barton replied. 'Ah yes of course,' said Lennox-Boyd, 'Manyani Detention Camp, 1954. Right?'[21] Not only would he remember the names and personal details of the people he encountered on his travels, but he would insist on making time to see them when they visited London. Likewise, on tours of the colonies, spaces would have to be carved in already crowded schedules to allow the Secretary of State to look up old acquaintances. During a visit to Cyprus for talks with Makarios, he made a point of seeking out a taxi driver he had met during a holiday on the island.[22]

Despite his position on the right of the Conservative party, Lennox-Boyd proved capable of working closely with colleagues of a variety of political persuasions and making full use of their abilities. Sir Hugh Foot, his inspired and courageous choice as Governor of Cyprus in 1957, spoke for many left-wing colleagues when he wrote of his former chief:

> In politics I probably disagree with him on almost every issue, but his good nature and his good humour and his generous fairness repeatedly rescue him from the consequences of his reactionary policies.[23]

Lennox-Boyd took pains to cultivate informal contacts with colonial politicians. To this end, as we have already seen, he regarded it as essential that Ministers should open their homes to overseas visitors. He felt that 'from every point of view, not least colour bar inhibitions, being asked to a private house is far more important than a pub – however grand'.[24] Indeed, when the Colonial Office passed to Iain Macleod, whose means ran only to a small flat in Hans Place, Lennox-Boyd along with Lyttelton tried to arrange for him to be provided with a more suitable private apartment in which to entertain. If, as Lennox-Boyd hoped, nationalist leaders in the colonial Empire were to be persuaded that a prolongation of British rule was desirable, it was essential that they should not believe Britain to be motivated by any sense of racial superiority. Yet the concern and generosity he displayed towards colonial leaders went well beyond any calculation of political advantage. Once, when the Malaysian leader, Tunku Abdul Rahman, was being treated in a Harley Street clinic, Lennox-Boyd visited him almost every other day bringing with him dishes he had bought from a nearby Indian restaurant. He told the Tunku that the condition for which he was being treated was bad enough without him also having to endure hospital food.[25]

Having considered Lennox-Boyd's general approach to colonial affairs and the manner in which he carried out his duties, it is now time to consider some of the problems which confronted him during his first two and a half years as Colonial Secretary.

Notes

1   Haya proverb from North West Tanzania collected by Lennox-Boyd, PBM, Mss. Eng. c. 3796, f. 271.
2   Lord Boyd interviewed about East Africa by Alison Smith, 13 Dec. 1974, PBM, Mss. Eng. c. 3433, f. 227.
3   Recent examples of this tendency in accounts of decolonization are Robert Shepherd, *Iain Macleod: A Biography* (London, Hutchinson, 1994) and Ritchie Ovendale, 'Macmillan and the Wind of Change in Africa, 1957–1960', *The Historical Journal*, 38, 2 (1995), pp. 455–477.
4   Macleod to Macmillan, 25 May 1959, PREM 11/2583.
5   Nigel Fisher, *Iain Macleod* (London, André Deutsch, 1973), p. 142.
6   Ovendale, p. 455.
7   Lennox-Boyd suggested this to a seminar in Oxford on 15 March 1978. See A.H.M. Kirk-Greene (ed.), *Africa in the Colonial Period, III – The Transfer of Power: The Colonial Administrator in the Age of Decolonization* (Oxford, University of Oxford, 1979), p. 5. Macleod's most famous defence of his actions as Colonial Secretary appears in his article, 'Trouble in Africa', *The Spectator*, 31 Jan. 1964.
8   Lord Boyd interviewed about the Colonial Service by A.H.M. Kirk-Greene, 13 Dec. 1974, PBM, Ms. Eng. c. 3432, f. 81.
9   Kirk-Greene, p. 29.
10 Lennox-Boyd to Lloyd, 27 Oct. 1958, 27 Oct. 1958, CO 1015/1918.
11 Michael Havinden and David Meredith, *Colonialism and Development: Britain and its Tropical Colonies 1850–1960* (London, Routledge, 1993), p. 253.
12 Havinden and Meredith, p. 267.
13 Havinden and Meredith, p. 257.

14 David Goldsworthy (ed.), *British Documents on the End of Empire, Series A, vol. 3, The Conservative Government and the End of Empire 1951–57*, Part I, p. lviii.
15 Macpherson to Lennox-Boyd, 6 Aug. 1959, PBM, Mss. Eng. c. 3467, f. 233.
16 Note by Lennox-Boyd, 15 March 1972, PBM, Mss. Eng. c. 3507, f. 74.
17 Sir John Johnston, *Recollections* (unpublished manuscript, 1997), p. 48
18 Sir John Macpherson interviewed about the Colonial Service by A.H.M. Kirk-Greene, 27 Feb. 1968, Rhodes House, Oxford, Mss. Brit. Emp. s. 487, p. 81.
19 Sir John Macpherson interviewed about the Colonial Service, Mss. Brit. Emp. s. 487, p. 83.
20 Johnston, pp. 62–3.
21 *The Overseas Pensioner*, no. 70, Autumn 1995, pp. 52–3.
22 Johnston, p. 54.
23 Hugh Foot, *A Start in Freedom* (London, Hodder and Stoughton, 1964), p. 152.
24 Lennox-Boyd to Lyttelton, 11 May 1952, CO 967/250.
25 *The Star*, 14 March 1983, PBM, Ms Eng. c. 3823, f. 109.

9

Pocket Handkerchiefs: The Mediterranean and the Far East, 1954–56

Better a clever enemy than a blundering friend.[1]

Part I: The Mediterranean

Cyprus

One of the most striking features of colonial affairs in the period 1954–59 is the lack of any apparent correspondence between the size and population of a territory and the amount of time the Colonial Secretary had to devote to it. Over vast areas of colonial Africa, conditions seemed remarkably peaceful and constitutional development required Lennox-Boyd to make only occasional interventions. Other relatively small territories, like Cyprus, Malta and

Singapore, posed extraordinarily complex administrative problems
and placed enormous burdens on Lennox-Boyd's time and patience.

Cyprus was leased to Britain by the Turks in 1878. Britain
annexed the island at the beginning of the First World War and 11
years later it became a crown colony. Britain had to contend, however, with an increasingly powerful campaign among the Greek
majority on the island for *Enosis* – union with Greece. This was
vigorously supported by the Greek government, and bitterly opposed by the Turkish minority on Cyprus and the government in
Ankara. The sympathies of the Churchill and Eden Governments
lay very largely with the Turks. Turkey had played a central role
in the establishment of the Baghdad Pact of 1955 and, as Arab
nationalism assumed an ever more hostile stance towards Britain,
her value as an ally increased. Furthermore, the Chiefs of Staff
regarded the maintenance of sovereignty over Cyprus as essential.
Conflicts with the Egyptian government over the Suez enclave had
demonstrated the dangers of relying on leased bases. With British
withdrawal from Egypt and the establishment of Middle East Headquarters on Cyprus, the importance of the island for Britain's military presence in the region seemed likely to increase.[2]

A constitution offering a large measure of internal
self-government had been proposed by the Governor of Cyprus in
1948. This failed to win local support, largely because *Enosis* was
not on offer. Faced with a constitutional stalemate, Sir Robert
Armitage, who took over as Governor of Cyprus in 1954, sought
to reactivate the political process with a new set of constitutional
proposals which actually reduced the influence of the elected representatives on the territory's Legislative Council.[3] These were endorsed by the Cabinet on 26 July 1954. It was decided that the
announcement of the new constitution should be combined with
a statement that Britain could not contemplate any change of sovereignty for Cyprus. This was never likely to be a popular step, but
the manner in which it was handled further aggravated the situation.

The statement on the Government's new policy came at the very
end of the Parliamentary session on 28 July, the day Lyttelton
formally tendered his resignation as Colonial Secretary. It was left
to his hapless Minister of State, Henry Hopkinson, to make the
announcement. His statement followed immediately after the announcement of the Anglo-Egyptian treaty under which Britain was
to withdraw her forces from the Suez zone. As such, Hopkinson
was under some pressure not to antagonize further the Imperial
wing of his party. Pressed on whether Cyprus could ever expect to
achieve complete self-determination, Hopkinson replied:

...it has always been understood and agreed that there are certain territories in the Commonwealth which, owing to their political circumstances, can never expect to be fully independent. [HON. MEMBERS: 'Oh.'] I think the Right Hon. Gentleman will agree that there are some territories which cannot expect to be that. I am not going as far as that this afternoon, but I have said that the question of the abrogation of British sovereignty cannot arise – that British sovereignty will remain.[4]

Hopkinson's use of the word 'never', albeit in a qualified way, provoked a storm of protests from the Opposition benches.

It was against this unpromising background that, the following day, Lennox-Boyd assumed formal responsibility for the affairs of Cyprus. They posed particular problems for the Colonial Office since the conventional bargaining process between the Government and colonial nationalists had to be subordinated to a broader set of international considerations. Indeed, even day-to-day decisions regarding the administration of justice and security on the island had frequently to be taken in the light of the state of negotiations between Britain, Greece and Turkey. Lennox-Boyd often had to defer not only to the views of the Foreign Secretary, but also, especially during Harold Macmillan's time at the Foreign Office, to those of the Prime Minister, Anthony Eden, who sometimes appeared determined to direct British foreign policy from 10 Downing Street. That this did not result in more serious conflicts at Cabinet level was due, at least in part, to the fact that Lennox-Boyd's personal sympathies were largely pro-Turkish.[5] Nevertheless, Lennox-Boyd recognized that political stability on the island could only be achieved if Britain made reasonable concessions to the demands of the Greek Cypriot majority.

In December 1954, Britain succeeded, with American help, in blocking an attempt by the Greek government to raise the question of Cyprus in the United Nations General Assembly.[6] This minor victory was bought at a high cost: frustrated in their diplomatic efforts, the government in Athens ceased to exercise a restraining influence over George Grivas, leader of the military wing of the nationalist movement. On 1 April 1955, EOKA (the National Organization of Cypriot Fighters) began its military campaign against the British presence on the island.

Much of the blame for the deteriorating situation in Cyprus fell on Armitage. Yet his ability to respond to unrest, either through conciliation or repression, was severely restricted by his masters in London. Well before EOKA launched its campaign, Armitage had decided that his original constitutional recommendations should be discarded, and that Cyprus should be offered a new

Legislative Council with a majority of elected members. He also
felt that Cypriot cooperation would only be forthcoming if Britain
were to hold out the prospect of self-determination at some later
date. To this end, he wanted to announce that, once the new
constitution was functioning effectively, the question of the future
status of the island could be agreed between the British Government and the elected representatives of the Cypriots. Lennox-Boyd
supported Armitage's proposals.[7] When, however, they were discussed in Cabinet on 19 April 1955, Harold Macmillan, the new
Foreign Secretary, persuaded Ministers to postpone a decision.[8]
A general election was due to take place in Britain the following
month and until this was over, Macmillan suggested, a statement
along these lines was unlikely to carry much weight. His main
concern, however, was the likelihood of a hostile reaction from the
Turkish government.

Two months later, with the Conservatives firmly back in power,
Macmillan and Lennox-Boyd presented their colleagues with a new
set of proposals. They wished to invite the Greek and Turkish governments to talks in London on the island's future.[9] Eden was
initially sceptical about the idea, fearing that it might be interpreted
as a sign of weakness. The deteriorating security situation on
Cyprus, however, soon convinced him of the need for action.[10] Ironically, the immediate effect of the Government's new initiative was
to restrict further Armitage's ability to combat the growing tide of
unrest. When he tried to persuade Lennox-Boyd to allow him to
declare a state of emergency, he was warned that this might prejudice the forthcoming talks.[11] Nevertheless, Lennox-Boyd recognized
that Armitage required some additional powers to deal with the
threat posed by EOKA. His Cabinet colleagues were keen, however,
that he should see for himself whether such measures were really
necessary.

Lennox-Boyd arrived in Nicosia on 9 July 1955, the first serving Colonial Secretary to visit Cyprus since Britain had taken control of the island 77 years before. His talks with Armitage persuaded
him that the governor did indeed require additional powers to
maintain order. Yet they also appear to have convinced him that
Armitage was the wrong man for the job. Lennox-Boyd later recalled, 'I don't think he would have been the sort of person who
would have been sent out if it had been anticipated it was going
to be a rough house.'[12] Perhaps the most significant meeting of
Lennox-Boyd's visit, however, was with Archbishop Makarios.
Makarios was the spiritual leader of the Greek Orthodox population of Cyprus, their principal political spokesman and – the British came ever more firmly to believe the guiding force behind EOKA.

1. RIGHT. Alan Lennox-Boyd, his mother, Florence, and his elder brother, George

2. BELOW. At the Oxford Union, 1926. (Back row, left to right) Dick Acland, Malcolm Brereton, Michael Franklin, Dingle Foot. (Front row, left to right) Roger Fulford, Henry Slessor, L. Fraser, Alan Lennox-Boyd, Playfair Price (Cross-legged) Aubrey Herbert

3. Three-quarters of the 'Lennox-Boyd Mutual Admiration Society'. (Left to right) Francis, Alan and Donald Lennox-Boyd at Henlow Grange in the 1930s.

4. RIGHT. Alan Lennox–Boyd with his mother at Sway in the 1930s.

5. BELOW. 'Problems of a Conqueror: I wonder if I'll ever get rid of these boots?' *Daily Herald*, 29 March 1938. Vicky's attack on Franco's British apologists featured prominently in the election literature of Lennox–Boyd's Labour opponent in Mid-Bedfordshire in 1945.

6. Alan Lennox-Boyd introducing his fiancée, Lady Patricia Guinness, to constituents in Mid-Bedfordshire in 1938.

7. ABOVE. Alan Lennox-Boyd with the crew of Motor Launch 113.

8. BELOW. Churchill, between Alan and Patsy Lennox-Boyd, addressing an election rally in Biggleswade Market Square during the 1955 General Election campaign.

9. ABOVE. Alan Lennox–
Boyd bidding farewell to
Kwame Kkrumah and his
Cabinet at the end of his
visit to the Gold Coast in
January 1957.

10. LEFT. The Secretary of
State downs a quart tankard
of tuak – the local rice wine
– in a longhouse in Sarawak
in one of his less formal
engagements during his tour
of the Far East in 1955.

11. ABOVE. A weekend at Chequers during the March 1957 Constitutional Conference on Singapore. (Left to right) John Profumo, Lim Choon Mong, Abdul Hamid, Alan Lennox-Boyd, John Johnston, Lim Yew Hock, Lady Martin, Margaret Moreton (holding Pip, the Lennox-Boyd family pet).

12. RIGHT. At the East African Governors' Conference at Chequers, January 1959. (Left to right) Sir Richard Turnbull, William Gorell Barnes, Lord Perth, Julian Amery.

13. ABOVE. The calm after the storm: Alan Lennox-Boyd sailing with his sons in August 1959. (Left to right) Simon, Mark, Christopher and Alan Lennox-Boyd.

14. BELOW. Alan and Patsy Lennox-Boyd with Nnamdi Azikiwe and his wife at the opening of the Guinness brewery in Ikeja, Nigeria, in March 1963

From the very first, the Archbishop inspired in him both fascina-
tion and exasperation. Lennox-Boyd later recalled:

> He was very small, very elegant, with quite beautiful hands. I remem-
> ber being fascinated by his hands, spotlessly clean; rather agreeable
> voice, very courteous and friendly, and I, in my innocence at that time,
> felt we might well do business together...But even then we never had
> agendas. He was allergic to agendas...There was no moment when you
> could say 'well, now we have dealt with one to five and let's sum up
> in this way and then we have got an agreement'. As soon as one hurdle
> was crossed another appeared and this subsequently really made
> negotiations pretty hopeless.[13]

Although the issue of self-determination for Cyprus was not officially on the agenda, Lennox-Boyd gave a heavy hint that this might
be the logical outcome of the Government's current constitutional
proposals. When Makarios complained that even the Gold Coast
was rapidly approaching independence, he replied that political
progress there had been achieved because of the willingness of the
people of the Gold Coast to cooperate in the development of representative institutions.[14]

The London talks on Cyprus began at the end of August while
Lennox-Boyd was still on a tour of the Far East. Macmillan seems
to have regarded them essentially as a piece of political theatre
designed to demonstrate that the deadlock was caused by the
sharply conflicting ambitions of Greece and Turkey rather than by
British colonial intransigence.[15] Lennox-Boyd was far from satisfied
with this approach and was keen achieve a more positive outcome.
On his return to London on 4 September, he felt that progress
might be within sight, but only if the Cypriots were offered the right,
at some point in the future, to express their views on the question
of self-determination. He therefore wanted Macmillan to make some
reference to the 'future status' of the island.[16] Macmillan, however,
was unwilling to give any commitment on the issue of
self-determination. He was fully supported by Eden, who felt that
any indication that self-determination might be negotiable would
forfeit Turkey's support for Britain and further embitter
Greco-Turkish relations. Lennox-Boyd was overruled.

The London talks finally broke down following anti-Greek riots
in Istanbul. Relations between Greece and Turkey deteriorated
further. Greece prepared once again to raise the issue of Cyprus
at the UN. The British Government hoped that the United States
would intervene for a second time to prevent the subject being discussed. They were therefore cautious about doing anything that
might alienate the Americans. Hence, when Armitage sought permission to deport the Bishop of Kyrenia, whose statements in

support of violent action were causing increasing concern in Government House, Lennox-Boyd insisted that he postpone the operation.[17]

On 18 September there was rioting in Nicosia in the course of which the British Institute was burned down, an action neither the army nor police made any serious effort to prevent. Armitage's freedom of action had clearly been restricted by British Ministers, but there was considerable feeling in Whitehall that he was failing to make adequate use of the resources available to him. A week later, it was announced that Armitage was to be relieved of his post. He was spirited off the island before the arrival of his successor in what was widely taken to be a very public indication of how little his views mattered in London.[18] By a supreme irony, Lennox-Boyd decided to send Armitage somewhere he thought would be less of a 'rough house' – Nyasaland, which in 1959 was itself to be placed under a state of emergency with damaging consequences for Lennox-Boyd and the Government of which he was a member.

Armitage's successor was Field Marshal Sir John Harding, Chief of the Imperial General Staff. The principal criticism which was made of Armitage both by Lennox-Boyd and by senior officials on Cyprus was not that he had failed to warn of the deteriorating security situation but that he had done so with insufficient force to influence policy makers in London. Harding, by contrast, as Britain's most senior ranking soldier, with experience of counter-insurgency operations in Malaya and Kenya, carried tremendous weight with the Cabinet. He set about a dual policy of intensifying the battle against EOKA and, at the same time, making every effort to reach a political settlement with Makarios.

For his talks with Makarios to stand any chance of success, Harding needed to be able to offer concessions on the issue of self-determination. British forces in the region were already overstretched, and the prospect of having to concentrate scarce resources in Cyprus provided Ministers with a powerful incentive to display some flexibility.[19] In November 1955, in response to pressure from Harding, they produced a policy statement which indicated, in the most oblique terms, their acceptance of the principle of self-determination for Cyprus at some later date. It was *not* the British Government's position, the statement claimed, 'that the principle of self-determination can never be applicable to Cyprus. It is their position that it is not now a practicable proposition'. Ministers felt that they had found a formula which could command the support of Turkey, Greece and the Greek Cypriots. They were therefore disappointed when Makarios dismissed it. Yet as Lennox-Boyd told his Cabinet colleagues, there was still the hope that if the talks between Harding and Makarios could be prolonged, the Greek government might be able to persuade the Archbishop to reach an agreement.

Talks carried on into February 1956.[20] On 24 February, Lennox-Boyd told Eden that Harding was keen for him to come out to Cyprus. His role would not be to conduct negotiations or even, necessarily, to meet Makarios. The point of the visit was, rather, to ensure that at this critical stage of the negotiations the Governor and Colonial Secretary were in complete agreement.[21] Harding also felt it was time to publish details of the offers made to the Archbishop in the course of their talks. Far from hoping that Lennox-Boyd might salvage an agreement, Harding seems to have decided by this stage that the breakdown of talks was inevitable and that it was time for the carrot to give way to the stick. Given the British Government's unwillingness thus far to sanction coercive measures, Harding wished to implicate Lennox-Boyd fully in the abandonment of negotiations so that he could not, thereafter, refuse to support the renewed use of force.[22] Eden was equally determined that Lennox-Boyd should not take any further initiatives in order to save the talks. The Prime Minister emphasized to him, 'we have gone as far in concessions to Makarios as it is reasonable to expect the Turks to accept at this stage'.[23]

On 27 February, following his arrival in Cyprus, Lennox-Boyd still seemed hopeful of being able to reach some sort of compromise with the Archbishop.[24] The following day, however, before talks between them had begun, he reported that Makarios had put forward new and unacceptable demands.[25] Lennox-Boyd knew that he would not be able to satisfy any of them. He therefore proposed to put before Makarios a statement which largely reiterated Britain's existing position. It was drafted with the expectation that the talks would fail. As he told Eden,

> ...it is clearly very desirable that I should speak to him in terms which can later be used in Parliament and which will then present our case to the world in the best possible light.[26]

The only significant concession to Greek Cypriot opinion in the document which Lennox-Boyd submitted for the Cabinet's approval was the assurance that the safeguards incorporated in any new constitution 'could not be such as to enable any one section to obstruct measures supported by the majority in matters which did not prejudice that community's particular interest'. The Cabinet, however, insisted on the excision of this line on the grounds that it would be unacceptable to the Turks.[27] It has been suggested that Lennox-Boyd wilfully wrecked the talks with Makarios which took place the following day in a display of 'old-fashioned imperial muscle'.[28] Yet as is clear from the foregoing, his room for manoeuvre was extremely limited, and any further concessions to Makarios would have proved unacceptable to Harding and to the Cabinet.

The venue for the meeting between Makarios and Lennox-Boyd did not bode well for their talks. Lennox-Boyd would not come to the Archbishopric, believing it to be a hive of subversive activity; nor would Makarios meet him at Government House. A neutral ground was provided by the dreary residence of the Anglican Archdeacon. Lennox-Boyd's sense of national and religious pride was offended by the shabbiness of the place. Worse still, a thorough search of the building failed to unearth any alcohol. As at their earlier meeting, Lennox-Boyd was irritated by the Archbishop's failure to stick to an agenda and by his habit of raising entirely new obstacles to a settlement as the existing ones were surmounted. Eventually, Lennox-Boyd informed Makarios that he saw no point in continuing with talks, and the meeting ended. Back at Government House, Harding announced, 'I have reluctantly come to the conclusion that there is no longer enough room in this island for His Beatitude and myself.'[29] Lennox-Boyd endorsed this decision, but warned him, presciently, 'If you get rid of the Archbishop, he will come back as Head of State.'

Having achieved the by no means simple task of convincing his Cabinet colleagues of the need to deport both Makarios and the Bishop of Kyrenia to the Seychelles, Lennox-Boyd faced some rather unexpected difficulties. The Governor of the Seychelles, Sir William Addis, reported that the most suitable place for the two men was *Sans Souci*, his summer residence. Sadly, however, the house had only one bathroom and lavatory. Makarios and the Bishop were known not to be the best of friends, and Addis feared that on top of deportation, it might be too much of an imposition to expect them to share these facilities. He therefore proposed placing them in another house with the unfortunate name of *La Bastille*. Lennox-Boyd, well aware of the amusement this would cause in Parliament and the press, was horrified by the idea. He told Addis:

> I had with great care and by producing photographs of it assured my colleagues of the charm and general suitability of Sans Souci. Indeed one or two of them would have liked the opportunity themselves. But La Bastille!! There will I fear be very awkward repercussions and as you can't rechristen it 'The Haven' without creating an even better news-story...[30]

Addis, a former colonial secretary in Bermuda, replied in the form of a calypso:

Well – in Sans Souci so let it be;
Thus denying Opposition opportunity
Of stating Archbishop
Ne peut pas rester tranquille
In a house with the name of La Bastille.[31]

Behind all this whimsy was a harsher reality. Makarios's deportation on 9 March was followed, as Lennox-Boyd and Harding knew it would be, by violent disorder in Cyprus and fierce criticism of the British Government at home and abroad. In response, Harding's administration intensified its battle against the rebels. The first executions of EOKA members served further to increase tension on the island. Yet Harding realized that military action had to be accompanied by constitutional and diplomatic progress. Signs that this might be possible appeared in May when the Greek Foreign Minister, Spyros Theotokis, resigned and was replaced by Evanghelos Averoff-Tossizza. The new Foreign Minister let the British Ambassador in Athens know that he wished to see a settlement of the Cyprus problem.[32]

Harding visited London in June and told the Cabinet that the Cypriots would only be ready to cooperate in a new constitution if they were assured that self-determination would be conceded at some point in the future.[33] He managed to persuade the Chiefs of Staff, for the first time, to accept the possibility of a change in sovereignty for Cyprus after a certain number of years.[34] The Colonial Policy Committee produced a new set of proposals based, in part, on plans submitted by Harding: Lord Radcliffe would be sent to Cyprus to prepare a new constitution. Britain would also seek a treaty with Turkey and Greece regulating their use of Cyprus for military purposes, and additional treaty arrangements to protect the interests of racial minorities. Once the new arrangements had been in operation for 10 years, NATO members would be asked to judge whether a change in the international status of Cyprus would be compatible with Western defence interests. If two-thirds of them replied affirmatively, there would be a plebiscite on self-determination.[35]

The Government's proposals were decisively rejected by the Turkish government. Radcliffe, however, went ahead with his preparations for a new constitution. His report, which was ready for publication in December 1956, offered the Greeks an elected majority in the legislative assembly. Turkish interests were to be protected by a series of constitutional guarantees. The only sense in which the Radcliffe proposals represented a retreat from the terms offered to Makarios earlier in the year was that, in accordance with the terms of reference he had been given, internal security was to remain permanently under official control.[36]

Lennox-Boyd was determined to secure Turkish approval for the constitution, but realized that this could only be achieved by offering substantial safeguards to the Turkish Cypriot minority in the event of any change in sovereignty. He therefore wanted to be able to make some public reference, on the day the Radcliffe report was published, to the possibility of Cyprus being partitioned. He told his colleagues, 'The prospect of partition as a possible ultimate solution would...give the Turks an effective veto against *Enosis*; and the Turks would not even acquiesce in our proposals if this possibility were not foreshadowed.'[37] Lennox-Boyd later claimed,

> I certainly never willingly embraced the idea of partition or thought it was a good idea in itself...but it seemed to me essential to reassure the Turks not to rule it out as being a possibility if intransigence on the Greek side continued indefinitely, and to make it clear that if self-determination was to be applied in practice it must be self-determination for both the communities.[38]

In the middle of December, in advance of the publication of the Radcliffe proposals, Lennox-Boyd paid a personal visit to Athens at the suggestion of the British Ambassador, Sir Charles Peake. If Peake imagined that Lennox-Boyd's long-standing friendship with the Greek King could be turned to Britain's advantage he was wrong. On the advice of the Greek government, King Paul refused to see him. The following day, still smarting from this diplomatic rebuff, Lennox-Boyd met Constantine Karamanlis, the Greek Prime Minister. He outlined the Radcliffe proposals and explained that if and when the British Government was ready to review the international status of Cyprus, the Turkish Cypriots no less than the Greek Cypriots would be free to decide upon self-determination. This was not well received by Karamanlis. The next day, the Greek Cabinet decided unanimously to reject the British proposals, although they did not announce their response until 19 December, following Lennox-Boyd's statement to the Commons.

After making another abortive attempt to see the King, Lennox-Boyd flew on to Ankara where his reception was a great deal warmer. He was met by a number of Turkish Ministers and taken straight to the Hilton hotel for talks. Lennox-Boyd revealed that the Government's gloss on the Radcliffe proposals would leave open the possibility of partition. Menderes, the Turkish Prime Minister, urged him to strengthen the statement. Rather than simply announcing that the Government 'would not exclude partition' as a solution, he wanted Lennox-Boyd to undertake that in the event of self-determination resulting in a change of Cyprus's sovereign status, 'the Turkish Cypriots would be given the option of electing for partition'. Were Britain to adopt this revised wording, Menderes suggested, his government would fully acquiesce to the Radcliffe proposals.

On his return to London, Lennox-Boyd urged his colleagues to accept this revision, arguing that it would not only ensure the support of Turkey but that it would gain the approval of the Government's supporters in Parliament.[39] The Cabinet rejected this suggestion, fearing that it would result in the issue of partition overshadowing the Radcliffe scheme. They were also concerned that it might encourage the movement in favour of partition on the island and provide a disincentive for Turkish cooperation with the new constitution. Instead, they agreed to a compromise formula which Lennox-Boyd adopted in his statement to Parliament two days later:

> ...Her Majesty's Government recognize that the exercise of self-determination in such a mixed population must include partition among the eventual options.[40]

In fact, the Greek government had already decided to reject the Radcliffe proposals. So 1956 ended with little hope of a solution to the problems of Cyprus. By that point, of course, the Eden government itself had been plunged into crisis by the failure of the Suez operation. Lennox-Boyd's own chances of presiding over a settlement therefore seemed doubly remote.

Malta

The island of Malta is only about eight miles wide and seventeen and a half across. Together with its smaller neighbours, Gozo and Comino, it contained, in the mid-1950s, just over 300,000 inhabitants. Yet the fate of these colonial subjects, among whom there was little resistance to British rule, was an issue which may well have occupied more of Lennox-Boyd's time than any other. The policy he attempted to advance throughout much of his time in the Colonial Office was a most unusual one: that of formally incorporating Malta into the United Kingdom. As Dennis Austin comments, 'it was as if a policy well tried out in Paris for *la France d'Outre-Mer* had suddenly taken flight and come to rest on the banks of the Thames'.[41]

The Malta Labour Party, under the leadership of Dom Mintoff, fought three elections between 1950 and 1955 on a platform of

integration with the United Kingdom. The Nationalist party led by
Georgio Borg Olivier, which was closely allied to the Catholic
Church, opposed integration fearing that union with nominally
Protestant but largely secular Britain would weaken the position
of the Church. In June 1953, Olivier's Nationalist government proposed that Malta be granted some form of qualified Dominion status under the Commonwealth Relations Office. Because of the
island's importance to her as a military base, however, Britain was
unwilling to grant the Maltese control over their defence and external affairs.[42] Instead, the possibility was raised of Malta being
transferred to the Home Office, to be administered in a similar
fashion to the Channel Islands and the Isle of Man. This proved
acceptable neither to Olivier nor Mintoff, and as Lennox-Boyd recalled, by the time he arrived at the Colonial Office in July 1954
the proposal was already something of 'a dead duck' which he had
no great desire to revive.[43]

The election of Mintoff's Labour Party in February 1955 put the
question of closer-association with Britain back onto the agenda.
Under Mintoff's plans for integration, the Maltese parliament would
retain responsibility for most areas of domestic policy, although its
overall power would be considerably reduced. In particular, control of financial affairs would pass to London, with British levels
of taxation eventually applying to Malta. In return, the Maltese
would be guaranteed standards of social services and rates of pay
roughly comparable to those in Britain. The Maltese people would
also be granted direct representation in the British House of
Commons.[44]

Rather to Lennox-Boyd's surprise, the majority of his Cabinet
colleagues required little convincing that the scheme should be
treated sympathetically. They were well aware of the danger that
Maltese representatives might exert a disproportionate influence
in a hung parliament, just as the Irish MPs had in the late nine-
teenth and early twentieth centuries. Yet with only three seats on
offer to the Maltese, this seemed a remote possibility. Furthermore, against the background of the incipient revolt in Cyprus and
criticism over the Simonstown agreement with South Africa, it
seemed ridiculous for the British Government to reject overtures
from the inhabitants of a strategically vital colony for closer association.[45]

In view of the very large amounts of Ministerial time that were
ultimately wasted on what now appears a somewhat eccentric
scheme, it is important to appreciate how widespread was the support for it at the time. For Lennox-Boyd the prospect of establishing a quasi-Imperial assembly had an obvious appeal.[46] Yet even

for those not imbued with the romantic Imperialism of Joseph Chamberlain, the arguments in favour of amalgamation seemed to make sense. There was a great warmth of feeling towards the island because of the heroic part its people had played during the Second World War. It was generally felt, on both sides of the House, that Malta was too small and too economically dependent on Britain to achieve full independence. At least until 1957, the Chiefs of Staff regarded Malta as vital to British defence, and with about 27% of the island's workforce employed in defence-related jobs there was little inclination locally to question their judgement.

In July 1955, the Cabinet decided to convene a Round Table Conference on Malta, taking as its model the Indian conferences of the 1930s.[47] This brought together representatives of all the main political parties in Britain. Its report endorsed the policy of integration and the scene appeared set for the acceptance and implementation of an unusually uncontroversial policy. Yet Lennox-Boyd and his colleagues had reckoned without Dom Mintoff.

In the middle of December 1955, just as the Round Table Conference was due to publish its report, Mintoff announced that he wished to hold a referendum in Malta on the integration plan. He was keen that it should take place before Lent when the capacity of the Church to propagate an anti-integration message would be at its height. Lennox-Boyd was concerned, however, that if the Maltese referendum occurred before the House of Commons had had the opportunity to debate the Round Table report, it might be perceived by MPs as an attempt to influence or prejudge their decision. He also believed, quite correctly, that it would provoke a head-on confrontation with both the Catholic Church on Malta and those political leaders on the island who opposed integration.

On 14 December, Lennox-Boyd told his Cabinet colleagues of Mintoff's request for a referendum and persuaded them that it should be refused. He was shocked and deeply angered when Mintoff subsequently revealed that he had already – on 13 December – tabled a dummy bill in the Maltese parliament for a referendum. Mintoff had not given London any advance warning and Lennox-Boyd was unable to prevent the bill from being given a second reading.[48] Lennox-Boyd's Cabinet colleagues took a fairly understanding view of this episode.[49] Nevertheless, it placed Lennox-Boyd in an extremely difficult position. Many Tory backbenchers were instinctively hostile towards integration, and the issue placed enormous strains on his normally extremely good relations with members of the Conservative backbench Commonwealth Affairs Committee. Lennox-Boyd had become so personally identified with the policy that a large-scale vote against the Round Table proposals by Conservative MPs would have been enormously damaging for him. During a meeting with Gaitskell in January, Lennox-Boyd told the Labour leader that he was close to resignation over the issue.[50]

The referendum which was held on the weekend of 11–12 February proved, as Lennox-Boyd had feared it might, both divisive and indecisive. The Archbishop of Malta urged his flock to boycott the vote. Borg Olivier for the Nationalists and Mabel Strickland, editor of the *Times of Malta* and leader of one of the smaller parties, also urged voters to stay at home. When the results were announced, Mintoff was able to claim a victory of sorts. Of those who voted, 74% were in favour of integration and 22% against. Yet only 59% of those eligible to vote had done so. The vote in favour therefore represented only about 44% of the electorate, roughly the same proportion as voted for the Malta Labour Party in the 1955 general election.

The Commons debate on the integration proposals took place on 26 March. The Government's motion backed away from a direct test of the loyalty of its backbenchers on the issue. It asked the House merely to take note of rather than to approve the report of the Round Table Conference. Winding up for the Opposition, James Griffiths suggested that the Government should proceed with preparations for integration but that the part of the bill dealing with representation at Westminster should await the outcome of a further general election in Malta. Lennox-Boyd appeared to reject this option. He pointed out that Malta had recently had both a general election and a referendum and suggested that there was nothing to be gained from a further delay. He would have liked to have wound up the debate with a clear statement that the Government would accept the Round Table report. His Cabinet colleagues were, however, inclined to be more cautious. So instead, he closed with that favourite device of British policy makers – the cautiously affirmative double negative:

> ...nothing has been said in the debate that gives me any ground for believing that for Her Majesty's Government to do something other than that proposed in the Report, or to do nothing at all, would find a fuller measure of agreement in Malta now, or hold out the prospect of achieving it in the future or be for the greater advantage of the British Commonwealth.[51]

Criticisms of the scheme voiced by Tory backbenchers in the course of the debate heightened unease within the Cabinet. At a meeting the following day, Lennox-Boyd rather optimistically told his colleagues that criticisms of the scheme had tended to be 'moderately expressed'.[52] Ministers were still, however, worried that a substantial number of Tory MPs might not support legislation for integration. They effectively endorsed the option suggested by Griffiths. The following day, Eden announced that the Government intended to introduce legislation giving effect to the recommendations of the Round Table Conference, but that the part of the scheme relating to representation at Westminster would not be implemented until the people of Malta had expressed their support for it in a further general election. This implied a recognition both of the strength of opposition to the scheme in Parliament and to the inconclusiveness of the February referendum.

The next aspect of the integration plan to cause difficulties was the scale of British financial aid to Malta. The Round Table Conference had assumed that a sum of £4–5 million a year in financial assistance from Britain would be sufficient to satisfy the Maltese. Mintoff was determined to increase this amount and, at least initially, Lennox-Boyd was sympathetic to his demands. He suspected that the Treasury had been determined from the start to thwart integration on economic grounds.[53] Yet even he quickly lost patience with Mintoff's intransigent approach. Mintoff demanded aid of £7–8 million in the coming financial year. Lennox-Boyd refused to sanction this and talks collapsed. On his return to Malta, Mintoff threatened to force a dissolution of the Maltese parliament and fight an election on a platform of self-determination for the island. The Cabinet put together a compromise proposal under which Malta would be offered £7.5 million over 18 months. A commission would also be sent out to examine Malta's longer term economic requirements and to advise on the extent to which the island should contribute to the costs of development.[54] This proved sufficient to persuade Mintoff to remain in office and to resume talks.

The whole episode clearly left Lennox-Boyd profoundly disillusioned. In the middle of July, he suggested that the Cabinet should have ready an alternative plan for Malta's future should the scheme for integration finally collapse. Since the degree of self-determination which could be offered to Malta was bound to be judged against the island's strategic importance, he suggested that the Chiefs of Staff should produce a reassessment of her role in the light of the recent enquiry into Britain's defence requirements.[55] They reported in September, by which time Malta was the site of a massive military build-up in preparation for the Suez operation. Not surprisingly, they advised that the strategic importance of Malta had actually increased over the previous year and was likely to increase further in the future.[56]

The reassessment of Britain's defence policy which followed the Suez Crisis seriously undermined Mintoff's bargaining position. In April 1957, the British Government published its Defence White Paper. This proposed reducing the size of the British armed forces from their current 690,000 to 375,000 by 1962. The size of the navy was also to be reduced, a move which would obviously lead to a decline in the amount of work likely to be undertaken in the Malta dockyards. In case the implications of these cuts were lost on Mintoff, he was treated to a characteristically blunt exposition of them by Duncan Sandys, the Minister of Defence. Sandys told Mintoff and his colleagues that although Malta was still a convenient naval base it did not, unlike Cyprus, play any major part in Britain's global strategy. Under the circumstances, Maltese workers could no more be spared the impact of defence cuts than could those in Britain. When Mintoff made vague threats about the possible consequences of a breakdown of the integration proposals, Sandys replied that 'quite frankly, many people in England thought Her Majesty's Government had been over generous, and they would heave a sigh of relief if we were released from this offer, through Maltese rejection'.[57]

Talks about the future of the island dragged on, in an increasingly acrimonious spirit, until April 1958, when Mintoff and his government resigned. This was followed by a general strike and the imposition of a state of emergency. In July, Lennox-Boyd sought to bring the main political parties around the table to begin work on a new constitutional settlement. Mintoff, Olivier, and Mabel Strickland of the Progressive Constitutional party all came to London, but refused to meet together. Only Strickland agreed to attend the plenary sessions, which thereafter became known in the Colonial Office as the 'Round Mabel' talks. After these had failed, legislation was introduced to enable the Governor to administer the territory with a nominated Executive Council.

Although Lennox-Boyd tried to put a brave face on the matter, this final breakdown in negotiations must have come as a severe disappointment to him. The enormous amount of time, effort and personal commitment he invested in the integration scheme had come to nothing. It was all too typical of a number of grand schemes which he sought to nurture during his time at the Colonial Office. Lennox-Boyd continued to monitor developments, even after his retirement from the Colonial Office. Ever the optimist, he retained the hope that the policy of integration might be revived and was only really prepared to admit defeat when Malta finally achieved her independence in 1964.

Part II: The Far East

Malaya

One of the central dilemmas Lennox-Boyd faced in the Mediterranean – namely how to reconcile popular nationalism with Britain's strategic interests and the views of neighbouring governments – was also to confront him across the world in the Far East. Once again, Lennox-Boyd sometimes found himself mediating between highly-strung colonial leaders and distinctly sceptical Cabinet colleagues.

At the end of the Second World War, the British attempted to re-establish control over Malaya in the wake of the Japanese occupation. Before the War, the four federated and five unfederated princely states of Malaya had enjoyed considerable autonomy. As Protectorates they came under the ultimate authority of a British High Commissioner who was also Governor of 'Straits Settlements' of Singapore, Penang and Malacca. In January 1946, Britain announced plans for the creation of the 'Malayan Union'. The government of Malaya was to be centralized, Singapore governed as a separate colony, and the influence of the Malay sultans much reduced. At the same time, the Chinese and Indian inhabitants, who jointly almost outnumbered the ethnic Malays, were to be granted proper rights of citizenship. The scheme met vigorous opposition from the Malay population and the British were forced onto the retreat. In 1948, they replaced the Malayan Union with the Federation of Malaya. This restored to the rulers some of their former authority and offered far more limited rights of citizenship to members of the Chinese and Indian communities. An upsurge in violence led to calls for a crack-down from the expatriate business community and in June 1948, the British authorities declared a state of emergency. At the time, they were unsure of the extent to which Communist influence lay behind the unrest. In retrospect, however, they justified their actions as a response to a carefully coordinated rising by the Chinese-dominated Malayan Communist Party (MCP).[58] Further constitutional progress was suspended.

By the time Lennox-Boyd became Colonial Secretary at the end of July 1954, the security situation in Malaya had greatly improved and arrangements were already underway for holding national elections. There had also been an important realignment among the political parties of Malaya. The three principal communal parties – the United Malays' National Organization (UMNO), the Malayan Chinese Association (MCA) and the Malayan Indian Congress (MIC) – had combined to form the Alliance. This brought into being a far more powerful organization, and British support shifted away from Dato Onn. Plans were put in place for the creation of a Legislative Council consisting of 98 members, 52 of them elected and 46 appointed. Despite the reservations of its leadership about the new constitution, the Alliance contested the election and won 51 of the 52 elected seats in the elections of August 1955, giving it a virtually unchallengeable mandate to press for further constitutional advance.

If the overwhelming victory of the Alliance came as somewhat of a surprise, Lennox-Boyd knew well before the elections that, with all the main parties campaigning on the basis of their capacity to deliver self-government, he was likely to come under intense pressure to make further concessions. He therefore payed a visit to Malaya and Singapore to coincide with the elections, leaving England on 23 July. Shortly before his departure, he put to the Cabinet the case for accepting Malayan calls for a swift transition to self-government. He told his colleagues:

> To leave the matter until there is strong pressure for the early appointment of a commission to consider these changes or until Malay nationalism has gathered further momentum or until the Emergency has petered out and is no longer a present threat to the security of Malaya might prejudice the satisfactory outcome of negotiations in regard to British bases and the fundamental issues of responsibility for external and internal defence.[59]

The 'satisfactory outcome' which he desired would include an agreement leaving the responsibility for defence in British hands and providing for the maintenance of British military bases in the Federation. Lennox-Boyd was also highly conscious of the extent of British investment in Malaya, particularly in rubber and tin. He told his colleagues that the Federation was 'one of the buttresses of the sterling area' and suggested that if Britain were required to provide her with substantial financial assistance over a long period, 'we should endeavour to ensure that the future security of our commercial interests in Malaya was safeguarded'.[60] That this economic consideration did not lead to greater delays in the transfer of power was due in part to the fact that British businessmen were generally confident about their capacity to operate without formal British protection.[61] Yet it was also due to a realization by Lennox-Boyd and his colleagues that, ultimately, the best safeguard for British interests was the goodwill of Malayan leaders.

Tunku Abdul Rahman, the leader of the Alliance and Malaya's new chief minister was precisely the sort of colonial politician with whom Lennox-Boyd most liked to do business. A member of one of the Malay ruling families, he had studied at Cambridge and trained as a barrister at the Inner Temple. His years in Britain had provided him with a taste for high living, a strong aversion to Communism and an exceptionally poor degree. He and Lennox-Boyd established a warm friendship which survived some difficult episodes, not the least of which was the Tunku's decision in October 1955 to go into the jungle and open talks with the MCP.[62] Both Lennox-Boyd and Sir Donald MacGillivray, the British High Commissioner, attempted to persuade the Tunku to drop this idea. Failing that, they were anxious that he should confine his talks to further exploration of the terms of the amnesty which had been offered in September.[63] The Tunku, however, refused to be deflected, and let it be known that if his attempts to reach a settlement were blocked, he might resign and accuse the British of having sabotaged his efforts to bring the Emergency to an end. Accompanied by David Marshall, the Chief Minister of Singapore, he met with the Communist leader, Chin Peng, in December. In the event, however, he proved his anti-Communist credentials by refusing Chin Peng's demand for recognition and insisting upon unconditional surrender. Negotiations collapsed and the Communists resumed their military campaign. The talks did not cause a significant hardening of opinion among British Ministers on the question of further transfers of power to the Malays. Indeed, the attitude displayed by the Tunku during the negotiations may have helped to accelerate this process.

During Lennox-Boyd's visit to Malaya in 1955, he had agreed to hold a conference in London on further constitutional advance. When the Alliance leaders arrived in Britain for these negotiations in January 1956, they brought with them a number of demands that seemed likely to prove controversial. Prompted by the more radical elements within the movement, they called for independence by August 1957. The British were still working on the basis that 'full self-government would not be reached before 1959'.[64] More disturbingly for the British, the Alliance wanted responsibility for internal security transferred to Malayan Ministers before independence had been attained.

So far as a date for independence was concerned, Lennox-Boyd was prepared to be flexible. He assumed that, in private, the Tunku did not really believe independence was possible by 1957. As such, he did not want to make this a sticking point in the negotiations.[65] It was the issue of control over internal security which proved most difficult for him. He did not accept that the battle against Communism within Malaya could be treated merely as an internal matter: it was of profound concern to Malaya's neighbours. Nevertheless, he was persuaded by MacGillivray that this point too would have to be conceded. The Tunku was under a great deal of pressure domestically to obtain this demand, not least because Chin Peng had undertaken to cease hostilities once complete control of internal security had passed to the elected government.[66] The Tunku had demonstrated that his government could be relied upon to take a firm line against the guerrillas. Of equal if not greater weight in British calculations was the fear that, if the Alliance failed to achieve their demands, the stable and moderate coalition of forces which seemed likely to inherit power would be shattered and replaced by a far less amenable set of negotiating partners. Lennox-Boyd made point forcefully to Eden shortly before the conference began:

> There is no doubt that both the Malays and the Chinese are united in a vehement desire for early self-government. This we shall have to grant since we cannot hope to govern the country without at least the acquiescence of the majority of the population; and that we will not long enjoy unless the territory is allowed rapidly to make moves towards self-government. There is therefore every advantage in granting quickly what is asked of us and using the goodwill which may be expected to flow from that to secure conditions which we want...[67]

The conference, which concluded on 8 February, effectively granted the Federation immediate *de facto* self-government, only seven months after her first national elections. It agreed that independence should be proclaimed 'by August 1957, if possible', a formula which proved sufficiently evasive for both sides. The key portfolios of Finance and Internal Defence and Security would henceforth be held by Malayan Ministers. The High Commissioner would, however, retain control over external defence, although he would consult with a new External Defence Committee composed of Malayan ministers. Britain's right to maintain forces in the Federation to meet her international obligations was recognized and a working party was established to prepare the details of a defence treaty. The conference also agreed on the composition of a constitutional commission to draw up the framework for full self-government. This was to include representatives from Britain and the other Commonwealth countries and was to be chaired by Lord Reid, a British Appeal Court judge. Reid, a former Conservative MP and an old friend of Lennox-Boyd was not a happy choice. He managed to fall out not only with Lennox-Boyd but with just about everyone else with whom he came into contact.[68]

Although the target date for independence of August 1957 had not been agreed in particularly good faith, once announced, all sides came under great pressure to meet it. The Reid commission published its report in February 1957. Three months later, a conference was held in London to secure agreement on various outstanding problems, in particular the thorny question of citizenship. On 31 August 1957, Malaya achieved her independence.

Singapore

In contrast to Malaya, the government of Singapore appeared to British Ministers to be weak, unpredictable, and incapable of maintaining order. Since the colony attracted large amounts of Western investment and provided Britain with her principal naval base in the Far East, this was a source of particular concern. Singapore's Chief Minister from April 1955 was David Marshall, a successful lawyer from Singapore's small but prosperous Jewish community. Marshall had fought against the Japanese during the war, was captured and put to work in the notorious Hokkaido coal mines. After the war he entered politics, working first with the Progressives and then, in 1954, establishing the Labour Front along with Lim Yew Hock and Francis Thomas.[69] In retrospect, Lennox-Boyd was characteristically generous about him, citing the courage and leadership he had displayed during the Japanese occupation.[70] At the time, however, he found Marshall a difficult and unpredictable negotiating partner. One Cabinet paper, signed by Lennox-Boyd, spoke of 'the levantine approach and almost psychopathic personality of the Chief Minister'.[71] One might suspect that this animosity was aroused not so much by any quirks in Marshall's character as by his passionate opposition to colonialism. Unlike the more pragmatic and deferential Malayan leaders with whom Lennox-Boyd got on so well, Marshall never displayed much willingness to 'play the game' of constitutional advance according to rules set down by the British.

Marshall's Labour Front won 10 of the 25 elected seats in the new Legislative Assembly in the 1955 elections. It maintained a majority with the support of a handful of ex-officio, elected and nominated members. Not only was its position within the Legislative Assembly relatively weak, but it faced growing pressures from outside the legislature, principally from the People's Action Party (PAP). Founded in November 1954, the PAP had strong links with the MCP which regarded it as a convenient front for its activities. The PAP's general-secretary, Lee Kuan Yew, was in the process of establishing himself as Singapore's outstanding political figure. Still only in his early 30s, Lee had been educated at Raffles College in Singapore and then at Cambridge where (in marked contrast to the Tunku) he had taken a brilliant law degree. Rather than allowing his party to be hijacked as a vehicle for Communist ambitions, Lee was determined to 'ride the tiger' of Communism.

The PAP used the April 1955 election to demonstrate their potential support without running the risk of having to form a government. They contested only four seats and won three of them.[72] Thereafter, they concentrated their efforts on destabilizing Marshall's government by extra-parliamentary means. The PAP were thought to be behind the wave of strikes which gripped the colony during April. The largest of these were at the Singapore Harbour Board and the Hock Lee Amalgamated Bus Company, the latter resulting in four deaths. There was also mass unrest in the Chinese schools of the territory.

The disruption placed Marshall in an extremely difficult position. If he accepted the Governor's advice and invoked Emergency regulations to deal with the unrest, he was likely as Chief Minister to bear the brunt of public criticism. Yet under the existing constitution, he was not directly responsible for administering these powers. His immediate response was to attempt to bring the strikes to an end. In the middle of May, under pressure from Marshall, the management of the bus company conceded almost all the strikers' demands. News of this settlement alarmed Eden, who demanded to know Lennox-Boyd's views on the matter.[73] Lennox-Boyd replied that he shared the Prime Minister's concern about the outcome of the strike.[74] At the same time, he offered a partial defence of Marshall's government, pointing out that it had 'shown firmness' by agreeing to the reintroduction of Emergency regulations providing for a curfew.

The situation was further complicated when Marshall's government proved unwilling to act against the organizers of unrest in the schools, despite the Governor's warning that another climb-down would weaken the administration.[75] Governor Nicoll offered to take full responsibility for the use of reserve powers, but Marshall and his Ministers refused. In the circumstances, Nicoll felt he could not insist on their use without provoking a constitutional crisis. Lennox-Boyd appreciated the reasons for the Governor's reluctance to act. He told Eden:

> If Marshall's coalition threw its hand in or were driven out of office it would be necessary either at once to suspend the constitution or to hold a fresh general election. The latter course would almost certainly secure the return of a government so much further to the left than the present one that the suspension of the constitution would still before long become unavoidable.[76]

The common perception of Marshall as a weak and disagreeable leader whose administration might be replaced by a more extreme government gave rise to two contradictory schools of thought among

British policy makers. On the one hand, it was suggested that if a constitutional crisis could be avoided through minor concessions, these were worth making in order to prevent an even more recalcitrant administration from taking power. Against this, it was argued that Marshall's government was bound eventually to fall whatever additional powers he was granted, and that these powers would ultimately be inherited by a more hostile administration. A refusal to offer concessions would hasten Marshall's departure. Although the immediate consequence of this seemed likely to be further unrest, in the longer term Britain had a good chance of finding a more moderate and amenable negotiating partner. In his dealings with Marshall, Lennox-Boyd appears to have wavered between these two approaches before finally opting for the second.

This ambivalent attitude towards Marshall's administration was apparent during Lennox-Boyd's visit to Singapore in August–September 1955. The unrest of April and May had highlighted the limitations on Marshall's powers as Chief Minister. On 9 July, in an effort to reinforce his authority, Marshall requested the appointment of four additional Assistant Ministers. The new Governor, Sir Robert Black, would only agree to appoint another two, arguing that there were already 10 Ministers in an Assembly of 32 members. Marshall then focused upon the broader question of ministerial powers, calling on the Governor to adopt a 'liberal interpretation' of the constitution. He suggested that on issues about which the Governor was obliged to consult the Chief Minister, he should accept the latter's advice.[77] Marshall threatened to resign if the principle was not conceded. Black, however, argued that this represented a departure from the existing practice which could only be effected by amending the constitution. On 25 July, two days after Lennox-Boyd departed for his visit to the Far East, Marshall called a special meeting of the Legislative Assembly which passed a resolution supporting his stand. This also asserted that the time had come for Singapore to be given a new constitution which would allow it full self-government.

Eden's initial reaction to the Assembly's resolution was that, since the colony's existing constitution had been in force for only three months, there was no justification for any immediate changes.[78] Black was, by contrast, prepared to take a more flexible approach. He believed that some of his discretionary powers were superfluous in so far as they seemed to involve him giving 'repetitious counsel patiently to a highly excitable prima-donna who can make a mountainous crisis out of a "junior" molehill'.[79] He suggested that by making some minor concessions on the issue of ministerial appointments the colonial administration would be in a stronger position to resist Marshall's more extreme demands. Malcolm MacDonald, the British Commissioner General for South East Asia, made a similar point to Lennox-Boyd in London shortly before the latter's departure for the Far East.[80]

Lennox-Boyd arrived in Singapore on 31 July. Marshall was due to make a statement to the Assembly on 2 August and both Black and MacDonald were keen that something should be done to mollify him before then. Lennox-Boyd accepted their advice and on Monday 1 August sent a telegram to Eden requesting authorization to accede to Marshall's request for the extra Assistant Ministers, subject to Cabinet confirmation. This he received some hours later. At 2.30 in the morning of 2 August, after an uncomfortable round of discussions the previous evening, Lennox-Boyd rang Marshall with the news.[81] Marshall was reassured and, as Black and MacDonald had hoped, the session of the Legislative Assembly later that day passed off without serious incident.

Before meeting Marshall again, Lennox-Boyd sought Cabinet approval for a package of concessions. Senior figures in London were concerned by his apparent readiness to respond to nationalist pressure. The three Chiefs of Staff were particularly uneasy, and Lord Salisbury, the Lord President, complained to Eden that 'Alan shows signs of giving way all along the line'.[82] Nevertheless, Lennox-Boyd was unrepentant. A paper circulated to the Cabinet by Hopkinson, the Minister of State, noted:

> The Colonial Secretary is convinced that nationalist feelings have risen so fast in Singapore that it is no longer possible unilaterally to control the pace of constitutional advance. The choice lies between a refusal to make concessions with what the Colonial Secretary has described as 'bloody and disastrous consequences' and meeting the demand for constitutional advance fast enough to keep the peace and retain a guiding influence over developments.[83]

The reforms for which Lennox-Boyd sought the Cabinet's approval were designed to give the Chief Minister greater control over the selection of ministers and ministerial committees. Lennox-Boyd also wanted to be able to promise talks in London the following year which 'would be comprehensive and include the timing of possible future constitutional advances'.

When the Cabinet met on 15 August to discuss these proposals, Lennox-Boyd's handling of the situation came in for serious criticism.[84] There was general agreement that it was too soon to talk of revising the constitution and that Britain should 'avoid the appearance of precipitate retreat under pressure'. Although Lennox-Boyd was authorized to make the substantive concessions he had proposed, the Cabinet refused to allow him to suggest that further constitutional concessions would be forthcoming at the talks scheduled to take place in London the following year. Ministers were also adamant that in no circumstances was the Chief Minister to be given the power to dissolve the Assembly.

By the time the next round of constitutional negotiations began in London in April 1956, Lennox-Boyd had reached the conclusion that major concessions to a Labour Front government would be counter-productive. The defection of two of Marshall's colleagues had reduced his party's strength in the Assembly to a minority of elected members. Lennox-Boyd warned his Cabinet colleagues that the PAP's leaders were playing a sophisticated waiting game. They would leave Marshall in charge of the country until after the talks in the hope that he would be able to obtain more concessions than they could themselves. On Marshall's return to Singapore, however, they would attempt to remove him and assume power in his place.[85] This message was hardly likely to encourage the Cabinet to agree to a significant transfer of responsibility in the colony. Lennox-Boyd also stressed the importance of safeguarding 'our vast trading interests in Singapore'. He argued, however, that since the failure of talks would lead to Marshall's resignation and the distinct likelihood of having to impose direct rule, it was important that the British Government should be ready to concede the fullest possible degree of self-government short of giving up control of external affairs, defence and security. If Britain were forced to impose direct rule she would be in a stronger position if she had shown herself ready to go to all reasonable lengths to reach agreement.

The main lines of the argument only fully emerged in April when the Singapore delegation submitted their proposals calling for the colony to be granted full sovereign independence. British strategic interests were to be safeguarded by a Defence and Security Council which was also to be responsible for internal security. Britain and Singapore were to have equal representation on this body, thus giving the Singapore representatives an effective veto over any initiative. The predominant view among the colonial administration in Singapore was that the demand for independence could not be resisted without damaging consequences. The majority of Black's senior advisers felt that independence should be conceded subject to a reinforcement clause and agreements about bases.[86] Black's own advice was that if Marshall fell as the result of the failure of talks, resentment against the British presence both domestically and across the region would grow, and the capacity of the authorities to resist Communism would be severely weakened.

The arguments against conceding the demands of the Singapore delegation came most forcefully from the Chiefs of Staff who

believed that the strategic importance of Singapore was actually
likely to increase in the next few years.[87] Their views were largely
endorsed by Sir Robert Scott, MacDonald's successor as British
Commissioner General. Scott felt that if a confrontation with the
government of Singapore over the question of independence was
inevitable, it was best undertaken while the authorities in the region still had sufficient British officers under their command to
make direct rule feasible. The governments of Australia and New
Zealand were also keen to impress upon the British Government
the strategic importance of Singapore.

Lennox-Boyd was sympathetic towards Black's concerns. He
warned his colleagues that Singapore might become another Cyprus
or even a Saigon 'with our scattered defence facilities the targets
for strikes and sabotage and our own people living behind barbed
wire'.[88] On the other hand, he accepted the arguments against a
full transfer of responsibility in 1956. He was sure the Chiefs of
Staff were correct in demanding that sovereignty had to be maintained for the security of the whole region.[89] Malaya was also a key
element in his calculations. He had taken a great risk in persuading the Cabinet to promise independence to Malaya before the
ending of the state of Emergency. Underpinning this settlement was
the Malayans' ability to call upon Britain's military forces in
Singapore. The British could not, at this stage, risk the possibility
of a Communist-infiltrated government achieving power in
Singapore and insisting on the removal of British military instal-
lations.[90] Under the circumstances, Lennox-Boyd could see little
possibility of the conference yielding a positive result. His main
concern for the duration of the talks from April 23 to May 15 was
to run them into the ground as gently as possible.

Lennox-Boyd succeeded in allowing the conference to fail in circumstances that did not reflect too badly on the British Government. All the members of the Singapore delegation except Marshall
and Lim Chin Siong were prepared to accept Lennox-Boyd's final
proposals on the composition of the proposed Defence and Security Council. Marshall's threat that the Singapore government
would resign *en masse* was quickly exposed as a sham. His Ministerial colleagues were not prepared to give up their jobs over the
failure of talks. Marshall returned to Singapore and submitted his
own resignation. The Labour Front chose Lim Yew Hock as his
successor and although there was widespread unrest, the breakdown of government which the Singapore authorities had predicted
failed to materialize.

Notes

1   Swahili proverb from Zanzibar collected by Lord Boyd, PBM, Mss. Eng. c. 3796, f. 278.
2   Evanthis Hatzivassiliou, 'Blocking *Enosis*: Britain and the Cyprus Question, March–December 1956', *Journal of Imperial and Commonwealth History*, vol. 19, no. 2, May 1991, pp. 247–9.
3   'Memorandum by the Secretary of State for the Colonies and the Minister of State', 21 July 1954, CAB 129/69, C (54) 245.
4   *HC Deb*, 531, cols. 504¯11, cited in A.N. Porter and A.J. Stockwell, *British Imperial Policy and Decolonization* (London, Macmillan, 1989), vol. II, pp. 319–25.
5   Lord Boyd interviewed about Cyprus, PBM, Mss. Eng. c. 3433, f. 7.
6   Evanthis Hatzivassiliou, 'The Cyprus Question and the Anglo-American Special Relationship, 1954–58', in Richard J. Aldrich and Michael F. Hopkins, *Intelligence, Defence and Diplomacy: British Policy in the Post-War World* (London, Cass, 1994), p. 152.
7   'Cyprus: Memorandum by the Secretary of State for the Colonies', 6 April 1955, CAB 129/74, C (55) 92; Diana Weston Markides, 'Britain's 'New Look' Policy for Cyprus and the Makarios–Harding Talks, January 1955–March 1956', *Journal of Imperial and Commonwealth History*, 23, 3 (1995), p. 483.
8   Cabinet Minutes, 19 April 1955, CAB 128/29, CM (55) 4, min. 8.
9   'Cyprus: Memorandum by the Secretary of State for Foreign Affairs and the Secretary of State for the Colonies', 11 June 1955, CAB 129/75, CP (55) 33.
10 Cabinet Minutes, 14 June 1955, CAB 128/29, CM (55) 14, min. 2; 28 June 1955, CAB 128/29, CM (55) 18, min. 8.
11 Cabinet Minutes, 7 July 1955, CAB 128/29, CM (55) 21, min. 1.
12 Lord Boyd interviewed about Cyprus, PBM, Mss. Eng. c. 3433, f. 9.
13 Lord Boyd interviewed about Cyprus, PBM, Mss. Eng. c. 3433, f. 31.
14 Lennox-Boyd to Martin, 12 July 1955, CO 926/190.
15 Cabinet Minutes, 15 Aug. 1955, CAB 128/29, CM (55) 28, min. 9.
16 Cabinet Minutes, 5 Sept. 1955, CAB 128/29, CM (55) 30, min. 1.
17 Outward telegram to Cyprus, 17 Sept. 1955, PREM 11/1248, f. 290.
18 Charles Foley, *Legacy of Strife: Cyprus from Rebellion to Civil War* (Harmondsworth, Penguin, 1964), p. 39.
19 Markides, p. 489.
20 Cabinet Minutes, 22 Feb. 1956, CAB 128/30, CM (56) 16, min. 11.
21 Lennox-Boyd to Eden, 24 Feb. 1956, FO 371/123872, 1081/347.
22 Markides, p. 496.
23 Eden to Lennox-Boyd, 25 Feb. 1956, FO 371/123871, 1081/325.
24 Lennox-Boyd to Eden, 27 Feb. 1956, FO 371/123871, 1081/325.
25 Three main points were at issue. First, the British were prepared to offer a new constitution under which there would be an elected majority in the legislative council. Makarios wanted an undertaking, in advance of any recommendations by a constitutional commission, that there would be a specifically Greek Cypriot majority in the legislature. Secondly, the British proposed that Ministerial responsibility for all internal affairs except security would pass as quickly as possible to elected Cypriots. Defence and foreign affairs would remain the responsibility of the Governor while internal security would be transferred to Cypriot ministers when conditions made it safe to do so. Makarios objected to the Governor being allowed this discretion over the allocation of responsibility for internal security. Thirdly, the British were prepared to offer an amnesty to those convicted of offences under emergency regulations, except those involving violence or the possession of arms or explosives. Makarios demanded an amnesty for all offenders.
26 Lennox-Boyd to Eden, 28 Feb. 1956, FO 371/123871, 1081/327.
27 Cabinet Minutes, 28 Feb. 1956, 128/30, CM (56) 17.

28 Lapping, p. 399.
29 Lord Boyd interviewed about Cyprus by Sir George Sinclair and others, PBM, Mss. Eng. c. 3433, f. 58.
30 Outward telegram to Seychelles, 7 March 1956, PREM 11/1248, f. 114.
31 Inward telegram from Seychelles, 8 March 1956, PREM 11/1248, f. 113.
32 Hatzivassiliou, 'Blocking *Enosis*', p. 250.
33 Cabinet Minutes, 12 June 1956, CAB 128/30, CM (56) 41, min. 6.
34 Hatzivassiliou, 'Blocking *Enosis*', pp. 250–1.
35 Cabinet Minutes, 19 June 1955, CAB 128/30, CM (56) 44, min. 5.
36 Foley, p. 86.
37 Cabinet Minutes, 12 Dec. 1956, CAB 128/30, CM (56) 99, min. 2.
38 Lord Boyd interviewed about Cyprus, PBM, Mss. Eng. c. 3433, ff. 2–3.
39 Cabinet Minutes, 17 Dec. 1956, CAB 128/30, CM (56) 102, min. 1.
40 *HC Deb*, 562, col. 1272, 19 Dec. 1956.
41 Dennis Austin, *Malta and the End of Empire* (London, Frank Cass, 1971), p. 2.
42 Austin, pp. 29–30.
43 Lord Boyd interviewed about Malta by Sir John Martin, 31 July 1975, PBM, Mss. Eng. c. 3432, f. 117.
44 Austin, p. 33.
45 Macmillan to Eden, 2 July 1955, PREM 11/1432, f. 552.
46 Lord Boyd interviewed about Malta, PBM, Mss. Eng. c. 3432, f. 129.
47 Cabinet Minutes, 5 July 1955, CAB 128/29, CM (55) 20, min. 5.
48 Johnson to Cairncross, 17 Dec. 1955, PREM 11/1432, ff. 131–2.
49 Cabinet Minutes, 20 Dec. 1955, CAB 128/29, CM (55) 47, min. 4.
50 Philip M. Williams (ed.) *The Diary of Hugh Gaitskell 1945–56* (London, Jonathan Cape, 1983), p. 430.
51 *HC Deb*, 550, col. 1931, 26 March 1956.
52 Cabinet Minutes, 27 March 1956, CAB 128/30, CM (56) 25, min. 7.
53 Lennox-Boyd interviewed about Malta, PBM, Mss. Eng. c. 3432, f. 131.
54 Cabinet Minutes, 28 June 1956, CAB 128/30, CM (56) 46, min. 8.
55 'Malta: Outcome of Financial Talks: Memorandum by the Secretary of State for the Colonies', 13 July 1956, CAB 129/82, CP (56) 169.
56 'The Strategic Importance of Malta: Memorandum by the Minister of Defence' 5 Sept. 1956, CAB 129/83, CP (56) 205.
57 'Record of meeting held on Friday, April 26th at the Office of the Prime Minister of Malta, Valetta', appended to 'Malta: Note by Minister of Defence', 3 May 1957, CAB 129/87, C (57) 114.
58 See A.J. Stockwell, '"A widespread and long-concealed plot to overthrow government in Malaya"? The origins of the Malayan emergency', *Journal of Imperial and Commonwealth History*, vol. 21, no. 3 (1993), pp. 66–88
59 'Federation of Malaya: Constitutional Development: Memorandum by the Secretary of State for the Colonies', 20 July 1955, CAB 129/76, CP (55) 81.
60 Cabinet Minutes, 21 July 1955, CAB 128/29, CM (55) 25, min. 3.
61 Lord Boyd interviewed about Malaya and Singapore by Sir David Watherston, 30 July 1976, PBM, Mss. Eng. c. 3432, f. 175.
62 Cabinet Minutes, 25 Oct. 1955, CAB 128/29, CM (55) 37, min. 4.
63 Lord Boyd interviewed about Malaya and Singapore, PBM, Mss. Eng. c. 3432, f. 173.
64 A. J. Stockwell, *British Documents on the End of Empire, Series B, vol. 3, Malaya, Part 1: The Malayan Union Experiment 1942–48* (London, HMSO, 1995) p. lxxvii.
65 MacKintosh to Martin, 16 Jan. 1956, CO 1030/70 no. 84, cited in Stockwell, *Malaya, Part 3: The Alliance Route to Independence, 1953–57*, p. 251.
66 Stockwell, *Malaya, Part 1*, p. lxxvii.
67 Lennox-Boyd to Eden, PM (56) 3, 5 Jan. 1956, PREM 11/1302, ff. 2–3.
68 Lord Boyd interviewed about Malaya and Singapore, PBM, Mss. Eng. c. 3432,

f. 177.

69 C. M. Turnbull, *A History of Singapore, 1819-1975* (Kualar Lumpar, OUP, 1977), p. 253.

70 Lord Boyd interviewed about Malaya and Singapore by Sir David Watherston, 30 July 1976, PBM, Mss. Eng. c. 3432, f. 190.

71 'Singapore: Memorandum by the Secretary of State for the Colonies', 23 March 1956, CAB 129/80, CP (56) 85.

72 John Drysdale, *Singapore: Struggle for Survival* (Hemel Hempstead, Allen and Unwin, 1984), p. 93.

73 Annotation by Eden, 18 May 1955, on inward telegram from Singapore, 14 May 1955, PREM 11/933, f. 26.

74 Lennox-Boyd to Eden, PM (55) 25, 18 May 1955, PREM 11/933, ff. 20-1.

75 Nicoll to Lennox-Boyd, 21 May 1955, PREM 11/933, f. 14.

76 Lennox-Boyd to Eden, PM (55) 27, 24 May 1955, PREM 11/933, ff. 11-13.

77 'Singapore: Constitutional Crisis: Memorandum by the Minister of State for Colonial Affairs', 10 Aug. 1955, CAB 129/76, CP (55) 97, Appendix A.

78 Cabinet Minutes, 26 July 1955, CAB 128/29, CM (55) 26, min. 5.

79 Black to Mackintosh, 27 July 1955, CO 1030/79, ff. 53-6.

80 MacDonald to Lennox-Boyd, 27 July 1955, CO 1030/79, ff. 48-9.

81 Black to Mackenzie, 3 Aug. 1955, CO 1030/79, ff. 41-2.

82 Salisbury to Eden, 'August 1955', PREM 11/874, f. 5.

83 'Singapore: Constitutional Crisis: Memorandum by the Minister of State for Colonial Affairs', 10 August 1955, CAB 129/76, CP (55) 97.

84 Cabinet Minutes, 15 Aug. 1955, CAB 128/29, CM (55) 28, min. 3.

85 'Singapore: Memorandum by the Secretary of State for the Colonies', 23 March 1956, CAB 129/80, CP (56) 85.

86 'Singapore: Memorandum by the Secretary of State for the Colonies', 14 April 1956, CAB 129/80, CP (56) 97.

87 Cabinet minutes, 17 April 1956, CAB 128/30, CM (56) 29, min. 5.

88 'Singapore: Memorandum by the Secretary of State for the Colonies', 14 April 1956, CAB 129/80, CP (56) 97.

89 Lord Boyd interviewed on Singapore, PBM, Mss. Eng. c. 3432.

90 Drysdale, p. 134.

10

'Ghosts Must be Silent': Africa and Suez 1954–56

Who will dance to the lion's roaring?[1]

Part I: Africa

<u>Uganda</u>

One of the first problems that Lennox-Boyd faced on becoming Colonial Secretary concerned the fate of Edward Frederick Mutesa II, the Kabaka of Buganda. Buganda was the richest and most important of Uganda's four 'kingdoms'. Its ruler, the Kabaka, governed, at least in theory, with the assistance of the Lukiko – the council of chiefs – and his ministers. In practice, however, his personal authority among the Baganda was largely unchallenged. His relations with the British were governed by the Protectorate Agreement of 1900 which made British recognition of the Kabaka conditional upon his continued loyalty to the government of the Protectorate.

A new Governor was appointed to Uganda in January 1952. He was Sir Andrew Cohen, a brilliant and innovative civil servant who as Assistant Under-Secretary at the Colonial Office had vigorously promoted the democratization of African local government. In 1945 and again in 1949, opponents of the Kabaka's autocratic government had provoked civil unrest in Buganda. For Cohen, the reform of the Bugandan administration was therefore no mere constitutional experiment but an urgent practical necessity. In March 1953, he appeared to have secured the Kabaka's agreement to a series of reforms aimed at making the government more representative and accountable.[2] Three months later, however, the political climate in Uganda was radically altered by a speech delivered in London by the Colonial Secretary, Oliver Lyttelton. Lyttelton raised the possibility of Uganda forming part of an East African Federation, something which provoked consternation throughout the Protectorate. Africans not unreasonably feared the prospect of European settler domination from Kenya along the lines of Southern Rhodesian control over the Central African Federation. For the Kabaka, this incident provided both an excuse to refuse to cooperate with the Governor in the democratization process, and a means of distracting his people from the issue of internal reform. The Bugandan government demanded undertakings from Cohen that there would never be federation in East Africa, that responsibility for Buganda be transferred to the Foreign Office, and that Buganda be given 'Independence'.

Despite a reassurance from the Governor on the first point, the Kabaka refused to back down. Lyttelton was confident that he could persuade the Kabaka to see reason and suggested that he be invited over to London. Cohen was sceptical. He wanted an assurance that, should the Kabaka refuse to cooperate, he would be detained in England. He argued that if the Kabaka was allowed back after having defied the Colonial Secretary, the safety of the Protectorate would be seriously imperilled. Lyttelton refused. In his view, to spring such a trap on a hitherto loyal traditional ruler – and a former captain in the Grenadier Guards at that – was simply not cricket.[3] He was therefore forced, reluctantly, to agree that Cohen should require the Kabaka to endorse the Government's position on independence. If he refused, he would be deposed and deported. The Kabaka proved unwilling to back down and on 30 November he was unceremoniously bundled onto an aircraft for England.

Lyttelton was distressed by having to order the exile of the Kabaka, whom he liked, and he blamed the crisis on Cohen's insensitive handling of Mutesa.[4] Lennox-Boyd's views on the situation were almost identical. He was at the Ministry of Transport when the deportation took place and remembered having been 'revolted' by the whole affair.[5] Like Lyttelton, he was well aware of all the Kabaka's personal foibles but retained a genuine affection for him. Also like Lyttelton, he regarded Cohen as a Labour partisan. His first encounter with tropical Africa had been his visit to

Buganda in 1934 and he retained a strong affection for its system of traditional rule. Lennox-Boyd remembered that on becoming Colonial Secretary he told Lyttelton: 'I am going to do my best to get the Kabaka back.'[6] In practice, however, this proved a difficult task.

In August 1954, barely a week after his return to the Colonial Office, Lennox-Boyd received an indication from Cohen that he was considering allowing the Kabaka to return. Professor Hancock, who had been sent out to Buganda by the British Government to help devise the basis of a new constitutional settlement, had told Cohen privately that he favoured this option. The long-term solution to the Buganda problem which Hancock recommended was the transformation of the Kabaka into a constitutional monarch. Real authority would be exercised in his name by six Bugandan Ministers. The Baganda government would accept the principle of the Protectorate as a unitary state and would participate fully in the Protectorate government. It would, in return, be guaranteed certain spheres of influence. Cohen suggested to Lennox-Boyd that on this basis, Mutesa's return would seem to constitute less of a threat than before. Furthermore, it appeared unlikely that a new Kabaka would be elected in the near future, and the probable consequence of a long interregnum would be to increase demands for the Kabaka to be allowed back.[7] Yet in setting down these considerations, Cohen added, as a serious proviso, that his most senior advisers closest to events in Buganda all took the view that the Kabaka's return would be 'disastrous'.

Cohen's change of heart divided opinion in Whitehall and left many there deeply disillusioned with the Governor. The initial response of Sir Thomas Lloyd, Permanent Under-Secretary at the Colonial Office, was that the balance of advantage lay in the Kabaka's continued exile.[8] He was, however, prepared to be persuaded otherwise by the Governor. Lennox-Boyd, by contrast, was instinctively sympathetic towards the new proposals. When he and his and senior officials discussed the matter with Cohen in London on 16 August, Lennox-Boyd stated that, on balance, he supported the view that the Kabaka should be allowed back to Buganda, subject to some major restrictions on his former powers.[9] The following month, he informed his Cabinet colleagues that his own inclination, 'looking at the future interests of Uganda only', was to allow the Kabaka to return.[10]

Lennox-Boyd knew, however, that there were powerful arguments against this course of action. He recognized that the Kabaka's return would be a severe blow to those Bugandans who had aligned themselves with the colonial administration. He also accepted the view of many of his senior officials that Cohen's behaviour had been so erratic that his current recommendations should be treated with extreme caution.[11] Above all, he had to consider the impact of any decision on British prestige elsewhere in Africa. He was advised by Lord Swinton, the Secretary of State for Commonwealth Relations, that the Kabaka's return would have 'serious and disturbing' repercussions for Britain's ability to justify the continued exile from Bechuanaland of Seretse Khama.[12] Lennox-Boyd's Assistant Under-Secretary, William Gorell Barnes, also stressed the harm that might be done in other parts of Africa:

> the feeling which was beginning to take root in Africa, that HMG are after all capable of taking difficult decisions and sticking to them will be dissipated; and doubts will at once revive about the seriousness and robustness of our intentions in regard to e.g. Kenyatta, Central African Federation, Lagos, etc.

Similar fears were later to be expressed by leading Conservative backbenchers.[13]

The Kabaka's exile was currently being challenged in the Ugandan High Court and Cohen and Lennox-Boyd decided await the Court's ruling before reaching a decision. In the meantime, Lennox-Boyd paid a visit to East Africa. His time in Buganda during October, far from confirming his initial view, raised new doubts in his mind about Cohen's judgement. He told Churchill he had been persuaded 'against my first disposition and my natural inclination', that to allow Mutesa's return as an act of policy 'would not be in the interest of either...this country or of our position in Africa'.[14] A reversal of policy would, he feared, so compromise the position of British officials and those 'moderate' Bugandans who had supported them, that 'the whole fabric of government' would be weakened.[15]

Salvation for Lennox-Boyd came in the form of the Ugandan High Court ruling on the appeal against the Kabaka's exile which was issued on 4 November. This provided the British Government with the best of both worlds. It was able to claim a moral victory in that all the declarations and injunctions sought by the plaintiffs were refused. Under Article 20 of the Protectorate Agreement the Government would have been justified in terminating its agreement with Buganda following Mutesa's refusal to cooperate with the administration. Yet the Government had invoked not Article 20 but Article 6 which, the Court ruled, was not applicable. As such, the Government had been technically in breach of the Agreement. This gave Lennox-Boyd his excuse.

He rejected the option of appealing against the judgement and told the Cabinet that in the circumstances he saw no option but to permit Mutesa's return under certain conditions: were the Lukiko to accept the full package of constitutional reforms they should be given the option of either electing a new Kabaka or obtaining the return of Mutesa.[16]

The Cabinet approved this option, subject to the Kabaka giving an assurance that he was prepared to cooperate in the new constitutional dispensation. There followed an extraordinary reconciliation between Mutesa and Cohen at Lennox-Boyd's house in Chapel Street. Lennox-Boyd arranged for them to appear together at a reception there. Mutesa had promised not to attempt to embarrass Cohen and on his arrival he announced to his followers, 'I have brought my friend the Governor.' The assembled Bugandan chiefs fell on their faces in a gesture of reverence which no doubt caused their ultra-monarchist host immeasurable delight.[17]

The omens for Mutesa's return were initially favourable. In July 1955 Lennox-Boyd reported that the Protectorate was peaceful and the Bugandans cooperating fully.[18] He was able to obtain the Cabinet's permission to announce that the Kabaka could return within two months of the constitution coming into operation, rather than the nine months originally stipulated.

Lennox-Boyd's optimism did not, however, long survive the arrival of Mutesa in Buganda. Before he left England, Lennox-Boyd had urged him to use his influence to prevent the victimization of those who had opposed his return. Even at that time, when a promise would have cost him nothing, Mutesa proved distinctly slippery.[19] Nevertheless, Lennox-Boyd did not wish to prolong his exile and in October he returned to Buganda. Almost immediately, reports began to emerge of a witch-hunt against chiefs who had remained loyal to the British administration during the Kabaka's absence. As evidence accumulated of violent attacks on chiefs accused of disloyalty to the Kabaka, suspicions grew that Bugandan ministers were orchestrating a general campaign of intimidation.[20] Cohen persuaded Mutesa to make a public appeal for an end to violence. The statement which Mutesa actually delivered, was however, far more equivocal in its condemnation of unrest than the one he had previously agreed with the Governor. When, shortly afterwards, four of the 20 Bugandan *saza*, or county chiefs, were invited by the Buganda Appointments Board to submit their resignations, there could be little doubt that the Kabaka's new regime was systematically rooting out elements it considered to have been disloyal.

In a less than reassuring explanation of recent events which Mutesa provided for Lennox-Boyd, he dismissed the victimization of the chiefs as 'administrative adjustments well within the regulations'.[21] This provoked a furious response from the Secretary of State:

> There is no one here – including myself – ready to believe that the four senior chiefs who resigned so soon after your return were not the victims of intimidation and reprisals which should have been officially discouraged and opposed by your ministers and yourself in the interests of the good name of Buganda.[22]

Lennox-Boyd told Sir Roy Welensky, the Prime Minister of the Central African Federation, that he had been 'very disturbed and indeed angry' about the witch-hunts.[23]

Ultimately, however, he could do little to halt the victimization. The most he could hope for was that Buganda would eventually settle down and play a full role in the affairs of the Protectorate. It did not. The rise of nationalism inside Uganda and its triumph in the Gold Coast at the expense of the traditional rulers in the Ashanti and Northern territories, persuaded Mutesa that his own survival depended on an ever more aggressive assertion of Bugandan separatism. A tough response by the British might have brought the Kabaka into line. Yet Lennox-Boyd and his senior officials remained remarkably sympathetic towards Mutesa's administration, seeing it as an important counterbalance to the forces of nationalism within Uganda. When, in October 1957, Cohen's successor, Sir Frederick Crawford, suggested attempting to weaken Mutesa's power by democratizing the Bugandan government, he encountered a remarkably cool response from his masters in London. W.A.C. Mathieson, head of the East Africa desk, noted that the Kabaka and his supporters among the traditionalists were likely to be hostile 'to the extreme forms of "democratic government"'.[24] As such, they might be persuaded to recognize that it was in their interests to cooperate with a Ugandan government which was keen to control the pace of constitutional advance in the face of nationalist pressure. Jock Macpherson, the Permanent Under-Secretary, made a similar point in a minute to Lennox-Boyd:

> We are always accused of dividing and ruling and of playing off one side against the other to delay constitutional advance. This accusation is basically unjust, but if opposing elements exist and this slows up political advance, we recognize the facts of life and note that the slowing down is, in the long term, in the best interests of the Territory![25]

Lennox-Boyd himself was inclined to follow this line of reasoning, not merely out of a desire to moderate the speed of constitutional change but also because of his long-standing belief that the general sum of human happiness was unlikely to be increased by replacing traditional forms of rule with neat, prefabricated replicas of the Palace of Westminster. In the margin beside Macpherson's assertion that the peoples of the other regions of Bunyoro, Toro and Ankole wanted to retain their chiefs, he commented, 'certainly v[ery] strongly'. His general conclusion on this correspondence was, 'I w[oul]d not favour ousting the chiefs'.[26]

When he left office in October 1959, Lennox-Boyd was no closer to solving the problem that had confronted the colonial administration ever since the Kabaka's return to Buganda in 1955: how to respond to an obstructive and defiant Bugandan nationalism which refused to be integrated into the political life of the Protectorate. He had been unusually indulgent towards the Kabaka; the Kabaka for his part proved consistently unwilling to compromise. He realized that his own position within Buganda was virtually unassailable and that the British would, in time, make further concessions. It was a pattern which was to continue after Lennox-Boyd's departure from office. In June 1960, the Kabaka's government announced that Buganda would not cooperate in Uganda-wide elections and demanded the end of British protection. The previous British strategy of holding back constitutional development in Uganda so as to avoid antagonizing Buganda had clearly failed to make the kingdom any less refractory. Hence, Macleod opted for the only other practical alternative: to off-load the problem of Buganda onto an independent Ugandan government. At the constitutional conference in September 1961 he managed to cobble together an agreement between the Kabaka and the territory's nationalist parties firm enough to see the country through to full independence in October the following year.[27] The Ugandan prime minister Milton Obote did not tolerate Buganda's semi-autonomous position for very long. In May 1966 he used troops to crush the Kabaka's regime. Mutesa escaped and fled to London where he died three years later. Yet even in death, Mutesa attracted political intrigue as Lennox-Boyd was to discover.

Kenya

On 21 October 1952, less than a month after his arrival in the territory, the new Governor of Kenya, Evelyn Baring, declared a state of emergency. His predecessor, Sir Philip Mitchell, had presided over a dangerous increase in racial tension. This arose partly as a result of the deteriorating economic position of African tenants on the European farms of Kenya's 'White Highlands'. Most of

these 'squatters' were members of the Kikuyu, Kenya's largest ethnic group. The failure of the authorities to provide Africans with
adequate legitimate outlets for political expression provided further
scope for conflict. By the time of Mitchell's departure from office,
the British authorities were becoming concerned by a rising tide
of violence most of which was aimed, not at the colony's European
population, but at Kikuyu elders and other Africans accused of
collaborating with the colonial regime. They attributed this unrest
to a secret organization among the Kikuyu which became known
as 'Mau Mau'.

Within the Colonial Office it was acknowledged that the Emergency had arisen, at least in part, because of the determination of
the settlers to monopolize political and economic power. Yet in the
short to medium term, the authorities were heavily dependent upon
the support of the settler community. This gave rise to a dual policy.
On the one hand, the Colonial Office was determined to press ahead
with social, economic and political reform. On the other hand, the
Kenya government, backed by the Colonial Office, was keen to
demonstrate to the settlers that it was vigorously suppressing terrorism and that it was not placing unnecessary legal restrictions
on the activities of those charged with that task.

In terms of reform, the Colonial Office took the opportunity of the
Emergency to push through the so-called 'Lyttelton Constitution' of
1954 which allowed the Africans a small increase in political representation. Along with this came programmes like the Swynnerton
Plan which sought to promote the creation of a prosperous class of
African landowners. The British were keen encourage 'moderates'
among the Kenya settlers, like Michael Blundell, who could help to
create some semblance of 'multi-racial' support for the reforms.
Running parallel to this was a ruthless policy of repression. The
Kenya African Union (KAU), the colony's leading inter-tribal nationalist movement, was suppressed and many of its leading members
detained. In 1953, the KAU's President, Jomo Kenyatta, was convicted of managing Mau Mau, after a trial which showed every sign
of having been 'fixed' by the Kenya government.[28] There was a complete ban on African political organizations from 1953 to 1955, and
thereafter Africans (except in those in the Central Province) were
allowed to organize only at a district level. The initial round-ups of
Mau Mau suspects proved counter-productive, driving thousands of
Kikuyu into the forests and turning a sporadic campaign of violence
into a full-blown guerrilla war. In the subsequent efforts of the Kenya
government to regain the initiative, 11,503 'terrorists' were killed
(about 1,000 of them executed); 1,920 African 'loyalists', 95 Europeans and 29 Asians also lost their lives.[29]

The treatment of those suspected of complicity in Mau Mau was to be a constant source of friction between Lennox-Boyd and his critics on the Labour benches. During 'Operation Anvil' in April 1954, around 30,000 members of the Kikuyu population of Nairobi were screened and 16,500 of these were subsequently detained.[30] By the end of 1954, the Kenya government had incarcerated 81,920 Mau Mau suspects in 176 camps.[31] The vast majority of these people were never charged with a specific offence but were held under Detention Orders. On their arrival at 'reception' camps, detainees were 'screened' by teams of interrogators and each was assigned to one of three categories, the names of which reflected, perhaps unconsciously, the colony's racial hierarchy. Those whose innocence could be established by witnesses were classified 'white' and were released as rapidly as possible. Detainees suspected of some degree of complicity with Mau Mau, who were nevertheless prepared to cooperate with the authorities, were classified 'grey'. After having confessed to taking the Mau Mau oath, 'greys' were to be fed through an elaborate 'pipeline' of rehabilitation camps, leading eventually to their release. Those classified 'black' – the supposedly irreconcilable Mau Mau extremists – were to be held indefinitely in exile camps.

The need to process and classify so many people created huge logistical problems. The two most important 'reception' camps were at Mackinnon Road and Manyani, both situated on the main railway line between Mombasa and Nairobi. Manyani, the largest of the two, was built from scratch over the space of four and a half months in 1954. By October 1954, it held over 16,000 men. Baring's initial reports to Lennox-Boyd about conditions in Manyani had been positive.[32] In mid-September 1954, however, Baring's government was forced to admit publicly that there had been 400 cases of typhoid at the camp over the previous five months resulting in 41 deaths.[33] The Labour Party's colonial specialists seized on this news. Fenner Brockway described the reported outbreak as 'appalling', and a question on the matter was tabled in Parliament.[34]

Anticipating further criticism, Lennox-Boyd took the opportunity of his visit to East Africa in October to make a well-publicized inspection of Manyani. He travelled there on 16 October, with Baring and other members of the Kenya government. The medical authorities had been given plenty of advance warning of the visit and were under strict instructions to get the situation under control before the Secretary of State arrived. Baring authorized the purchase from the United States of Chloromycetin, a new and extremely expensive drug which was highly effective against typhoid fever.[35] While at Manyani, Lennox-Boyd went out of his way to impress upon reporters that he had complete confidence in the way the camp was being managed, praising the 'Herculean effort' that was being made to deal with the situation.[36] Back in London four days later, Lennox-Boyd told the Commons, in reply to a Labour question, that 63 people had died of typhoid at Manyani since the end of August and that there were 760 other proven or suspected cases. He claimed that conditions in the camp were good and that he was satisfied that the outbreak 'was not due to the camp water supply or sanitation, or to any failure to take proper health measures'.[37] Rather, he suggested, it had probably been spread by personal contact with detainees who were already infected with a mild form of the disease.

Even in terms of the information then available to him, Lennox-Boyd's Parliamentary answer was seriously incomplete.[38] Investigations by the Kenya government had pointed to the distinct possibility that exposure to urine, used in secret Mau Mau oathing practices within the camp, had been an important element in spreading the infection. Yet Lennox-Boyd's statement made no mention of this, no doubt because it carried the disturbing implication that the camp authorities were not fully in control, and that Mau Mau continued to operate freely within Manyani.

A more important question is whether the medical evidence presented to Lennox-Boyd gave an accurate picture of conditions in Manyani. Official medical findings, which were not committed to a final report, suggested that poor sanitary conditions, and the abuse of detainees, may have contributed significantly to the spread of the disease.[39] The staff employed at Manyani and the other camps had to be recruited rapidly and were often of a low calibre. Training was poor, and corruption and brutality against detainees, on the part of both Europeans and African loyalists on the screening teams, appear to have been widespread.[40] Giving typhoid fever as the official cause of death seems to have been a fairly common method by which camp authorities sought to disguise the murder of detainees.[41] Josiah Mwangi Kariuki witnessed such a cover-up at Manyani early in 1955 after six detainees died following a punitive attack by warders.[42] There was certainly to be a disturbing echo of Manyani five years later when, following the beating to death by guards of 11 inmates at the Hola detention camp, the Kenya government issued a statement implying that the loss of life had been due to the men drinking poisoned water.

His handling of the deaths at Manyani suggests that Lennox-Boyd's main priority was to maintain the momentum of the rehabilitation process. Accusations of neglect or brutality on the part of the Kenya government had to be rebuffed quickly before they could endanger that key objective. A lack of alternative sources of information meant that Labour MPs had little choice but to accept the explanation Lennox-Boyd had given in the Commons. As time passed, and as reports of abuses perpetrated against detainees became more widespread, Lennox-Boyd's support for the actions of Baring's administration was questioned ever more aggressively by some Labour members.

The degree to which agents of government should be accountable for abuses of power was a question which took up a great deal of the Colonial Office's time during Lennox-Boyd's first months as Secretary of State. One event that brought matters to a head was the arrival in Kenya of a new Commissioner of Police, Sir Arthur Young. Young was no stranger to colonial affairs. He had previously reported on police reorganization in the Gold Coast and had played an outstandingly important role in the Malayan counter-insurgency campaign as commissioner of police there from 1952–53. Young's experience in Malaya had convinced him that success against a guerrilla army could only be achieved if the authorities won the confidence of the people from whom the guerrillas drew their support; and that the establishment of a fair, impartial police service was an important prerequisite for this. As such, he was deeply disturbed by the apparently widespread use of violence against Mau Mau suspects by members of the Home Guard and the tribal police. Yet far from aiding the police in their investigations of such abuses, he found that, all too often, administrative officers were actually implicated in this violence. He was therefore determined to implement one of the key recommendations of a recent Police Commission report, that police officers in Kenya should be given the status of constable in common law, allowing them, in effect, to act independently of administrative officers in the conduct of criminal investigations.

This project encountered fierce opposition from Baring and a majority of his ministers who feared that the capacity of local Kikuyu chiefs and headmen to maintain order might be damaged if the police acted against them without reference to local administrative officers.[43] Baring maintained, 'if we have a weak Police force we have a strong Administrative service; and I am convinced that we cannot and should not weaken the position of our Administrative officers'.[44] His view prevailed, and in the middle of December, the Kenya Government publicly rejected the idea of making each police officer a constable in common law, declaring that ultimate responsibility should rest with the Provincial and District

Commissioners.[45] 'Constable status' was extended only to the level of inspectors. Young resigned.

Young's letter of resignation was a potentially explosive document. It cited, among other things, the reliance of Baring's administration on the rule of fear rather than the rule of law. Young referred to instances of brutality against detainees in screening camps and Home Guard posts. Having received no response from Baring, Young followed this letter up two weeks later by sending him a report, compiled by his Assistant Commissioner in charge of the CID, Duncan Macpherson, listing a sickening catalogue of torture, rape and murder perpetrated by members of the Home Guard against Mau Mau suspects. In some of these cases, police investigations appeared to have been hampered by administrative officers.[46] The most serious case mentioned by Macpherson concerned a flagrant attempt by the Provincial Commissioner, C.M. Johnston, to prevent the CID from prosecuting an African chief accused of murdering a prisoner. Baring himself also appears to have played a part in this particular cover up.[47]

When, after Young's return to London in January 1955, he visited the Secretary of State to agree a Parliamentary statement about his resignation, he was left in no doubt that he no longer enjoyed Lennox-Boyd's confidence. Lennox-Boyd knew that, were he to refer to Young's letter of resignation in the Commons, he would be forced by Parliamentary protocol to disclose the document.[48] He therefore made no mention of it either in his statement or on subsequent occasions when he was challenged to do so by Labour MPs.

It is not difficult to understand why Lennox-Boyd acted as he did in this matter. To have supported Young would have been to display a marked lack of confidence in Baring, a friend since Lennox-Boyd's time at Oxford. Furthermore, there were legitimate grounds for fearing that the reforms championed by Young would have created administrative confusion at a time when the Kenya government appeared to be fighting for its life. The publication of Young's allegations would, of course, have unleashed a storm of domestic and international condemnation. Nevertheless, Young's defeat set an extremely dangerous precedent. Aside from the detailed proposals under debate, the question of police reform tended to divide opinion between those who regarded the maintenance of the rule of law as a priority, and those who felt that, under the conditions of the Emergency, a strict adherence to the law was sometimes unrealistic and unhelpful. If the former view was idealistic, the victory of the latter view contributed to creating the climate in which agents of the government could be fairly

confident that the use of illegal force against those implicated in
Mau Mau would go unnoticed and unpunished.

The clash with Young was swiftly followed by another development which served to undermine the principle of the impartial
application of the rule of law. On 13 January 1955, Lennox-Boyd
presented the Cabinet with proposals for an amnesty for Mau Mau
fighters as part of a strategy to encourage a general surrender.[49]
In what was clearly an effort to ease settler suspicions, the Kenyan
War Council recommended that the amnesty should be extended
to members of the Kikuyu guard and other supporters of the government for misdemeanours committed in the course of
counter-insurgency operations. Lennox-Boyd told the Cabinet that
he agreed with this recommendation. During this same Cabinet
meeting, the question of the removal of the Director of military
operations, General Sir George Erskine, was also raised for the
first time. Antony Head, the Secretary of State for War, later explained that although Erskine had done a good job in Kenya there
had been 'quite a lot of friction with the civil authorities'. In the
circumstances he thought there was 'nothing to lose and possibly something to be gained' by Erskine's departure.[50] Erskine had
made no attempt to disguise his contempt for the settlers, whom
he once, vividly described as 'middle class sluts'.[51] He had also
acted firmly against the indiscriminate and illegal killing of suspects by British and Kenyans troops. It is difficult not to see his
replacement as yet another important concession to settler opinion in Kenya.

The Cabinet initially raised some objections to the idea of ex-
tending the amnesty to loyalist troops and particular concern was
expressed about likely reactions in England to such a move. In the
end, however, Ministers accepted Lennox-Boyd's view that the surrender terms 'would be resented in Kenya' unless government personnel were also exempted from prosecution.[52] One problem that
remained was whether the legal actions against loyalists that had
already been initiated could be halted. The major stumbling block,
as Lennox-Boyd explained to his Cabinet colleagues, was the refusal of John Whyatt, the Kenya Attorney General, to enter a plea
of *nolle prosequi* in such cases. In the circumstances, the Cabinet
decided that they could not intervene to terminate existing prosecutions of loyalists. What Lennox-Boyd did not tell Ministers at
this meeting was that arrangements had already been set in hand
for the removal of Whyatt from Kenya. The Colonial Office admitted that a consideration behind this action was that Whyatt's 'relationship with some of the unofficial Ministers has not always been
easy'.[53]

Under great pressure from Baring, Lennox-Boyd allowed there to develop in Kenya a situation in which the rights of those suspected of involvement in Mau Mau were subordinated to the objective of maintaining the support of the settlers and loyalist Kikuyu. It was a state of affairs which Lennox-Boyd would have defended. He regarded the defeat of Mau Mau as being in the long-term interests of all the people of Africa. Yet many of Lennox-Boyd's fellow MPs, including some on the Government benches, were to prove far less sanguine about assuming moral responsibility for British actions in Kenya; and a vocal section of the anti-colonial Left made increasing efforts to bring some of these actions to public attention. In the longer term this was to cause Lennox-Boyd immense problems.

The Gold Coast

The Gold Coast had already travelled a great distance on the path to independence by the time Lennox-Boyd became Secretary of State in 1954. The principal concern of this study is not to describe the process in detail but to chart Lennox-Boyd's attitude towards it and consider what influence he had upon its final stages. A short answer might be that his attitude was deeply pessimistic but that this had remarkably little impact upon the political progress of the Gold Coast. If he viewed the achievement of independence by Ghana with apprehension, subsequent events did nothing to persuade him that his doubts had been misplaced. In retrospect he liked to portray himself as an unhappy and largely powerless onlooker, a 'prisoner of the past'.[54] There is plenty of evidence to suggest that this was not a serious misrepresentation.

At the beginning of 1951, a new constitution had come into force which greatly increased African representation in the colony's legislature and produced a majority of African ministers in its executive council. Elections in February were decisively won by the territory's radical nationalist movement, the Convention People's Party (CPP). Its leader, Kwame Nkrumah, was in prison at the time of the election, having been arrested in the January of the previous year following the CPP's attempt to orchestrate a general strike. In a move which was both bizarre and entirely typical of Britain's dealings with nationalist politicians, Nkrumah was released from jail on 12 February and appointed 'leader of government business', prime minister in all but name. A year later, Nkrumah obtained the title of 'prime minister' as part of a further set of concessions reluctantly approved by Oliver Lyttelton.[55]

Lennox-Boyd was clearly unhappy at the pace of political development in the Gold Coast. When in November 1951 the Colonial Office discussed reforms to the system of local government in the Gold Coast, Lennox-Boyd, as Minister of State, commented,

> No doubt in common with others who have seen this file, I wish that changes in *local* government had preceded and not followed virtual self-government at the centre.[56]

By the time Lennox-Boyd became Colonial Secretary in July 1954, the Gold Coast's swift transition to independence under a CPP government seemed assured. Following elections in June, when the CPP won 72 out of the 104 seats in the Assembly, the Gold Coast achieved full internal self-government. There were, however, already signs that Lennox-Boyd's reservations about the speed of constitutional reform might have some justification.

The Governor of the Gold Coast presided over a series of administratively distinct territories. To the south was the Gold Coast colony itself where the nationalists of the CPP were at their strongest. To the north of this was the separate protectorate of Ashanti and further north still there was the Northern Territories protectorate. To the east, also under the control of the Gold Coast's Governor, was the British Trusteeship territory of Togoland.

By the time of the 1954 elections, it was clear that the Governor's broad acceptance of the political agenda of the southern nationalists was leading to resentment elsewhere. An opposition movement, the Northern People's Party, founded in April, won 12 of the 17 seats it contested in the Northern Territories. In September 1954, another opposition movement was founded – the National Liberation Movement (NLM) – this time based largely in Ashanti. Virtually without representation in the Assembly and with no realistic chance of defeating the CPP in future national elections, the NLM concentrated on obstructing progress towards full independence and on campaigning for a federal constitution under which there would be a substantial devolution of powers to regional assemblies. It drew support outside the Gold Coast, largely from politicians and businessmen who opposed the liquidation of colonial rule in the Gold Coast. Even on the Conservative back benches, the NLM proved unable to gather any very significant following. Yet although they could not deflect the British Government from its chosen path they could encourage violence and instability within their own strongholds.

Opposition to the CPP had both an economic and a political aspect. Farmers in Ashanti were unhappy that the CPP government was acting to keep the price they received for their cocoa crop artificially low at a time when world prices were rising. On

the political side, 'traditional' rulers resented attempts by Southern politicians to extend their control over the Ashanti region.[57]
Lennox-Boyd was particularly sensitive to the concerns of the
peoples of Ashanti and the Northern Territories. From the time
of the disputes over the Government of India Bill, Lennox-Boyd
had tended to sympathize more with 'traditional' rulers than with
Westernized nationalist leaders. He also felt an instinctive sense
of loyalty towards those regions which had supplied dispropor-
tionately large numbers of troops for the colonial armies. During
the 1930s, this had led him to favour the men of the Punjab over
the 'clerks of Bengal'. In the case of the Gold Coast in the 1950s
it made him sympathetic towards Ashanti and the Northern Territories.[58] The Ashantehene shrewdly chose to emphasize this element in his own past in an encounter with the Colonial
Secretary. He told a delighted Lennox-Boyd that modern politics
were very difficult and that his happiest memories were of his days
as a junior NCO in the West African Rifles, serving drinks to the
English officers.

Personally then, Lennox-Boyd was sympathetic towards the
NLM's federalist approach. The advice he received from his officials was, however, dismissive of these proposals. He himself accepted that political developments had already gone too far along
the lines of unitary government to make a federalist solution a
viable option; but he did so with regret.[59] He liked Nkrumah and
found him immensely charming. Yet he shared the fears of the
NLM and the Northern People's Party that the nationalist politicians of the south would act with high-handed disregard for 'traditional' forms of government. He was particularly infuriated when
in December 1955, Nkrumah's government enacted a bill designed
to weaken the authority of the Asanteman Council over which the
NLM exerted a strong influence.[60] Lennox-Boyd described the timing of the bill as 'criminally inept' and raised questions about what
he regarded as the excessively close relations between the Governor and the CPP.

Sir Charles Arden-Clarke, the Governor of the Gold Coast since
1949, had developed a strong rapport with Nkrumah. As the only
party in the Gold Coast capable of delivering the consent and cooperation of the great mass of the population, it is hardly surprising that the Governor should have made every effort to work with
the CPP. Lennox-Boyd was quite aware of this and made no serious attempt to interfere in the running of the territory. In common
with some others in London, however, he felt that Arden-Clarke's
relations with Nkrumah had become rather *too* friendly, and that,
together, the two wished to be able to dictate constitutional

development in the Gold Coast with the minimum interference by
the Colonial Office. He later recalled,

> I think the Governor had worked out what he thought was the only
> possible tolerable constitution, and he was rather worried that some-
> one like myself, with a natural preference or interest in minorities,
> perhaps a sort of instinctive interest in the armed forces and that sort
> of thing, should come to disturb the pattern he had worked out.[61]

Lennox-Boyd understood Arden-Clarke's fears that his authority
within the colony might be undermined by the arrival of the Secretary of State. Yet Lennox-Boyd's instinctive reaction when serious problems arose in a particular territory was to get on a plane
and make a personal visit to the trouble-spot. In July 1955, at a
time when NLM agitation was proving to be particularly disruptive,
Lennox-Boyd told a meeting of senior figures in the Colonial Office of 'the importance he attached to personal contact and his
regret that the Governor advised against a Ministerial visit to the
Gold Coast'.[62]

In September 1955, in an attempt to bridge the gap between the
NLM and the CPP, Lennox-Boyd sent Sir Frederick Bourne, a former
Governor of East Bengal, to investigate the situation in the Gold
Coast and make constitutional recommendations. The NLM, how-
ever, refused to meet Bourne and rejected his proposal for the establishment of regional assemblies on the grounds that the central
government would retain too much power. With the situation in
Ashanti showing no signs of improvement, Lennox-Boyd accepted
Arden-Clarke's proposal that the CPP should be required to prove
its electoral mandate in a further general election. Nkrumah was
unhappy about this, claiming it would give the impression that the
NLM's programme of disruption had succeeded in wresting this
concession from the government in Accra. He agreed, however, on
condition that Lennox-Boyd should state publicly that the elections
were taking place at the insistence of the British Government and
not as the result of NLM pressure.

On 11 May 1956, Lennox-Boyd told Parliament that if the CPP
won the forthcoming election and a 'reasonable majority' was obtained in the new legislative assembly for a motion calling for independence within the Commonwealth, then the British
Government would set a date for the transfer of sovereignty. In the
elections of July 1956, the CPP won a decisive majority while the
NLM proved unable to attract any significant support outside
Ashanti. Far from accepting defeat, however, the NLM increased its
policy of disruption. By the end of the year, with the situation deteriorating and the date for independence fast approaching,
Arden-Clarke's resistance to Ministerial visits broke and he

prevailed on the Secretary of State to stop off in the Gold Coast on his return from Central Africa.

Lennox-Boyd's visit to the Gold Coast in January 1957 was a political success largely, it seems, because the leaders of the NLM had by this stage finally recognized that independence was inevitable, and that their best hope lay in reaching some accommodation with the CPP government.[63] A few days after Ghana achieved her independence, Arden-Clarke wrote to Lennox-Boyd to compliment him on his handling of local politicians and chiefs.[64] For Lennox-Boyd himself, however, this brief tour of the Gold Coast was the source of deeply unhappy memories. He later recalled his sense of sadness and humiliation at having to tell the Paramount Chiefs of the Northern Territories that the Queen's protection over them would be withdrawn within a matter of weeks.[65] He also found it both strange and disconcerting that Arden-Clarke did not feel able to join him on a visit to Ashanti, so closely was the Governor now associated with the unpopular government in Accra.

On 6 March 1957, the day Ghana achieved her independence, Lennox-Boyd attended a service in St. Martin-in-the-Fields to mark the event. As he left the church at the end of the service he received warm and entirely unwelcome congratulations from Geoffrey Fisher, the Archbishop of Canterbury. 'God will thank you for all you have done,' Fisher confidently predicted. 'It is my suspicion,' Lennox-Boyd replied, 'that the Almighty will take a little longer to make up his mind than you apparently have done.'

Part II: Suez

Towards the end of January 1957, as he sailed for New Zealand, Anthony Eden contemplated the events of the previous months which had culminated in the disastrous invasion of Egypt and in his own resignation. He conveyed his thoughts in a handwritten letter to Lennox-Boyd, one of his most loyal and enthusiastic supporters throughout the whole affair. Eden was unrepentant. 'I am sure,' he claimed, ' – more than I have ever been in my life – that we have only to uphold the decision we took in Egypt to be proved a hundred times right.'[66] He added that it was 'the least that is due to the Israelis' that Britain should defend their right to free passage through the Gulf of Akaba; but he did not want to be quoted to this effect. 'Ghosts,' he lamented, 'must be silent.'

The regime of Gamal Abdel Nasser was frequently cited in the months before the Suez crisis as a leading sponsor of anti-British unrest in parts of Africa and the Middle East. British Ministers were particularly concerned by the threat of Egyptian subversion in the

strategically important areas of Aden and the Horn of Africa. In
March 1956, Lennox-Boyd warned his Cabinet colleagues of the
possibility that the British Protectorate of Somaliland might fall
under Egyptian influence on attaining its independence and that
'if Egyptian influence also extended to the Sudan, the security of
all British territories in East Africa would be threatened'.[67] In June,
he told Eden that anti-British sentiment in the Aden colony was
'due mainly to the growth of the spirit of Arab nationalism fomented
by broadcasts from Cairo'.[68] A few weeks before, Lord Lloyd had
noted the dismay of the Protectorate rulers that Britain was not
doing more to combat Egyptian propaganda.[69] Lennox-Boyd thus
had good reasons to wish to see the Egyptian leader overthrown;
and when, in July 1956, Nasser announced the nationalization of
the Suez Canal, he was very much to the fore in urging decisive
action.

The news that Nasser had decided to nationalize the property
of the Suez Canal Company reached London on the evening of 26
July, just as Lennox-Boyd was preparing to take a much-needed
holiday after months of intense pressure. Not only was Lennox-Boyd
not included in the original Cabinet committee on Egypt which
Eden convened to deal with the crisis, but the Prime Minister saw
no reason for him to postpone his vacation. Indeed, Eden allowed
him to extend it by four days commenting, 'far more restful for
you'.[70]

As events began to unfold, Lennox-Boyd became uneasy at
Eden's willingness to spare him direct involvement in the Suez
affair. On 29 July, he told Eden that 'the events of the last few days
will, I imagine, alter everyone's plans' and that he himself had
abandoned the idea of taking an extra few days holiday.[71] During
the next couple of days, the deliberations of the Egypt Committee
began to impinge directly on Lennox-Boyd's departmental responsibilities. On 30 July, unbeknownst to the rest of the Cabinet, the
explicit aim of bringing down Nasser was raised in the Committee
and a preliminary timetable for action discussed.[72] The following
morning, the Committee, meeting with the Chiefs of Staff, decided
to jam Egyptian broadcasts to Cyprus and send an artillery regiment to the island.[73] This was apparently the final straw. William
Clark, Eden's press officer, recorded in his diary that 'those Cabinet members outside the "Egypt Committee" are not kept in the
least informed so that Alan Lennox-Boyd...has revolted and asked
if he could please have some information because it affects his
colonies'.[74]

Lennox-Boyd was not brought into the Egypt Committee as a
full member at this stage. He does, however, appear to have been

taken into the Committee's confidence sufficiently to allay his mis-
givings. Lennox-Boyd was, in any case, still committed to leaving
England for his holiday in the Mediterranean. He did so on 4 August, telling Eden that he was 'very guilty about going away at such
a moment'.[75] Lennox-Boyd promised, however, that he would 'rush
back home at the least sign that I am needed' adding that Eden's
handling of the affair had been 'superb'.

His absence from London coincided with an important phase in
the preparation of military action. On 10 August, the Egypt Committee approved a plan drawn up by the Chiefs of Staff, codename
'Musketeer'. This envisaged a bombing campaign to knock out the
Egyptian air force followed by a large-scale seaborne assault on
Alexandria.[76] British forces would then advance, perhaps through
Cairo, to the Suez Canal itself. The principal objective of the operation was clearly to topple Nasser, freeing the Canal in the process. The Colonial Office was inevitably going to be directly affected
by these plans. The bulk of the invasion force would sail from Malta.
Some military operations would also be conducted out of Cyprus
although this had neither the airfield nor the harbour facilities
necessary to launch the main thrust of the attack.[77] The political
situation in both these islands was unstable and it seemed likely
that unrest in Cyprus would be exacerbated were it to be the base
for an assault upon Nasser.

On 12 August Eden instructed Norman Brook to arrange for
Lennox-Boyd's recall. The Colonial Office dispatched a radio telegram 'Pl[ease] return immediately with minimum publicity'.[78] On
receiving these instructions Lennox-Boyd, whose yacht was then
in harbour at Bastia, abandoned his holiday and travelled back
through France under a false name. On his arrival in London he
was handed a letter from Eden. The Prime Minister apologized for
having disrupted his plans, but emphasized that the Egyptian situation was likely to have a direct impact on several colonies. There
were already problems with radio broadcasts in Malta.[79] Eden explained that he had been concerned by the fact that the Colonial
Office was temporarily without a Permanent Under-Secretary, John
Macpherson not yet having taken up his post. He had not realized
that the Minister of State, John Hare would be out of the country
at the same time as Lennox-Boyd and felt that at least one of them
should be on hand.

Having been summoned back to London in such haste,
Lennox-Boyd was surprised and annoyed to find that his services
were not, apparently required. Twenty-four hours after his return
to London, there had still been no Cabinet meeting and he had
received no information. He rang Norman Brook and demanded to

know why he had been told nothing. If the situation was not sufficiently important for him to be consulted then why, he asked, had
he been called back from the Mediterranean.[80] Eden swiftly responded by asking Lennox-Boyd to join the Egypt Committee.

In terms of the role he played in the preparation of the military
operation, Lennox-Boyd was not an important member of the Committee. His principal role was to canvas opinion within the colonial territories, particularly among Moslem communities. He
remembered there being very little opposition from this quarter to
the use of force against Egypt. The Aga Khan was strongly in favour
and none of the Islamic rulers of Northern Nigeria raised objections.
In more general terms, his significance within the Egypt committee was as a voice urging the adoption of a tough line against
Nasser.

One of the first matters in which Lennox-Boyd became involved
on his return to London was a dispute with the BBC. On 15 August, the Corporation broadcast an attack on the Government by
Major Salah Salem, one of the Nasser regime's most ebullient
spokesmen. They defended their broadcast in the name of balanced
reporting. This infuriated Lennox-Boyd, who had little time for the
Corporation's claims to journalistic impartiality. He told the Prime
Minister,

> ...I think it is an outrage that a body widely believed to be in part at
> least associated with the British Government should broadcast at such
> a moment a speech by a notorious enemy.[81]

His report to Eden about the matter provoked, according to William Clark, a determination in Downing Street to teach the BBC a
lesson.[82] As a result, Sir Ian Jacob, the Director General of the BBC,
was summoned to see the Prime Minister. Clark noted that Eden
'was being heated up' by Lennox-Boyd and Macmillan in advance
of the meeting and he did his best to calm matters somewhat.[83]

On 24 August, Lennox-Boyd sent Eden a remarkably 'hawkish'
letter. 'I remain convinced,' he asserted 'that if Nasser wins, or even
appears to win, we might as well as a government (and indeed as
a country) go out of business.'[84] He was very unhappy at the course
of the Egypt committee meeting that morning, fearing that some
of his colleagues might be having 'second thoughts as to a tough
policy'. In particular, he was 'horrified' by the reservations expressed
by the Minister of Defence, Walter Monckton. Above all, he had no
doubts about the critical importance to Britain of emerging from
the crisis with her prestige clearly restored and reinforced:

> You call international control of the Canal a matter of life and death
> for us. This though true of Suez itself is still more true if this outrage

is, as we believe, a step in a careful plan to drive us out of the Eastern Mediterranean and the Middle East.

Lennox-Boyd suggested that the Cabinet's resolve might be strengthened if they were told more about the reasons for Eden's overriding concern to defeat Nasser. He promised to provide any information from the colonial angle which might help.

He was also keen to rally public support by stressing the threat which Nasser's seizure of the Canal posed to the British Empire. The nature of this threat was one of the themes of a party political broadcast he made over the Home Service of the BBC on Sunday 22 September. He portrayed the nationalization of the Canal both as an attack upon the economic sinews of Empire and as a test of Britain's will to rule.[85] He told his listeners,

> There are some people who believe – and many more who say – that we have lost our resolution. Great Empires in the past, they say, and, they add, it might be true of our Commonwealth, have always decayed from within when beset by weariness and the desire to give way in the struggle. If an individual or a people, it has been said, ceases to believe in itself, its aims and ideals, others with firmer aims and beliefs will climb into the saddle.

The military preparations in the Mediterranean occasionally impinged upon Lennox-Boyd's Ministerial responsibilities in unexpected ways. At the beginning of September, Eden expressed concern about plans to move the 24th Infantry Brigade from Gibraltar to Malta in order to replace troops due to be transferred to Cyprus as anti-aircraft artillery. He feared that the Spanish might take advantage of this reduction of British defences in Gibraltar to launch an attack. 'I do not suppose,' he told Monckton, 'that the Spanish would take action but after two hundred years we should not tempt them to do so.'[86] The Colonial Office was, however, more sanguine about the threatened withdrawal of troops from Gibraltar. Lennox-Boyd replied that although he did not like the situation he was ready to accept it. The Governor of Gibraltar had been consulted and did not appear unduly perturbed given that reinforcement could be flown from Britain in about five hours.[87]

Unlike some of his Cabinet colleagues, Lennox-Boyd almost certainly knew in advance of plans for British and French collusion with the Israelis. On 21 October, Selwyn Lloyd met Eden at Chequers and was told that the arrival of the Israelis in France was imminent and that he should travel there incognito. The following day, Lloyd met with the French and Israelis at Sèvres, outside Paris. Two days later, two British officials went to France and put their names to a document which confirmed the conclusions of the

Sèvres meeting: that the Israelis would attack Egypt on 29 October and would hope to reach the Canal zone the following day. The British and French Governments would respond to the Israeli attack by appealing to the two sides to withdraw 15 kilometres from the Canal zone. If, as was expected, this call was rejected, an Anglo-French force would attack Egypt on 31 October.[88] On 22 October, the Cabinet Secretary informed Eden, 'I have told the Colonial Secretary what passed at Chequers yesterday. He is in full agreement with what is proposed.'[89]

On 29 October, as had been agreed, the Israelis invaded Egypt. At dawn on 5 November, the Anglo-French force landed at Port Said. Lennox-Boyd's initial reaction was one of elation. When, later that day, it was reported in the Commons that the Egyptian forces in Port Said were discussing surrender terms, Conservative members greeted the news with a noisy standing ovation. One dissident Tory MP, J.J. Astor, remained seated. He was reportedly rounded on by Lennox-Boyd who shouted at him to stand up.[90] The day after these triumphant scenes in the Commons, Lennox-Boyd told Eden, 'I can't find words to express my admiration for your courage, fortitude and skill.'[91] Yet by midnight on the same day the Cabinet had halted the operation. Ministers had been impressed by warnings from the Chancellor of the Exchequer, Harold Macmillan, that the Americans were selling sterling at such a rate that the pound might have to be devalued. They also wished to avoid a hostile resolution in the UN Assembly and were worried about the possibility of a Soviet invasion of Syria.[92]

As the British sought to salvage what dignity they could from the operation, Eden's health broke and he was advised by his doctor to take a holiday in order to recuperate. Eden's wife, Clarissa, appears to have been responsible for suggesting 'Goldeneye', the Jamaican house of the novelist Ian Fleming, as a suitable retreat. She was one of the oldest friends of Fleming's wife, Ann, and godmother to the Flemings' son.[93] Yet in the atmosphere of intense secrecy surrounding the Prime Minister's departure from London, Clarissa had no opportunity to discuss with Ann whether 'Goldeneye' was a suitable place of refuge. Instead, the approach to the Flemings was made by Lennox-Boyd. He asked Ian Fleming whether he might borrow the house himself for a holiday. Fleming readily agreed and suggested that Ann could contact Lennox-Boyd's wife to make the necessary arrangements. 'Oh, you mustn't tell Patsy,' insisted Lennox-Boyd. 'I quite understand, old boy,' replied Fleming, jumping to entirely the wrong conclusion.

Eden only returned to London in mid-December. In the meantime, his Government's attempts to save face internationally following the halting of the attack proved a dismal failure. On 24 November, the UN Assembly passed a vote of censure against Britain and France. Selwyn Lloyd responded by promising the withdrawal of forces within four weeks. This did not go far enough to restore international confidence and rescue the pound. At a Cabinet meeting on 29 November, at which Macmillan impressed on his colleagues the full extent of Britain's financial crisis, the decision was made to undertake a full and unconditional withdrawal of forces from Egypt. This appears to have been the final straw for Lennox-Boyd who had invested so much emotional and political capital into the operation. Not for the first time in his career – and certainly not for the last – he decided to resign. He was, however, persuaded that this would be a mistake. His old friend, Lord Selkirk, Chancellor of the Duchy of Lancaster, told him that his popularity was such that his resignation would bring down the Government.[94] Selkirk also argued that the main object now was to put the Government in a strong enough position to be able to influence events both in Syria and elsewhere. Lennox-Boyd accepted the logic of this plea. In retrospect, however, he wished he gone ahead with his resignation.[95]

Another factor behind Lennox-Boyd's decision to remain in office was almost certainly the extent to which he felt himself to be personally embroiled in the affairs of the colonies. One of the most pressing issues he faced was the future of the Central African Federation. He had already postponed a visit to the Federation and was now determined that the trip should take place. At the end of December 1956, he boarded a plane for Africa with his wife Patricia and son Simon, and flew far away from the political crisis in London.

Notes
1   Swahili proverb from Zanzibar collected by Lennox-Boyd, Mss. Eng. c. 3796, f. 277.
2   S. R. Karugire, *A Political History of Uganda* (Nairobi, Heinemann, 1980), p. 151.
3   Lord Chandos, *The Memoirs of Lord Chandos* (London, Bodley Head, 1962), pp. 418–9.
4   Lord Chandos interviewed by Max Beloff, Rhodes House, Oxford, Mss. Brit. Emp. s. 525, pp. 24, 49.
5   Lord Boyd interviewed about East Africa by Alison Smith, 13 Dec. 1974, PBM, Mss. Eng. c. 3433, f. 270.
6   Lord Boyd interviewed about East Africa, PBM, Mss. Eng. c. 3433, f. 270.
7   Cohen to Lennox-Boyd, 8 Aug. 1954, CO 822/751.
8   Comments upon Sir Andrew Cohen's letter of 8 August 1954 by Sir Thomas Lloyd, 13 Aug. 1954, CO 822/751.
9   Discussion on the question of Mutesa's return, 16 Aug. 1954, CO 822/751.
10 'The Kabaka of Buganda: Memorandum by the Secretary of State for the Colonies', 9 Sept. 1954, CAB 129/70, C (54) 287.
11 Lennox-Boyd to Hopkinson, 18 Aug. 1954, CO 822/751.

12 Swinton to Lennox-Boyd, 17 Sept. 1954, CO 822/751.
13 Minutes of the Commonwealth Affairs Committee, 26 Oct. 1954, CCO 507/1/1.
14 Lennox-Boyd to Churchill, 13 Oct. 1954, PREM 11/1070, f. 132.
15 'Uganda Protectorate: the Kabaka of Buganda: Memorandum by the Secretary of State for the Colonies', 20 Oct. 1954, CAB 129/71, C (54) 317.
16 'Uganda Protectorate: Memorandum by the Secretary of State for the Colonies', 9 Nov. 1954, CAB 129/71, C (54) 336.
17 Lord Boyd interviewed about East Africa, PBM, Mss. Eng. c. 3433, p. 73.
18 Cabinet Conclusions, 14 July 1955, CAB 128/29, CM (55) 23, min. 11.
19 Lennox-Boyd to Welensky, 30 Jan. 1956, WP 592/8, f. 19.
20 Inward Telegram from Cohen, 20 Nov. 1955, CO 822/815.
21 Mutesa to Lennox-Boyd, 15 Dec. 1955, CO 822/815.
22 Lennox-Boyd to Mutesa, 16 Jan. 1956, CO 822/815.
23 Lennox-Boyd to Welensky, 30 Jan. 1956, WP 592/8, f. 21.
24 Mathieson to Crawford, 30 Jan. 1958, CO 822/1439.
25 Macpherson to Lennox-Boyd, 27 Jan. 1958, CO 822/1439.
26 Internal minute by Lennox-Boyd, 29 Jan. 1958, CO 822/1439.
27 John Darwin, *Britain and Decolonisation* (London, Macmillan, 1988), p. 259.
28 Baring as much as admitted to the then Colonial Secretary, Oliver Lyttelton, that witnesses at Kenyatta's trial had been bribed; and the judge who presided over the trial received a mysterious ex gratia payment of £20,000 on Baring's instructions from an emergency fund (Charles Douglas-Home, *Evelyn Baring* (London, Collins, 1978) pp. 246–8).
29 Bruce Berman, *Control and Crisis in Colonial Kenya: The Dialectic of Domination* (London, James Currey, 1990), p. 352.
30 Randall W. Heather, 'Intelligence and Counter-Insurgency in Kenya, 1952–56', *Intelligence and National Security*, vol. 5, no. 3, 1990, p. 71.
31 Robert B. Edgerton in *Mau Mau: An African Crucible* (London, I.B. Taurus & Co. Ltd., 1990), p. 267. Edgerton suggests that the total number of people detained during the course of the Emergency may be as high as 90,000.
32 Baring to Lennox-Boyd, 31 August 1954, CO 822/799, f. 140.
33 *Daily Telegraph*, 17 Sept. 1954.
34 Brockway to Lennox-Boyd, 28 Sept. 1954, CO 822/801.
35 W.L. Barton, 'Which Colony?', *The Overseas Pensioner*, no. 70, Autumn 1995, p. 53.
36 Press Office handout, Nairobi, 16 Oct. 1954, CO 822/801.
37 *HC Deb*, 531, col. 1192, 20 Oct. 1954.
38 Stott to Director of Medical Services, 14 Sept. 1954; Stott to Director of Medical Services, 20 Sept. 1954; Stott to Director of Medical Services, 12 Oct. 1954, CO 822/801.
39 I am grateful to Terence Gavaghan for drawing my attention to the critical part played by medical and health officers, on the urgent intervention of the Governor, in controlling and remedying the epidemic conditions at Manyani.
40 Berman, p. 360. For a personal account of detention in Manyani, see Josiah Mwangi Kariuki, *'Mau Mau' Detainee* (Oxford, Oxford University Press, 1963), pp. 63–78.
41 Edgerton, p. 186.
42 Kariuki, pp. 68–9.
43 Baring to Gorell Barnes, 4 Nov. 1954, CO 1037/2.
44 Baring to Gorell Barnes, 6 Nov. 1954, CO 1037/7.
45 *Reuters*, 14 Dec. 1954, CO 1037/7.
46 Young to Baring, 28 Dec. 1954; Macpherson to Young 23 Dec. 1954, Papers of Sir Arthur Young, Rhodes House, Oxford, Mss. Brit. Emp. s. 486, 5/3, ff. 100–107.
47 Douglas-Home, pp. 254–5.
48 Unpublished memoir by Arthur Young on his service in Kenya, Young Papers, Mss. Brit. Emp. s. 486, 5/1, pp. 27–8.

49 Cabinet Minutes, 13 Jan. 1955, CAB 128/28, CC (55) 3, min. 1.
50 Head to Churchill, 29 March 1955, PREM 11/1424, f. 107.
51 Douglas-Home, p. 242.
52 Cabinet Conclusions, 13 Jan. 1955, CAB 128/28, CC (55) 4.
53 Hopkinson to Churchill, PM (55) 5, 17 Jan. 1955, PREM 11/1424, f. 126.
54 Lord Boyd interviewed about West Africa by A. H. M. Kirk-Greene, 12 Dec. 1974, PBM, Mss. Eng. c. 3433, f. 161.
55 'Amendment of the Gold Coast constitution', Cabinet memorandum by Mr Lyttelton, PREM 11/1367, C(52)28, 9 Feb. 1952, in Richard Rathbone (ed.), *British Documents on the End of Empire, Series B, vol. 1, Ghana, Part 1, 1941–1952* (London, HMSO, 1992), pp. 372–4.
56 Rathbone, *Ghana, Part 1*, p. 361.
57 Rathbone, *Ghana, Part 1*, pp. lix–lx.
58 Lord Boyd interviewed about West Africa, PBM, Mss. Eng. c. 3433, f. 166.
59 Lord Boyd interviewed about West Africa, PBM, Mss. Eng. c. 3433, f. 164.
60 Rathbone, *Ghana, Part II*, p. 197.
61 Lord Boyd interviewed about West Africa, PBM, Mss. Eng. c. 3433, f. 177.
62 Rathbone, *Ghana Part II*, p. 139.
63 Rathbone, *Ghana Part I*, p. lxvii.
64 Arden-Clarke to Lennox-Boyd, 11 March 1957, PBM, Mss. Eng. c. 3463, f. 219.
65 Lord Boyd interviewed about West Africa, PBM, Mss. Eng. c. 3433, f. 164.
66 Eden to Lennox-Boyd, 28 Jan. 1957, PBM, Ms. Eng. c. 3571, ff. 5–6.
67 Cabinet Minutes, 29 March 1956, CAB 128/30, CM (56) 26, min. 1.
68 Lennox-Boyd to Eden, 28 June 1956, PREM 11/2616, f. 71.
69 Millard to Eden, 20 June 1956, PREM 11/2616, f. 73.
70 Lennox-Boyd to Eden, 27 July 1956, PREM 11/1957, f. 44.
71 Lennox-Boyd to Eden, 29 July 1956, PREM 11/1957, f. 43.
72 Keith Kyle, *Suez* (London, Weidenfeld and Nicolson, 1991), pp. 148, 153–4.
73 Robert Rhodes James, *Anthony Eden: A Biography* (London, Weidenfeld and Nicolson, 1986), p. 467.
74 Extract from diary of William Clark, 31 July 1956, cited in William Clark, *From Three Worlds* (London, Sidgwick and Jackson, 1986), p. 167
75 Lennox-Boyd to Eden, 4 Aug. 1956, PREM 11/1957, f. 40.
76 Kyle, pp. 174–5.
77 Kyle, p. 169.
78 Note by Freddie Bishop, 12 Aug. 1956, PREM 11/ 1957, f. 39.
79 Eden to Lennox-Boyd, 13 Aug. 1956, PREM 11/1957, f. 36.
80 Lord Boyd interviewed about Prime Ministers, PBM, Mss. Eng. c. 3432, f. 70.
81 Lennox-Boyd to Eden, 16 Aug. 1956, PREM 11/1089, ff. 11–12.
82 William Clark's diary, 16 Aug. 1956, cited in Clark, p. 175.
83 William Clark's diary, 17 Aug. 1956, cited in Clark, p. 175.
84 Lennox-Boyd to Eden, 24 Aug. 1956, PREM 11/1152, ff. 39–41.
85 Text of a Party Political Broadcast by Lennox-Boyd, 22 September 1956, PBM, Mss. Eng. c. 3795, ff. 307–314.
86 Eden to Monckton, 1 Sept. 1956, PREM 11/1368, f. 5.
87 'D.N.' to Cairncross, 1 Sept. 1956, PREM 11/1368, f. 4.
88 John Turner, *Macmillan* (London, Longman, 1994), p. 112.
89 Brook to Eden, 22 Oct. 1956, PREM 11/1140, f. 2.
90 Hugh Thomas, *The Suez Affair* (Harmondsworth, Penguin, 1967), p. 158.
91 Lennox-Boyd to Eden, 6 Nov. 1956, PREM 11/1154, f. 15.
92 Richard Lamb, *The Macmillan Years 1957–63: The Emerging Truth* (London, John Murray, 1995), pp. 19–20.
93 John Pearson, *The Life of Ian Fleming* (London, Coronet, 1989), p. 391.
94 Selkirk to Lennox-Boyd, 29 Nov. 1956, Mss. Eng. c. 3499, f. 73.
95 Lord Boyd interviewed about British Prime Ministers, PBM, Mss. Eng. c. 3432, f. 74.

11

'All this "Liquidation of Colonialism"': Colonial Affairs, 1957 – 1958

Caution is not cowardice; even the ants march armed.[1]

Part I: 'Profit and loss'

On the evening of the 9 January 1957, while dining in Salisbury with Lord Llewellin, the Governor General of the Central African Federation, Lennox-Boyd learned of Anthony Eden's resignation.[2] He made immediate arrangements to return home, hoping to be able to participate in the choice of a new premier. Yet by the time his plane touched down in Cairo en route to London, Macmillan had already been confirmed as Prime Minister. Lennox-Boyd was surrounded by journalists who had heard reports that Macmillan intended to make him Foreign Secretary. In response to their questions, he replied that he hoped the rumours were untrue and that all he really wanted was to continue as Colonial Secretary and return to Nyasaland. When he arrived back in London, Macmillan told him that he had read a transcript of his comments to the press in Cairo and was pleased to confirm Lennox-Boyd in his existing post. Whether Macmillan had really considered him for the Foreign Office remains unclear.[3]

Lennox-Boyd was uneasy at the speed with which Eden had been replaced. If he regarded Eden's successor with some suspicion, this cannot have been assuaged by the new Premier's first major policy initiative in the field of colonial affairs. On 28 January, Macmillan requested an assessment of probable constitutional advance in the colonies in the years ahead. He wished to know which territories would be 'ripe' for independence or   as he put it   'even if they are not ready for it, will demand it so insistently that their claims cannot be denied'.[4] He also wanted to see 'something like a profit and loss account' for each of the colonies, to enable Britain to judge whether she would gain or lose from a particular transfer of power.

In a preliminary response to Macmillan's request for a 'balance sheet of Empire', Lennox-Boyd and his officials were keen to stress that premature British withdrawal from any given territory would not necessarily save the Exchequer money:

> ...if in any territory HMG were to withdraw without being able to hand over to a successor government which could be expected to govern reasonably well in the interests of all its inhabitants, the repercussions would be serious and widespread.[5]

Civil Servants from the Commonwealth Relations Office, the Foreign Office, the Board of Trade and the Treasury as well as the Colonial Office, all had the opportunity to shape the resulting study, produced under the aegis of the Cabinet's Official Colonial Policy Committee. On the basis of an examination of the main papers that emerged from the study and the preliminary work behind them, one commentator has recently identified 'a major change in Conservative policy', with the Treasury forcing upon the Colonial Office 'a new central principle' expounded in the September draft: 'the economic and financial implications of the grant of independence to Colonial territories do not flow from the grant of independence itself but from the policies which may be followed by the particular countries after independence'.[6] Hence, Macmillan's policy review marked a significant shift towards Britain's acceptance that, in the future, her economic interests would increasingly be secured by informal rather than formal means. It was thus a major step in the direction of rapid decolonization and a defeat for Lennox-Boyd's more gradualist approach.

This interpretation of the policy review depends upon a rather caricatured view of Lennox-Boyd's existing policy as being 'in essence, to hold what we already had'.[7] Yet he had already applied this supposedly revolutionary new doctrine a year earlier in the preparations for Malaya's independence. In January 1956, he had been pressed by some of his Cabinet colleagues to seek formal safeguards for British economic interests there at the forthcoming constitutional

conference.[8]   After consultations with the Treasury, the Board of
Trade and the CRO, Lennox-Boyd reported back to Cabinet that it
would not be practical to protect those interests through formal
assurances. He explained that the well-being of British commercial
interests would essentially depend upon a friendly relationship with
Malaya and that this might well be jeopardized if the Government
were to impose unwelcome legal undertakings on Malayan leaders.[9]
Indeed, the basic position of the Colonial Office, both before and after
1957, was that, in most instances, a peaceful and amicable transfer of power was the best means of securing the post-independence
economic interests of Britain herself and of individual Western firms.

The general conclusion of the 'audit of empire' of 1957 was that,

> the economic considerations tend to be evenly matched, and the eco-
> nomic interests of Great Britain are unlikely in themselves to be deci-
> sive in determining whether or not a territory should become
> independent. Although damage could certainly be done by the prema-
> ture grant of independence, the economic dangers to Great Britain in
> deferring the grant of independence for her own selfish interests after
> the country is politically and economically ripe for independence would
> be greater than any dangers resulting from an act of independence
> negotiated in an atmosphere of goodwill such as has been the case with
> Ghana and the Federation of Malaya.[10]

This   conclusion   was   one   that   Lennox-Boyd   could
whole-heartedly endorse. Indeed he claimed that, thereafter, he
always kept a copy of the report to hand in case the issue should
again arise. If the conclusion suited his purposes, however, this was
not because he was oblivious to Britain's economic interests. The
defence of those interests was one of his central concerns, a fact
he never sought to disguise in his discussions with nationalist leaders. He recognized, however, that to advance or delay constitutional
development in a colony merely on the basis of some abstract notion of its cost-effectiveness could prove counter-productive.
Political instability might result, with damaging consequences for
British economic interests.

Part II: Solutions: Cyprus & Singapore

Cyprus

The period from the beginning of 1957 to the end of 1958 witnessed
political breakthroughs in the strategically important colonies of
Cyprus and Singapore. In the case of the former, this appeared
suddenly and unexpectedly. In the latter case, it followed more
directly from Lennox-Boyd's own efforts to reach a solution. Yet the
deal which he finally struck in Singapore contained one element
that caught him by surprise.

In February 1957, against the wishes of the British Government, the UN debated the issue of Cyprus. During the course of the debate, Lester Pearson, the Canadian Foreign Minister, suggested that NATO might be invited to consider the question. Lord Ismay, the Secretary General of NATO, took up this call, offering to intercede between the British, Greek and Turkish governments. Lennox-Boyd thought that this was premature given the seriousness of the security situation on the island, but he recognized that it would be embarrassing for the Government to reject the offer.[11] While the Government was framing its response, EOKA announced that it would suspend operations as soon as Makarios was released. This appeared to offer the prospect of a breakthrough, although the decision to release Makarios was likely to arouse Turkish hostility and encounter criticism from within the Conservative Party.

The question was considered on 15 March by a committee of Ministers, chaired by Macmillan, and a package of proposals was agreed upon. This consisted of three main elements: first, the British Government would announce that it wished to use the good offices of Ismay to reach agreement with the Greek and Turkish governments. Secondly, a conference would be held in London on constitutional development to which representatives of the Cypriot communities would be invited. Thirdly, in the light of the offer by EOKA, Makarios would be asked to call publicly for an end to terrorist activity. If he complied, he would be released from the Seychelles and the British Government would not object to him taking part in the London talks. There was no commitment as to when he would be allowed back to Cyprus.[12] Macmillan was, by this stage, determined to 'get clear of Cyprus' and ready to surrender sovereignty over the island should this prove necessary.[13] After the issue had been discussed by the full Cabinet on 18 March, a revised statement was prepared which, in deference to Turkish objections, made no mention of a London conference or of Makarios's involvement therein.[14] The principal opponent within Cabinet of the offer to the Archbishop was the Lord President, Lord Salisbury. Two days after this Cabinet meeting, Macmillan noted in his diary that Salisbury and Lennox-Boyd 'took diametrically opposing views. At one time both had offered – or threatened – to resign...'[15]

Despite this clash, the omens for peace – both on Cyprus and within the Cabinet– appeared encouraging when Makarios privately indicated that he might accept the Government's proposals. Yet when it finally materialized, Lennox-Boyd and his colleagues were presented by the Archbishop with a statement which fell short of the call for an unconditional end to violence which they had demanded. Macmillan was in Bermuda for his meeting with Eisenhower, an important attempt by the Prime Minister to mend fences in the wake of the Suez crisis. Against this background, Makarios became an important bargaining counter. Macmillan not only agreed to Eisenhower's request that Makarios be released but indicated that Britain was no longer interested in retaining sovereignty over Cyprus.[16] Following his return to London, Macmillan told his Cabinet colleagues that the balance of advantages lay in releasing Makarios. Salisbury made it clear that he could not associate himself with a policy 'which, in his view, would be a prelude to a process of gradual retreat in the face of pressure which the Archbishop would mobilize as soon as he was at liberty'.[17] Nevertheless, the Cabinet approved the decision to release Makarios. Salisbury resigned. As the Cabinet's foremost critic of decolonization, Salisbury's departure from the Cabinet probably served to give Lennox-Boyd greater room for manoeuvre. Yet the two men shared a strong commitment to the Empire, and, unlike Macmillan, Lennox-Boyd appears to have been genuinely saddened by the resignation.

The release of Makarios did not bring about the unconditional cessation of EOKA violence and the British Government was no closer to finding a political settlement to the problems of Cyprus. In July, Macmillan put forward a new proposal under which sovereignty over the island would be shared between a 'Tridominium' of Britain, Turkey and Greece. The Greek government, however, refused to take part in tripartite talks on the issue and the scheme came to nothing.

As 1957 neared its end, Lennox-Boyd was faced with the difficult task of choosing a successor to Sir John Harding as Governor of Cyprus. In March 1957, when for a short while an end to violence seemed within reach, Harding told Lennox-Boyd he feared that his continued presence on the island might be an obstacle to a political settlement. In addition, he was beginning to feel that he could not give his job the concentration it required and his doctors were worried about his health. Under the circumstances, Lennox-Boyd had little choice but to 'relieve him of his responsibilities'.[18] His choice of Hugh Foot to succeed Harding was a bold and imaginative one. Foot was a humane, liberal man from a family with outstanding left-wing credentials. Indeed, his brother, Dingle, provided legal assistance to a number of nationalist leaders in the colonies, including Makarios. Lennox-Boyd told Macmillan that the new Governor's approach might be somewhat unorthodox, a warning that was to be fully justified by subsequent events. He recognized, however, that if the emphasis of British policy was henceforth to be on negotiation rather than repression, Foot was eminently suited for the job.

Foot replaced Harding in December 1957. He had made it plain to Lennox-Boyd before accepting the post that his aim would be to end the state of emergency as quickly as possible, facilitate contacts between members of the two Cypriot communities and minimize foreign interference in the island's affairs. Yet his own outline for a political settlement, which formed the basis of the constitutional proposals which Lennox-Boyd submitted to the Cabinet a month after Foot's arrival in Cyprus, proved no more successful than previous British initiatives in attracting the necessary level of cross-communal support. In May, after extensive discussions in the Colonial Policy Committee, Macmillan brought forward yet another scheme which included elements both of Foot's proposals and of his own ideas for 'Tridominion'.[19] Meanwhile, in April, without the knowledge or the permission of Lennox-Boyd, Foot made his own private attempt to end the conflict. He had written to the EOKA leader, George Grivas offering to meet him, alone and unarmed, at any time or place; but although his letter resulted in a temporary suspension of violence, talks did not take place. When, two months later, they were informed of these contacts, Lennox-Boyd's Cabinet colleagues were horrified. They demanded that he deliver a severe reprimand to the Governor who was due back in London for talks on the new constitutional proposals. On Foot's arrival at his office, Lennox-Boyd adopted his sternest manner. This proved difficult to sustain, however, as Lennox-Boyd later recalled:

> [I] said that this was an outrageous thing to do – consorting with the Queen's enemies behind the back of the Secretary of State and putting him in an intolerable position and why did he do it? Then he said, 'Can I ask you a question? Are you as indignant with me as you are saying – are you really sorry that I did get in touch with him?' And I said, 'You mustn't ask me embarrassing questions. No, I am not.'[20]

The Secretary of State then took his contrite governor home and gave him lunch.[21]

At the end of July, having been ordered to take a long rest, Lennox-Boyd left with his family for the Rocky Mountains in Canada. He remained there throughout August and was not sent official papers. Meanwhile, Macmillan engaged in an energetic personal effort to 'sell' the new scheme, visiting Athens, Ankara and Cyprus. In Canada, Lennox-Boyd read a report in the Sunday paper that Macmillan was now running his department. The story linked Macmillan's behaviour with rumours that Lennox-Boyd was about to retire and become Managing Director of Guinness.[22]

Determined that these rumours should not gain further credence, Lennox-Boyd returned to London and sought to regain the initiative.

On the face of it, the situation Lennox-Boyd encountered on his return to England appeared unpromising. Yet forces were already at work which were to lead to a settlement. The summer of 1958 witnessed the outbreak of an even more worrying form of violence on Cyprus. As well as having to deal with renewed EOKA activity, British troops were confronted with the task of having to protect members of both communities from a wave of more random communal violence. This seemed in danger of developing into a full-scale civil war. Furthermore, although Turkey had been persuaded to accept the new constitutional proposals, Greek resistance to a compromise settlement appeared to be hardening. There was also, from the British point of view, a sharp deterioration in the situation in the Middle East. In the middle of July, a coup by radical elements in the army toppled the pro-Western regime in Iraq, shattering the Baghdad Pact. In the immediate wake of the coup, American troops were sent to Lebanon and British troops to Jordan at the request of their respective rulers.

Events in Iraq were a severe personal blow to Lennox-Boyd. The Regent of Iraq, Prince Abd al-Ilah, who was murdered along with his nephew, King Feisal, was an old and valued friend.[23] Yet the repercussions of events in the Middle East were to strengthen Britain's hand in Cyprus. Fearful that the virus of revolution might spread across her southern border, Turkey became increasingly concerned to avoid confrontation with her British ally over Cyprus.[24] The Americans, who had previously been sympathetic to Greece, responded to the crisis by moving closer towards the British position over Cyprus. In December 1958, for the first time at the UN, the Americans opposed a Greek item calling for Cypriot independence.[25] Pressures were clearly mounting on Turkey and Greece to reach an accommodation and in the course of their stay in New York for the UN session in December, their Foreign Ministers agreed between themselves to work for a solution.

The sudden improvement in relations between Greece and Turkey appears to have taken Lennox-Boyd by surprise. This was despite the fact that he had received a number of indications that the Greeks were prepared to compromise. In October, he had a meeting with the Labour MP, Barbara Castle, who had visited Athens, Ankara and Cyprus the previous month. She told Lennox-Boyd that in the course of three encounters with Makarios she had become convinced that the Greek Cypriots were prepared to forego *Enosis* and accept some form of guaranteed independence. Lennox-Boyd was dismissive. He sent Macmillan a record of their encounter along with a note implying that the meeting had been a bit of a bore.[26]

Yet he was to receive a similar message from members of his own party. In November, shortly before the UN debate, a group of Tory MPs including Peter Kirk and Antony Lambton, met the Greek Ambassador in London. The Ambassador apparently told them, quite accurately, that his government was ready to drop demands for *Enosis* and accept independence for Cyprus at some later date. Lennox-Boyd warned Edward Heath, the Chief Whip, that the Greeks were probably seeking to sow division in Tory ranks in advance of the UN vote.[27] When Lennox-Boyd addressed the members of the Commonwealth Affairs Committee, he suggested that the dropping of *Enosis* by Makarios and the Greeks was a means of achieving their objectives by the back door.[28] In response to the comments of some members who hoped that the option of partition would remain open, Lennox-Boyd apparently referred to a study carried out in May into the feasibility of partition. He seems to have suggested that although this option was practicable it was likely to result in severe hardship and could therefore be considered only in extreme circumstances.[29] This was not, however, the way in which his remarks were reported. A leak to the press led to widespread fears among the Greek Cypriot community that Lennox-Boyd had revealed a secret plan for partition, and did nothing to ease tensions on the island.[30]

Although Lennox-Boyd played no direct role in it, the reconciliation between Greece and Turkey produced a suitably melodramatic climax to his dealings with Cyprus. During a NATO meeting in Paris in December, Selwyn Lloyd received a request from Fatin Zorlu, Turkey's Foreign Minister, for Britain to spare the lives of two Greek Cypriot murderers due to be executed on Cyprus the following day. Zorlu and his Greek counterpart, Evanghelos Averoff-Tossizza, were about to put forward their own proposals for Cyprus: independence with British sovereign bases. Zorlu warned that agreement would be impossible if the executions took place. These were the first death sentences Foot had confirmed as Governor of Cyprus. Although he was strongly opposed to the death penalty, the crime for which the two Greeks had been convicted was particularly horrible, and Foot could find no grounds on which to commute the sentences. Yet in addition to his objection to the executions on ethical grounds, he realized that if they went ahead they would provoke violent reprisals and probably fatally undermine his capacity as Governor to achieve a settlement.[31] It was therefore with the greatest foreboding that he cabled to Lennox-Boyd the code-word 'Daffodil', the signal that he was not recommending clemency. Lennox-Boyd conveyed this message to the Queen and preparations for the executions were set in motion.

Lennox-Boyd heard of the news from Paris only hours before the executions were due to take place. He decided not to attempt to speak to the Governor on an open line, fearing that EOKA informers in the Cyprus Post Office would leak details of the conversation. Instead, he made use of a ticker-tape system in the basement of the Admiralty. He told Foot of the new conditions, but added that if he reprieved the two men he would never be able to use the death penalty again on the island. Whatever Foot decided, he promised to support him. There was a brief pause before the machine in front of Lennox-Boyd punched out Foot's reply: 'I will reprieve'.[32]

The settlement of the Cyprus issue, details of which were agreed at a conference in London in February 1959, was a source of the greatest satisfaction to Lennox-Boyd. Yet this sense of triumph was quickly to give way to bitter indignation at what he regarded as the Greek-Cypriot majority's abuse of power. In April 1964 he told the Prime Minister, Alec Douglas-Home, that he was 'horrified' by the way the situation was developing in Cyprus. He added,

> I cannot believe there is now any long-term solution other than partition. It would be shameful for the Turks to be given no alternative but to live under Greek domination or emigrate to the Turkish mainland.[33]

When, ten years later, a Turkish invasion of the island resulted in *de facto* partition, there was little doubt as to where his sympathies lay.

Singapore

March 1957 witnessed the resumption of constitutional negotiations over the future of Singapore. Lennox-Boyd felt far more comfortable with Lim Yew Hock as Chief Minister, than he had done with Lim's predecessor, David Marshall. He regarded Lim as 'shrewd and courageous' and admired his firm response to unrest in the colony's schools.[34] He was someone, Lennox-Boyd felt, to whom 'it was possible to make concessions'. Britain was prepared to grant the elected government of Singapore full authority in all matters except external affairs, defence and internal security. Foreign affairs and defence would remain the responsibility of the United Kingdom, while internal security would be under the control of a special council. This was to be composed of an equal number

British and Singaporean representatives. The casting vote was to be given to a representative of the government of Malaya.

The main focus of disagreement at the March talks was the scope of the security council's business. Britain wanted to be able to exercise a veto over the issues discussed in the council. Lim's delegation demanded that the council itself should be able to decide what matters lay within its competence. They argued that with pro-Communist elements in the colony seeking a pretext to attack the government, they could not afford to concede powers which might be represented as a continuation of colonial rule. Lennox-Boyd was persuaded of their sincerity and their determination to combat internal subversion. He feared that if he refused to concede their demands, Lim would resign and the subsequent elections would be conducted on bitterly anti-British lines, something that could only benefit the far left.[35] These arguments were of course, very similar to those which, the previous January, had persuaded him of the need to hand over control of internal security to the Tunku's government in Malaya.

Shortly before agreement was reached, Lim visited Lennox-Boyd at his home in Chapel Street and told him that he would not sign a final deal unless Lennox-Boyd made one further and quite extraordinary concession: the Colonial Secretary must insist that during the interim period before new elections took place, a general warrant would be issued under which subversives, who did not need to be named, could be proscribed and placed in detention. Those identified as having been engaged in subversive activities would not be eligible for membership of the Legislative Assembly. Lim warned that he would attack Lennox-Boyd publicly for demanding this measure, but that unless he undertook to do so there would be no agreement. Lennox-Boyd suggested to Lim that Lee Kuan Yew, leader of the People's Action Party and Lim's likely successor after the next general election, was unlikely to support such a move. To Lennox-Boyd's surprise, Lim told him that Lee was also a party to his demand.[36]

Fearing the reaction of the Labour Opposition, Lennox-Boyd asked Lee Kuan Yew to tell Aneurin Bevan of the secret request. This he did. Lennox-Boyd faced a difficult task persuading the Cabinet of the need to consent to this strange conspiracy. Lord Kilmuir, the Lord Chancellor, claimed that it was one of the most improper suggestions he had ever heard. Lennox-Boyd was characteristically unperturbed. He told his colleagues that 'it was the price of admiralty and our shoulders were broad'.[37] In the end, he managed to obtain the Cabinet's permission. The following day, he informed the constitutional conference that the internal security situation made it necessary for him to introduce the clause against subversives. The delegates ritually denounced this as an act of fascist repression and then, after a brief adjournment, announced that they would sign under pressure. This incident served, quite unfairly, to bolster Lennox-Boyd's image as a stubborn reactionary. Indeed, he was criticized in *The Times* for having almost wrecked the conference.

The impression that Lennox-Boyd had been responsible for this last-minute problem was reinforced by the more than ritual protests of the Singaporean political leaders when they returned home. So strenuous were their attempts to shift the opprobrium onto the British Government that Lim was forced to give a pledge to the Legislative Assembly that he would again raise the matter with Lennox-Boyd and urge him to lift the ban. When Harold Macmillan passed through Singapore in February 1958, Lim took the opportunity to reassure him on this point. His demand would be for public consumption only and if, when he visited London in the spring, the British Government refused to lift the ban, 'there would be no difficulty'.[38] When talks did open in May they proved fruitful, clearing the way for full internal self-government in 1959.

Part III The Federations: the West Indies, Central Africa, Nigeria and Southern Arabia

The years 1957 to 1958 saw Lennox-Boyd grappling with the problem of creating or sustaining federal political structures in the Caribbean, Southern Arabia, Central Africa and Nigeria. The Federation of the West Indies and the Federation of the Arab Emirates of the South were both inaugurated during Lennox-Boyd's time in office, in January 1958 and February 1959 respectively. The Central African Federation, which had been established in 1953, witnessed important political changes during this period in which Lennox-Boyd was closely involved. Nigeria would achieve her independence in 1960 on the basis of a federal constitution the final form of which was agreed during these years. The practice of federating colonial territories seems in retrospect a defining feature of Lennox-Boyd's period at the Colonial Office. It was certainly a policy with which he whole-heartedly agreed. It appeared to offer the small territories of the Caribbean and the Western Aden Protectorate the opportunity to pool their economic resources and to form politically viable entities. For the large and ethnically diverse colony of Nigeria, a federal system seemed the obvious solution to the problem of how to achieve unitary independence. In Central Africa it offered a means of maintaining European access to the region's mineral resources while halting the northward spread of South African-style apartheid.

Yet for all their attractions from a British perspective, these four federal experiments, to which Lennox-Boyd devoted so much of his time, proved conspicuous failures. By 1968, the federations in the Caribbean, Southern Arabia and Central Africa had ceased to exist and Nigeria had collapsed into bloody civil war. Lennox-Boyd narrowly avoided being implicated in a fifth ill-fated federation. In 1961, shortly after having left the House of Commons, he was asked by Macmillan to lead a commission of enquiry into the feasibility of including Sarawak and North Borneo in a federation with Malaya and Singapore. He declined, partly because he feared that the commission was being allowed insufficient time to accomplish its task, and Lord Cobbold was chosen in his place. Inaugurated in September 1963, the Federation of Malaysia survived in its original form for less than two years. In August 1965, Singapore was expelled and became an independent state.

It is difficult to point to any single common flaw in these various federal experiments which could explain their failure. One might be tempted to conclude, with apologies to Tolstoy, that each unhappy federation is unhappy in its own way. Yet certain recurring themes do emerge from the cases examined below. Federations were sometimes too obviously instruments of British policy for them to establish sufficient internal or external legitimacy. In some cases, the aims of the British Government were wildly at variance with those of local political leaders. Most common and most corrosive, however, was the fear that one section of a federation – be it a territory, a region or, in the case of Central Africa, a racial group – would subordinate all other interests to its own. Lennox-Boyd, whose belief in the essential wisdom of these federal experiments survived much evidence to the contrary, cannot be entirely absolved of the charge of complacency. Yet he was quite aware of the problems they faced and his efforts to solve them were often impeded by the intransigence and short-sightedness of his senior colleagues. In particular, Macmillan's own, highly ambivalent attitude towards decolonization greatly complicated Lennox-Boyd's task.

The Federation of the West Indies

The British Government had already moved ahead quite rapidly with constitutional reform in the Caribbean by the time Lennox-Boyd became Colonial Secretary. This occurred partly on the recommendations of the Moyne Commission and partly under pressure from the Americans whose involvement in the

British West Indies increased significantly during the course of the Second World War. Universal adult suffrage was introduced in Jamaica in 1944, and in the neighbouring colonies shortly afterwards. The British also revived the idea of a federation of the West Indies. At a constitutional conference held in 1947 at Montego Bay in Jamaica, political leaders from the West Indian territories accepted federation in principle. From the beginning, however, there was a fundamental conflict of interests between the British Government and local politicians. While Whitehall was primarily interested in creating a more efficient system of government, the West Indians were concerned above all to achieve a rapid transition to independence.[39]

As plans for federation progressed, the degree of control Britain would be able to exercise over the new structure diminished as the leaders of the individual territories sought to protect the constitutional gains they had already achieved. The Montego Bay conference established a Standing Closer Association Committee to produce concrete proposals for federation. Its report, published in March 1950, advocated placing a considerable amount of power in the hands of a Governor-General, including the right to appoint all members of the Upper House of the federal legislature and six of the 14 members of the Council of State.[40] At a conference held by Oliver Lyttelton in 1953 to discuss the proposals, West Indian delegates insisted on major reductions in the powers of Britain and her representative in the federation, and a further weakening of the already extremely limited powers of the federal government itself, particularly its capacity to raise revenue. Both here and at the constitutional conference presided over by Lennox-Boyd at Lancaster House in February 1956, West Indian leaders proved to be extremely jealous of any encroachments on their powers by Britain, by a future federal government, or indeed by each other.

Two relatively minor but highly symbolic issues served to sour relations between the British Government and West Indian leaders. The first of these was the choice of Governor-General. Macmillan decided to appoint Patrick Buchan-Hepburn (thereafter Lord Hailes), an old friend of Lennox-Boyd's and a former Conservative Chief Whip. Norman Manley and Eric Williams, the chief ministers of Jamaica and Trinidad respectively, were unhappy with the appointment, believing that the post should be filled by someone with proven experience of and sympathy for the political aspirations of the West Indian people. Meanwhile, at home, the British Government came under fire for using the new federation to provide 'jobs for the boys'.

Even more trouble was caused by the question of where to locate the federal capital. In May 1957, the West Indies Standing Federation Committee, composed of representatives from the Caribbean governments, selected the Chaguaramas Peninsula of Trinidad, an area leased to the United States as a base under the 1941 Destroyers for Bases Agreement. The Americans had already made it clear that they had no intention of abandoning the base and that they would regard the choice of Chaguaramas as an unfriendly and provocative act. After further negotiations, the West Indians were persuaded to accept proposals for a joint British, American and West Indian commission to examine possible alternative sites for a military base. The Americans were, however, unwilling to do anything which might suggest a willingness to surrender the existing site. Macmillan made a personal request to Eisenhower asking him to display some flexibility in the matter. In a mischievous departure from the draft prepared for him by the Foreign Office, Macmillan claimed 'all this "liquidation of colonialism" is going so well that I would be sorry if there was any hitch, especially one in the Caribbean'.[41] Eventually, and with great reluctance, the Americans agreed terms of reference for the Joint Commission.

In May 1958, four months after the federation had formally been inaugurated, the commission recommended that the United States should be allowed to retain Chaguaramas. West Indian leaders had already indicated that they might be prepared to consider alternatives to Chaguaramas and were keen to avoid a row over the issue.[42] The question of the capital's location could probably have been settled fairly amicably given sensitive handling. As such, Lennox-Boyd made a major error of judgement in publicly accepting the commission's report within a week of its publication, without making even a pretence of consultation with the West Indian governments. His decision caused enormous resentment and did nothing to increase confidence in the federation.

Port-of-Spain in Trinidad was selected as the federation's capital and served as such during the four years of its existence. Manley and Williams proved unwilling to join the government there, preferring to concentrate on leading their own territories to full independence.[43] As a result, the federation became the creature of the smaller and poorer islands. Without the wholehearted support of Jamaica and Trinidad, it had little chance of success. Its fate was sealed in September 1961 when the people of Jamaica rejected federation in a referendum called by Manley. Eight months later, the federation was formally dissolved by the British Parliament. The arithmetic of federation was explained with cruel accuracy by Eric Williams: 1 from 10 does not leave 9; it leaves 0.[44]

Central African Federation

Ghana's achievement of independence in March 1957 whetted the appetites of the Central African Federation's European Ministers for complete autonomy. When the Federal Prime Minister, Roy Welensky, visited London the following month, he obtained from Lennox-Boyd and Lord Home, the Commonwealth Secretary, a virtual promise of independence for the federation within three or four years. He was told that the federal constitutional review conference would be held no later than 1960 and that it would consider a programme for the attainment 'of such status as would enable the Federation to become eligible for full membership of the Commonwealth'. Yet it was painfully obvious by this stage that Welensky and his colleagues, for all their talk of 'partnership' and 'multi-racialism' had little or no intention of allowing the African majority in the Federation a significant share of political power. They conclusively demonstrated this in the course of 1957 when they introduced into the federal parliament two bills – The Constitutional Amendment Act and the Federal Electoral Bill – which further entrenched white control. The effect of these bills was to dilute the relative strength of effective African representation in the Federal assembly, from an extremely low starting point.[45] Sir Arthur Benson, the Governor of Northern Rhodesia, was scathing in his criticism of the Federal Electoral Bill and furious at Lennox-Boyd's failure to force changes to it. He told his old friend William Gorell Barnes, Assistant Under-Secretary of State at the Colonial Office, 'You know it is wrong and I know it is wrong and what is more our masters know that it is wrong. But they don't give a damn.'[46]

It was against that background that in 1958, Benson attempted to obtain agreement for a relatively small but important increase in African representation in the legislature of his own territory, Northern Rhodesia. Under the conditions which pertained at the beginning of that year, the Africans of Northern Rhodesia were effectively debarred from participation in direct elections to the legislative council. The franchise was open only to British citizens over 21 subject to certain property qualifications. Since the Africans occupied the status of British Protected Persons they were not eligible to vote. Hence, the 12 directly elected seats in the Northern Rhodesian Legislature were all held by Europeans, while four African members were returned via a system of electoral colleges. There were no African members on the Executive Council. In March 1958, after extensive consultations with Lennox-Boyd and with political leaders in his territory, Benson published a White Paper containing proposals for a new constitution. This provoked considerable opposition both from Europeans and Africans.

In July, Lennox-Boyd invited representatives from the main groups on the colony's legislative council to London for talks on the constitution. He failed to achieve agreement, but came away from the talks convinced that, with certain amendments, the March proposals could form the basis of a settlement. The revised plan which emerged in September was bewilderingly complex. Its basic consequence was likely to be that, initially, 14 of the 22 elected seats would go to Europeans and eight to Africans with the prospect of a gradual increase in the African element on the common roll. Although this was certainly a step forward for the Africans, they still had every reason to feel dissatisfied given that they outnumbered Europeans by 2,300,000 to 71,000. In what Lennox-Boyd and the Northern Rhodesian members of the United Federal Party clearly hoped would be an obstacle to 'extremist' African leaders, the proposals also stipulated that candidates in the 'special' constituencies – which comprised six of the eight seats likely to be won by Africans – should obtain permission to stand from at least two-thirds of the recognized local chiefs. The Executive Council was to contain 10 Ministers, of whom 4 would be officials, four elected Europeans and two elected Africans.

Despite the very limited political advance these proposals represented for the Africans of Northern Rhodesia, they were vigorously opposed by Welensky. He was able to deploy his usual argument against imaginative political concessions; namely that these would encourage European electors in the Federation to shift their support away from his United Federal Party (UFP) to the more explicitly racist Dominion Party. Lord Home accepted the logic of Welensky's argument and urged that the publication of the proposals be postponed until after the Federal elections. He was, however, persuaded 'very reluctantly' to accept Lennox-Boyd's argument that there was a need for African political advancement in Northern Rhodesia and that delays would be counter-productive.[47] Lennox-Boyd therefore pressed ahead, publishing his proposals in the form of a despatch on 17 September. The Government's refusal to be deflected drew from Welensky the accusation that British Ministers had acted in breach of their undertaking at the inception of the Federation to consult the Federal government about changes to territorial constitutions. Lennox-Boyd assured his Cabinet colleagues that the Federal government had been adequately consulted and that he had made at least one important concession to the Federal government's objections.[48] Despite this, by October Welensky was threatening that he would denounce Benson and the British Government for 'anti-Federal activities'.[49]

Lennox-Boyd felt that the Government could safely ride out Welensky's vocal opposition. Elsewhere in Whitehall, however, the angry noises emanating from the office of the Federal premier caused greater consternation. Home in particular believed that Welensky had to be pacified. In November he submitted to the Cabinet a paper formally endorsing Lennox-Boyd's policy but implicitly inviting his colleagues to offer concessions to settler opinion. He noted that, through a series of pledges and less formal undertakings, the British Government was faced with mutually incompatible commitments.[50] On the one hand, its undertakings of April 1957 had appeared to offer the Federation independence by 1960 or shortly after. This, of course, could only come about once Britain had withdrawn Protectorate Status from Northern Rhodesia. Yet in 1953, the Government had pledged not to do this without the consent of the inhabitants of the northern territories. Were Britain to withdraw protection before establishing governments that commanded African support, she would be accused of disregarding her pledges.

Home implied that if the Government had to choose between the concerns of the Africans and the Europeans, its support should go to the latter. In order to satisfy the Europeans' desire for autonomy, Britain might, Home suggested, have 'to stretch the interpretation of the 1953 pledges, so as to be able to hand over in the Northern Territories within a reasonable time'. Above all the British Government should not be deflected by 'factious' African opposition: it was their duty to lead African opinion, not to follow it. Home's message was clear: Welensky was being pushed too hard in the name of satisfying African demands.

Burke Trend, the Deputy Secretary to the Cabinet, agreed with Home. On 17 November, he told Macmillan that the question of the Northern Rhodesian constitution should be viewed in the context of Britain's broader policy towards Africa. He noted Welensky's oft repeated warning of an Egyptian and Soviet drive against Southern Africa and his assertion that only a white-dominated politico-military bloc could stem the tide of subversion. Trend continued:

> If we accept his views in principle – and given the increasing strategic importance of the air reinforcement route across Central Africa it is difficult to contest them – we should surely lean as far towards him as possible without compromising the discharge of our responsibilities towards the black peoples.[51]

These views were echoed by Macmillan himself the following day when the Northern Rhodesian constitution was discussed in Cabinet. Lennox-Boyd defended the proposals and repeated his view that no significant concessions should be made to the scheme's opponents beyond, perhaps, dropping the stipulation that African candidates – specifically those standing in 'special' constituencies – should be vetted by local chiefs. Macmillan, however, made it clear that more extensive concessions might be necessary. Given, he argued, 'the very important contribution to the maintenance of our position in Central Africa' that the Federation could make, Britain should make every effort to avoid prejudicing its interests.[52] If Welensky was not prepared to accept Lennox-Boyd's proposals, it might, Macmillan suggested, be necessary to reconsider them.

Negotiations with Welensky and the Northern Rhodesian representatives of his UFP dragged on into December. Ultimately, Macmillan backed his Colonial Secretary and Lennox-Boyd emerged with the principal features of his September proposals intact. It is clear, nevertheless, that before 1959, Macmillan was even less convinced than Lennox-Boyd of the need to offer substantive political concessions to the Federation's African population.

When elections in Northern Rhodesia took place in March 1959, the UFP won 13 of the 22 contested seats. The Northern Rhodesian African National Congress (ANC) split over the issue of whether to contest the elections. Kenneth Kaunda led a break-away by those members opposed to participation, and established the Zambia African National Congress (ZANC). The ZANC was banned on 12 March, shortly before the elections, and Kaunda was detained. The ANC, led by Harry Nkumbula, fought the election but won only one seat. If Lennox-Boyd's aim was for the new constitution to produce a firm and growing base of African support for the Northern Rhodesian government, it was clearly a complete failure. Moreover, by the time the elections took place, the affairs of Northern Rhodesia had been overshadowed by the emergency in Nyasaland, a development which was cast serious doubts on the viability of the Federation itself.

Nigeria

The problems posed by the question of constitutional advance for the Central African Federation also served to complicate Lennox-Boyd's negotiations with the Nigerians. In 1951, a federal constitution had been established in Nigeria. The country was divided into three regions, each with its own assembly. These assemblies in turn elected members to a federal House of Representatives. The three regions broadly corresponded to the location of Nigeria's

three principal ethnic groups: the population of the Northern region was largely Hausa-Fulani, the Western region Yoruba, and the
Eastern region Ibo. The 1951 constitution encouraged the development of politics along ethnic lines, and a dominant political party
emerged in each region: in the North, the Northern People's Congress (NPC) led by Sir Ahmadu Bello; in the West, the Action Group
led by Chief Obafemi Awolowo; and in the East, the National Council of Nigeria and the Cameroons (NCNC) led by Dr Nnamdi Azikiwe.
In 1953, the constitution was revised at a conference in London
chaired by Oliver Lyttelton. Lyttelton faced strong pressure from
the Action Group and the NCNC for Nigeria to be granted 'Dominion Status' by 1956. He responded with the offer of internal
self-government by 1956 for those Regions that desired it. A conference to consider this question was to have been held in the
autumn of 1956 but this was postponed while an investigation took
place into charges of corruption against Azikiwe, the Premier of the
Eastern Region.

Britain's hopes of resisting pressure for rapid constitutional
change rested largely on exploiting the tensions between the
Northern Region and the two Southern Regions. Lacking an educated administrative class to govern its 18 million inhabitants, it
seemed likely that self-government would make the Northern
Region heavily dependent upon expatriates and Southerners.
Furthermore, the Northern Premier, the Sardauna of Sokoto, was
worried about the impact of democratic politics upon the North's
traditional aristocracy.[53] It seemed possible then, that the North's
suspicions of the southerners could delay Nigerian independence.
Lennox-Boyd not only regarded the attitude of the Northerners as
a useful bargaining counter but also, characteristically, was genuinely sympathetic towards their wish to retain their existing institutions. He later recalled that he was far happier among the
Northerners than among the inhabitants of the Southern or Western Regions.[54]

By the time the postponed conference was held, in the late
spring of 1957, it was clear that the Northerners could no longer
be relied upon to resist further constitutional advance. Delegates
from the two other regions were relieved to hear the Sardauna
express the wish that the North should attain self-government in
1959.[55] Furthermore, in March 1957, the Federal House of Representatives, with the full support of the Northern delegates, had
unanimously passed a motion calling for full independence for the
Federation by 1959. Lennox-Boyd had no doubt that such rapid
political development was undesirable. He warned his colleagues
that the country might disintegrate and that administrative chaos

was already likely in the Eastern Region 'thanks to the largely corrupt, inept and opportunist rule of Dr Azikiwe's NCNC'.[56] At the same time, however, he was clear that Britain could not continue to rule Nigeria and protect her sizable economic interests there without the good will and cooperation of the Nigerian people. He told his colleagues that if Britain were to resist overtly a demand for independence by the leaders of the three Regions, this would simply unite the Nigerians against her and increase the pressure for change. In a version of the familiar argument that a concession now would ultimately assist Britain in maintaining her position, Lennox-Boyd suggested that if Nigerian demands were met, there was a chance that the transfer of power might be delayed until 1961 or even 1962.

He wanted to be able to offer an assurance that the British Government would consult with all the Nigerian governments in 1959 about arrangements for a final transfer of power. Other members of Colonial Policy Committee were, however, concerned that this would leave open the possibility of Nigeria achieving her independence before 1960. The Committee decided that if 'consultations' about independence did take place in 1959, these should be accompanied by the establishment of a Constitutional Commission.[57] That the Commission was essentially a delaying tactic is clear from the Cabinet's discussion of this issue. It was stressed, probably by Lord Home, that there was considerable hostility from within the Commonwealth – particularly from South Africa, but also from Australia and New Zealand – to the admission of additional 'coloured' states.[58] Furthermore, the government of the Central African Federation had recently been persuaded that their own admission to the Commonwealth should be deferred until the Federal Review Conference, which would probably take place in 1960. The Cabinet agreed that, if at all possible, Lennox-Boyd's objective in the forthcoming conference should be to avoid putting any date to Nigeria's independence.

Somewhat to Lennox-Boyd's surprise, the 1957 constitutional conference proved successful in settling a variety of issues. The Eastern and Western Regions were granted self-government, the Federal House was enlarged and a new post of federal Prime Minister was established. This led to the creation of a national government supported by all of the three major parties, led by Alhaji Abubakar Tafawa Balewa, the deputy president of the NPC. Far less easily resolved was the issue of Nigerian independence. Any hopes Lennox-Boyd might have harboured that the Northern Nigerians would break the consensus in favour of independence proved illusory. He was faced with a formal request from the three

Regional Premiers for independence within the Commonwealth in 1959. Following further talks, they proposed a compromise: after the next elections, which they promised would not be until the end of 1959, the new parliament would pass a motion setting a specific date for independence and the British Government would endorse this. Lennox-Boyd felt that this was a significant advance on their previous position and told Macmillan he would have been inclined to accept this, were it not for the likelihood that the government of the Central African Federation would object.[59] He consulted Home and they agreed on the following response: were such a motion to be passed, the British Government would be prepared to fix a date for independence although they could not promise that it would be the same as the one requested in the resolution. This did not satisfy the Nigerians. They effectively took note of Lennox-Boyd's statement under protest and reserved the right to press for independence by 2 April 1960.[60] Despite, or indeed perhaps because of the stalemate on the question of the timing of independence, the Colonial Office felt that the conference had been a success.

Another issue that remained outstanding after the 1957 conference was the position of the minorities and the question as to whether the three existing regions should be broken down into smaller states. Non-Muslim peoples in the Northern region were demanding the creation of a 'Middle Belt' state, outside Hausa-Fulani control, while non Yoruba-speaking peoples in the West sought the establishment of a separate 'Mid-West' state. There was also pressure for the creation of a non-Ibo 'Calabar-Ogoji-Rivers' state in the East. At the 1957 Conference it was decided to refer this issue to a commission led by Sir Henry Willink. When Willink's group reported the following year, it rejected the idea of creating new states and recommended that minority rights could best be protected through the establishment of local representative bodies and by entrenched human rights clauses in the constitution.

Looking back some years later, with the 1966 *coup* and subsequent Civil War very much in his mind, Lennox-Boyd wondered whether he had been right to accept the recommendations of the Willink Commission. At the time, however, he had no doubt. He saw few advantages in 'Balkanizing' Nigeria. Furthermore, he was keen that the influence of the North over Federal politics should not be weakened. As he later explained, 'I felt strongly that the conservatism of the North in a predominant position would be more likely to ensure stability and slow down constitutional change...'[61] Although his decision to accept Willink's recommendations was not popular with the leaders of the two main southern parties, Lennox-Boyd had little difficulty in persuading them to accept it when constitutional talks resumed in London in October 1958. As Lennox-Boyd told his colleagues shortly before the Conference ended, none of the main parties could afford to seem to be retarding the achievement of independence by insisting upon the re-drawing of regional boundaries.[62]

As the 1958 talks approached, Lennox-Boyd came under increasing pressure to move beyond his statement of the previous year and announce that Nigeria would achieve independence in 1960. The arguments against such a statement were advanced by Burke Trend, the Deputy Cabinet Secretary. Trend argued that the practical difficulties involved in constitutional change, the opposition of other Commonwealth members, particularly South Africa, and the prospect of the Central African Review Conference in 1960 all made it 'desirable that we should not, if possible, go beyond the statement made at last year's conference'.[63] When the matter was discussed in Cabinet on 11 September, no decision was made on the date of independence, but close attention was paid to the military implications of British withdrawal. Duncan Sandys, the Minister of Defence, stressed the strategic importance of Nigeria and the need to reach firm agreements over the future of British defence facilities.[64] It was even suggested that Britain might maintain a military enclave under her sovereignty.

Obtaining firm undertakings from the Nigerians on the issue of defence proved to be one of Lennox-Boyd's biggest problems. In consultation with Sandys he produced a list of the facilities Britain would want from Nigeria after independence, but had difficulty persuading Abubakar and the Sardauna to sign a formal agreement. As Lennox-Boyd later recalled:

> I was under great pressure from Duncan Sandys...to produce a signed document, and I said that when you are dealing with gentlemen it is not always necessary to have everything signed; this was an approach that Duncan Sandys, not unnaturally, found was a little too emotional for him, and it didn't satisfy the Chiefs of the Defence Staff.[65]

In the end, after some cajoling, the Nigerians put their signatures to the Defence Agreement.

With a solution to the defence issue in sight, Lennox-Boyd returned to his Cabinet colleagues to seek their agreement to a statement promising independence by 1960. His assessment of the situation in Nigeria was extremely sombre and he made no effort to disguise his reluctance to grant independence so swiftly. He told the Cabinet that the differences between the peoples of the

different regions were 'probably irreconcilable' and that there was
a chance that the North might break away from the Federation.[66]
'I would certainly not like to assert,' he added, 'that self-government
will in Nigeria be good government.' After much thought, however,
Lennox-Boyd had concluded that Britain would gain nothing by
postponing a decision on independence. The essential point was
that, with the granting of self-government to the three regions and
the steady haemorrhage of European personnel, political development in Nigeria would be almost entirely dependent on the will of
the people there:

> To continue to govern a discontented and possibly rebellious Nigeria
> would...present well-nigh insoluble administrative problems in view of
> the transfer of effective power that has already taken place in the
> domestic field. It might even need substantial military forces.

The Cabinet accepted this gloomy assessment and on 25 October
Lennox-Boyd informed the final session of the Nigeria Conference
that the colony would achieve her independence in October 1960.
He told the Prime Minister that the negotiations had ended 'in an
atmosphere of great goodwill'.[67]

This atmosphere of goodwill did not long survive the grant of
independence. The decision made at the 1958 conference to allo-
cate seats in the Federal Assembly in relation to the size of the
populations of the three regions seemed, on the face of it, a fair
and sensible one. Yet, in practice, it gave the North a permanent
majority which, so long as politics in Nigeria continued to operate on ethnic-regional lines, was bound to create conflict. The two
Southern regions found themselves having to compete with each
other for the privilege of being the junior partner in a coalition
dominated by Northern politicians.[68] At the same time, the
ethno-regional power bases of the three main parties made them
highly suspicious of attempts by their rivals to attract votes on a
genuinely national basis. Tensions finally exploded in January
1966 with a coup by Southern army officers. This was followed
in July by a counter-coup by Northern officers. In May 1967, the
Eastern region began its struggle to secede from the federation
as the independent state of 'Biafra', sparking a three-year-long
civil war.

With the benefit of hindsight, it is arguable that the British
should have made greater efforts to encourage political alliances
across ethnic lines in the final years of colonial rule, rather than
pursuing their traditional policy of using the conservative North as
a bulwark against the ambitions of Southern politicians.
Lennox-Boyd must take some responsibility for perpetuating this

policy of divide-and-rule. Yet he no doubt sincerely believed that any delay to the transfer of power achieved by this method would allow Britain to prepare Nigeria more fully for independence. It might also be argued that Lennox-Boyd should have given more thought to the possibility of dividing Nigeria's three regions into smaller units, just as General Gowon did in the wake of the 'Biafran' war when he established a federation of twelve states. Yet aside from Lennox-Boyd's concern that this would weakened the influence of the North, it would certainly have created huge administrative problems and might have actually have exacerbated ethnic tensions on the eve of decolonization. In practice, by the time Lennox-Boyd became Colonial Secretary, the ethnic divisions which poisoned Nigerian politics and which Britain had done so much to foster, were already firmly entrenched. He knew better than anyone else the dangers these posed for the future. Once, when his son Simon asked him why he always prayed at night, he replied, 'If you were responsible for the government of fifty million Nigerians, you'd pray.'

The Southern Arabian Federation

Britain captured the Aden Colony in 1839 and over the following 75 years extended her control over the surrounding area through a series of protectorate treaties with local rulers. The twenty protected states that constituted the Eastern and Western Aden Protectorates appeared too small to achieve independence on their own. A federal solution was suggested in 1952 by the Governor of Aden, and his proposals were subsequently discussed with the rulers of the Western Protectorate.[69] There was, however, no more enthusiasm for this scheme than there had been for a similar British initiative in 1928. The Government decided not to press the matter further.

In September 1955, Lennox-Boyd raised the prospect of reopening negotiations.[70] He circulated to his colleagues a departmental memorandum which argued that, although Britain could not contemplate independence for the Colony in the foreseeable future, she had a strong historical obligation to foster self-determination in the Protectorates:

> HMG ought to have no selfish wish to continue to impose their rule, even through protectorate and advisory treaties, on these states longer than is absolutely necessary; and their object should be solely to assist these states to reach the degree of stability necessary for them to attain a genuine form of independence, if and when they become ready for it.

This independence would only be viable, however, given some form of association between the constituent states. The Governor of Aden should, therefore, be authorized to carry out general consultations with the rulers with the object of promoting closer association, but without seeking to impose a particular form of federation upon them.

These proposals met with a distinctly cool response from some of Lennox-Boyd's colleagues. A highly sceptical few words in Eden's ear were provided by Guy Millard, the Prime Minister's private secretary, who expressed the fear that moves towards self-government by a federated Protectorate would encourage calls for independence from the inhabitants of the Colony.[71] Other critics of the proposals included Harold Macmillan, the Foreign Secretary, who was far from happy to disclaim any 'selfish wish' to hold on to the Protectorates. He told Lennox-Boyd that although guiding colonies towards self-government was an established British aim, 'surely we ought not to make a fetish of this'.[72] He began with the assumption that the Aden Colony was vital to Britain's strategic interests and that, in so far as federation in the Protectorates would encourage demands for independence from the Colony's inhabitants, it was undesirable. About Britain's relations with the rulers, Macmillan was brutally frank:

> In the Protected States I suppose our real interest in them is the possibility that there might be oil. If we want to hold on there, surely it is better to leave the local Sheikhs and Rulers in a state of simple rivalry and separateness, in which they are glad of our protection and can, where necessary, be played off one against the other rather than to mould them into a single unit which is most likely (and indeed expressly designed) to create a demand for independence and 'self-determination'.

Eventually, the Government gave its distinctly luke-warm support to a new initiative by the Governor of Aden. The British Government's lack of enthusiasm for the scheme was more than matched by that of the local rulers, and negotiations over federation again ran into the ground.

In the immediate wake of the Suez crisis, the prospects for federation appeared to diminish further. A new Governor in Aden, Sir William Luce, concluded that the policy was fundamentally misguided. At the same time, Aden gained an enhanced significance in Britain's post-Suez strategic calculations.[73] The Middle East Command was moved to Aden and the number of troops stationed there was increased fourfold from 1957 to 1959. As a consequence, Ministers became even more suspicious of any developments that seemed likely to encourage demands for Adeni independence.

As so often happened, however, events on the ground followed a logic of their own. As attacks from the Yemen intensified, the

rulers of the Western Protectorate began to see greater advantages
in some form of association. In June 1958, Lennox-Boyd told the
Cabinet that, in response to the threat of foreign intervention, the
Western rulers had agreed among themselves on the desirability
of federation. Such a federation would, he suggested, be bound by
treaty relations with Britain in the same way as were the current
Protected states, but would be offered independence in due course.[74]
There was broad approval in Cabinet for this although Lord Home
was worried about offering the prospect of 'independence' to the
proposed federation before political and military powers had been
precisely allocated. Macmillan shared Home's fears about the use
of the word 'independence' and summoned Lennox-Boyd for a talk
about the matter. As Macmillan recorded at the time in a passage
worthy of the late Peter Cook:

> I impressed on him…that we must get rid of this horrible word 'indepen-
> dence'. What we wanted was a word like 'home rule'. The thing to do was
> to think of the Arabic for 'home rule' and then work backwards from it.[75]

It seems that in terms of the arrangement Lennox-Boyd had in
mind, the word 'independence' would, in any case, have been misleading. Lennox-Boyd assured the Prime Minister that a defence
agreement would be integral to the federation's constitution and
that if any attempt were made to repudiate it, the inhabitants of
the federation would lose their rights of self-government.

Objections were also raised by the Treasury to the cost of establishing federation. They questioned the Colonial Office's original proposals for expenditure on the federation and were alarmed
when, in the course of talks between Lennox-Boyd and the Rulers
in July, the amounts increased.[76] Nevertheless, Lennox-Boyd was
able to present the Rulers with an acceptable package of aid, and
in the middle of July, he reached an agreement with them on the
financial, military and political aspects of federation. His talks coincided with news of the coup in Iraq. Lennox-Boyd was initially
concerned that the coup might give the Rulers 'cold feet' by providing a grim warning of the fate that could befall Arab leaders who
were seen as too closely aligned to the West. In fact, as he discovered, it served further to cement their commitment to federation
and their desire for British military protection. In February 1959
he proudly presided over the establishment of the Federation of
Arab Emirates of the South.

At this stage, the Federation included only the Western Protectorate and one of the Eastern Protectorate states. The future of the
Colony remained uncertain. When, in 1955, Lennox-Boyd raised the
issue of federation, he assured Macmillan, 'I want us to hang on

to the Colony...indefinitely'.[77] By the end of 1958, however, he had been persuaded by Luce that nationalist pressure within Aden could not be resisted for much longer. He therefore supported the Governor's view that Britain's best hope of retaining the use of defence facilities there lay in offering the Colony the opportunity to join the Federation and transferring sovereignty.[78] The Chiefs of Staff continued to insist, however, that the maintenance of the Aden base was essential to British strategic interests, and a study by the British Government concluded that it would not be feasible to partition off a separate military enclave from the rest of the Colony. Trapped between the competing demands of nationalist leaders in Aden and the defence chiefs in London, Lennox-Boyd and Luce had little option but to 'play for time', neither committing Britain to a merger nor ruling out the possibility.[79] Indeed, it was not until September 1962 that proposals for a merger with the Federation and the transfer of sovereignty 'as soon as practicable' were put before the Aden Legislative Assembly. Yet although it narrowly voted in favour of merger, Macmillan's hope that the conservative influence of the Protectorate rulers would neutralize Adeni radicalism proved illusory. Nationalist leaders in Aden rejected independence on the basis of the current constitution and demanded the establishment of universal suffrage throughout the Federation.[80] Unrest continued to mount as did the influence of radical nationalism. In 1967, the Emirs were deposed, Britain withdrew from Aden and the National Liberation Front seized control of the whole area. The Federation was swiftly replaced by the avowedly Marxist People's Democratic Republic of Yemen.

The prospects of success for a federation based upon the traditional rulers of the Western Protectorate were never particularly good. They faced a formidable threat from the growing influence of radical Arab nationalism both within the Colony and in neighbouring states. Under the circumstances, it seems reasonable to suggest that the British Government failed to recognize the urgency of the situation. Had they pressed ahead with federation in a determined fashion, included the Colony within it at an earlier stage, and rapidly transferred sovereignty, they might have defused some of the unrest within the Colony and enhanced the federation's legitimacy among its Arab neighbours.[81] Instead, as we have seen, British policy during Lennox-Boyd's term in office was characterized by confusion and vacillation, and continued to be so in the years after 1959. Lennox-Boyd himself, however, deserves little of the blame for this. Unlike Macmillan, he recognized that the old game of divide-and-rule in Southern Arabia could no longer guarantee the maintenance of British influence there. Despite his own feelings of ambivalence towards the project he was, from 1955 onwards, prepared to give his support to federal initiatives in the face of objections from Downing Street and the Foreign Office. It is difficult to see how he could have expedited the establishment of the Federation, given the lack of enthusiasm for the scheme among the Southern Arabian rulers themselves. Lennox-Boyd also recognized that Britain's best hope of retaining her defence facilities in Aden was by reaching some kind of accommodation with the growing forces of nationalism and opening the way for the transfer of sovereignty. Had Lennox-Boyd and Luce prevailed over this matter at the time of the Federation's establishment, its chances of survival and those of British influence in the region would surely have been enhanced.

Notes

1   Ganda proverb from Uganda collected by Lennox-Boyd, PBM, Mss. Eng. c. 3796, f. 273.
2   Lord Boyd interviewed about Central Africa by Kenneth Kirkwood, 21 Feb. 1975, PBM, Mss. Eng. c. 3433, f. 124.
3   Bryan Magee, Lennox-Boyd's Labour opponent in the 1959 General Election, was told that a delegation of Conservative back benchers led by Angus Maude had visited Macmillan at this time to demand an assurance that Lennox-Boyd would not be sent to the Foreign Office. According to the story, they believed his private life left him vulnerable to blackmail. I have been unable to find any evidence to substantiate this rumour. Macmillan's diaries for these days are not available for consultation. In retrospect, Macmillan was certainly keen to give the impression that he had always been determined to keep Selwyn Lloyd at the Foreign Office (Alistair Horne, *Harold Macmillan, 1957-1986* (London, Macmillan, 1989), p. 7).
4   Macmillan to Salisbury, 28 Jan. 1957, PREM 11/2617.
5   Lennox-Boyd to Salisbury, 15 Feb. 1957, PREM 11/2617.
6   Tony Hopkins, 'Macmillan's audit of empire, 1957', in Peter Clarke and C. Trebilcock (eds.), *Understanding Decline* (Cambridge, Cambridge University Press, 1997), pp. 247, 251
7   Hopkins, p. 253.
8   Cabinet conclusions, 17 Jan. 1956, CAB 128/30/1, CM 4(56)3, cited in David Goldsworthy (ed.), British Documents on the End of Empire, Series A, vol. 3, *The Conservative Government and the End of Empire 1951-57*, part 2 (London, 1994), pp. 389–90.
9   Draft Cabinet Memorandum by Lennox-Boyd, Feb. 1956, cited in A.J. Stockwell (ed.), British Documents on the End of Empire, Series B, vol. 3, *Malaya*, part 3 (London, 1995), p. 258.
10 Cabinet Official Committee on Colonial Policy, 'Future Constitutional Development in the Colonies', CP(O)(57)6, 4 July 1957, CAB 134/1551.
11 Cabinet Minutes, 7 March 1957, CAB 128/31, CC (57) 16, min. 8.
12 'Cyprus: Note by the Secretary of State for the Colonies', 16 March 1957, CAB 129/86, C (57) 71.
13 Harold Macmillan's diary 15 March 1957, cited in Horne, *Macmillan 1957-1986*, p. 100.
14 'Cyprus: Note by the Secretary of State for the Colonies', 19 March 1957, CAB 129/86, C (57) 72.

15 Horne, *Macmillan, 1957 1986*, p. 36.
16 Evanthis Hatzivassiliou, 'The Cyprus Question and the Anglo-American Spe-
    cial Relationship, 1954 58', in Richard J. Aldrich and Michael Hopkins, *Intelli-*
    gence, Defence and Diplomacy: British Policy in the Post-War World (London,
    Cass, 1994), p. 160.
17 Cabinet Minutes, 28 March 1957, CAB 128/31, CC (57) 25, min. 4.
18 Lord Boyd interviewed about Cyprus, PBM, Mss. Eng. c. 3433, ff. 13–17.
19 Cabinet Minutes, 13 May 1958, CAB 128/32, CC (58) 42, min. 2.
20 Lord Boyd interviewed about the Colonial Service, PBM, Mss. Eng. c. 3432,
    f. 112.
21 Foot, pp. 155–6.
22 Lord Boyd interviewed about Cyprus, PBM, Mss. Eng. c. 3433, f. 55.
23 Lennox-Boyd attempted to arrange a memorial service for the murdered mem-
    bers of the Iraqi royal family, and was enraged when the Archbishop of Can-
    terbury, Geoffrey Fisher, tried to prevent this (Memoir by W.R. Moore, PBM, Mss.
    Eng. c. 3455, pp. 37–8). Lennox-Boyd's close links to the Iraqis generated some
    rather unsavoury rumours in the wake of the coup. The 9 August 1958 edi-
    tion of the German magazine, *Der Stern,* carried an extraordinary article claim-
    ing that a note from Lennox-Boyd had been discovered in the ruins of the royal
    palace which revealed that he had been supplying girls to the young Prince
    Feisal. The story seems to have been based on a wildly inaccurate translation
    of one of Lennox-Boyd's visiting cards, and *Stern* subsequently published a
    full apology (see CO 967/339).
24 Horne, p. 101.
25 Evanthis Hatzivassiliou, 'The Cyprus Question', p. 163.
26 Note of a meeting between Barbara Castle and Alan Lennox-Boyd at Lancaster
    House, 13 Oct. 1958, PREM 11/2251, ff. 7–11.
27 Lennox-Boyd to Heath, 21 Nov. 1958, PBM, Mss. Eng. c. 3465, f. 267.
28 Commonwealth Affairs Committee Minutes, 11 Dec. 1958, CCO 507/1/1.
29 Lennox-Boyd to Foot, 12 Dec. 1958, PREM 11/2257, f. 7.
30 *The Times*, 15 Dec. 1958.
31 Foot, pp. 178–9.
32 Lord Boyd interviewed about Cyprus, PBM, Mss. Eng. c. 3433, f. 75–6.
33 Boyd to Douglas-Home, 29 April 1964, PREM 11/5011.
34 Lord Boyd interviewed about Malaya and Singapore, PBM, Mss. Eng. c. 3432,
    f. 190.
35 'Singapore Conference: Progress Report: Memorandum by the Secretary of State
    for the Colonies', 26 March 1957, CAB 129/86, C (57) 78.
36 Lord Boyd interviewed about Singapore, PBM, Mss. Eng. c. 3432, ff. 191–2.
37 Lord Boyd interviewed about Singapore, PBM, Mss. Eng. c. 3432, ff. 191–2.
38 'Prime Minister's meeting with Lim Yew Hock at Singapore on 12 February 1958',
    PREM 11/2296.
39 Franklin W. Knight, *The Caribbean: The Genesis of a Fragmented Nationalism*
    (Oxford, Oxford University Press, 1990), p. 301.
40 Trevor Munroe, *The Politics of Constitutional Decolonization: Jamaica, 1944–62*
    (Jamaica, University of the West Indies, 1972), p. 123.
41 Macmillan to Eisenhower, 19 July 1957, PREM 11/2880, f. 76.
42 J. Mordecai, *The West Indies: the Federal Negotiations* (London, 1968), p. 116.
43 Nigel Fisher, *Iain Macleod* (London, André Deutsche, 1973), p. 187.
44 Fisher, p. 189.
45 Patrick Keatley, *The Politics of Partnership* (Harmondsworth, Penguin, 1963),
    pp. 438–9.
46 Benson to Gorell Barnes, 20 Dec. 1957, Papers of Sir William Gorell Barnes,
    Churchill College, Cambridge, BARN 3/6.
47 Home to Macmillan, 5 Sept. 1958, PREM 11/2477, ff. 71–2.
48 This was the provision that 'ordinary' votes should not be devalued in 'special'
    constituencies ('The Federation of Rhodesia and Nyasaland: Northern

Rhodesian Constitution: Memorandum by the Secretary of State for the Colonies', 11 Nov. 1958, CAB 129/95, C (58) 231).
49 Internal memorandum to Macmillan, 25 Oct. 1958, PREM 11/2477, f. 51.
50 'The Federation of Rhodesia and Nyasaland: Note by the Secretary of State for Commonwealth Relations', 12 Nov. 1958, CAB 129/95, C (58) 232.
51 Trend to Macmillan, 17 Nov. 1958, PREM 11/2477, f. 34.
52 Cabinet Conclusions, 18 Nov. 1958, CAB 128/32, CC (58) 81, min. 8.
53 Michael Crowder, *The Story of Nigeria* (London, Faber and Faber, 1978), p. 241.
54 Lord Boyd interviewed about West Africa by A. H. M. Kirk-Greene, 12 Dec. 1974, PBM, Mss. Eng. c. 3433, f. 181.
55 Crowder, p. 241.
56 'Nigeria: Note by the Secretary of State for the Colonies', 14 May 1957, CAB 129/87, C (57) 120.
57 'Nigeria: Note by the Lord Chancellor', 16 May 1957, CAB 129/87, C (57) 122.
58 Cabinet Minutes, 22 May 1957, CC (57) 42, min. 4.
59 Lennox-Boyd to Macmillan, PM (57) 24, 22 June 1957, PREM 11/2436, ff.20– 3.
60 Moreton to Ramsden, 28 June 1957, PREM 11/2436, ff. 14–15.
61 Lord Boyd interviewed on West Africa, PBM, Mss. Eng. c. 3433, ff. 180 1.
62 'Nigeria: Note by the Secretary of State for the Colonies', 20 Oct. 1958, CAB 129/95, C (58) 213.
63 Trend to Macmillan, 5 Sept. 1959, PREM 11/2436, ff. 10–11.
64 Cabinet Minutes, 11 Sept. 1958, CAB 128/32, CC (58) 71, min. 5.
65 Lord Boyd interviewed about West Africa, PBM, Mss. Eng. c. 3433, f. 185.
66 'Nigeria: Note by the Secretary of State for the Colonies', 20 Oct. 1958, CAB 129/95, C (58) 213.
67 Lennox-Boyd to Macmillan, 25 Oct. 1958, PREM 11/2436, f. 4.
68 Ali A. Mazrui and Michael Tidy, *Nationalism and New States in Africa* (London, 1984), pp. 234–238.
69 Glen Balfour-Paul, *The End of Empire in the Middle East: Britain's Relinquishment of Power in her Last Three Arab Dependencies* (Cambridge, Cambridge University Press, 1991), p. 65.
70 Lennox-Boyd to Macmillan, 23 Sept. 1955, enclosing the paper 'HMG's Long Range Policy in the Aden Protectorate and Aden Colony', 22 Sept. 1955, PREM 11/2616, ff. 139–152.
71 Millard to Eden, 30 Oct. 1955, PREM 11/2616, ff. 129–31.
72 Macmillan to Lennox-Boyd, 14 Oct. 1955, PREM 11/2616, f. 136.
73 Wm Roger Louis and Ronald Robinson, 'The Imperialism of Decolonization', *Journal of Imperial and Commonwealth History*, vol. 22, no. 3 (1994), p. 484.
74 Cabinet Minutes, 26 June 1958, CAB 128/32, CC (58) 50, min. 6.
75 Note by Macmillan, 28 June 1958, PREM 11/2616, f. 46.
76 Lennox-Boyd to Heathcoat Amory, 8 July 1958, PREM 11/2616, ff. 38–42.
77 Lennox-Boyd to Macmillan, 1 Nov. 1955, PREM 11/2616, f. 125.
78 CPC (58) 27, 'Aden Colony and Protectorate', Dec. 1958, PREM 11/2616, ff. 18– 20.
79 Bishop to Macmillan, 8 Sept. 1959, PREM 11/2616, f. 4.
80 Balfour-Paul, pp. 75–80.
81 The best discussion of the causes of the Federation's failure is Glen Balfour-Paul, pp. 49–95.

12

'A Great Administrative Disaster': Colonial Affairs, 1959

Where there is a corpse, there the vultures assemble.[1]

Part I: The future

In November 1958, Lennox-Boyd bowed to pressure from his family and decided to leave Parliament at the next general election in order to succeed Sir Hugh Beaver as Managing Director of Guinness.[2] He had already served for over four years as Colonial Secretary and had no strong desire to occupy any other Cabinet post. He wanted to be able to leave the Colonial Office soon after he had told his constituency association of his intention not to seek re-election. As he told the Prime Minister, he felt that his authority as Colonial Secretary would be seriously undermined once it was known that he was not to continue in the post for much longer.[3] Yet Macmillan was in no hurry to get rid of him. When they discussed the matter early in 1959, he would not hear of Lennox-Boyd resigning before the next election. He even tried to persuade him to remain in government as Commonwealth Secretary or Lord President.[4] He repeatedly asked Lennox-Boyd's Minister of State, 'Can't you possibly get Alan to stay?'.[5] Alan, however, was determined to go.

He had hoped to be able to announce his decision to the annual general meeting of the Mid-Beds constituency party on 11 April. Yet somehow the news leaked out. During his visit to Aden in February, the *Daily Mail* revealed that he did not plan to stand again and that he was about to resign his post as Colonial Secretary. Faced with the inevitable barrage of questions, he told reporters that he had no intention of resigning. He would not be drawn, however, on whether he intended to contest the next election. As a result of these comments, the executive committee of his local association met and begged him to tell them of his intentions within the next fortnight. So far, only the President of the Mid-Beds Conservatives had been informed. Lennox-Boyd agreed to meet them on Saturday 14 March. He proposed telling them that he would not be putting himself forward as a candidate at the next election, but that his immediate future as Colonial Secretary was entirely in the hands of the Prime Minister.[6] Macmillan agreed to this. He suggested that if the preliminary steps to find a new candidate could be kept secret then so much the better; but if there was any chance of a leak, Lennox-Boyd had better make a statement to the press.[7]

On the morning of 14 March, only hours before he was due to meet with his constituency party, Lennox-Boyd received a grave piece of news from the Governor of Kenya, Sir Evelyn Baring. On 3 March, 11 inmates had died in the Hola detention camp. The Kenya government had initially sought to portray the deaths as a tragic accident caused by a contaminated water supply. Baring now had to tell Lennox-Boyd that his initial information had been incorrect and that the deaths had probably been due to violence. Realizing that a storm of protest was about to be unleashed, Lennox-Boyd immediately contacted Macmillan. As he later recalled,

> [Macmillan] said...'Poor Alan, what a bore – we will discuss this on Monday.' I said Monday was a bit late. 'I have got my President and Chairman here and I am going to announce this afternoon I shall not stand at the next election.' 'You are still on to that silly plan are you?', he said. I said, 'Well, I am and it is what you promised.' 'Well,' he said, 'you cannot go now, can you?' And I said, 'No, I cannot, but it is very awkward.'[8]

Lennox-Boyd's immediate and extremely embarrassing task was to explain to his constituency party President and Chairman that he would, after all, be seeking re-election.

When Lennox-Boyd finally did return to the back benches by mutual consent after the 1959 election, Macmillan had warm words for him in his diary:

> Alan Lennox-Boyd leaves us, much to my regret. He has been an outstanding Colonial Secretary, for 5 years of growth and development in all the Overseas Territories. If he had bad luck over Kenya (the Hola Camp) and Nyasaland, these are very small affairs in comparison to the wonderful work which he has done.[9]

The timing of Lennox-Boyd's decision to leave the Government and Macmillan's repeated efforts over the course of 1959 to persuade him to stay put, tend to disprove the common assumption that he was eased out of the Colonial Office in order to open the way for the rapid liquidation of Britain's colonial empire.[10] Nevertheless, there are unmistakable signs that during Lennox-Boyd's final year in office, Macmillan was becoming dissatisfied with the general direction of British policy towards Africa and was eager to play a more active role in its formulation. An early indication of this was his decision, in November 1958, to assume the chairmanship of the Cabinet Colonial Policy Committee and to expand its remit.[11] Initially, Lennox-Boyd was in full agreement with this suggestion, although he was subsequently disturbed by a note to Ministers which described the role of the Committee as being 'to assist the Cabinet in controlling constitutional development in the colonial territories'.[12] He was clearly worried that the policy-making process was about to become more centralized.

Macmillan's interest was inevitably aroused by the colonial policy initiatives of Britain's European neighbours. In January 1959, riots in the Belgian Congo were swiftly followed by the first firm declaration from the Belgian government that it intended to prepare the territory for independence. Elsewhere in Africa in the early months of 1959, France's sub-Saharan colonies were adopting new and more democratic constitutions under the terms of Charles de Gaulle's short-lived scheme for a French 'Community'.[13] At a meeting of the Colonial Policy Committee on 17 April 1959, Macmillan implied that Britain could learn lessons from these political experiments:

> Recent developments in other countries had raised the question whether our form of parliamentary democracy was necessarily the best for these territories, or whether some other form of democratic government might lead to their acquiring greater stability when they became independent of the United Kingdom.[14]

Macmillan developed this theme in the summer of 1959 during discussions about *Africa: The Next Ten Years*. Produced by the

Cabinet's Official Africa Committee, this document set out the long-term considerations which seemed likely to shape British policy over the following decades and suggested some of the forms it might take. It grew out of talks at Brize Norton between Selwyn Lloyd and American Secretary of State, Foster Dulles, at which they agreed that Britain and the United States should seek to undertake a joint examination of the future of Africa.

Africa: the Next Ten Years was circulated in its final form at the beginning of June 1959.[15] It combined a conventional defence of the policy of gradual constitutional development in East Africa with a more gloomy assessment of the prospects for success of the Central African Federation. If agreement could be reached at the 1960 constitutional conference then European leadership in Central Africa would probably be maintained; if not, then the Federation might well decline into racial conflict and could even disintegrate, with Southern Rhodesia drifting into the orbit of apartheid South Africa. Among the threats to continued Western influence identified by the document were Pan-Africanism, Soviet penetration and the possible growth of a Pan-Islamic movement encouraged by Egyptian propaganda. It was also extremely apprehensive about the likely effect on British colonies of the preferential trading agreements made under the Treaty of Rome between France and Belgium's territories in Africa and the members of the EEC. The document's authors could see few lessons for Britain in the French and Belgian models. Understandably, they claimed to be more optimistic about the likely impact of growing American interest in Africa, arguing that Britain could benefit considerably from increased cooperation with the United States in this sphere.

Despite the fact that it adhered closely to Lennox-Boyd's own views, *Africa: The Next Ten Years* did not meet with an enthusiastic response from Downing Street. Macmillan's private secretary, Philip de Zulueta, complained that the paper was 'permeated by the spirit of colonial administration in decadence'.[16] In particular, Zulueta felt that insufficient attention had been paid to the administrative practices of other colonial powers in Africa. Given, he argued, that the French had managed to produce 'a higher type of politician' in their colonies than had the British, might not Britain benefit from adopting the French habit of breaking down tribal structures and encouraging Africans to participate in their own administrative systems? He also wondered whether more thought might be given to devising some alternative form of post-independence government to Western-style parliamentary democracy, which had so clearly failed in Ghana. Zulueta questioned the whole notion of coordinating policy with the Americans, arguing that American policy was geared, essentially, to gaining access to Africa's mineral resources. He implied that the other European colonial powers might have a common interest in seeking to block the spread of American influence in Africa.

Macmillan echoed much of what Zulueta had to say in his own response to the document. He began from the optimistic assumption that over the following decade Africa would be 'one of the few parts of the world in which the European powers still have direct influence'.[17] He suggested that Britain might explore the possibilities of coordinating her colonial policy with the other European powers in Africa, perhaps in the process adjusting some anomalies in her territorial boundaries.[18] Secondly, echoing de Zulueta, he asked whether Britain could learn from the French method of 'breaking down indigenous tribal arrangements'. In that connection he wondered about the role the English language might play and whether there might be benefits in educating African students in England rather than at home. Thirdly, Macmillan suggested that 'more thought ought to be given to the role of Christianity in keeping the Africans orientated towards Western ideas'. He also suggested that the economic division of Europe which he agreed might be a consequence of the development of the EEC could be averted by greater cooperation between the colonial powers.

Lennox-Boyd was not enthusiastic about Macmillan's suggestion of joint talks with the other European powers on economic and other matters, fearing that this would be seen as Europe 'ganging up' on the Africans. As to the respective merits of other forms of administration, he told Macmillan, 'I honestly don't think that any of them is better able, or as able as ours to develop stable African governments well disposed towards the West'.[19] He felt that this was about 50 years too late to begin thinking about adjusting Africa's territorial boundaries. Lennox-Boyd agreed that Christianity could play an important role in binding Africa to the West, but added 'I doubt whether the Archbishop of Canterbury would agree that this was its role!'

Yet by the time Lennox-Boyd made this stout defence of the *status quo*, Macmillan had already begun to explore alternative approaches. In the late spring and early summer of 1959, he had conducted informal discussions with the then Minister of Labour, Iain Macleod, the founder of the Capricorn Africa Society, David Stirling, and the Commonwealth Secretary, Lord Home, about new policy initiatives in Africa, possibly along the lines of a general statement of intent.[20] Like Macmillan's gloss on *Africa: The Next Ten Years*, the ideas they examined were largely characterized by their extreme impracticality and were largely forgotten as the pace of African decolonization accelerated. Nevertheless, by the spring of 1959, Macmillan's impatience with the general direction of British policy in Africa was palpable, and it owed much to two separate developments that, by chance, both occurred on 3 March 1959 – perhaps the most important single date in the story of Britain's withdrawal from Africa.

Part II: The Past – The Devlin Report and Hola Camp

July 1958 witnessed the return to Nyasaland of its most distinguished son: Dr Hastings Kamuzu Banda. Born into a peasant family in 1902, Banda had already achieved great things. Having made his way to the United States, he studied history and political science at Chicago University, and medicine in Nashville Tennessee. He then took diplomas in Glasgow and in Edinburgh where he also became an Elder of the Church of Scotland.[21] Banda practised in Tyneside with the Mission for Coloured Seamen, and then from 1945 to 1953 in London where he was widely known and respected. During his time in London he led opposition among Nyasaland's Africans to the imposition of federation. He refused to play any part in the politics of the new federation, preferring instead to practise medicine in the Gold Coast. Finally, in the summer of 1958, he was persuaded to return to his homeland and take up the leadership of the nationalist struggle. Shortly before departing for Nyasaland, Banda had cheerfully boasted to Lennox-Boyd, 'I am going to bust your damned federation'.

Banda's arrival in his home-land acted as a catalyst for unrest. In October 1958, a disturbance in Blantyre by a crowd which had just been addressed by Banda, led to calls by the local press and settlers for a government clamp-down. On 20 January 1959, police used tear gas on a crowd in Zomba which had marched on the police station. Again, the incident followed a speech by Banda. These incidents served to shake the Federal government out of their initial complacency. On the same day as the incident in Zomba, Bob de Quehen, director of the Federal Intelligence and Security Bureau, recommended to Welensky that the Nyasaland government should engineer a confrontation with Banda following which they could deport him.[22] When Welensky wrote to Lennox-Boyd on 23 January, he echoed de Quehen's sentiments. He argued that there were two issues on which 'we could possibly have a show-down'. These were the proposals for a new constitution and the federalization of African agriculture. Welensky suggested that Banda was far more likely to take a stand on the former, and in particular the continued existence of Nyasaland within the Federation. For that reason 'the sooner an announcement can be made about the Nyasaland constitution, the better, because it would bring matters to a head'.[23] As such, Lennox-Boyd can have been under absolutely no illusions about Welensky's intentions.

As unrest in the territory increased in late January and early February 1959, the Nyasaland Special Branch obtained reports of a secret meeting of Banda's African National Congress which had supposedly taken place on 25 January. Banda had not been present. The meeting had allegedly discussed what action they would take if Banda was arrested, and had agreed the following plan: D.K. Chisiza, H.B. Chipembere and Rose Chibambo, all leading members of Congress, would assume the leadership of the movement. They would then designate a day, 'R-Day', upon which they would launch a campaign of sabotage and would carry out the murder of Asians and Europeans including Governor Robert Armitage. This was chilling stuff, but the Nyasaland government was sufficiently familiar with Congress rhetoric to take it with a pinch of salt and wait to see how the Congress responded. For Welensky, however, it was the opportunity he wanted to engineer a 'show-down'. He put the Federal army on alert and invited Armitage to discuss the situation with him. Armitage was not prepared to be rushed into action by the Federal Prime Minister. He told Welensky that his latest information indicated that Congress did not contemplate a serious confrontation until Banda was arrested or constitutional changes were announced.[24] He wanted to do nothing which might cause the postponement of the impending visit by the Minister of State for the Colonies, Lord Perth. Nor was Armitage in any hurry to pass on details of the murder plot to London. When, on 10 February, Perth provided Macmillan with a brief appraisal of the situation in Nyasaland, he made no mention of any 'plot'.[25] Lennox-Boyd himself was away from London for much of February and thus in a poor position to judge the seriousness of the situation.

On 19 February, Armitage reported to the Colonial Office that the internal security situation in his territory, particularly in the Central and Northern provinces, had deteriorated further. In response, he had requested a battalion of the King's African Rifles and two platoons of riot police from Northern Rhodesia. He hoped that this display of force would prevent a further deterioration of the situation. In seeking to justify his actions he referred to the disturbances being 'part of Congress programme now known to have been determined at meeting in bush [sic] held on 25 January'.[26]

The following day, as attempts were being made to control fresh rioting in the Karonga district, Armitage and Sir Arthur Benson, the Governor of Northern Rhodesia, attended a Heads of Government meeting in Salisbury. Armitage described the intelligence report he had received about the Congress meeting in the bush on 25 January. Sir Edgar Whitehead, the Southern Rhodesian Prime Minister, told the meeting that he was thinking of imposing a state of emergency in his territory. He was, therefore, concerned by the prospect of troops moving from Southern Rhodesia to act as reinforcements in Nyasaland. According to Benson, he thought it better 'to clean up all the subversionists in Southern Rhodesia first and get them inside' before sending troops to Nyasaland.[27] Benson told the meeting that his territory was under control and that he could enforce order without recourse to a state of emergency.

At this point, accounts of the meeting differ. Benson claimed that by the time he and Armitage left the meeting, Welensky and the other Federal Ministers present had given no indication that they agreed with Whitehead. Since there seemed to be no immediate threat to public order in Southern Rhodesia, Benson assumed that the idea of declaring an emergency was a non-starter. Yet according to the minutes of the meeting and to Welensky's memoirs, it was decided to establish an inter-governmental committee on which Welensky, Whitehead, Benson and Armitage would all sit, to coordinate action. Whitehead would declare a state of emergency on 27 February, and Armitage would take action thereafter.[28]

All the evidence suggests that at this stage Armitage still felt that there was no immediate reason to impose a state of emergency in his own territory and wanted Perth to go ahead with his visit. On 24 February, however, there was more violence. Armitage responded by appealing for further reinforcements. Meanwhile, Banda was citing the arrival of Southern Rhodesian troops in Nyasaland as evidence of a European plot to dominate his territory and using this as a reason to refuse to condemn outbreaks of violence. Welensky seized upon these developments, and urged that Perth's visit be postponed.[29] Perth told Armitage that when reinforcements were available he hoped Armitage would take any action he thought necessary, irrespective of whether this prejudiced the success of constitutional talks during his own forthcoming visit to Nyasaland.[30]

At midnight on 25–26 February, to what Benson claimed was his complete surprise, the government of Southern Rhodesia declared a state of emergency. As well as being deeply disturbed by this development, Benson also felt that he was not being fully informed about the situation in Nyasaland.[31] Some hours after the emergency in Southern Rhodesia had come into force, Armitage told Perth that further outbreaks of rioting, and the threat of Congress escalating their campaign of violence, made it necessary for him to consider declaring a state of emergency in Nyasaland. He thought this should probably be done at midnight on 2–3 March.[32] In the circumstances, he felt that constitutional talks with Perth would not be appropriate.

The following day, the Cabinet discussed the situation in Nyasaland. Standing in for Lennox-Boyd, Julian Amery, the Under-Secretary of State, told Ministers of Armitage's intentions. In seeking to justify the declaration of another state of emergency, Amery emphasized the more alarming aspects of the Nyasaland government's intelligence reports. He claimed that the recent disturbances had been part of 'an organised threat to the European community'. Having succeeded in making his colleagues' flesh creep, Amery was faced with the inevitable question as to why, if the situation really was so dangerous, Armitage could not bring forward the declaration of the emergency. He replied that reinforcements from Southern Rhodesia could not be made available until 2 March.[33]

It was not until the evening of 1 March that Lennox-Boyd finally arrived back in London, having broken his journey from Aden with a brief stop-over in Cyprus. Both visits seemed to set the seal on important political initiatives. They left Lennox-Boyd with a strong sense of being at the height of his powers. On his return, he was met by Amery who gave him what he later suspected was 'a slightly too vivid description' of the situation in Nyasaland.[34] In retrospect, Lennox-Boyd admitted to having been 'a little overconfident' and confessed that this, combined with confusing signals from Nyasaland which Amery's interpretation did little to clarify, might have clouded his judgement. With the benefit of hindsight, he wished he had got straight back on a plane and flown out to Nyasaland to assess the situation for himself.[35]

Lennox-Boyd's response to events in Nyasaland may also have been shaped by a certain sense of guilt about the way which he had treated Armitage in the past. During Armitage's unhappy spell as Governor of Cyprus, Lennox-Boyd had repeatedly denied his requests for a security clamp-down. Were he to do so now, he would effectively be signalling a complete lack of confidence in the Governor. So instead of getting back on a plane, he returned to the Colonial Office and telegraphed Armitage asking him to confirm that the declaration of a state of emergency would go ahead as planned. Armitage replied that he intended to declare the state of emergency at 15 minutes past midnight on the morning of 3 March. About 180 people would be arrested. These would be Congress office holders and other activists. Special 'VIP attention' was promised for

Congress leaders Banda, Chipembere and Chisiza.[36] In a separate situation report Armitage warned,

> Intelligence reports over last few days show widespread activity by Congress branch officials to get people to create disturbances and prepare for the general plan of violence.[37]

No explicit reference was, however, made to a 'murder-plot' or to 'R' day.

Armitage went ahead with his declaration early on 3 March. Probably influenced by Amery's vivid account of recent developments, Lennox-Boyd told the House that he had evidence of plans by Congress 'to carry out widespread violence and murder of Europeans, Asians and moderate African leaders; that in fact a massacre was being planned'. Amery went further, making comparisons with Mau Mau and raising the spectre of a 'blood-bath'. Armitage was 'staggered' when he heard of this. He had made no reference in his announcement of the emergency either to a 'massacre' or a 'murder plot'. He later claimed that his actions had been informed by a desire to put an end to what he regarded as a campaign of sabotage and to curtail the escalating violence towards loyalist Africans. He regarded the Europeans as being quite capable of looking after themselves.[38]

The total number of people arrested by the police and troops in 'Operation Sunrise' was not 180 as Armitage had promised, but 1,322. If they could be dismissed as an unrepresentative minority, they were unrepresentative partly by virtue of including the African community's most highly educated and articulate members, the very people whose cooperation was vital if stable government was to be maintained. Among them were 34 out of the 35 Nyasas who possessed a university degree.[39] The arrests of the major Congress leaders went ahead smoothly. Banda was flown to a jail in Southern Rhodesia, and the feared reprisals did not materialize. Yet the round-ups did provoke spontaneous protests, to which the police and army responded with force. Within a week of the declaration of the emergency no Europeans had been harmed, but 48 Africans had been killed by the security forces. The worst incident occurred at Nkata Bay, where prisoners were being loaded into a ship. A crowd, intent on freeing the prisoners, advanced on troops who fired, killing 20 people.

The violence used during the operation, and the fact that the Governor of Nyasaland and the Colonial Secretary appeared to disagree about why it had been initiated, led to Opposition calls for an enquiry. The Government responded by announcing the creation of a commission to examine the affair. The person eventually chosen to lead it was Sir Patrick Devlin, a distinguished High Court judge. Devlin was not Lennox-Boyd's first choice – he had unsuccessfully attempted to persuade Lord Morton, an Appeal Court judge, to accept the job.[40]   But Devlin and his three colleagues were all regarded as being 'sound', establishment figures with broadly Conservative sympathies. As such, Ministers felt that they had little to fear from the commission.[41]

On 14 March, just as Lennox-Boyd was considering what form the Nyasaland enquiry should take, he received a further massive setback, this time from Kenya. As we have already seen, on the very day he was to announce his intention not to stand at the next general election, Evelyn Baring, the governor of Kenya, revealed the shocking news about the true circumstances behind the deaths of 11 detainees at Hola detention camp on 3 March.

In order to understand what happened at Hola, one needs to appreciate the way in which principles governing the treatment of 'Mau Mau' detainees evolved over time. By 1956, the Kenya government had developed a relatively sophisticated system of 'rehabilitation'. In theory, this consisted of a mixture of political and religious indoctrination, and hard physical labour. In practice, even one of the architects of the system is prepared to admit that the controlled application of psychological pressure sometimes gave way to incidents in which detainees were 'illegally assaulted and even killed'.[42] Indeed, there is ample evidence to suggest that detainees were routinely subjected to vicious attacks and systematic torture by their captors.[43] This was not merely the result of junior 'screeners' getting out of control: several camp commandants acquired reputations among the detainees for their sadism. The Fairn Commission, established by Lennox-Boyd to report on the camps in the wake of the Hola massacre, claimed to have heard 'impressive testimony from responsible people on all sides that violence, not just corporal punishment, was often used in the past by 'screening teams' to compel confessions.'[44]

By the end of 1956, this system had succeeded in 'processing' the majority of those arrested by the authorities. Yet this still left over 20,000 detainees within the system who had so-far failed to cooperate with their 'rehabilitation'. Their continued presence in detention came to be seen as an impediment to constitutional progress and the Kenya government came under increased pressure from London to speed them through the rehabilitation process.

Officially, prison regulations prohibited the use of force against detainees except in response to violence or resistance to escort, and then 'no more than is absolutely necessary'. Yet under political pressure to speed up the rehabilitation of detainees, senior figures in Baring's administration decided that the regulations as they stood were unduly restrictive. Officers should, they believed, have greater discretion to use a limited amount of force to overcome the resistance of the 'irreconcilables'. In November 1959, shortly after taking over from Lennox-Boyd as Colonial Secretary, Iain Macleod told his Cabinet colleagues that the Kenyan Minister for African Affairs, C.M. 'Monkey' Johnston, had been responsible for the unofficial change of policy. Macleod suggested that Johnston had 'condoned illegal methods of 'persuading' detainees to confess and co-operate', without the knowledge of Baring and in direct contravention of his orders.[45] Yet according to one of those at the heart of the rehabilitation process, the new policy was known about and approved at the highest level.[46]

The initiative for the new policy certainly appears to have come from Johnston as the Minister jointly responsible for the detention camps. In 1957, Johnston, with the approval of Baring, decided that a new, more intensive effort was required drastically to reduce the number of detainees still in captivity. He appointed a single officer to coordinate the process, who was to report directly to Johnston and to Johnston only. The officer – Terence Gavaghan – was given no written instructions, but understood from Johnston that he had considerable latitude in the way he discharged his duties.[47] On a visit to one of the camps, Eric Griffiths-Jones, the Kenya Attorney General, agreed that the existing Prison Regulations did not allow Gavaghan and his staff sufficient scope to deal with recalcitrant detainees. He ruled that they might legitimately use 'compelling' as opposed to 'punitive' force to induce detainees to obey instructions. This might, he added, include a kick to the front of the body or a blow delivered to the head with the open hand. Again, nothing was committed to paper.

Baring provided Lennox-Boyd with enthusiastic reports of Gavaghan's progress. In April 1958, he told the Secretary of State that he had recently visited the Mwea filter camps and had been 'enormously impressed by the remarkable work done during the period of exactly one year by Mr Gavaghan'.[48] Baring gave Gavaghan much of the credit for the fact that the number of detainees had been reduced to between 10,000 and 11,000. Gavaghan relinquished control of the rehabilitation process well before the Hola incident and bears no responsibility for this or any other instances of violence against inmates. Yet the tacit relaxation of the rules governing the use of force which had accompanied his appointment provided a dangerous amount of licence for less scrupulous officers. One can be fairly confident that Lennox-Boyd knew that an unofficial change of policy had taken place. In an

interview conducted shortly after Lennox-Boyd's death, W.A.C.
Mathieson, head of the Colonial Office's East Africa desk from 1955–
59, guardedly admitted that Lennox-Boyd had expressed concern
about the use of violence against Mau Mau suspects.[49]
Characteristically, Lennox-Boyd himself was far more candid. In one
of a series of interviews conducted in the 1970s, he recalled,

> I went the week after I left the Colonial Office, to stay with Alec Home
> at Dorneywood for the day and Iain Macleod was there. I brought out
> all the skeletons for Iain's perusal, of people other than those
> concerned with the Hola thing whose breaches of discipline I had
> tolerated on Evelyn's advice. So I said, 'Now you will know all the cover
> up operations that I have made.' There were three or four others –
> unauthorized beatings under extreme provocation, and various crimes
> that people had made against others under the cover of the emergency.
> I had the whole lot there and I gave them all to Iain. He was very
> shocked. I said, 'Well if you can apply the canons of the cloister to a
> battle in tribal Africa, good luck to you,' or words to that effect.[50]

A steady stream of reports alleging the torture and murder of detainees reached the ears of anti-colonial campaigners in London.
Pressure from the Opposition culminated on 24 February 1959 in
a full Commons debate on the issue. A Labour motion signed by
almost 200 members demanded an independent inquiry into the
conditions and administration of Kenyan prisons. Lennox-Boyd
argued that an inquiry was unnecessary. He had been advised by
Baring that the latest spate of allegations were unfounded and that
a formal investigation would undermine the morale of his officers.[51]
The Government opposed the Labour motion and it was defeated
by 288 votes to 232. It was against this background that the Hola
tragedy took place.

In November 1958, Lewis, the Kenya Commissioner of Prisons, had
visited Hola, a detention area on the Tana River, consisting of an
irrigation settlement, an open camp and a closed camp. The closed
camp had become the final dumping ground for those 'hard core'
detainees who were thought to be beyond the reach of the
rehabilitation process. Lewis concluded that a tougher approach to
these irreconcilables was needed.[52] When the new camp commandant,
Sullivan, was about to take up his post in January 1959, Lewis briefed
him and impressed upon him the need to tighten discipline. By
February 1959, there were 208 detainees in the closed camp, about
half of whom were working. Of the rest, 32 were certified unfit to work
and the other 66 refused to do so. A further intake of 'hard-core'
detainees was due to arrive shortly. The numbers of cooperative
detainees were insufficiently large in proportion to recalcitrant ones
to enable the standard procedures of 'dilution' to be applied. Indeed,
it was feared that the militants already inside the closed camp might

'reinfect' the others.[53]   On 7 February, Cowan, the Senior Superintendent of Prisons, was sent to Hola to assess how best to deal with the situation. Cowan briefed Sullivan verbally as to his conclusions but did not show him any written instructions. He then drafted a memorandum for Lewis, dated 11 February, setting out his ideas on how the Hola militants could be induced to begin working. He envisaged confronting the detainees with hundreds of riot police and armed guards in a massive show of force. A small group of detainees – less than 20 – would then be ordered to undertake a form of agricultural work not requiring the use of tools. Cowan went on,

> It is assumed that the party [of detainees] would obey this order [to go to work] but should they refuse to work they would be manhandled to the site of work and forced to carry out the task.

Although Lewis's recommendations appeared to contravene the Prison department's own regulations, they were broadly in accord with the notion of 'compelling force'. The fact that Sullivan was not given written instructions was also wholly characteristic of the way in which the unofficial policy was managed. On the basis of the information they had received verbally, Sullivan and his colleagues at Hola had doubts about the viability of the plan. In a situation report which Sullivan drafted for his superiors on 13 February, Sullivan made clear the extent of their concern. He reported that the representative of the Ministry of Works on the site had asked to be 'dissociated entirely' from the plan.

Sullivan's report was seen by Lewis, who was sufficiently concerned to send it and a copy of Cowan's memorandum to Cusack, the Minister of Internal Security and Defence. He noted that the Cowan plan might result in someone getting 'hurt or even killed' and suggested that it be brought to the notice of the Security Council. At the same time, however, he did not take the most elementary of precautions, namely to supply Sullivan with a copy of Cowan's memorandum. The papers which Lewis submitted to Cusack were also considered by Johnston who had joint responsibility for the rehabilitation process. Despite the serious warnings they had received, Cusack and Johnston decided to authorize the plan without reference to the Security Council, subject only to the proviso that Lewis should ensure a sufficient number of warders were available at Hola to deal with all eventualities.

On 25 February, Sullivan was instructed to proceed with the scheme. The timing of this instruction was, for British MPs on both sides of the House, to carry the disturbing implication that the defeat the previous day of Labour's motion calling for an enquiry into the prison camps had been taken by the Kenyan government as a signal to initiate the Cowan plan. Sullivan put the plan into operation on 3 March. He reportedly told his African staff in Swahili, 'If people make trouble you will hit him. But you will only hit on the legs. Don't entirely hit.' Like Cowan's written injunction this was ambiguous, and Sullivan must have been aware of the grave danger of suggesting the use of force without making very clear the limits within which it could legally be applied. Having done this, his ignorance of the details of the Cowan plan led him into an error which contributed to the scale of the tragedy. Cowan had envisaged that there would be 66 'hard-core' detainees involved in the plan and that they should be moved in four batches. He expected trouble and believed that resistance would be easier to control if the prisoners were in relatively small groups. Sullivan, however, simply ignored this part of the plan. He managed to persuade 85 'hard-core' prisoners, to leave the camp willingly and march towards the work place in a single group.

When the group reached its destination, trouble arose. The guards responded by beating the detainees with rifles and batons. The violence briefly subsided before the guards resumed the beating. Witnesses at the subsequent inquest gave widely varying reports as to the cause of the confrontation. Sullivan claimed that his men had been seriously provoked and that he had done his best to restrain them. Other witnesses, however, recalled that the detainees had squatted on the ground, offering merely passive resistance, and that during the second round of beatings Sullivan had done little to intervene.[54] Sullivan then left the scene and returned to the camp. During his absence, the guards again attacked their charges. By the following morning, 10 of the detainees were dead and a further prisoner died shortly afterwards as a result of his injuries. Many more were injured.

Although Baring claimed not to have been told in advance of the Cowan plan, his behaviour following the deaths earned him little credit. On hearing of the deaths, he immediately sent three officials to investigate. On the basis of a brief and thoroughly inadequate inspection of Hola, they concluded that 'the compelling exercise was in no way connected with the cause of death' of the detainees. Coutts, the deputy commandant at Hola, had told the officials that he had seen a detainee collapse near a water cart from which he had been drinking, and this evidence was presented so as to imply that the deaths had been due to poisoning. Baring, Cusack, Johnston, Lewis, the Chief Government Doctor, and Griffiths-Jones met to discuss their report. Cusack, Johnston and Lewis had all been present when Griffiths-Jones gave his definition of 'compelling force', and they were also fully aware of the details of Cowan's report. Nevertheless, although the possibility that the deaths were the result of violence was discussed, the meeting decided to endorse the officials' conclusions. They issued a statement which made no mention of violence and contained the following passage:

> The deaths occurred after they had drunk water from a water cart which was used by all members of the working party and by their guards.

Baring and his colleagues had been careful not to say that the detainees had died *as a result of* drinking poisoned water, but the implication was clear.

As we have already seen, when Baring heard from the pathologists that there was clear evidence that the Hola deaths had resulted from violence, he informed Lennox-Boyd. This news reached the Secretary of State on 14 March. An inquest into the deaths opened in Mombasa on 18 March under W.H. Goudie, the Senior Resident Magistrate, and thereafter a fuller picture of the terrible events in Kenya gradually emerged. D.N. Pritt, who was in Kenya for the trial of Rawson Macharia, tipped off Barbara Castle that a major scandal was breaking.[55] On 26 March, Castle asked Lennox-Boyd whether Kenyan officials had attempted a cover-up over the Hola deaths and made the first mention in Parliament of the existence of the Cowan plan. In response to her demand for a full judicial enquiry, Lennox-Boyd would only say that he could not anticipate the findings of the current inquest.[56]

Goudie's findings, which were published on 6 May, did little to apportion proper responsibility for the deaths at Hola. He found that the deaths had been caused by shock and haemorrhage due to multiple bruising. Yet he also concluded that, although illegal force had been employed, there was insufficient evidence to bring specific charges against any individual. After consulting Baring, Lennox-Boyd decided that in order to counter the growing demands for a full judicial inquiry into the circumstances of the Hola deaths, the Government should appoint two experts to advise the Governor on the future administration of the detention camps, with particular reference to the investigation of complaints. They were to be Duncan Fairn, the Director of Prisons Administration, and Sir George Beresford-Stooke, a former governor of Sierra Leone. As a sop to the Labour Party, Lennox-Boyd persuaded Baring to accept the appointment of an additional commission member, Canon Bewes, the Africa Secretary of the Church Missionary Society.[57] Any credit which might have followed from this, however, was almost immediately cancelled by the decision of Griffiths-Jones not to proceed with any prosecutions against those implicated in the Hola incident. Disciplinary proceedings were to be brought against Sullivan and Coutts, but no action was to be taken against the African guards.[58] Callaghan telephoned the Colonial Office later that day to express his 'astonishment' and 'indignation'.[59]

The decision not to prosecute exacerbated Lennox-Boyd's problems and did nothing to stem growing Parliamentary criticism. In June, the Government was faced with a Labour motion deploring the Hola deaths and demanding the immediate establishment of a public enquiry. In a further effort to blunt demands for such an enquiry, they published a White Paper on 10 June which included Goudie's conclusions and a list of the charges against Sullivan and Coutts. On the eve of its publication, Macmillan was in a pessimistic mood, complaining in his diary that the Government were 'in a real jam'.[60] When the White Paper came out, however, he was relieved by what he regarded as the sensible press reaction to it.[61] His principal concern was to keep his Cabinet steady and united. On 4 June, the Cabinet discussed Hola. Lennox-Boyd had not yet returned from a visit to West Africa and Perth was left to put forward the Colonial Office viewpoint. The Cabinet was divided on the desirability of instituting a full enquiry as Labour was requesting. Some Ministers were keen that such an inquest should extend to the circumstances surrounding the production of the Kenya government's water-cart communiqué.[62] There was broad agreement within Cabinet that a great deal of the blame for Hola should be pinned firmly on the Kenya government itself rather than onto individual officers.

On his return from West Africa, however, Lennox-Boyd sought to guide opinion within Cabinet away from this position and towards a more forthright defence of the Kenya Government. The new approach followed a familiar pattern: Baring, who had returned to England for a prolonged visit, was keen to protect his senior officials from criticism, while Lennox-Boyd saw it as his duty to defend the Governor's line to his Ministerial colleagues. Baring made his position quite clear on 4 June at a meeting with Perth, Amery and Macpherson. He told them that blame should not be attached either to Cowan or to Cusack who had authorized the plan, and that he would not be a party to making 'scape-goats' of them.[63] On 8 June, after a meeting with Lennox-Boyd and the Chief Whip, Macmillan set down their new position. This was that the Government should refuse to establish any enquiry into the recent past and stress instead the importance of the Fairn Committee in establishing guidelines for the future. Rather than seeking to blame Baring's administration, the Government would stress its success in the war against terrorism.[64] Macmillan's belief that he could carry the Cabinet and parliamentary party with him on this basis was dented somewhat on 13 June when, quite incredibly, it was announced that Cowan had been awarded an MBE. Macmillan could hardly warrant the stupidity of the Colonial Office in recommending Cowan for an honour and remarked in his diary (not for the first time) that it was 'a badly run office'.[65]

The debate on Labour's motion about Hola took place on 16 June. Macmillan confessed himself satisfied with the Government's defence. He complimented Lennox-Boyd on his speech and told him that what had really got the Government through had been his own character and reputation.[66] In the privacy of his diary, Macmillan was a little more restrained, recording that the debate 'has gone off 'as well as could be expected' but it has been an anxious day'.[67] He thought that Lennox-Boyd's speech had been 'in the main' successful, and that his high standing within the Commons had helped to deflect some of the more barbed personal criticisms. Yet doubts about the Government's handling of the affair remained, and not only on the Opposition benches. Members of the Conservatives' Commonwealth Affairs Committee continued to express grave concerns about the issue.[68]

At around this time, Lennox-Boyd's most dangerous adversary over the Hola incident entered the fray. This was Enoch Powell, then on the back benches after having left the Government in January 1958. He had resigned along with fellow Treasury Ministers Peter Thorneycroft and Nigel Birch over Macmillan's refusal to sanction sufficiently far-reaching deflationary measures. As well as being hostile to the Government's handling of the economy, Powell had also been evolving a powerful critique of British colonial policy. Despite having entered politics in 1945 with the avowed intention of helping to save India for the Empire, by 1957 Powell was arguing that the Conservative Party had to be 'cured' of its attachment to Imperialism.[69] Hola provided an opportunity for Powell to expand further upon his attitude towards the British Empire. On 18 June, he told Lennox-Boyd,

> After the many ways in which we have been associated for ten years past, I am sure you do not think I could have any feelings towards yourself but those of admiration and the warmest goodwill. It is not in spite of this but because of it that I believe the matter of Hola Camp must not remain where it was at the end of Wednesday's debate. A large slice of responsibility for this administrative disaster lies at a high level in Kenya, and I trust that it is going to be accepted publicly and in the only possible way. If I have the opportunity, I feel I must say this in the 1922 Committee.[70]

If by 'the only possible way' Powell meant the resignation of the Colonial Secretary, Lennox-Boyd privately endorsed these sentiments. On 22 June, he urged Macmillan to accept his resignation. Macmillan refused to do so, citing among his reasons the damage this would do to the British and Kenya Governments and the fear that it 'might make the more extreme Africans feel that they had now got the white man on the run'.[71] Lennox-Boyd accepted the logic of these arguments and remained at his desk.

Criticism of Lennox-Boyd from within the Conservative party continued to mount. On 9 July 1959, the maverick Tory MP Lord Lambton published an article in the *Evening Standard* which, while stopping short of demanding Lennox-Boyd's resignation, suggested that his loyalty towards some of those implicated in the Hola affair was misplaced and that heads should roll. Although Lambton was the first Tory member to break ranks in public, plenty of his colleagues privately agreed with him. Yet Baring remained determined that heads should definitely *not* roll and Lennox-Boyd continued to support this view. The disciplinary committee into the actions of the Commandant of Hola and his deputy found that the charges against Sullivan were established while those against Coutts were unproven. The evidence gathered by the committee cast further doubt on the competence of Sullivan's superiors, but Baring was adamant that disciplinary actions should not extend beyond Hola's staff.

Taking his lead from the Governor, Lennox-Boyd persuaded Macmillan that only the most limited of consequences should follow from the disciplinary enquiry. Sullivan would merely be asked to retire with no loss of gratuity. No action would be taken against Coutts who had been exonerated by the disciplinary committee. Lennox-Boyd wanted Lewis, who had been criticized in the disciplinary committee's report, to be offered six months leave until the time when his retirement was due to take place. He felt sure, however, that, on being shown the report, Lewis would offer to resign as soon as possible. This he did. Campbell, who had been responsible for the misleading report into the Hola deaths, was not to be subject to any action. These proposals may have avoided a confrontation with the Kenya government, but they drew criticisms from some of Lennox-Boyd's colleagues, principally Reginald Manningham-Buller, the Attorney General, who felt that much stronger action needed to be taken against those implicated in the scandal.[72]

Just as Lennox-Boyd was becoming embroiled in a serious argument with the Attorney General over the Hola affair, the Nyasaland Emergency came back to haunt him with a vengeance.

Lord Devlin and his team, who had been sent to Nyasaland to investigate the circumstances of the Emergency, had discharged their task with devastating rigour. Having seen an advance copy of the report, Lennox-Boyd told Armitage that it was, as they had both expected, 'very hostile'.[73] On 13 July, the day on which the page proofs were flown to the Federation, Lennox-Boyd met with Macmillan, Home, Perth and Sir Norman Brook to discuss the report. Perth told the gathering that he had already talked to Devlin and had asked for amendments to be made. In particular Perth had requested changes to the summary of the report's conclusions, which the Commission's authors had added as an appendix. His colleagues felt that this did not go far enough and that the appendix should simply be deleted.[74] They were keen that journalists should not be presented with a ready-made series of headlines for the next morning's newspapers. Devlin subsequently agreed to this and the appendix was dropped. Curiously, however, Perth neglected to demand the deletion of what was undoubtedly to become the report's most famous, and, to the Government, deeply embarrassing, passage:

> Nyasaland is – no doubt temporarily – a police state, where it is not safe for anyone to express approval of the policies of the Congress party, to which the vast majority of politically-minded Africans belonged, and where it is unwise to express any but the most restrained criticism of government policy.

By the time it dawned on Perth quite how very damaging the phrase 'police state' was likely to be, the final report had already been printed and the only way of altering the passage would be to add a corrigendum slip. The effect of this would, of course, have been approximately the same as underlining the original words in red ink.[75]

There was far more than this passage to embarrass the Government in the final version of the Devlin commission's report. The document contained three, extremely damaging conclusions: first, that 'illegal force' had been used in making arrests and in the subsequent campaign of pacification.[76] Secondly, the commission was highly sceptical about the idea of a 'murder-plot'.[77] It accepted that a policy of violence had been adopted at the meeting on 25 January (without the knowledge of Banda himself), that there had been talk of beating and killing Europeans, and that, under the circumstances, the Nyasaland government had either 'to act or to abdicate'; but it concluded that the plans of the Malawi ANC fell far short of a cold-blooded programme of assassination or massacre. Thirdly, and perhaps most significantly, the report endorsed the view that opposition to the Federation among Nyasaland's Africans 'was deeply rooted and almost universally held'.[78]

Macmillan held a meeting about the Devlin report in Downing Street on 14 July. Lennox-Boyd, Home and Brook were again present, as was Edward Heath, the Chief Whip.[79] Parliamentary tactics were the focus of the discussion and in particular the timing of the report's publication. The Government was faced with a difficult situation: the House would be sitting for eight more days before the recess. Of these, five would be taken up by Opposition-sponsored debates. In addition to the Devlin report, the Government was due to publish a second White Paper on the Hola Camp affair. Ministers feared that the Opposition might attempt to repeat its tactics at the time of the Suez crisis and use each of the five days to debate Hola and the Devlin report. In order to evade this threat, it was decided that the publication of both documents, and a response to the Devlin Report, should be postponed until Wednesday 22 July. The following day, the Government would announce that it was ready to concede a debate on East and Central Africa on Monday 27th and possibly also Tuesday 28th.

As to the form which the response to the report would take, it would clearly be difficult for the Government to become involved in direct criticism of the Commission. The solution suggested by Macmillan was that the counter-attack should be framed as a series of preliminary observations by the Governor of Nyasaland. Hence, rather than merely defending himself against the report when the issue was debated in Parliament, Lennox-Boyd (having, of course been heavily involved in the drafting of the Governor's 'observations') could give the appearance of dealing 'in a balanced way' with the conflicting views of Devlin and Armitage. Macmillan thought that the Governor's reply should be 'of a robust nature'. It was decided that the report 'should be subjected to the sort of merciless ridicule F.E. Smith would apply where appropriate'.[80]

The Prime Minister lent Lennox-Boyd Chequers for the weekend of the 18–19 July. A formidable team was assembled there, including not only Lennox-Boyd, Armitage, Kilmuir and Amery but also Perth and Macpherson, the Permanent Under-Secretary. Charles Hill, Chancellor of the Duchy of Lancaster and the Government's resident expert on public relations, was also invited to attend. In advance of the weekend sessions, two teams of Colonial Office officials began to draft sections of the document; a 'political' group dealing with the status and functions of the Nyasaland government and a 'security' group dealing with the 'murder plot'.[81] Clearly, nothing was to be left to chance in the Governor's 'preliminary observations'.

The 'merciless ridicule' which Ministers had decided to adopt was aimed principally at the distinction the Devlin commission sought to draw between 'talk of beating and killing Europeans' and the planning of 'cold-blooded assassination or massacre'.[82] Yet in the face of the Devlin report's remarks about the degree of opposition to the Federation among Nyasas, the Government had no credible defence. Indeed, the despatch noted that the Governor had 'always recognized the existence of strong opposition to Federation in Nyasaland' and had often brought it to the attention of Lennox-Boyd.[83]

For all the effort that had been invested in it, Lennox-Boyd must have known that the Governor's despatch would do little to detract from the impact of the Devlin Report. He was also facing continued pressure from Manningham-Buller to take a tougher line against those implicated in the Hola scandal. On 18 July, Macmillan predicted in a characteristically melodramatic diary entry, 'The Attorney General may well drive the Colonial Secretary to resignation and so break up the Government.'[84] Seeking some room for manoeuvre, Lennox-Boyd told Baring that some of his ministerial colleagues believed that Campbell – author of the misleading report on the Hola deaths – should face disciplinary charges.[85] Entirely predictably, Baring strongly opposed any action being taken against Campbell, citing among other reasons the adverse effect this would have on morale within the prison service.[86]

By the morning of Monday 20 July when the Cabinet was due to discuss both Devlin and Hola, Lennox-Boyd was feeling tired and dejected. He was determined to back Baring, but felt that the Governor's refusal to sacrifice his subordinates, coming on top of the Devlin Report, put him in an impossible position. Once again, however, Macmillan had other ideas. The Prime Minister choreographed the events of that Monday with great care. From 10.30 to 11.00 am, he discussed tactics with Butler. Then both of them had a meeting with Lennox-Boyd who was keen that they should accept his resignation. According to Macmillan, he and Butler told Lennox-Boyd that this would be both damaging to the colonial administration and highly inconvenient to the Government.[87] In the face of Lennox-Boyd's continued doubts, Macmillan assured him that he would not give the Cabinet a lead on this issue but would leave them free to decide whether to endorse the actions of the Secretary of State and the Nyasaland government. He had, however, done his best to prepare the ground. At 11.15, a quarter of an hour before the meeting was due to begin, Ministers were asked to read the Governor's despatch. Macmillan therefore ensured that the Government's counterblast was fresh in their minds when the meeting began. Having introduced the issue of Nyasaland, he then asked each Minister in turn to express his view, beginning with Kilmuir and Manningham-Buller.[88] To Macmillan's profound relief, each in turn argued that the Government should stand by the Nyasaland administration and the Colonial Secretary. Following the meeting, Lennox-Boyd wrote to Macmillan, 'that was brilliantly done and I am greatly strengthened and reassured'.[89]

The culmination of the political confrontation over Hola and the Nyasaland emergency came during two days of highly charged Parliamentary debate on 27–28 July. First on the agenda was a Labour motion on the Hola affair. The debate began on Monday 27 July and lasted into the early hours of the following day. It came only five days after Lennox-Boyd had been called upon to respond at length to a debate on Central Africa and a day before he was again called upon to defend his actions in Parliament, this time against the criticisms made in the Devlin Commission's report. The debate on Hola contained two outstanding interventions both highly damaging to the Government. The first came from Barbara Castle, who by her own account was 'trembling so much from anger' that she could barely articulate the facts of the case.[90] Nevertheless she was able to cite an impressive catalogue of incompetence and deception. She was followed by Enoch Powell whose speech was couched in less emotive terms but was no less effective. During a meeting of the 1922 Committee on 22 July, Powell had openly suggested that Lennox-Boyd had a duty to resign over the deaths at Hola. Now, with cold, forensic skill, Powell deployed the evidence contained in the Government's two White Papers to demolish their argument that responsibility for the deaths lay essentially with Sullivan and to a lesser extent with Lewis. Powell absolved Lennox-Boyd from any personal blame for what he again referred to as 'a great administrative disaster'. Yet in the name of Lennox-Boyd's outstanding record as Colonial Secretary, Powell called on him 'to ensure that the responsibility is recognized and carried where it belongs, and is seen to belong'. He concluded:

> We cannot say, 'We will have African standards in Africa, Asian standards in Asia and perhaps British standards here at home'…We cannot, we dare not, in Africa of all places, fall below our own highest standards in the acceptance of responsibility.[91]

This, in a sense, went to the heart of Baring's stewardship in Kenya. Whyatt, his first Attorney General and Young, the Commissioner of the City of London Police who had been sent to Kenya to advise on changes in policing, had both tried to apply this principle. Both had been frustrated in their efforts to impose metropolitan standards of justice and investigation on Baring's administration. Baring, and Lennox-Boyd himself, believed that their approach was both naive and impracticable within the context of a counter-insurgency campaign, and more specifically an *African* counter-insurgency campaign. In terms of maintaining the structures of consent and cooperation upon which British rule rested, their objections were probably justified. Yet the logical corollary of this was that British Ministers would preside over a system which was prepared, in practice, to tolerate the use of a degree of illegal force by its personnel.

At 1.55 on the morning of 28 July, Lennox-Boyd rose to reply for the Government on the Hola affair. In an eloquent, although not entirely convincing speech, he sought to persuade the House that the Kenya government had not fallen short of the highest standards of administration. In Macmillan's view, Lennox-Boyd put up a good case, but was not helped by the Kenya government's management of the affair. He clearly believed, however, that the Government's survival owed more to the Labour party's poor handling of the debate than to the skill of his front bench. The Opposition had arranged for the issue to be debated on an Appropriation Bill which meant it could not be put to a vote. Macmillan believed, with good reason, that had Hola been the subject of a division 'quite a number of Conservatives' would have either voted against the Government or abstained.[92] Furthermore, by having the debate late at night – something the Opposition could have avoided – they ensured that their efforts to embarrass the Government would not be reported in the following morning's papers.

Yet if the late-night sitting was in some sense fortunate for the Government, it imposed a severe strain on Lennox-Boyd. The debate went on until 3.00 in the morning and Lennox-Boyd had to make another speech in the debate on the Devlin Report later that day. His predecessor, Oliver Chandos, commiserated with his plight and offered what encouragement he could:

> I am sure you would agree that our experience shows how ill the Labour Party takes to sitting up late. Once trained to go to bed at 9.30, they can never compete with people like you and me, who are trained to sit up late at night in 'chambering and wantonness' or, if you prefer it, in playing bridge and going to parties...I have been through one or two of these 'incidents' myself, so my rejoicings are hardly those of an onlooker. When you have the ermine around your neck, you and I will go to Baiae, like Pontius Pilate, and discuss the troubles which so often assail Procurators, though our provinces were a bit bigger than Judea.[93]

Supporting evidence for Chandos's thesis was scarce when, later on 28 July, the House debated the Devlin Report. Lennox-Boyd's

Labour opponents were sufficiently wide awake to give him another rough ride. Lennox-Boyd knew that this might be the last time he addressed the Commons and he rose to the occasion with a defence not just of his handling of the Nyasaland crisis but of his stewardship at the Colonial Office over the previous five years. Bevan had concluded his speech with a fierce attack on Macmillan's Government, describing the Conservatives' performance over the previous four years as 'squalid'. Lennox-Boyd replied that those years had seen independence for Ghana and Malaya, preparations for the imminent independence of Nigeria, rapid strides in that direction for the West Indies and the construction of racial 'partnership' in East Africa. In the subsequent division even Lennox-Boyd's critics within the Conservative Party like Powell and Astor voted with the Government.

At the same time as time as he was attempting to deal with the political repercussions of Hola and the Nyasaland emergency, Lennox-Boyd also faced the problem of how to prevent any more skeletons from falling out of Baring's well-stocked cupboard. Shortly before he left the Colonial Office, the alarming possibility arose that the unofficial policy regarding the treatment of hard-core detainees might become public. Prosecutions were pending of a District Commissioner and a District Officer, for unauthorized punishments inflicted on eight detainees at the Aguthi camp in January 1959. The two men refused to give statements to the CID, apparently because they believed that their testimonies would indicate that the offences took place with the knowledge, or even implicit authority of 'Monkey' Johnston and their Provincial Commissioner.[94] A trial threatened to reignite the Hola scandal and open a flood of new prosecutions. This could best be averted, Baring decided, by the introduction of a general amnesty as part of the ending of the state of emergency. Yet the practical difficulties of doing this proved too much for Lennox-Boyd during his final months in office.

On 18 June, Lennox-Boyd told members of the Cabinet Colonial Policy Committee that the Governors of both Kenya and Nyasaland wished to bring to an end the states of emergency in their territories. The problem was that they were not prepared to release many of those currently detained without trial under emergency powers. It would therefore be necessary for the British Government to introduce special legislation to allow for the continued detention of such people. Lennox-Boyd felt, quite understandably, that with Parliament in such a belligerent mood over Africa it was the wrong time to introduce legislation of this kind.[95] When the issue was reconsidered by the Committee at the beginning of July it was decided to leave the matter until after the summer recess. Hence, it was Lennox-Boyd's successor, Iain Macleod, who in November sought the Committee's permission to bring the emergency in Kenya to an end. It was decided that the Governor should act through a local Preservation of Public Security Ordinance which would give the him limited powers of detention without trial, while avoiding the need for British legislation. The ending of the emergency so soon after Macleod's arrival at the Colonial Office appeared to herald a new policy towards Kenya. In fact, it was at least in part the legacy of Baring's efforts to cover his tracks and was decided upon despite continued concerns on the part of Manningham-Buller about the propriety of the Kenya government's actions.[96]

Macleod's arrival at the Colonial Office in October 1959 also seemed to herald a more general change of policy towards constitutional development in East and Central Africa. Yet as we shall see in the final part of this chapter, the political situation within Africa had developed in such a way by the autumn of 1959, that change was virtually irresistible.

Part III: The Present

Kenya

In November 1957, largely as a response to concerted African pressure, Lennox-Boyd imposed a new constitution in Kenya. African representation was to be increased so as eventually to give them the same number of elected seats as the Europeans in the Legislative Council. Lennox-Boyd made the – in retrospect laughable – promise that there would be no further changes in the proportions of communal representation for another 10 years. The legislature would sit as an electoral college to nominate twelve additional 'Specially Elected Members', four of them from each of the European, Asian and African communities. Their method of selection was clearly intended to blunt the edge of the African nationalist presence in the Council: the fact that nominated as well as elected members of the legislature would choose the 12 extra members meant that Europeans would play a dominant role in the selection process.[97] There was also to be a 'Council of State' with powers of delay, revision and reference. The precise composition, function and powers of this body were not defined. Finally, the importance of the portfolios held by the two African ministers was to be increased, although the 2:2:4 breakdown of African, Asian and European ministers was left unaltered.

If Lennox-Boyd had hoped to establish conditions of stability and 'multi-racial partnership' through the new constitution, there were few immediate signs of either. The African Elected Members, led by the young and dazzlingly talented Luo politician, Tom Mboya, attempted to organize a boycott of the 'Specially Elected' seats. A dangerous split also emerged in the European community centring around the figure of Ernest Vasey, the Minister for Finance and Development. Baring regarded Vasey, the most progressive of European politicians in Kenya, as an important bridge between the races. As such, he was keen to keep him in the government and hoped he could secure one of the Specially Elected seats.[98] Yet following the publication in March 1958 of comments attributed to Vasey supporting the establishment of an African majority government, his European colleagues in the legislature – among them the Minister of Agriculture and key 'moderate', Michael Blundell – made a concerted and ultimately successful effort to prevent Vasey from being elected.

In general terms, the creation of the 'Specially Elected' seats produced mixed results. Although Mboya and his supporters had urged a boycott of the seats, a number of Africans did stand for them and Baring hoped that they would form the core of a 'moderate' African presence in the Legislative Council.[99] Yet the actions of the Europeans in blocking Vasey's election had given credence to Mboya's claims that the Specially Elected Members were bound to be pro-European stooges. Mboya continued to focus on the sole objective of obtaining African majority rule in Kenya, and showed no inclination to cooperate with Lennox-Boyd's project of 'multi-racial' social engineering. In November 1958, all fourteen African elected members began a boycott of the Legislative Assembly.

During the first half of 1959, it became clear that some further increase in political representation for Kenya's Africans was inevitable in the near future. In January 1959, Lennox-Boyd had convened a meeting of the East African governors at Chequers. In the course of their discussions it was tentatively agreed that Tanganyika would achieve her independence first, some time around 1970, with Kenya and Uganda following in about 1975.[100] Baring had brought up the question of whether the British Government should make a statement about its ultimate objectives in Kenya.[101] Over the following months, the case for such a statement was strengthened by the threat of renewed instability.

Lennox-Boyd was due to give a general statement on constitutional advance in East Africa, but the Kenyan administration felt that this should be preceded by a separate statement on their own colony. On 22 February, W.F. Coutts, the Chief Secretary of Kenya, submitted to the Colonial Office a proposed text of such a statement.[102] This bore a close resemblance to that statement which was eventually made by Lennox-Boyd on 22 April. It reaffirmed that the Secretary of State did not think it possible that the British Government could abandon their ultimate responsibility for the administration of Kenya in the foreseeable future. Any future transfer of responsibility would require a number of preconditions. These included a viable parliamentary system, multi-racial cooperation, and a reasonable prospect of economic prosperity. The draft statement also raised the prospect of some form of constitutional discussions following the next British general election. Yet it made no specific reference to power eventually passing to the African majority, something which attracted adverse comment from within the Colonial Office.[103] When Lennox-Boyd produced his response to Coutts's draft on 26 March he sought to address this problem. He told Baring that the draft,

> lacked the 'punch line', by which I mean that in not coming out clearly with the idea that the Africans, given satisfactory fulfilment of the conditions, would progressively take more share in affairs until they actually found themselves in the majority, the whole impact of the statement would fail...It really boils down to this, that if we cannot face up to saying anything as positive as this about African advancement, we had better not make a statement at all.[104]

Yet Lennox-Boyd's objection to the draft statement was quickly over-taken by events. In mid-March, he had been informed by Baring that Blundell was planning to resign as Minister of Agriculture in order to lead a political movement of his own. Baring felt that the balance of advantages lay in allowing him to go. In the light of the 'political war of nerves' being waged by Mboya, he believed that Blundell was the only person capable of rallying 'moderate' opinion against the claims of African nationalism.[105] After some hesitation, Lennox-Boyd agreed that if Blundell could strengthen his position by announc-ing his intention to resign in the near future he should do so.

Baring was considering Lennox-Boyd's proposal for the 'punch-line' in his Parliamentary statement, when, on 1 April, Blundell informed him that he could not postpone the announcement of his resignation any longer. He was concerned that rumours of his intentions were appearing in the press and he was determined to retain the initiative. On the same day, he held a press conference to launch a policy statement which called, among other things, for the extension of voting rights to 'responsible people' of all races, and the removal of racial restrictions on the sale of land. Blundell and his supporters in the legislature named themselves the New Kenya Group. They included 21 nominated members, most of the elected European members and all of the 'specially elected' African and Asian members. The African elected members

responded by announcing the formation of the Constituency Elected
Members Organization (CEMO) which included the elected Asian
and Arab members and one progressive European.

The emergence of the New Kenya Group had an immediate impact
on the shape of Lennox-Boyd's proposed statement. Baring informed
him that Blundell felt 'his chances of rallying European moderate
opinion would be destroyed and the moderate group he had just
formed broken up' if the reference to African advancement were to
be included in the statement.[106] Under the circumstances, Baring
was clear that it had to go. For Lennox-Boyd and his advisers, this
settled the matter. They regarded Blundell as their best chance of
creating a 'multi-racial' counterbalance to African nationalism, and
they were determined to do nothing that might weaken his position.

A revised version of the statement was worked out between the
British and Kenyan Governments. One of the most important
revisions agreed was the insertion of a definite undertaking to hold
a constitutional conference in advance of the 1960 Kenyan General
Election. The British Government was anxious to give the impression
that the concessions contained in Lennox-Boyd's statement were the
result of Blundell's initiative and not the product of pressure from
the CEMO. In advance of the statement, British embassies were told:

> After the debate discreet emphasis should be laid on the extent to
> which Colonial Secretary's speech is a response to policy call of 46
> Member multi racial group of moderates in Kenya, now led by Michael
> Blundell...(We hope what is said will strengthen force of Blundell
> group's appeal to the Kenya public.)[107]

The same impression was conveyed in the brief which the Colonial
Office prepared for Sir Roland Robinson, a senior Conservative back
bencher whose 'inspired' motion for an adjournment debate provided the excuse for Lennox-Boyd's statement. Robinson, who adhered closely to the text he had been given, referred to the 'dramatic change in the political situation in Kenya' which was brought
about by the 'well thought-out and constructive statement' of the
Blundell group.[108] Robinson tabled his motion late on 22 April, after
a long and lively debate on the subject of prostitution. Lennox-Boyd,
in his reply, began by paying his own tribute to Blundell. He spoke
of Lord Perth's recent visit to Kenya and his meeting with representatives of all the main groups and implied that his subsequent
remarks were a response to the reports he had received from Perth.
He then moved on to the statement agreed with the Kenya government. Although at the time the statement appears to have been well
received on all sides of the House, it is now best remembered for
one supposedly short-sighted section in which Lennox-Boyd stated:

I have on many occasions made it clear that I cannot now foresee a date at which it will be possible for any British Government to surrender their ultimate responsibilities for the destinies and well-being of Kenya. To that view I still adhere.[109]

In fact, this closely follows the draft submitted by Coutts in February. The preconditions which Lennox-Boyd set down for any future transfer of responsibility were very largely those outlined by Coutts although additional emphasis was placed on the need for a strong Civil Service. As he had agreed with the Kenya government, he also announced that there would now be a constitutional conference on Kenya well before the elections there in 1960.

The announcement of a conference, and the largely favourable impression Lennox-Boyd had made on a recent CEMO delegation to London, brought one immediate benefit from Lennox-Boyd's point of view: the boycott of the Legislative Assembly by African and Asian elected members was ended. There were also signs that Lennox-Boyd's announcement had sown divisions among the African elected members, with Mboya taking a notably more hostile line towards the initiative than some of his colleagues.[110]

Lennox-Boyd's main concerns during the summer of 1959 were that divisions among the non-European politicians in Kenya should be amplified and exploited and that, conversely, every attempt should be made to build up Blundell's New Kenya Group. The strategy was threatened when, in July, plans were made to subsume CEMO within a new supposedly non-racial 'Kenya National Party' (KNP). This was in response to rumours that the government was about to drop its ban on colony-wide political associations, so long as the new political movements could prove themselves to be genuinely 'multi-racial'. Lennox-Boyd was concerned by this development. He realized that if the party were to have the appearance of a genuinely non-racial organization it would be difficult to refuse it registration, but that this would make things extremely difficult for Blundell's group. He suggested to Baring that 'the most reasonable course from the moderate point of view might well be to try to swamp the party and capture it from Mboya'.[111]

The threat of a united non-European challenge to Blundell receded somewhat when on 23 July Mboya dramatically refused to put his name to the KNP's newly drafted statement of policy, claiming that it lacked sufficient concrete proposals. Unwilling to be perceived as being less radical than Mboya, three other prominent African elected members – Oginga Odinga, Lawrence Oguda and Julius Kiano – refused to associate themselves with the new movement. This left a clear split between the 'moderate', non-Kikuyu Africans allied with Cooke and the Asians, and the four 'radical' Kikuyu and Luo Africans. In August, having detached two African elected members from the KNP, Mboya and his colleagues established the Kenya Independence Movement (KIM) committed to narrowly defined African nationalist goals. In accordance with their regulations concerning multi-racial movements, the Kenya government granted registration to the KNP while denying it to the KIM.

This was entirely the sort of division Lennox-Boyd hoped would emerge. Although the Europeans had themselves split, with the more conservative of their representatives organizing under the banner of the United Party, the British Government appeared to have the prospect of entering the forthcoming constitutional talks without facing the concentrated pressure for independence of a united African nationalist movement. When Lennox-Boyd left office in October this situation had not changed. As such he might, with some confidence, have expected that his successor would be in a strong position to win agreement for some revised form of 'multi-racial' constitution for Kenya which stopped considerably short of the concession of an African majority in the legislature. Yet on 19 November, less than a month after his departure from the Colonial Office, the African elected members achieved the miraculous feat of burying their differences and constructing a united movement in advance of the Lancaster House Conference. This represented a significant shift in the balance of power and limited the range of options open to Iain Macleod, Lennox-Boyd's successor. These options were further curtailed by developments in Tanganyika during Lennox-Boyd's final months in office.

Tanganyika

Despite the timetable for constitutional change agreed at Chequers in January 1959, according to which Tanganyikan independence was not expected for another decade, it was already clear that very gradual political development on the 'multi-racial' model was going to be extremely difficult to achieve in the territory. The existing constitution in Tanganyika had been announced by the then Governor, Sir Edward Twining, in April 1957. This had provided for a Legislative Council consisting of 67 members, 30 of whom were to be elected, the Africans, Europeans and Asians each receiving 10 seats. The elections took place in two phases, the first in September 1958 and the second in February 1959. They resulted in an overwhelming victory for the country's main African nationalist party, the Tanganyika African National Union (TANU). TANU won nine of the 10

African seats, and of the Asian and European candidates returned, the majority were supported by TANU. The United Tanganyika Party (UTP), which was established during Twining's governorship with a great deal of official support to promote 'multi-racialism', had effectively collapsed by the time of the elections.

On 17 March 1959, Twining's successor, Sir Richard Turnbull, announced further constitutional changes. The territory's Executive Council would be replaced by a Council of Ministers consisting of 12 members, seven of whom would be officials and five unofficials. Of the latter, three would be Africans, one European and one Asian. In addition, he announced the terms of reference of a constitutional committee which would consider changes to the franchise and to the composition of the Legislative Council. At this stage, Turnbull was still expecting to operate broadly on the 'Chequers' time-table, with an unofficial majority on the Council of Ministers only being attained in 1965.[112] Yet he was by no means confident that the concessions he was to offer in his March statement would achieve its principal aim of securing the cooperation of Julius Nyerere, the leader of TANU.

Turnbull's fears were fully justified. At the beginning of May, he reported to London that TANU and the other members of the Tanganyika Elected Members Organization (TEMO) were still proving hostile towards his administration. They had accused the government of obstructing the formation of the constitutional committee, due to be headed by Sir Richard Ramage, in order to delay a statement on further constitutional reform. Turnbull concluded that the best way to defuse this criticism was to try to bring forward the date of Ramage's arrival in Tanganyika to later that month.[113] He also feared that if Nyerere failed to obtain a promise of constitutional advance, his authority would be undermined and he might be 'replaced by an extremist'.[114]

This immediately set alarm bells ringing inside the Colonial Office. One of Lennox-Boyd's officials predicted, quite accurately, that within the next few months Turnbull would recommend to London that the cooperation of unofficial members of the legislature could only be secured by the promise of an unofficial majority on the Council of Ministers not later than 1961.[115] Another civil servant suggested that if this were to happen, there would be obvious implications for the prospect of phased constitutional advance not only in Tanganyika but also in Uganda, Kenya and Zanzibar.[116] Lennox-Boyd himself described the recent correspondence from Tanganyika as 'disturbing' and commented:

> We gave consent at Chequers to the phased programme for Tanganyika
> on the assumption, almost the assurance, that there was a very good
> chance of delaying the approach of virtual internal self-govt until 1969.
> I agree that it is essential to test the depth of Sir R. Turnbull's
> convictions.[117]

Lennox-Boyd told Turnbull of his disquiet and requested an outline of how the Governor saw events developing. Turnbull replied
that TEMO was remarkably united and disciplined in its campaign
for further constitutional reform. He envisaged a statement before
the end of the year, in which elections would be announced for
September 1960 to be followed by the creation of an unofficial
majority of one in the territory's Council of Ministers.[118] There was
some sympathy within the Colonial Office for Turnbull's approach.
Gorell Barnes pointed to the stark fact that TANU had the support
not only of the Africans, including the chiefs, but also of almost
all Asian and European politicians. As such, there were virtually
no other forces capable of resisting the demand for rapid moves to
internal self-government. If the British resisted TANU's claims and
encountered widespread resistance, the disorder in the territory
would be attributed to their intransigence.[119] Gorell Barnes was not
inclined to oppose Turnbull's request that the Ramage Committee's
work be brought forward. Lennox-Boyd, by contrast, felt that
Turnbull was needlessly expediting the process and informed him
that Ramage should begin work at the end of June as originally
planned.[120]

Yet Turnbull was not to be deflected and, indeed, his arguments
in favour of a radical departure from the 'Chequers' timetable
became more emphatic. On 3 July, he wrote to Gorell Barnes
setting out his position with painful clarity. He noted that a great
deal of creative energy which could better have been directed
towards developing the territory, had been channelled into the
conflict over constitutional reform.[121] The key to solving the
present difficulties was, he believed, to bring Nyerere into the
government, something his March statement had singularly failed
to achieve. He was clear about what this would involve: an
announcement of elections for September 1960 to be followed by
the creation of a majority of 6:5 or preferably 7:5 of unofficials
over officials in the Council of Ministers. There would also, quite
regardless of what Ramage might decide, have to be an unofficial
majority in the Legislative Council. So long as they were able to
induce Nyerere to join their ranks, the government would not in
these circumstances face any problem in securing a majority for
its legislation. Turnbull further predicted that by 1962, pressure
for further reform would be unavoidable and it would be necessary

to introduce full responsible self-government and to accept Nyerere as Chief Minister. He recognized that Gorell Barnes would find his conclusions 'thoroughly disagreeable and sadly out of key with many of the conclusions we reached at Chequers'. He also noted that the announcement of an unofficial majority in 1960 was likely to cause embarrassment in Uganda which was undertaking its own constitutional review and was intending to proceed far more slowly. Yet he felt that for the reasons he had set out, the case for rapid political development in Tanganyika was overriding.

Over the next three months until Lennox-Boyd's retirement, the Colonial Office resolutely failed to make any firm response to Turnbull's request. Hence, when Macleod arrived at the Colonial Office a decision on Tanganyika was still pending. In retrospect, Lennox-Boyd maintained that a major shift of policy had occurred at around the time of the 1959 General Election and that both Macleod and Macmillan were determined to withdraw from East Africa.[122] Certainly, as we have seen, in the course of 1959 and particularly after the Hola massacre and the Nyasaland emergency, Macleod and Macmillan had come to see colonial affairs as a major source of problems for the Government. Both men were keen for the Government to regain the initiative in this area of policy. Yet it seems unlikely that the constitutional reforms which occurred in Tanganyika and Kenya after October 1959 were the result of a comprehensive reassessment by Macleod and Macmillan of the general direction of British policy. The choices were, as we have seen above, extremely stark by the autumn of 1959 when Lennox-Boyd left the Colonial Office. If the British were not to resort to a policy of wholesale repression (and this was hardly likely following the political outcry over Devlin and Hola) their room for manoeuvre was limited. To maintain the existing policy of extremely gradual constitutional advance in East Africa, it would be necessary at the forthcoming constitutional conference on Kenya to reach a settlement which fell some way short of an African elected majority in the Colony's legislative council. For this to be possible, there would almost certainly need to be serious splits among African political leaders with some prepared to side with Blundell's 'moderate' Europeans. Yet by November 1959, African elected members were united (albeit temporarily) behind calls for rapid constitutional advance.

In Tanganyika, Turnbull was clear that Nyerere's cooperation could only bought by rapid progress towards self-government. Under these circumstances, the Colonial Office was almost bound to accept Turnbull's recommendations. If they did not, they risked undermining peaceful political evolution in Tanganyika in the name of holding back change in Kenya, something they were, in any case, by no means certain of being able to achieve. Concessions in Tanganyika would render impossible a substantially more limited constitutional settlement in Kenya, whether they occurred before or after the Kenyan conference. If before, then Kenya's African nationalists would be prepared to settle for nothing less. If after, they would almost certainly serve to unravel any agreement reached at the Kenyan conference.

Macleod, in effect, accepted the logic of the situation and opted for the policy of the 'lesser risk'; namely to go ahead with constitutional reform in Tanganyika and to follow this with the concession of an African majority in Kenya's legislative council at the Lancaster House Conference in January–February 1960. His approach was informed, not by a sudden decision to liquidate British power in East Africa, but by a determination to retain control of a rapidly changing situation by offering concessions to those African politicians most likely to be able to deliver the cooperation of their compatriots. The same rationale emerges from many of Lennox-Boyd's own policy decisions, and had he remained as Colonial Secretary after the 1959 General Election, it seems quite likely that he would have been forced to adopt a similar approach.

Lennox-Boyd did not, however, remain in government. As such, he was freed from the pressures which exerted such a powerful influence on his successor, and allowed to dwell, with increasing frustration, on the growing gap between his ideals for Africa and the policies he saw being enacted there.

Notes

1 Giryama proverb from Kenya collected by Lennox-Boyd, PBM, Mss. Eng. c. 3796, f. 305.
2   Beaver to Iveagh, 23 Nov. 1958, PBM, Mss. Eng. c. 3397, f. 5.
3 Lord Boyd interviewed about East Africa by Alison Smith on 13 Dec. 1974, PBM, Mss. Eng. c. 3433, f. 249.
4 Lord Boyd interviewed about East Africa, PBM, Mss. Eng. c. 3433, ff. 249–50.
5 Interview with Lord Perth, 2 June 1995.
6 Lennox-Boyd to Macmillan, 7 March 1959, PREM 11/3051.
7 Macmillan to Lennox-Boyd, 8 March 1959, PREM 11/3051.
8 Lord Boyd interviewed about East Africa, PBM, Mss. Eng. c. 3433, f. 251.
9 Harold Macmillan's diary, 18 Oct. 1959, Macmillan Papers, Bodleian Library, Oxford, Mss. Macmillan dep. d. 37, ff. 35–6.
10 For an example of the conventional view, see Julian Amery's rather cryptic entry on Lennox-Boyd in Lord Blake and C.S. Nicholls (eds.), *Dictionary of National Biography* (Oxford, Oxford University Press, 1990), p. 238.
11 Macmillan to Lennox-Boyd, 14 Nov. 1958, PREM 11/4117.

12 Bishop to Martin, 4 Dec. 1958, PREM 11/4117.
13 Raymond F. Betts, *France and Decolonisation* (London, 1991), p. 126.
14 Cabinet Colonial Policy Committee Minutes, 17 April 1959, CAB 134/1558, CPC (59) 1.
15 'Africa: The Next Ten Years', 3 June 1959, CAB 134/1355, A.F. (59) 28.
16 Zulueta to Macmillan, 1 July 1959, PREM 11/2587, ff. 25–7.
17 Macmillan to Lloyd, 3 July 1959, PREM 11/2587, ff. 18–20.
18 Macmillan to Lloyd, 3 July 1959, PREM 11/2587, ff. 18–20.
19 Lennox-Boyd to Macmillan, PM (59) 39, 30 July 1959, PREM 11/2587, ff. 5–7.
20 For an account of these discussions, see Ritchie Ovendale, 'Macmillan and the Wind of Change in Africa, 1957–60', *The Historical Journal*, vol. 38, no. 2 (1995), pp. 471–473.
21 Ronald Segal, *African Profiles* (Harmondsworth, Penguin, 1962), pp. 98–9.
22 de Quehen to Welensky, 20 Jan. 1959, WP 592/8, f. 62.
23 Welensky to Lennox-Boyd, 23 Jan. 1959, WP 592/8, f. 64.
24 Sir Roy Welensky, *Welensky's 4000 Days* (London, Collins, 1964), p. 118.
25 Perth to Macmillan, PM (59) 5, 10 Feb. 1959, CO 1015/1520, f. 1.
26 Armitage to Morgan, 19 Feb. 1959, CO 1015/1515, f. 16.
27 Benson to Gorell Barnes, 2 March 1959, CO 1015/1516, f. 139.
28 Welensky, p. 120–1; J.R.T. Wood, *The Welensky Papers* (Durban, Graham Publishing, 1983), p. 641.
29 Wood, pp. 642–3.
30 Perth to Armitage, 25 Feb. 1959, CO 1015/1515, f. 30/31.
31 Inward telegram from Benson, 26 Feb. 1959, CO 1015/1515, f. 40.
32 Armitage to Perth, 26 Feb. 1959, CO 1015/1515, f. 36; Inward telegram from Perth, 26 Feb. 1959, CO 1015/1515, f. 39.
33 Cabinet Minutes, 27 Feb. 1959, CAB 128/33, CC (59) 13, min. 1.
34 Lord Boyd interviewed about Central Africa, PBM, Mss. Eng. c. 3433, f. 131.
35 A.H.M. Kirk-Greene (ed.), *The Transfer of Power: The Colonial Administrator in the Age of Decolonisation* (Oxford, University of Oxford, 1979), p. 3.
36 Armitage to Lennox-Boyd, 2 March 1959, CO 1015/1515, f. 60.
37 Armitage to Morgan, 2 March 1959, CO 1015/1515, f. 63.
38 Brian Lapping, *End of Empire* (London, Paladin, 1989), p. 563.
39 Patrick Keatley, *The Politics of Partnership* (Harmondsworth, Penguin, 1993), p. 442.
40 Kirk-Greene, *Transfer of Power*, p. 3.
41 Lapping, p. 564.
42 Tom Askwith, *From Mau Mau to Harambee: Memoirs and Memoranda of Colonial Kenya* (Cambridge, Cambridge African Monographs, 1995), p. 118.
43 This evidence is presented in shocking detail by Robert B. Edgerton in *Mau Mau: An African Crucible* (London, I.B. Taurus & Co. Ltd., 1990), pp. 173–201.
44 Edgerton, p. 199.
45 Colonial Policy Committee, Memorandum by the Secretary of State for the Colonies, 3 Nov. 1959, CPC (59) 19, CAB 134/1558.
46 Terence Gavaghan's account appears in his privately published novel, *Corridors of Wire: A Saga of Colonial Power and Preventive Detention in Kenya* (1994). The narrative is a lightly fictionalized version of Gavaghan's personal recollections in which names have been changed and dialogue reconstructed. Questions of historical fact have been clarified in conversations and correspondence between Gavaghan and the author.
47 *Corridors of Wire*, p. 31.
48 Baring to Lennox-Boyd, 8 April 1958, CO 822/1252.
49 W.A.C. Mathieson interviewed by Allan Segal, End of Empire Interviews, Rhodes House Library, Oxford, Mss. Brit. Emp. s. 527/8, vol. 2, f. 158.
50 Lord Boyd interviewed about East Africa, PBM, Mss. Eng. c. 3433, f. 264.
51 Lennox-Boyd to Amery, 22 Feb. 1959; Baring to Lennox-Boyd, 22 Feb. 1959,

CO 822/1269.
52 Much of the following information on the events preceding the Hola massacre is taken from the Government's two White Papers on the affair cited in Commons debates on 16 June and 27 July 1959.
53 *HC Deb*, 607, col. 277, 16 June 1959.
54 Edgerton, p. 196.
55 Barbara Castle, *Fighting all the Way* (London, Macmillan, 1993), p. 288.
56 *HC Deb*, 602, cols. 1502–3, 26 March 1959.
57 Lennox-Boyd to Baring, 13 May 1959, CO 822/1269.
58 Lennox-Boyd to Gaitskell, 12 May 1959, CO 822/1269.
59 Moreton to Buist, 12 May 1959, CO 822/1269.
60 Horne, *Harold Macmillan 1957–1986*, p. 174.
61 Harold Macmillan, *Riding the Storm* (London, Macmillan, 1971), p. 733.
62 Cabinet Minutes, 4 June 1959, CAB 128/33, CC (59) 33, min. 4.
63 Gorell Barnes to Webber, 4 June 1959, CO 822/1261.
64 Note by Macmillan, 8 June 1959, CO 822/1261, f. 211A.
65 Horne, p. 175.
66 Macmillan to Lennox-Boyd, 17 June 1959, Mss. Eng. c. 3395, f. 3.
67 Macmillan, *Riding the Storm*, p. 734.
68 Murphy, p. 177.
69 Murphy, p. 164.
70 Powell to Lennox-Boyd, 18 June 1959, PBM, Mss. Eng. c. 3470, f. 313.
71 Macmillan's diary 22 June 1959, Mss Macmillan dep. d. 36, ff. 26–7; Macmillan, *Riding the Storm*, p. 734. It is interesting to note that the version of this entry published in Macmillan's memoirs omits the passage, 'it might make the more extreme Africans feel that they now had the white man on the run'.
72 Manningham-Buller to Lennox-Boyd, 13 July 1959, CO 822/1263.
73 Lennox-Boyd to Armitage, 13 July 1959, CO 1015/1545, f. 5A.
74 'The Devlin Committee', note by Tim Bligh, 13 July 1959, PREM 11/2783, ff. 106–7.
75 Perth to Devlin, 28 Sept. 1959, CO 1015/1547, f. 77.
76 *Report of the Nyasaland Commission of Inquiry*, Cmnd. 814 (London, HMSO, 1959), para. 286.
77 Cmnd. 814, para. 170.
78 Cmnd. 814, para. 43.
79 Minutes of meeting at 10 Downing Street, 14 July 1959, CO 1015/1545, f. 18.
80 Moreton to Macpherson, 14 July 1959, CO 1015/1545, f. 24.
81 Morgan to Macpherson, Amery and Lennox-Boyd, 16 July 1959, CO 1015/1545, f. 30A.
82 *Despatch by the Governor Relating to the Report of the Nyasaland Commission of Inquiry*, Cmnd. 815 (London, HMSO, 1959), para. 26.
83 Cmnd. 815, para 10.
84 Horne, p. 175.
85 Lennox-Boyd to Baring, 18 July 1959, CO 822/1263
86 Baring to Lennox-Boyd, 19 July 1959, CO 822/1263.
87 Macmillan, *Riding the Storm*, p. 737.
88 Cabinet Minutes, 20 July 1959, CAB 128/33, CC (59) 43, min. 1.
89 Lennox-Boyd to Macmillan, 20 July 1959, PREM 11/2783, f. 18.
90 Castle, p. 288.
91 *HC Deb*, 610, col. 237, 27 July 1959.
92 Macmillan, *Riding the Storm*, p. 734.
93 Chandos to Lennox-Boyd, 29 July 1959, PBM, Mss. Eng. c. 3467, f. 197.
94 Colonial Policy Committee, Memorandum by the Secretary of State for the Colonies, 3 Nov. 1959, CPC (59) 19, CAB 134/1558.
95 Colonial Policy Committee Minutes, 18 June 1959, CPC (59) 2, CAB 134/1558.
96 Douglas-Home, p. 297.

97 Trend to Macmillan, 13 Nov. 1957, PREM 11/3030.
98 Baring to Lennox-Boyd, 8 April 1958, CO 822/1252.
99   Baring to Lennox-Boyd, 12 June 1958, CO 822/1426, f. 272.
100   Douglas-Home, 283–4.
101   Internal memorandum by F.D. Webber, 25 Feb. 1959, CO 822/1861.
102   Coutts to Webber, 22 Feb. 1959, CO 822/1861.
103   Buist to Webber, 27 Feb. 1959, CO 822/1861.
104   Lennox-Boyd to Baring, 26 March 1959, CO 822/1861.
105   Baring to Lennox-Boyd, 12 March 1959, CO 822/1861, f. 163.
106   Baring to Lennox-Boyd, 2 April 1959, CO 822/1861, f. 201.
107   Commonwealth Relations Office outward telegram, 21 April 1959, CO 822/
        1862, f. 239.
108   *HC Deb*, 604, col. 555, 22 April 1959.
109   *HC Deb*, 604, col. 563, 22 April 1959.
110   David Goldsworthy, *Tom Mboya: The Man Kenya Wanted to Forget* (London,
        Heinemann, 1982), p. 116.
111   Lennox-Boyd to Baring, 16 July 1959, CO 822/1426, f. 314D.
112   Macpherson to Turnbull, 20 Feb. 1959, CO 822/1448.
113   Turnbull to Gorell Barnes, 1 May 1959, CO 822/1449, f. 225A.
114   Turnbull to Ramage, 1 May 1959, CO 822/1449.
115   Internal minute by B.E. Rolfe, 5 May 1959, CO 822/1449.
116   Internal minute by J. L. F. Buist, 5 May 1959, CO 822/1449.
117   Internal minute by Lennox-Boyd, 7 May 1959, CO 822/1449.
118   Turnbull to Lennox-Boyd, 10 May 1959, CO 822/1449, f. 227.
119   Internal minute by Gorell Barnes, 12 May 1959, CO 822/1449.
120   Lennox-Boyd to Turnbull, 14 May 1959, CO 822/1449, f. 228.
121   Turnbull to Gorell Barnes, 3 July 1959, CO 822/1450, f. 241.
122   Lord Boyd interviewed about Central Africa, PBM, Mss. Eng. c. 3433, f. 156.

13

In a Perfect World

Age repeats youth like the red onion.[1]

The October 1959 General Election was to be the last of
Lennox-Boyd's political career. Yet although he had held on to
Mid-Bedfordshire for nearly 30 years, the result there was by no
means a foregone conclusion. He had never succeeded in turning
it into a safe seat, and the combined effects of boundary changes
and the relentless press criticism he had had to face over Hola
Camp and the Nyasaland Emergency, seemed likely to render
Lennox-Boyd's position more than usually precarious. He also hated
the subterfuge involved in seeking re-election while intending to
leave politics at the earliest opportunity. Harold Macmillan almost
gave the game away when he came to the constituency to speak
on his behalf. At one point, he began to say, 'Send Alan back to
help us in...', and was about to add 'the Cabinet', when he suddenly remembered, and instead said 'in Parliament'. Afterwards, he
muttered to Lennox-Boyd, 'That was a near thing, wasn't it?'

Standing against Lennox-Boyd for Labour was Bryan Magee.
Like Lennox-Boyd in 1929, Magee had recently graduated from
Oxford and was having his first taste of a parliamentary election.
If Magee had hoped to make some political capital out of his
opponent's recent problems, he was to be disappointed. He found
the electors of Mid-Beds to be remarkably unconcerned about the
finer points of the Hola Camp massacre or the Devlin Report.[2] On
polling day, the Conservative and Labour candidates met by chance
on a country road, and for the first time in the campaign exchanged
a few friendly words. When Magee asked how he thought the election had gone, Lennox-Boyd responded, 'I think you might have
won.' In fact, Lennox-Boyd's fears were misplaced. He not only

236

regained the seat but increased his majority from 3,964 in 1955 to 5,174. Nationally, the Conservatives were returned to power with a majority of 100 seats.

With the General Election safely out of the way, Macmillan fulfilled the promise he had made six months earlier and relieved Lennox-Boyd of his Cabinet position. His departure from the Colonial Office was long desired and long delayed but none the less a source of sorrow when it finally occurred. His deep sense of loyalty and affection for the colonial service was conveyed in a very personal statement about his resignation which was telegraphed to the Governors of Britain's colonial territories:

> The times that I have spent as a Minister and then as Secretary of State for the Colonies have been the happiest and most interesting and, I hope the most worthwhile periods of my life. As I said in my letter to the Prime Minister, this office is one which I have always wanted to hold and it is with deep regret that I now leave it.[3]

Among Lennox-Boyd's friends there were already fears that his departure from office might presage a weakening of Government policy. Julian Amery confessed to feeling a strange sense of foreboding which he could not shake off.[4] His former chief, Anthony Eden, by then Lord Avon, told him that the firmness he had shown both in domestic and colonial affairs would be missed in government. Avon clearly felt that his successor as Prime Minister needed to be kept in check, adding that, 'to take the short and easy way seems the national failing of the day in too many external problems'.[5]

Having fought the 1959 election on sufferance, Lennox-Boyd was not prepared to devote a great deal of time to Parliamentary affairs. Indeed, he spent much of his remaining time as an MP abroad. In October and November he visited Italy on family business, and from January to March he accompanied Patsy on a tour of the Pacific. He was understandably dismissive when Martin Redmayne, the Government Chief Whip, tried to persuade him that his proper place was in the division lobbies supporting the Government.[6] He told Redmayne,

> You will know the circumstances under which I was obliged, much against my will, to fight another election and I really must now do everything I can to help my family affairs first.[7]

Lennox-Boyd was duly rewarded for his long service to the Government and for the manner of his leaving it. He was made a Companion of Honour in the 1960 New Year's Honours List and, in July, he accepted a viscountcy. The newly created Viscount Boyd of Merton had, of course, to vacate his seat in the Commons. His

successor in Mid-Beds was Stephen Hastings, an MI6 officer whose
final posting had been on Cyprus. Julian Amery, who was closely
involved in the final negotiations for the island's independence
settlement, had met Hastings there. He commended him to Boyd
and the Mid-Beds constituency association and subsequently spon-
sored Hastings's first appearance in the Commons after his election in November 1960.

Soon after Boyd's departure from government, he and Patsy began to search for a home outside London. Appropriately enough,
the new inhabitants of their house in Chapel Street were to be the
staff of the Nigerian High Commission. The transfer was not an easy
one. Grosvenor Estates, who owned the lease of the building, did
everything possible to prevent the Nigerians from taking the property. Boyd himself was both embarrassed and outraged by this
blatant display of racial prejudice, and it was only after a personal
intervention by the Prime Minister himself that the matter was finally settled. Alan and Patsy's new home was Ince Castle in
Cornwall. They had come across the house quite by chance while
inspecting another property nearby. Its owner was keen to sell, and
the Boyds wasted no time in making an offer for it. It is not difficult to imagine why Ince should have made such a strong and
immediate impression upon them. Situated at the end of a peaceful peninsular overlooking the Lynher estuary, Ince is a strikingly
unusual building. It was probably built by Henry Killigrew the
younger, son of the Elizabethan diplomat Sir Henry Killigrew. Appropriately enough, Killigrew was an ardent Royalist. He held out
for the King during the civil war and constructed earthworks for
the defence of the Ince peninsular. If, as seems likely, he built the
house some time between 1640 and 1645, its fortress like design
– with castellated walls and a tower at each of its four corners –
requires little explanation.

The Boyds restored Ince and designed and planted new gardens. As A.L. Rowse noted, in his memorial address for Alan, the
gardens were really Patsy's creation but 'they both loved Ince, that
island paradise they filled with flowers and rare flowering shrubs,
where they were so welcoming to us all'.[8] The house had many
incidental pleasures for the visitor. The long, upper corridor was
used by Boyd to display his large collection of antique walking
sticks. His unusual hobby was widely known, and he regularly
received letters from all over the world offering him rare and interesting specimens. The magnificent new garden to the south of
the house, patrolled by Patsy's fierce white peacocks, contained an
octagonal shell-house, which the Boyds decorated with brightly
coloured rocks and shells gathered from their many travels. Yet

what tended to impress itself most forcefully on the many guests who made their way to Ince, was the extraordinary care and attention with which the Boyds set about arranging weekend parties. Not even the smallest detail escaped Alan's attention. One visitor to Ince in the 1970s remembers his host's distress on discovering a less than fresh vase of flowers. As he had done throughout his political career, Alan continued to use the wealth at his disposal to keep innumerable friendships in good repair.

Boyd's main preoccupation after leaving the Cabinet was to acquaint himself with the running of Arthur Guinness & Co. Ltd. Following his marriage to Patsy, he had served as a director of the firm during two spells on the back benches, the first during the war and the second from 1945 to 1951. Now, he rejoined both the main Guinness board and those of the firm's Dublin and Park Royal subsidiaries. He served initially as Joint Managing Director, and then, following Sir Hugh Beaver's retirement at the beginning of January 1961, as sole Managing Director.[9] He remained in the post until 1967 and then served as joint vice-chairman until 1979.

Alan Boyd's style of management and the principles which he carried over into the world of business would have been familiar to anyone who had seen him at work in the Colonial Office. He surprised his new colleagues by demanding that, in addition to his three secretaries at the Park Royal Brewery and his personal secretary, Kay Kentish, he should be provided with a personal assistant; not merely a secretary but someone to run his office, sit in on meetings and accompany him on his travels. The post was filled successively by three junior employees of the firm: David Sandys-Renton, Nigel Salmon and Peter Banner. Another of Boyd's requests was for a personal aircraft. He apparently disliked staying in hotels, and wanted to be able to tour his new domain and still sleep in his own bed.[10] He was duly presented with a six-seater Piper Aztec. Sandys-Renton was given the job of recruiting a pilot and providing him with a uniform.[11] Since the Guinness logo – the harp – closely resembled an inverted version of Ireland's national symbol, the uniform of an Irish customs officer was swiftly transformed into that of a Guinness pilot simply by reversing the badge.

The Guinness plane operated from RAF Northolt and made use of a rather primitive grass air-strip at Plymouth which had to be lit with kerosene flares during the winter. On one occasion, when Boyd was about to join the plane at Northolt in the company of Nigel Salmon, he spotted Princess Alexandra and Sir Angus Ogilvy across the tarmac. He rushed over to greet them. After having exchanged a few words, Boyd and the Royal couple boarded their respective planes. Salmon takes up the story:

> Captain Grummitt taxied to the end of the run-way to take off first.
> Lord Boyd began to remonstrate loudly and insisted that we let the
> royal couple go in front. Captain Grummitt responded he had clear
> instructions from the Control Tower to go first and proceeded to take
> off. Shouting over the noise of the engine, Lord Boyd immediately began
> to dictate to me a letter of sincere apology to the Ogilvies for this 'dis-
> courtesy', whilst we sped down the run-way.[12]

While this story has distinct shades of Beachcomber about it, there
can be little doubt as to its veracity. It would have been entirely
characteristic of Boyd to put royal protocol before the more mundane conventions of civil aviation.

As in his political career, Boyd's easy charm and willingness to
delegate made him extremely popular with his staff. For those who
worked closely with him, he introduced an irresistible sense of
adventure into the world of business. If there were drawbacks to
being among his entourage, these were largely due to the fact that
Boyd did not always make allowances for those who could not keep
up with his frenetic life-style. Salmon recalls one occasion when
Boyd was due to fly to Dublin for a board meeting. He had to leave
for Northolt before he had finished dictating in his office. So he took
a couple of secretaries with him to the airfield in his Rolls Royce
in order to complete the process. He had still not finished when
they reached Northolt. The unsuspecting two secretaries were therefore invited onto the plane. 'Two hours later,' according to Salmon,
'they found themselves in Dublin with no over-night clothes, and
no way of getting back to London.'[13]

The visits Boyd undertook for the company took on the character of his tours as Colonial Secretary. His notebook was always at
the ready to record names and comments. Those who crossed
Boyd's path in almost any capacity were virtually guaranteed a
follow-up letter, sometimes a carefully selected gift. At public functions he rarely missed the opportunity to work the crowd in the
manner of a politician on the campaign trail rather than of a captain of industry. Might he have been tempted back into politics?
It seems that Macmillan would have welcomed his return in some
capacity. In July 1962, the *Daily Express* carried the story that
Boyd had been offered the Chairmanship of the Conservative Party
and that he had made known his interest, subject to certain conditions. That Boyd was offered the party chairmanship at least once
and rejected it, is confirmed by one of his Personal Assistants at
Guinness.[14] Boyd would have found it extremely difficult to persuade the Guinness family to accept his departure from the firm
so soon after becoming Managing Director. Nevertheless, it must
have been with some regret that he declined the post.

Although he resisted the lure of politics, Boyd showed unmis-takable signs of wishing to replace his business colleagues with old associates from his political career. In the summer of 1962, he wrote to Sir Gerald Templer, former High Commissioner of Malaya, inviting him to take the job of assistant managing director in charge of the St. James's Brewery in Dublin. Despite an attractive salary, Templer declined the offer.[15] Another old acquaintance he tried to bring into Guinness was Anthony Montague Browne, Winston Churchill's last private secretary. Boyd invited him to a number of lunches at Park Royal, the firm's London headquarters, to intro-duce him to his colleagues. He then, apparently, told them that he wanted Montague Browne to succeed him as Managing Director and suggested that he be provided with a specially tailored course at the Harvard Business School in preparation for the task. Presum-ably, he felt that the skill with which he had organized Churchill's funeral marked Montague Browne out as an obvious candidate for the job. His colleagues and the Guinness family seem, however, to have felt that this great achievement could not entirely compen-sate for his total lack of business experience, and Boyd's sugges-tion was quietly dropped.[16]

There can be little doubt that Boyd missed politics, and that he was not by nature an entrepreneur. Yet his performance as man-aging director was certainly dynamic and in many ways far-sighted. Like many other Western companies, Guinness's market share in some of Britain's former colonies was threatened by the advent of independence, as successor governments sought to promote domes-tic manufacturing through the use of subsidies and high import duties. Boyd recognized that Guinness could no longer simply rely on exporting its produce, but had to invest in manufacturing within the developing world. His contacts amongst post-independence political leaders and Western businessmen placed him in a good position to supervise this transition. In March 1963, he attended the opening of Guinness's first brewery outside the United King-dom and Ireland at Ikeja in Nigeria. The £2 million plant was a joint venture with the United Africa Company which, like Guinness, was keen to diversify its operations in West Africa. For the official open-ing, Boyd obtained the services of Dr Azikiwe, by that time Governor-General of Nigeria, who commended the brewery as 'an-other step forward on Nigeria's road to economic reconstruction'.[17] Boyd's contacts in Malaysia also proved helpful to Guinness. In March 1966, Tunku Abdul Rahman opened a new Guinness brew-ery in Petaling Jaya with Boyd at his side. During Boyd's time as Managing Director, agreements were also reached for licensed pro-duction in South Africa, Trinidad and Kenya. New ventures were to follow in Ghana, Jamaica and Cameroun.[18] They represented, for Boyd, the essence of enlightened self-interest. As displays of confidence in the post-independence regimes, he could feel that he was playing a continuing role in the economic development of their countries. At the same time he was safe-guarding the future prosperity of Guinness. The small parent company – the Overseas Planning Group – which the firm maintained to supervise such operations was expanded by Boyd to form Guinness Overseas Ltd.

As well as Guinness, Boyd took on a string of other directorships, many of them of firms in Canada where his family had large investments. As we have seen, Guinness benefited enormously from Lennox-Boyd's knowledge of the developing world. Yet he was keen not to appear to be exploiting his position as a former Colonial Secretary for financial gain. Shortly after leaving office, he was asked by Sir Ian Lyle to join the board of Tate and Lyle, a firm with extensive interests in the West Indies. In reply, Boyd pointed out that there was a very strict rule preventing colonial governors from taking up directorships in firms which operated in the former territories until three years after the termination of their governorships. He noted that he had had to apply this rule in relation to at least one former governor of a West Indian territory. For that reason, despite the fact that no restrictions applied to former Ministers, he felt he could not accept the position.[19] Sir John Macpherson, the former Permanent Under-Secretary at the Colonial Office, whom he consulted about this, felt that Boyd was being over-punctilious. Nevertheless, when the offer was repeated a year later, Boyd again turned it down and it was only in April 1966 that he finally joined the company as a non-executive director.

Despite his extensive business commitments, Boyd found it difficult to refuse requests for help from other organizations. Shortly after leaving government, he became President of the British Leprosy Relief Association (later LEPRA) and of the Save the Children Fund, a post he retained until 1967. Towards the end of September 1960, he explained to the Earl of Dundee that the pressure of work upon him prevented him from accepting any other appointments:

> It may sound absurd but having left the Colonial Office where I was certainly very busy I now seem to have no time at all for duties other than those which I have already assumed. Yet I fear it is true.[20]

Nevertheless, over the next few years he added to his list of responsibilities. He served as President of the Overseas Employers, Federation in 1962, as Chairman of the Royal Commonwealth Society from 1961 to 1964 and President in 1965, and as Chairman of Voluntary Service Overseas (now VSO) from 1962 to 1964. He also established a trust in his old constituency of Mid-Bedfordshire to send young people overseas as VSO volunteers. Until the time of his death he served as President of both the Corona Club and the Overseas Pensioners' Association.

Boyd devoted a considerable amount of time and effort to the affairs of the British Museum. Under the Act governing the Museum, the Secretary of State for the Colonies was an *ex officio* Trustee. Few of his predecessors had bothered very much about this, but with characteristic diligence, Boyd regularly attended Trustees' meetings. Since these took place at noon on Saturday, they proved, for the rest of the family, a rather irritating source of disruption to their weekends. In 1962, Boyd was invited to continue as a Trustee, an office he retained until 1978. He also served as a Trustee of the Natural History Museum. In addition, he became a governor of Sherborne School in 1962 and President of its board of governors in 1968. In the same year was made an Honorary Student of his old Oxford college, Christ Church, having taken an active part in its fund-raising activities. In 1964, he served as Prime Warden of Gold-smiths Company and took on the Presidencies of the Mid-Bedfordshire Conservative Association and the RNVR Officers Association. A common feature of most of the organizations with which he became involved was that they served as a link to earlier stages in his career. Many were associated with his first great love – Commonwealth and colonial affairs – but they also provided links to his school, his college, his naval career and his constituency. It was typical of a man who never sought to apologize for his past and who remained intensely loyal to the institutions with which he had been associated and the people he had known.

In April 1965, his friend, Bill Astor, warned him that unless he cut back on some of his commitments he was in danger of damaging his health.[21] Astor's fears were at least in part justified. A year later, Boyd suffered from a severe attack of cystitis and was forced to undergo surgery on his prostate. Following the operation, his doctors insisted upon a long period of convalescence and Boyd retired to Ince for a much-needed rest. He made a good recovery and resumed a heavy schedule of activities. His workload did decrease somewhat especially after he ceased to be Managing Director of Guinness in 1967. Nevertheless, he continued to pursue a startling range of activities for a man of his age.

In political terms, Boyd took something of a vow of silence immediately after leaving office. He had always believed that Britain should speak with one voice over colonial affairs, and he did not want to make statements that might prove unhelpful to his successors. In public at least, he refrained from criticizing the

Government for a couple of years, even when he found its policies disagreeable. Ultimately, however, Boyd remained too much absorbed in the fate of the colonies to have any hope of honouring that vow. Freed from the responsibility of having to implement policy, his approach underwent a distinctly rightward shift. He was no longer so concerned with what *could* be done as with what *should* be done. In public and private he gave the distinct impression that he would have dealt with events in a quite different manner to that adopted by his successors. In effect, he began the process of re-writing the history of his own years at the Colonial Office.

Boyd's first public intervention was, characteristically enough, a defence of the pension rights of colonial service personnel. The Government maintained that the responsibility for paying these pensions rested entirely with the territories in which the colonial officers had formerly served. Critics argued that in cases where those territories failed to keep pensions in line with UK levels, Britain had a responsibility to step in and top up the incomes of those concerned.[22] The Government's response was that such an assurance would remove any incentive for overseas territories to use their own funds to provide pensions. During a Lords debate on the matter in February 1962, Boyd pointed out that the Colonial Secretary had ultimate authority over the general conditions of employment of colonial servants.[23] The Government could not, therefore, simply shuffle off responsibility onto the territorial governments. He returned to the fray in a further debate on the matter in June. A number of former Colonial ministers and governors rose to challenge the Government, and Boyd himself made one of the most telling interventions. Lord Listowel's motion calling on the Government to increase the basic rate of pensions paid to former colonial servants and their dependents, was carried despite Government opposition.

Boyd's role in this affair aroused the indignation of Michael St. Aldwyn, the Conservative Chief Whip in the Lords. St. Aldwyn told Macmillan's private secretary,

> I deplore the fact that one who has so recently been in a position to influence Government policy on this issue should take an early opportunity after resigning his office of voting against the very policy which he himself defended as a Minister.[24]

Macmillan suggested that if Boyd raised the matter again in a debate, St. Aldwyn should point out that he had served as Colonial Secretary for longer than anyone since Joseph Chamberlain 'and if he thinks things are wrong it is a bit late to say so now'.[25]

As to the general course of the Government's colonial policy, many of Boyd's concerns focused upon East and Central Africa.

The promise of African majority rule in Kenya given at the Lancaster House Conference of January–February 1960 had, he recognized, increased the likelihood of Jomo Kenyatta's release. He found the prospect so disturbing that when the Foreign Secretary asked him to take part in an official lecture tour of the United States at some point between December 1960 and March 1961 he declined. He claimed that the pressure of work made it impossible for him take part.[26] In fact, he was more concerned that Kenyatta might be released while he was in America and that, as a Government-sponsored speaker, he would have to defend this action. In January 1961, he reminded Macmillan of the public undertaking he had made while Colonial Secretary that 'irreconcilables' like Kenyatta would not be allowed to return to the Kikuyu reserves. This statement had, he maintained, encouraged many Africans to assist the British in the campaign against Mau Mau. He told Macmillan:

> You will realize my feeling of personal responsibility in this matter. This feeling would be in no way diminished if some of those for whose sake in part the promise was made should now say that they would rather see him released without restrictions by Her Majesty's Government than by an African Nationalist Government if such should emerge.[27]

Yet when the announcement of Kenyatta's release did come, in the summer of 1961, Boyd reacted generously towards his successor. He was informed of the decision personally by Iain Macleod. Boyd remembered telling Macleod, 'Well I couldn't have done it, but I don't doubt you are right.'[28]

In February 1962, on the eve of the second Lancaster House Conference on Kenya, Boyd again intervened, this time to urge a postponement of the granting of independence to Kenya. He told Macmillan that although he had as Colonial Secretary been opposed to setting timetables for constitutional advance, he now thought it 'might well be essential' for the Government to announce a three to five year moratorium before the final transfer of sovereignty in Kenya. This would allow for an intensive programme of economic development particularly in the area of African land settlement which Boyd believed was proceeding far too slowly. He acknowledged, however, that it was 'an open question' whether anyone would trust the Government to adhere to such a timetable.[29]

Boyd also kept a worried eye on the affairs of Uganda. Perhaps the strangest epilogue to Boyd's time as Colonial Secretary concerned the sad fate of Edward Mutesa, the Kabaka of Buganda. In February 1966, Uganda's prime minister, Milton Obote, staged what amounted to a coup. He abrogated the constitution and

dismissed Mutesa from the presidency, the post he had been
granted under Uganda's independence settlement. Three months
later, in response to Bugandan protests, Obote ordered troops to
storm the Kabaka's palace. Amidst the fighting and general confusion, Mutesa was able to make his escape. For the second time
in 13 years, Mutesa faced the prospect of exile in England. As in
1953, his presence was an embarrassment to the British authorities, although for different reasons. Uganda currently occupied a
seat on the United Nations Security Council, and the British Foreign Office was keen to retain her support over the issue of Rhodesia. It therefore discouraged high-level contacts with the man
Obote had so brutally expelled from office. It was left to a few
friends, among them Alan Boyd, to offer the Kabaka sympathy and
assistance. The philanthropist, Richard Carr-Gomm, provided him
with a flat in East London and the Department of Social Security
supplied a weekly maintenance allowance of £4, plus £4 for his
rent.[30] Meanwhile, the Bermondsey labour exchange did its best to
find suitable employment for a recently dismissed African president.

Mutesa dealt with this radical change of life-style with remarkable stoicism, but still lapsed into periods of depression and heavy
drinking.[31] On the evening of 21 November 1969 he was discovered
dead in his Bermondsey flat. The coroner concluded that he had died
of alcoholic poisoning, and the police were, understandably, unwilling to pursue the matter further. Some of the Kabaka's supporters,
however, were suspicious about the circumstances surrounding the
case. The inquest had discovered that his body contained a huge
amount of alcohol – 408 milligrams per 100 millilitres of blood. This
suggested a prolonged, suicidal binge. Yet Carr-Gomm and another
friend, Mark Amory, had dined with him the day before his death
and had found him composed and drinking only moderately. He was
alone for most of the following day, but his adjutant, who lived with
him, was convinced that the Kabaka had had only wine to drink;
and it seems unlikely that he could have absorbed such a large
amount of alcohol into his blood stream merely by drinking wine.
Finally, the Kabaka had believed that his life was in danger, and had
been warned specifically that a woman, with contacts in the Ugandan High Commission, had been sent to kill him.

Alan Boyd, who was in Cornwall at the time of the Kabaka's
death, was one of the first people to ring Carr-Gomm on the morning of 22 November to find out more details of the tragedy. Over
the next few months, Carr-Gomm and Ronnie Owen, another of the
Kabaka's closest friends, supplied Boyd with what they regarded
as convincing proof of foul-play. Accompanied by Carr-Gomm, Boyd
met the Commissioner of Police, Sir John Waldron, and sought to

persuade him to re-open the enquiry into the Kabaka's death. Waldron did not seem particularly impressed. He had been fully briefed on the Kabaka's fondness for alcohol and was sceptical about their allegations. The police did open a new investigation, but after preliminary enquiries they decided that there was no reason to regard the Kabaka's death as suspicious.[32]

The most bizarre and macabre aspect of this saga was yet to come. Obote wanted the Kabaka's body returned to Uganda for a ceremonial burial, but Mutesa's family and Bugandan elders were adamant that it should remain in England. There were even rumours that the Ugandan government intended to destroy the corpse the moment it arrived in Entebbe. So the funeral took place in London. On 3 December, a memorial service was held for the Kabaka in the Guards Chapel at Wellington Barracks, the home of his old regiment. After that, his body was buried in catacombs under the chapel of Kensal Green Cemetery. Yet fears remained, among the Kabaka's supporters, that Obote's government might actually attempt to steal the remains and fly them to Uganda. So Boyd performed one final service for his old friend. A day or two after the funeral, the Kabaka's body was removed from its initial resting place and reinterred in the Boyd family grave in another part of the cemetery. The original coffin was replaced by an empty 'decoy'. Among his papers, Boyd left a note directing that if, after his own death, the Kabaka's successor or his heirs requested that the body be handed over to the family for re-burial in Uganda, their wishes should be respected.

In the event, Edward Mutesa's final return to Uganda was not to be long delayed. In January 1971, Obote was overthrown in a military coup led by General Idi Amin, the man who had super-vised the storming of the Kabaka's palace five years earlier. Keen to consolidate his support among the Baganda, Amin persuaded Mutesa's friends and family to return his body for burial. At the end of March, Boyd left for Uganda where, as the official represen-tative of the British Government, he witnessed the Kabaka being laid to rest in the tombs of his ancestors. It was the end of a long and difficult association.

The part of Africa which caused Boyd perhaps the greatest con-cern in the years immediately following his departure from the Colonial Office was the Central African Federation. In February 1961, Macleod published proposals for a new constitution in North-ern Rhodesia which would supersede the one established by Boyd in 1958. These proposals appeared likely to give Africans a nar-row majority in the territory's Legislative Council. Given that the Africans of Northern Rhodesia, like those of Nyasaland, were

solidly opposed to the Federation, an African majority of one was
enough to spell its death. Macleod's White Paper presented his
opponents both in Africa and in the Conservative Party with the
opportunity for which they had been looking to challenge him on
a single, clearly defined issue. Supporters of the Federation on the
Tory backbenches attracted over 100 signatures for an early day
motion calling for a return to the 'multi-racial' principles of the 1958
constitution.

Boyd left the Government in little doubt about his own lack of
enthusiasm for the new proposals. His short intervention on the
matter in the Lords on 21 February was superficially conciliatory,
attributing to Macleod his own 'non-racial' approach. Yet, as he had
warned the Prime Minister in advance, it contained a sting in its tail:

> In conclusion may I say that in any debate we may have, I am sure
> that we shall be told by Her Majesty's Government why, after only two
> years, any changes other than ordinary evolutionary changes, were
> necessary. I know that Her Majesty's Government recognise that con-
> stitutional changes or a Bill of Rights or some assurances of this kind,
> to have validity and confidence placed in them, must have an air of
> permanence about them.[33]

Lord Perth answered Boyd's point about evolutionary changes by
showing him a memorandum which attempted to calculate the likely
consequences were the 1958 constitution allowed to run its course.
This estimated that the gradual increase in Africans qualifying for
membership of the two electoral rolls was likely to be extremely slow.
Even by 1968 they would probably be insufficiently numerous to
elect candidates of their choice in any of the 14 constituencies that
currently returned European candidates. As the paper noted, this
assumed that voting would continue to be on broadly racial lines and
that Northern Rhodesia would not have experienced 'the emergence
and success' of a genuinely multi-racial party which could attract
African and European votes in equal proportion. In the margin, Boyd
scribbled 'but it was to ensure that that was one of the purposes of
the constitution'.[34] He retained the hope that a 'multi-racial' constitution could engineer a genuine change of attitudes among members of both communities. For Macleod, it was clear that the
'multi-racial' experiment had failed at least in its current form.

Boyd remained unconvinced by the Government's logic. In
March, the Northern Rhodesian constitution was the subject of one
of the most impassioned House of Lords debates in the post-War
period. During the course of this Lord Salisbury made a sharp
personal attack on Macleod accusing him of being 'too clever by
half' in his dealings with the European settlers. Boyd decided not
to speak, but his sympathies were firmly with Salisbury.

Following the debate he complimented Salisbury on having drawn attention 'to the feelings of most Europeans and many Africans'.[35] He continued to support the Federation, despite the fact that by the end of 1962 the governments of Northern and Southern Rhodesia and Nyasaland were all determined to extricate themselves from it. In December 1962, he gave public expression to his frustration at the Government's policy. In a House of Lords debate, he joined with Lords Chandos, Colyton and Salisbury in questioning the right of British Ministers to dissolve the Federation without the consent of Welensky's government.[36] Their protest did nothing to delay the inexorable process of dismantling the Federation. On 29 March 1963, Butler signalled its official demise by announcing the right of all the Federal territories to secede. To Boyd, this represented the abandonment by the British Government of one of his most cherished political projects. He told Welensky,

> I can hardly find words to express my feelings of shame and distress at the events of the last few weeks which are the culmination of a long period of disastrous surrenders.[37]

Following the break-up of the Federation, Welensky's allies within the Conservative party turned their attention to the future of Southern Rhodesia. Boyd was a member of a 'Watching Committee' established under the chairmanship of Lord Salisbury early in 1961. Initially its purpose was to monitor affairs in the Federation, but from 1963 it concentrated on Southern Rhodesia. It provided the principal means by which the Conservative supporters of the European settlers in both Houses of Parliament could coordinate their activities and it remained in existence up to the time when Rhodesia achieved her formal independence as Zimbabwe in 1980. From 1963 to 1965, the Committee sought to persuade the Government to grant Southern Rhodesia independence without requiring that she first deliver a significant increase in political representation to her African majority.

Following Rhodesian premier, Ian Smith's, Unilateral Declaration of Independence (UDI) on 11 November 1965, members of the Committee put considerable pressure upon the leadership of the Conservative party, by then in Opposition, to resist the imposition of economic sanctions upon Rhodesia. In the immediate wake of Smith's declaration they were particularly alarmed by the possibility that the Wilson Government might employ military force to defeat the revolt. On 25 November, Boyd led a delegation of like-minded Conservative parliamentarians to see the party leader Edward Heath. They sought an undertaking that the party would withdraw their support for Wilson over Rhodesia if British troops were moved into neighbouring Zambia.[38] Heath refused to give them the firm assurance they required.

Boyd's own feelings towards Smith's Rhodesian Front government were distinctly ambivalent. Like many Conservatives who were broadly sympathetic towards the European settlers, he found the plodding, charmless Smith a far less sympathetic figure than the ebullient Roy Welensky. He did not meet Smith until he went out to Zimbabwe-Rhodesia to monitor the elections there in 1979. From a distance, however, he judged him to be 'not my style of person'.[39] Yet his sense of loyalty towards the Rhodesian settlers, whom he regarded as having received a raw deal from successive British governments, tended to override both his antipathy towards Smith and his concern for Commonwealth unity. In 1967, he explained his attitude towards UDI in a letter to a member of the Rhodesian Constitutional Commission:

> While I lamented UDI...I none the less recognised the responsibility of some people in the UK of all political parties, for the growth of suspicion and frustration and lack of confidence in the UK which was, I assume, the main cause for the declaration of UDI.[40]

Boyd's sense of disillusionment with Government policy attracted him to a new political group: the Monday Club. The Club was established in 1961 by Paul Bristol, a 24-year-old former army officer. Bristol's intention was to provide a home for young Conservatives on the right of the party who felt uncomfortable with the more liberal ethos of the Bow Group. Nevertheless it soon fell under the control of Welensky's circle of friends in the Watching Committee. In 1962 both Boyd and Salisbury agreed to act as joint patrons of the Club. From the start, the Club took a keen critical interest in Government policy towards Africa and was, throughout the 1960s and 1970s, to provide another important base for the Conservative party's 'Rhodesia Lobby'. It was this which initially attracted Boyd. Yet the Club's essentially authoritarian analysis of the failings of the Tory party – that it had been too eager to adopt modern 'progressive' values, and needed to preach the old-fashioned virtues of patriotism and discipline – had a wider appeal for Boyd.

Problems began to arise for him when the Monday Club moved from arguments about policy to attacks on the party leadership. It fired its first direct salvo at Harold Macmillan early in 1963 shortly after his efforts to obtain Britain's entry into the European Community had been wrecked by de Gaulle's use of the veto. In a memorandum published by the Club in February, it was suggested that 'a change in the Conservative leadership may be necessary'. Launching the document, Bristol told the *Daily Mail*, 'I am sure that the feeling that it is time for Macmillan to go is held by a great many people'.[41] It was not, however, held by Boyd, whose name featured prominently in the *Mail*'s coverage as a supporter of the Monday Club. Despite Boyd's dissatisfaction with developments in Africa, he remained loyal to his former chief and was embarrassed at being associated with this kind of personal attack.

If Boyd hoped that the Club's vendetta against Macmillan might subside, he was to be disappointed. On 6 October, the Sunday before the start of the Conservatives' Annual Conference, the press published details of a Monday Club pamphlet which was being circulated to all Tory MPs. The document, written by Lord Newry and Robin Garran, was advertised as a 'manifesto' of the Club's beliefs, but what attracted the attention of journalists was its fierce condemnation of the Prime Minister. 'Mr Macmillan' it argued 'has lost the confidence of the elector because of his inability to communicate, or rather of his unconscious desire not to'. In his comments to reporters Bristol suggested that the Club wanted Lord Hailsham to replace Macmillan as party leader.[42] Once again, Boyd's name featured prominently in reports of the Club's activities. This time, the irritation which Boyd angrily communicated to the Club's chairman was accompanied by a very public rebuke. On 8 October, a leader in the *Daily Telegraph* implicitly criticized both Boyd and Salisbury for having been implicated in this attack upon Macmillan. Boyd responded with a letter to the editor in which he entirely dissociated himself from the Club's comments adding, 'I am one of the very many people who hope that Mr. Macmillan will continue as our leader, and carry the Conservative party to victory in the next Election'.

Boyd continued as patron of the organization, his confidence in its leaders severely dented. What finally persuaded him to part company with them was the issue of immigration. As Colonial Secretary, Boyd's commitment to 'multi-racial' ideals in Africa was matched by a reluctance to see restrictions imposed on Commonwealth immigration into Britain. He had opposed moves in the mid-1950s to tighten the immigration laws on the grounds that this would provoke resentment against Britain both within the colonies and among the leaders of some independent Commonwealth countries. Initially, the rhetoric of the Monday Club was similarly shaped by an apparent adherence to 'multi-racial' principles. From 1964, however, the Club moved rapidly towards supporting immigration controls, identifying this as an issue on which they could attract a mass membership. In a speech in Birmingham on 20 April 1968, under the pretence of supporting the opposition of his front bench to the Labour Government's Race Relations Bill, Boyd's old adversary, Enoch Powell, dragged the public debate on this issue to hitherto unimagined depths. The former classics professor, whose humane attack on the abuses perpetrated at Hola camp is justly remembered as one of the great Parliamentary occasions of the twentieth century, spoke in inflammatory terms of a terrified white woman surrounded by coloured neighbours being followed by 'wide-grinning piccaninnies' and having excrement pushed through her letter-box. Boyd was appalled by the speech and when the Monday Club publicly endorsed Powell's position, he resigned as the organization's patron.

Following his unhappy experiences with the Monday Club, Boyd was notably reluctant to become too closely associated with any of the right wing pressure groups which proliferated in the 1970s. He did, however, take a close interest in the more mainstream elements of the Conservative right. Since the 1960s, he had been an enthusiastic supporter of the free-market evangelists of the Institute of Economic Affairs and was gratified to see their ideas being taken up by the party leadership. In the course of the 1970s, he also had the very personal satisfaction of seeing his youngest son, Mark, retracing his steps to the Commons. Like his father 45 years before, Mark's first Parliamentary contest on behalf of the Conservatives was for a safe Labour seat, Brent South. He stood here, unsuccessfully, in the General Election of October 1974. Boyd was naturally delighted to be able to visit a meeting in the constituency and speak on his son's behalf. In 1979, Mark was elected to Parliament for Morecambe and Lonsdale. He served as Parliamentary Private Secretary (PPS) to Nigel Lawson, first at the Department of Energy and then at the Treasury. In the late 1980s, he was PPS to the Prime Minister. Then, for four years from 1990, Mark served as Parliamentary Under Secretary at the Foreign Office. Boyd lived to see only the first few years of his son's Parliamentary career. It was a great source of pleasure and pride for him.

Boyd would have been delighted at Mark's selection by Margaret Thatcher as her PPS. He had been unhappy about the challenge to Edward Heath in 1975, but was pleased when Tory MPs selected Mrs Thatcher as Heath's successor. At an early stage in her career, Boyd seems to have recognized in Thatcher something of his own political outlook. While neither was particularly censorious on moral issues, both distrusted the current liberal consensus in British politics, fearing a general erosion of respect for authority. They also shared a belief that successive governments had squandered British influence in the world in the name of political expediency, just as they had surrendered to socialism at home. As a young candidate in the early 1950s Mrs Thatcher had been invited by Boyd to address meetings in his constituency. In the mid-1990s, she could still recall how kind and encouraging he had been 'to a mere candidate'.[43]

Shortly before she was elected Prime Minister, Mrs Thatcher repaid Boyd's solicitude in a way that was to bring him pleasure and frustration in almost equal measure: she invited him to visit Rhodesia as head of a team of observers to report on the April 1979 elections. The chance to play a part in resolving a major piece of outstanding colonial business was one he accepted with relish. The elections took place against the background of efforts by the illegal settler regime of Ian Smith to deliver the country from international isolation and civil war. Since 1972, his government had faced a concerted campaign by nationalist guerrillas. These forces received an enormous boost when, following a coup in Lisbon in April 1974, Portuguese rule in Mozambique was replaced by an African nationalist government. Rhodesia lost a valuable ally in the region and the guerrillas were able to launch incursions across her 760 mile long eastern border from bases inside Mozambique.[44] Smith's position was further weakened by the determination of the South African premier, John Vorster, to reach a settlement in Rhodesia as part of a broader strategy of improving his country's relations with her African neighbours. The United States was also keen to force Smith to reach agreement with his opponents. After a series of abortive talks, Smith found a couple of amenable negotiating partners in Bishop Abel Muzorewa, leader of the ANC and Ndabaningi Sithole, head of what was, in effect, a breakaway faction of the Zimbabwe African National Union (ZANU). ZANU's leader, Robert Mugabe, was still waging a guerrilla campaign against the Rhodesian government. In March 1978, Smith reached agreement with Muzorewa and Sithole for a new constitution under which the whites would notionally surrender their exclusive grip on power. A new parliament would be elected under which the whites would be guaranteed 28 of the 100 seats. This provided for a formal transition to majority rule; but the whites would effectively retain control of the main levers of political and economic power and would have a right of veto over changes to the entrenched clauses in the constitution.

The settlement proved acceptable neither to Mugabe nor to Joshua Nkomo, leader of the Zimbabwe African People's Union (ZAPU) whose forces were fighting in alliance with those of ZANU as part of the Patriotic Front. Far from ending the civil war, the 'internal settlement' encouraged the Patriotic Front to intensify its campaign against the Rhodesian government. The constitution was too obviously a piece of window dressing to commanded any significant international support. In Britain, the Labour Government refused to endorse the settlement. The Foreign Office recognized that any major new initiative to resolve the situation would have to await the results of Britain's own impending general election.[45] With the Rhodesian elections fixed for April 1979 and the British elections due in May, it was clear that one of the first foreign policy decisions that the new Government of Britain would have to make would be whether to recognize the regime in Rhodesia.

The attitude of the Conservative Opposition to the Rhodesian settlement placed the future course of British policy in doubt. It seemed quite possible that an in-coming Tory government would defy world opinion and recognize the new regime. There had always been a hard core of white supremacists within the party who had given the Smith government their unwavering support. A far more widespread view was that, although UDI had been a mistake, the British Government had consistently mishandled the Rhodesian situation, particularly in imposing sanctions against the country. Those who maintained this position probably formed a majority within the party. They certainly included Boyd, and also, at least instinctively, the party leader, Margaret Thatcher. Proponents of this view tended to feel that whatever its faults, the 'internal settlement' would establish in Rhodesia a far more democratic system than prevailed elsewhere on the continent. They were also highly suspicious of the leaders of the Patriotic Front, particularly Mugabe, and broadly accepted Smith's view that the guerrillas were 'terrorists' and that a victory for them would be a further stage in the Marxist penetration of Africa.

In addition to these arguments for recognizing the settlement, there was the question of consistency. The principles upon which the British Government had conducted their negotiations with Smith in the past had been based upon a vague commitment to majority rule at some point in the future and an insistence that any settlement should be acceptable to the people of Rhodesia as a whole. Boyd himself felt that the principle of acceptability was an unrealistic one, and he had been frustrated when, in 1972, it had stood in the way of a settlement.[46] Nevertheless, even this condition now seemed likely to be satisfied, so long as a majority of the population cast a vote. Britain would then, it was argued, no longer have any excuse to withhold recognition.

This line of reasoning was incorporated in the Conservatives' election manifesto, published in February 1979 which stated: 'If the Six Principles, which all British Governments have supported for the last 15 years, are fully satisfied following the Rhodesian

elections, the next Government will have a duty to return Rhodesia to a state of legality, move to lift sanctions, and do its utmost
to ensure that the new independent state gains international recognition.'[47] This commitment was implicit in Mrs Thatcher's decision to send a team to monitor the Rhodesian elections on behalf
of the Conservative Party. She and her colleagues said merely that
they would be 'guided' by the team's findings.[48] Yet in asking it to
report solely on the election itself, she seemed to be sending a signal to the party that, so long as it could be proved that the poll
was fairly conducted and commanded wide-spread support, a Conservative administration would recognize Rhodesia's new government. This was despite the fact that the election seemed unlikely
to solve Rhodesia's two overriding problems: her international isolation and her bloody civil war. In this respect, Boyd cannot be
blamed for the fact that his report proved such an embarrassment
to the Government. The project itself was fundamentally flawed.

The fact that the Rhodesian poll took place in the middle of the
British general election campaign made it impossible to send a team
of observers from the Commons. Among Tory peers, Boyd was certainly one of the best qualified in terms of his long experience of
African affairs. Yet he also had long-standing associations with
some of Smith's most active sympathizers, both openly up to 1968
through the Monday Club, and more covertly through his continued membership of the Watching Committee. He had never made
any secret of his opposition to the use of sanctions against Rhodesia. Hence, Mrs Thatcher's choice of Boyd to lead the team was
another sign of her determination to re-establish normal relations
with Rhodesia once the elections there were over. Accompanying
Boyd to Rhodesia were two other peers: Lord Elton, and Viscount
Colville of Culross who had served as Minister of State at the Home
Office in Edward Heath's Government. Also in the team were Sir
Charles Johnston, a former governor of Aden, and the writer, Miles
Hudson. John Drinkwater, a member of the Parliamentary Bound-
ary Commission, travelled with them as an 'apolitical' advisor and
did not sign their subsequent report.

They arrived in Salisbury on 14 April, the day before polling for
the 72 common roll seats was due to begin. It is clear from their
report that the team carried out their task with remarkable rigour.
The Rhodesian authorities initially offered them a place on an organized tour for visiting journalists and dignitaries. They refused,
fearing, quite reasonably, that their conclusions would carry less
weight were it known that the Rhodesians had been guiding their
steps.[49] Instead, they were provided with a Cheetah helicopter from
the Rhodesian Air Force and a Dakota for longer trips, and were

allowed to devise their own tour. Working at times in pairs, they were able to cover a great deal of ground. They claimed to have travelled over 2,000 miles, to have visited 66 polling stations and observed the counting of votes in 17 centres. It was an exhausting schedule for a man of 74; but Boyd appears to have equalled if not surpassed his younger colleagues in energy and enthusiasm.

When Boyd left Rhodesia on Sunday 29 April, Bishop Muzorewa was firmly set to become the country's new prime minister. His United African National Congress had gained 51 of the 72 common roll seats giving it an outright majority. Later that week, the Conservative party was returned to power in the British general election. Boyd's verdict suddenly took on a new importance. He and his colleagues presented their report to Mrs Thatcher on 16 May and published it eight days later. They concluded, on the basis of 'the strictest Western European criteria', that the poll had been a fair one 'in the sense that the electoral machinery was fairly conducted and above serious reproach'.[50]

The Rhodesian authorities had, of course, no incentive to attempt to rig the elections. It was of little consequence to them how the common roll seats were distributed since the African parties contesting them were all committed to upholding the new constitution. What really mattered was that the turnout should be   sufficiently high to enable them to claim overwhelming popular support for the 'internal settlement'. This they appeared to have achieved. There was no electoral register, and unofficial estimates of the size of the potential electorate varied. Yet at the very least, it was possible to claim with some confidence that a majority of those eligible to do so had cast a valid vote. The real question was whether the votes had been cast freely or whether coercion had been employed. On this point, the Boyd report was more guarded. It admitted that the conditions of the civil war made it 'impossible to hold a fully free election in the sense that everyone qualified to vote could either do so or abstain precisely as he or she wished'.[51] Nevertheless, it concluded that the pressures on voters were not sufficient to invalidate the election; nor, it argued, was the absence of candidates from the Patriotic Front. Boyd and his colleagues pointed to the overwhelming desire of African voters for peace, implying that it was this, rather than coercion, which explained the high turnout.

The report was received in Britain as a ringing endorsement of the new constitutional settlement. Within the Foreign Office, however, there was greater scepticism. The new Foreign Secretary, Lord Carrington, recognized that as 'a man of great experience and probity', Boyd's views carried considerable weight within the Conservative party.[52] Yet Carrington himself, as a former director of RTZ (Rio Tinto Zinc Corporation), was no stranger to the complexities of African politics and was acutely aware of the difficulties that might arise from a decision to recognize Muzorewa's government. Carrington's instincts were confirmed by soundings taken by Lord Harlech. These suggested that no black African state and no other member of the European Community would join Britain in recognizing the new regime. A move in this direction by Britain would almost certainly be subject to a hostile vote in the UN and might well lead to the break-up of the Commonwealth. It would, in short, do little to help Rhodesia and much to harm Britain's international standing. Yet in his attempts to persuade Mrs Thatcher of the need to devise a new constitutional settlement in Rhodesia, the Boyd Report proved a major obstacle for Carrington.

Meanwhile, Boyd was becoming increasingly irritated by the Government's failure to adopt a clear policy towards the Muzorewa regime. When the subject was debated in the Lords on 10 July, he implicitly critical of this apparent indecision, adding that 'time is not all on our side'.[53] His impatience was understandable. Mrs Thatcher had still not even formally acknowledged his report. She finally did so on 30 July just as she was about to leave for the Commonwealth conference at Lusaka. Even at this stage, however, her letter to Boyd gave little indication of the position she would adopt with Britain's Commonwealth partners. Indeed, right up to the time of her departure for Africa, she and Carrington appear to have been at odds over the issue. Her own instinct was to go ahead with recognition and in the course of what Carrington euphemistically described as their 'spirited discussions' she cited the Boyd Report in support of her case.[54]

At the Lusaka conference in August, a combination of Carrington's lobbying and pressure from other Commonwealth leaders persuaded Mrs Thatcher that an entirely new constitutional settlement was needed, one which would command the support of the Patriotic Front. Britain was given a free hand in this matter. Negotiations between the different sides in Rhodesia opened at Lancaster House in London on 10 September. They were to drag on for 14 weeks during which time the Rhodesian civil war claimed still more victims. At the Conservative Party Conference in October, the Boyd report provided ammunition for those on the right of the party who accused Carrington of having betrayed Rhodesia. Finally, on 21 December, agreement was reached at Lancaster House for a cease-fire and a new constitution. Rhodesia reverted temporarily to being a British colony. Elections held the following March resulted in a clear victory for Mugabe's ZANU. The following month, Zimbabwe, as the country was now called, achieved her formal independence bringing to an end the most tortuous chapter in the history of British decolonization.

An uncharitable view of this episode would be that it formed an appropriate conclusion to a career in which Boyd had displayed an unenviable gift for backing the wrong horse in African politics; from the doomed Central African Federation to the leaders of the 'multi-racial' parties in East Africa. Perhaps it would be fairer to say that he should never have been called upon to undertake the task, but that he discharged it in a thoroughly professional and judicious manner. For her part, Mrs Thatcher, who was genuinely fond of him, seems to have felt some remorse about the way in which Boyd had been treated. 'It was hard on Alan', she later recalled, 'wasn't it?'[55]

If Boyd's faith in Mrs Thatcher was somewhat dented by the transfer of power in Zimbabwe, it was restored by her performance during the Falklands campaign of 1982. Boyd had been a vocal member of the so-called 'Falkland Islands lobby', which during the 1970s and early 1980s proved remarkably effective in hampering the British Government's efforts to reach some kind of deal with Argentina over the Islands' future.[56] At the end of March 1982, the Argentine government decided to settle the matter by force with a full-scale invasion of the Falklands. Boyd was able to add his own personal endorsement of Mrs Thatcher's handling of the subsequent campaign. The Prime Minister had been invited to attend a dinner in his old constituency to celebrate the Conservatives having held the seat for an unbroken 50 years. It was due to be held, rather belatedly, on Friday 30 April. When the Falklands Crisis erupted, the Mid-Bedfordshire Conservatives assumed that the Prime Minister would cancel the engagement. She did not. She later recalled that the sitting MP, Stephen Hastings, and Boyd, his predecessor, 'spoke magnificently. I was given a wonderful reception. No one present had any doubt of the justice of our cause'.[57] The subsequent success of the operation must have allowed Boyd to feel that he had been right to maintain that Britain's leaders did not have to accept as inevitable their country's gradual retreat from global responsibilities.

Boyd entered the 1980s in good spirits. Politically, he might have been forgiven for believing that some of his own political views were coming back into fashion. His personal life was settled and happy. Alan's eldest son, Simon, who married Alice Clive in 1962, had built a home of his own, Wivelscombe, on the Ince estate. Simon and Alice presented Alan with four grandchildren whose presence at Saltash during the school holidays was a great source of joy to him. A constant stream of rather older visitors continued to make their way to Ince. Among them was Macmillan, who made a number of visits. Boyd's relations with his former chief were probably never better than during the final years of his life. Macmillan would later claim that he missed Alan Boyd more than any other of his former colleagues.

Alan and Patsy had continued to travel during the 1970s and early '80s. They made regular visits to East Africa, hosted and organized by their old friend Michael Blundell. They also toured India for several weeks. Ironically, given the amount of time and effort he had invested during the 1930s in the activities of the India Defence League, this was Boyd's first visit to the subcontinent.

1983 looked likely to be another eventful year. At 78 Boyd was fit and although not quite as busy as he had been 20 years before, he was still dividing his time between a remarkable number of interests and organizations. In January, he and Patsy fulfilled a life-long ambition to explore the Galapagos Islands. Back in London, on the evening of 8 March, Boyd dined with Lord Moyne, his wife's cousin and a friend from his days at Oxford. After leaving the restaurant, they decided to look in the window of a nearby antiques shop. As Boyd was crossing the Fulham Road he was hit by a car driven by a young, uninsured, student. He was rushed to St. Stephen's Hospital but was found to be dead on arrival.

The fact that Boyd had remained so active during his final years, his commanding personality and great enthusiasm for life seemingly undimmed, made it all the more difficult for those who loved him to come to terms with his sudden death. The shock and grief of those closest to him were widely shared. His family was inundated by letters of commiseration from every corner of the world. A day or two after Boyd's death, his son, Simon, received a telephone call from Lee Kuan Yew, the Prime Minister of Singapore. 'I just wanted you to know,' Lee told him, 'that without your father, my country would not exist.'

Boyd was cremated in a private ceremony and his ashes buried in the grounds of St. Stephen's parish church in Saltash. Two months later, leading figures in the post-war Conservative Party gathered at Westminster Abbey to pay tribute to their distinguished colleague. The ranks of the mourners were swelled by representatives of the countless voluntary organizations which Boyd had supported, from the National Appeal for Dominica to the Friends of Friendless Churches. This was not, however, an especially bi-partisan event. Unlike the memorial service for Rab Butler a year earlier, Labour politicians were few and far between. In the highly polarized political climate of the time, they were perhaps reluctant to be seen paying their respects to a figure so firmly identified with the right wing of the Conservative party. It was also undoubtedly the case that, however magnanimous they might have been about him in public, a number of his former opponents never forgave him for his strident advocacy of causes with which they violently disagreed. Amid otherwise glowing obituaries, the *Daily Telegraph* recalled that as a young MP, Boyd's 'barbed and often ill-judged' wit meant that he was 'not universally popular' in the Commons.[58] Those who encountered Boyd later in his life sometimes had difficulty reconciling this kindly old man with the sharp-tongued right wing maverick of the 1930s. When the historian, Piers Brendon, was staying at Ince in the mid-1970s, he made a casual remark about Franco and was quite taken aback when his host revealed himself to have been one of the General's leading supporters in the Commons.[59]

To forget his past would be to underestimate the extent of Boyd's personal achievement. He was not blessed with the placid nature of a saint, but with the more acerbic gifts of a forceful political operator. Yet his legacy was not to be the grandiose political projects which he had sought to promote in government – few, if any of these survived into the 1980s. Rather, it was to be the genuine and deep affection which this 'very rude' young politician had managed to inspire in so many people by the end of his long career. In his address at Boyd's memorial service, Lord Home remembered him thus:

> A man of stature, charged with an abundance of energy and a zest for living; a man of presence and authority; a man of intellect and intuition which took him to the heart of the matter in hand; a natural leader of men, a man of loyalty and service which he placed at the disposal of his country; a man of generosity and hospitality carried far beyond the calls of duty and friendship. All these aspects of his character were displayed in peace and war, in official life and private business, in his relationships with countless people at home and overseas. To these qualities all responded with respect, affection and love.

This was a remarkable epitaph for professional politician, and all the more so for being fully deserved. The love he generated enabled him to attain a degree of happiness and inner peace which the stark contradictions in his character and the cruelty of fate might otherwise have denied him.

The day after Boyd's memorial service, the *Daily Express* carried a photograph of Mrs Thatcher emerging from Westminster Abbey under the headline 'SO CHIC MAGGIE FIVE YEARS ON'. The accompanying story noted that Mrs Thatcher was embarking upon her fifth year as Prime Minister 'in black but still radiant'. It neglected even to mention that her fetching velvet pillbox hat had been worn in honour of a man who once presided over an empire of 80 million people. As a past master of the photo-opportunity, Boyd would probably not have minded very much. After all, the general election was little over a month away. The past could look after itself, and there was much to be done.

Notes

1 Ganda proverb from Uganda collected by Lord Boyd, PBM, Mss. Eng. c. 3796, f. 273.
2 Interview with Bryan Magee, 20 June 1995.
3 Lennox-Boyd to all Colonial Governors, 18 Oct. 1959, PBM, Mss. Eng. c. Mss. Eng. c. 3397, f. 134.
4 Amery to Lennox-Boyd, 20 Oct. 1959, PBM, Mss. Eng. c. 3468, f. 191.
5 Avon to Lennox-Boyd, 21 Oct. 1959, PBM, Mss. Eng. c. 3397, f. 86.
6 Redmayne to Lennox-Boyd, 20 Oct. 1959, PBM, Mss. Eng. c. 3468, f. 199.
7 Lennox-Boyd to Redmayne, 21 Oct. 1959, PBM, Mss. Eng. c. 3468, f. 208.
8 Memorial address by A. L. Rowse in Truro Cathedral, 5 May 1983, PBM, Ms. Eng. c. 3823, ff. 162–5.
9 Paper by Nigel Salmon, 'Alan Lennox-Boyd: The Guinness Years', 11 Oct. 1996.
10 Jonathan Guinness, *Requiem for a Family Business* (London, Macmillan, 1997), p. 73. Perhaps not surprisingly, Guinness questions whether this was an entirely cost-effective use of company funds.
11 Interview with David Sandys-Renton, 22 July 1996.
12 Salmon, 'The Guinness Years'.
13 Salmon, 'The Guinness Years'.
14 Salmon, 'The Guinness Years'.
15 John Cloake, *Templer: Tiger of Malaya* (London, Harrap, 1985), p. 396.
16 Anthony Montague Brown, *Long Sunset: Memoirs of Winston Churchill's Last Private Secretary* (London, Cassell, 1995), p. 342.
17 *West Africa*, 16 March 1963, p. 287.
18 Salmon, 'The Guinness Years'.
19 Boyd to Lyle, 4 Jan. 1960, PBM, Mss. Eng. c. 3469, f. 9.
20 Boyd to Dundee, 28 Sept. 1960, PBM, Mss. Eng. c. 3471, f. 318.
21 Astor to Boyd, 26 April 1965, PBM, Mss. Eng. c. 3476, f.228
22 *HL Deb*, 237, cols. 659–666, 20 Feb. 1962.
23 *HL Deb*, 237, cols. 668–75, 20 Feb. 1962.
24 St. Aldwyn to Bligh, 22 June 1962, PREM 11/3905.
25 Bligh to St. Aldwyn, 25 June 1962, PREM 11/3905.
26 Lennox-Boyd to Lloyd, 22 July 1960, PBM, Mss. Eng. c. 3471, f. 91.
27 Boyd to Macmillan, 12 Jan. 1961, PREM 11/3177.
28 Lord Boyd interviewed about East Africa by Alison Smith, 13 Dec. 1974, PBM, Mss. Eng. c. 3433, f. 255.
29 Note by Boyd, 8 Feb. 1962, PREM 11/3856.
30 Richard Carr-Gomm, *Push on the Door: An Autobiography* (London, The Carr-Gomm Society, 1982), p. 170.
31 Mark Amory, *The Sunday Times Magazine*, 22 Oct. 1972, p. 36.
32 Carr-Gomm, pp. 180–182.
33 *HL Deb*, 228, col. 975, 21 Feb. 1961.
34 Perth to Boyd, 16 March 1961, enclosing undated Colonial Office memorandum, Mss. Eng. c. 3403, ff. 19–23.
35 Boyd to Salisbury, 9 March 1961, Mss. Eng. c. 3473, f. 187.
36 *HL Deb*, 245, col. 1209–1210, 19 Dec. 1962.
37 Murphy, p. 197.
38 *The Guardian*, 26 Nov. 1965.
39 Lord Boyd interviewed about Central Africa, PBM, Mss. Eng. c. 3433, f. 149.
40 Boyd to W.R. Whaley, 21 June 1967, WP 736/4, f. 31.

41 *Daily Mail*, 5 Feb. 1963.
42 *Observer*, 6 Oct. 1963.
43 Interview with Lady Thatcher, 10 Aug. 1995.
44 Martin Meredith, *The First Dance of Freedom: Black Africa in the Postwar Era* (London, Hamish Hamilton, 1984), p. 310.
45 David Owen, *Time to Declare* (Harmondsworth, Penguin, 1992), p. 315.
46 Boyd to Lord Salisbury, 16 Feb. 1972, PBM, Ms. Eng. c. 3506, f. 277.
47 John Dickie, *Inside the Foreign Office* (London, Chapmans, 1992), p. 134.
48 Lord Carrington, *Reflect on Things Past* (London, Collins, 1988), p. 291.
49 *Report to the Prime Minister on the Election held in Zimbabwe/Rhodesia in April 1979* (the 'Boyd Report'), para. 5.
50 Boyd Report, para. 132, conclusion b.
51 Boyd Report, para. 132, conclusion c.
52 Lord Carrington, *Reflect on Things Past* (London, Collins, 1988), p. 289.
53 *HL Deb*, 401, col. 795, 10 July 1979.
54 Carrington, p. 292; Dickie, p. 135.
55 Interview with Lady Thatcher, 10 Aug. 1995.
56 Peter Hennessy, *Whitehall* (London, Fontana, 1990), p. 339.
57 Margaret Thatcher, *The Downing Street Years* (New York, HarperCollins, 1993), p.212
58 *Daily Telegraph*, 10 March 1983.
59 Interview with Piers Brendon, 19 July 1996.

Select Bibliography

LENNOX-BOYD PAPERS

The bulk of Alan Lennox-Boyd's papers are held by the Bodleian Library, Oxford. They are indicated in the text by the abbreviation 'PBM' followed by the full reference. Lennox-Boyd's extensive scrapbooks of photographs and press cuttings are held at Ince Castle, Cornwall. They are not currently available for public consultation, although they will, eventually, also be transferred to the Bodleian Library. They are indicated in the text by the abbreviation 'SB'.

GOVERNMENT PAPERS

Public Record Office, Kew. These are indicated in the text by the following abbreviations:
(ADM) Admiralty
(CAB) Cabinet Office
(CO) Colonial Office
(PREM) Prime Minister's Office

PAPERS OF OTHER INDIVIDUALS AND ORGANISATIONS

Papers of Lord Beaverbrook, House of Lords Record Office, Hist. Coll. 184
Minutes of the Canning Club, Bodleian Library, Oxford, Dep d. 782
Minutes of the Chatham Club, Bodleian Library, Oxford, Mss. Top Oxon d. 727
Papers of Sir Winston Churchill, Churchill College, Cambridge
Minutes of the Commonwealth Affairs Committee, Conservative Party Archives, Bodleian Library, Oxford, CCO 507/1/1
Papers of David Gammans, Rhodes House, Oxford, Mss. Brit. Emp. s. 506
Papers of Sir William Gorell Barnes, Churchill College, Cambridge
Papers of Harold Macmillan, Bodleian Library, Oxford
Papers of Sir Roy Welensky, Rhodes House, Oxford
Papers of Sir Arthur Young, Rhodes House, Oxford, Mss. Brit. Emp. s. 486

UNPUBLISHED MANUSCRIPTS

Lennox-Boyd, Alan, *The Development of the Idea of Trusteeship in the Government of Backward Peoples* (1926)
Lennox-Boyd, Alan (et al.), *Report to the Prime Minister on the Election held in Zimbabwe/Rhodesia in April 1979* (1979)
Gavaghan, Terence, *Corridors of Wire: A Saga of Colonial Power and Preventive*

Detention in Kenya (1994)

Johnston, Sir John, *Recollections* (1997)

Salmon, Nigel, *Alan Lennox-Boyd: The Guinness Years* (1996)

TRANSCRIPTS OF INTERVIEWS

Lord Chandos interviewed by Max Beloff, Rhodes House, Oxford, Mss. Brit. Emp. s. 525

Sir John Macpherson interviewed about the Colonial Service by A. H. M. Kirk-Greene, 27 Feb. 1968, Rhodes House, Oxford, Mss. Brit. Emp. s. 487

W. A. C. Mathieson interviewed by Allan Segal, End of Empire Interviews, Rhodes House, Oxford, Mss. Brit. Emp. s. 527/8

OFFICIAL PUBLICATIONS

Hansard, indicated in the text by the following abbreviations:

(*HC Deb*) House of Commons Debates

(*HL Deb*) House of Lords Debates

Report of the Nyasaland Commission of Inquiry, Cmnd. 814 (London, HMSO, 1959)

Despatch by the Governor relating to the Report of the Nyasaland Commission of Inquiry, Cmnd. 815 (London, HMSO, 1959)

JOURNALS

Bedfordshire Standard

Bedfordshire Times and Independent

Biggleswade Chronicle and Bedford Gazette

Daily Express

Daily Mail

Daily Sketch

Daily Telegraph

Daily Worker

Guardian

Isis

Leighton Buzzard Observer

Luton News

Lymington Times

Newcastle Journal

News Chronicle

New York Times

Observer

Overseas Pensioner
Oxford City Chronicle
Sherborne Register
South Wales Daily Post
The Spectator
Sunday Despatch
Sunderland Echo
The Times
Tribune

BOOKS AND ARTICLES

Askwith, Tom, *From Mau Mau to Harambee: Memoirs & Memoranda of Colonial Kenya* (Cambridge, Cambridge African Monographs, 1995)

Austin, Dennis, *Malta and the End of Empire* (London, Frank Cass, 1971)

Balfour-Paul, Glen, *The End of Empire in the Middle East: Britain's relinquishment of power in her last three Arab dependencies* (Cambridge, Cambridge University Press, 1991)

Berman, Bruce, *Control and Crisis in Colonial Kenya: The Dialectic of Domination* (London, James Currey, 1990)

Boyd, Mark, *Reminiscences of Fifty Years* (London, Longmans, Green and Co., 1871)

Boyd-Carpenter, John, *Way of Life* (London, Sidgwick and Jackson, 1980)

Brendon, Piers, *Head of Guinness: The Life and Times of Rupert Guinness, 2nd Earl of Iveagh* (privately published, 1979)

Bridge, Carl, *Holding India to the Empire: The British Conservative Party and the 1935 Constitution* (New York, Envoy Press, 1986)

Buchan, William, *John Buchan: A Memoir* (London, Harrap, 1982)

Butler, R. A., *The Art of the Possible* (London, Hamish Hamilton, 1971)

Canner, W. H. P., *The Air Transport Industry* (London, Brown, Son, Ferguson Ltd., 1986)

Carr-Gomm, Richard, *Push on the Door: An Autobiography* (London, The Carr-Gomm Society, 1982)

Carrington, Lord, *Reflect on Things Past* (London, Collins, 1988)

Castle, Barbara, *Fighting all the Way* (London, Macmillan, 1993)

Chandos, Lord, *The Memoirs of Lord Chandos* (London, Bodley Head, 1962)

Charmley, John, *Lord Lloyd and the Decline of the British Empire* (London, Weidenfeld and Nicolson, 1987)

Chisholm, Anne and Davie, Michael, *Beaverbrook: A Life* (London, Hutchinson, 1992)

Clark, William, *From Three Worlds* (London, Sidgwick and Jackson, 1986)

Cloake, John, *Templer: Tiger of Malaya* (London, Harrap, 1985)

Cross, Colin, *The Fascists in Britain* (London, Barrie and Rockliff, 1961)

Crowder, Michael, *The Story of Nigeria* (London, Faber and Faber, 1978)

Darwin, John, *Britain and Decolonisation* (London, Macmillan, 1988)

Day Lewis, C., *The Buried Day* (London, Chatto & Windus, 1960)

Day Lewis, Sean, *C. Day Lewis: An English Literary Life* (London, Weidenfeld & Nicolson, 1980)

Diamond, Marion, *The Sea Horse and the Wanderer: Ben Boyd in Australia* (Carlton, Melbourne University Press, 1988)

Dickie, John, *Inside the Foreign Office* (London, Chapmans, 1992)

Douglas-Home, Charles, *Evelyn Baring* (London, Collins, 1978)

Driberg, Tom, *Ruling Passions* (London, Jonathan Cape, 1977)

Drysdale, John, *Singapore: Struggle for Survival* (Hemel Hempstead, Allen and Unwin, 1984)

Edgerton, Robert B., *Mau Mau: An African Crucible* (London, I B Taurus & Co Ltd, 1990)

Fisher, Nigel, *Iain Macleod* (London, André Deutsch, 1973)

Foley, Charles, *Legacy of Strife: Cyprus from Rebellion to Civil War* (Harmondsworth, Penguin, 1964)

Foot, Hugh, *A Start in Freedom* (London, Hodder and Stoughton, 1964)

Gilbert, Martin, *Winston S. Churchill, Vol. 5, Companion, Part 2* (London, Heinemann, 1981)

Goldsworthy, David, *Tom Mboya: The Man Kenya Wanted to Forget* (London, Heinemann, 1982)

Goldsworthy, David (ed), *British Documents on the End of Empire, Series A, vol. 3, The Conservative Government and the End of Empire 1951-57, Parts I-III* (London, HMSO, 1994)

Griffiths, Richard, *Fellow Travellers of the Right: British Enthusiasts for Nazi Germany, 1933-39* (Oxford, Oxford University Press, 1983)

Guinness, Jonathan, *Requiem for a Family Business* (London, Macmillan, 1997)

Hatzivassiliou, Evanthis, 'Blocking Enosis: Britain and the Cyprus Question, March-December 1956', *Journal of Imperial and Commonwealth History*, vol. 19, no. 2, May 1991

Hatzivassiliou, Evanthis, 'The Cyprus Question and the Anglo-American Special Relationship, 1954-58', in Aldrich, Richard J. and Hopkins, Michael F., *Intelligence, Defence and Diplomacy: British Policy in the Post-War World* (London, Cass, 1994)

Havinden, Michael, and Meredith, David, *Colonialism and Development: Britain and its tropical colonies 1850-1960* (London, Routledge, 1993)

Hennessy, Peter, *Whitehall* (London, Fontana, 1990)

Holt, Oliver, *Nowell Smith and his Sherborne: A Memoir* (private publication, 1955)

Tony Hopkins, 'Macmillan's audit of empire, 1957', in Clarke, Peter, and Trebilcock, C. (eds.), *Understanding Decline* (Cambridge, Cambridge, 1997)

Horne, Alistair, *Macmillan 1957-1986* (London, Macmillan, 1989)

Izzard, Molly, *Freya Stark: A Biography* (London, Hodder and Stoughton, 1993)

Jeal, Tim, *Baden-Powell* (London, Hutchinson, 1989)

Kariuki, Josiah Mwangi, *'Mau Mau' Detainee* (Oxford, Oxford University Press, 1963)

Karugire, S. R., *A Political History of Uganda* (Nairobi, Heinemann, 1980)

Keatley, Patrick, *The Politics of Partnership* (Harmondsworth, Penguin, 1993)

Kirk-Greene, A. H. M. (ed), *Africa in the Colonial Period, III-The Transfer of Power: The Colonial Administrator in the Age of Decolonization* (Oxford, University of Oxford, 1979)

Knight, Franklin W., *The Caribbean: The Genesis of a Fragmented Nationalism* (Oxford, Oxford University Press, 1990)

Kruse, Juanita, *John Buchan and the Idea of Empire: Popular Literature and Political Ideology* (Lampeter, The Edwin Mellon Press, 1989)

Kyle, Keith, *Suez* (London, Weidenfeld and Nicolson, 1991)

Lamb, Richard, *The Macmillan Years 1957-63: The Emerging Truth* (London, John Murray, 1995)

Lapping, Brian, *End of Empire* (London, Paladin, 1989)

Lees-Milne, James, *Caves of Ice* (London, Faber and Faber, 1983)

Lees-Milne, James, *Midway on the Waves* (London, Faber & Faber, 1985)

Lees-Milne, James, *Diaries 1942-1945: Ancestral Voices and Prophesying Peace* (London, John Murray, 1995)

Louis, Wm Roger, and Robinson, Ronald, 'The Imperialism of Decolonization', *Journal of Imperial and Commonwealth History*, vol. 22, no. 3 (1994)

McKenzie, R. T., *British Political Parties* (London, Mercury Books, 1964)

Macleod, Iain, 'Trouble in Africa', *The Spectator*, 31 January 1964.

Macmillan, Harold, *Riding the Storm* (London, Macmillan, 1971)

MacNeice, Louis, *The Strings are False: An Unfinished Autobiography* (London, Faber and Faber, 1965)

Manchester, William, *The Caged Lion: Winston Spencer Churchill, 1932-1940* (London, Michael Joseph, 1988)

Markides, Diana Weston, 'Britain's 'New Look' Policy for Cyprus and the Makarios-Harding Talks, January 1955-March 1956', *Journal of Imperial and Commonwealth History*, vol. 23, no. 3 (1995)

Masters, Anthony, *The Man Who Was M* (London, Grafton, 1986)

Mazrui, Ali A., and Tidy, Michael, *Nationalism and New States in Africa* (London, 1984)

Meredith, Martin, *The First Dance of Freedom: Black Africa in the Postwar Era* (London, Hamish Hamilton, 1984)

Middlemas, Keith, and Barnes, John, *Baldwin: A Biography* (London, Weidenfeld and Nicolson, 1969)

Montague Brown, Anthony, *Long Sunset: Memoirs of Winston Churchill's Last Private Secretary* (London, Cassell, 1995)

Mordecai, J., *The West Indies: the federal negotiations* (London, 1968)

Morgan, Kenneth O., *Labour in Power 1945-1951* (Oxford, Oxford University Press, 1985)

Munroe, Trevor, *The Politics of Constitutional Decolonization: Jamaica, 1944-62* (Jamaica, University of the West Indies, 1972)

Murphy, Philip, *Party Politics and Decolonization: The Conservative Party and*

British Colonial Policy in Tropical Africa, 1951-1964 (Oxford, Oxford University Press, 1995)

Ovendale, Ritchie, 'Macmillan and the Wind of Change in Africa, 1957-1960', *The Historical Journal*, vol. 38, no. 2 (1995)

Owen, David, *Time to Declare* (Harmondsworth, Penguin, 1992)

Pakenham, Lord, *Born to Believe* (London, Jonathan Cape, 1953)

Parker, John, 'Oxford Politics in the Late Twenties', *Political Quarterly* vol. 54, no. 2, (April-June 1974)

Parker, R. A. C., *Chamberlain and Appeasement: British Policy and the Coming of the Second World War* (London, Macmillan, 1993)

Pearson, John, *The Life of Ian Fleming* (London, Coronet, 1989)

Porter, A. N. and Stockwell, A. J., *British Imperial Policy and Decolonization, vol. II* (London, Macmillan, 1989)

Rathbone, Richard (ed.), *British Documents on the End of Empire, Series B, vol. 1, Ghana Parts I-II, 1952-1957* (London, HMSO, 1992)

Rhodes James, Robert (ed.), *Chips: The Diaries of Sir Henry Channon* (Harmondsworth, Penguin Books, 1970)

Rhodes James, Robert, *Anthony Eden: A Biography* (London, Weidenfeld and Nicolson, 1986)

Rich, Paul B., *Race and Empire in British Politics* (Cambridge, Cambridge University Press, Second Edition, 1990)

Roberts, Andrew, *Eminent Churchillians* (London, Weidenfeld and Nicolson, 1994)

Segal, Ronald, *African Profiles* (Harmondsworth, Penguin, 1962)

Shepherd, Robert, *A Class Divided: Appeasement and the Road to Munich, 1938* (London, Macmillan, 1988)

Shepherd, Robert, *Iain Macleod: A Biography* (London, Hutchinson, 1994)

Stark, Freya, *Dust in the Lion's Paw* (London, John Murray, 1961)

Stark, Freya, *Letters, Vol. 3, The Growth of Danger 1935-1939* (Tisbury, Compton Russell, 1976)

Stockwell, A. J., '"A widespread and long-concealed plot to overthrow government in Malaya"? The origins of the Malayan emergency', *Journal of Imperial and Commonwealth History*, vol. 21, no. 3 (1993)

Stockwell, A. J., *British Documents on the End of Empire, Series B, vol. 3, Malaya, Parts I-III* (London, HMSO, 1995)

Taylor, A. J. P., *Beaverbrook*, (London, Hamish Hamilton, 1972)

Taylor, A. J. P., *My Personal History* (London, Coronet edn., 1984)

Trelawny-Ross, A. H., *Their Prime of Life: A Public School Study* (Winchester, Warren & Son, 1956)

Turnbull, C. M., *A History of Singapore, 1819-1975* (Kualar Lumpar, OUP, 1977)

Turner, John, *Macmillan* (London, Longman, 1994)

Watkinson, Harold, *Turning Points: A Record of Our Times* (Salisbury, Michael Russell, 1986)

Waugh, Alec, *The Early Years of Alec Waugh* (London, Cassell, 1962)

Welensky, Sir Roy, *Welensky's 4000 Days* (London, Collins, 1964)

Williams, Philip (ed), *The Diary of Hugh Gaitskell 1945-56* (London, Jonathan Cape, 1983)

Williamson, Philip, *National Crisis and National Government: British politics, the economy and Empire, 1926-1932* (Cambridge, Cambridge University Press, 1992)

Wood, J. R. T., *The Welensky Papers* (Durban, Graham Publishing, 1983)

Index